WebLogic Multitenancy

WebLogic as a Platform & Foundation for Cloud Services

Oracle In-Focus Series

Martin Heinzl

Dedicated to my wonderful wife Lourdes

WebLogic Multitenancy

WebLogic as a Platform & Foundation for Cloud Services

By Martin Heinzl

Printed in the United States of America.

Published in Kittrell, North Carolina, USA.

Oracle In-Focus Series: Book #52

Series Editor: Donald K. Burleson

Production Manager: Janet Burleson

Editor: Jennifer Kittleson

Production Editor: Jennifer Kittleson

Cover Design: Janet Burleson

Printing History: August 2016 for First Edition

ISBN 13: 978-0-9861194-2-2

Table of Contents

Foreword - Our world of CaaS

My name is Martin Heinzl and since 1998 I have been working with Enterprise (Middleware) Systems based on Common Object Request Broker Architecture (CORBA), Java Enterprise Edition (JEE) and other similar technologies. During my assignments in many different companies and various sectors as principal consultant and architect I have frequently observed administrators busily writing their own shell scripts, tinkering with configuration files or even using graphical configuration tools to repeatedly alter the same settings across multiple servers in production environments.

In the last years I have been using WebLogic in many different and complex environments with hundreds of applications and thousands of WebLogic instances. Technologies like WebLogic Scripting Tool (WLST) and Java Management Extension are always helping a lot to make the life of all administrators, operators and also for deplorers much easier.

In the last months and years, a new buzzword is getting more and more popular: Cloud and cloud infrastructure. Whenever cloud is mentioned, hundreds of new abbreviations are immediately shouted out: IaaS, PaaS, SaaS, XaaS and many more.

For me these are all part of CaaS. If you now think CaaS stands for "Cloud as a Service" then you are wrong (at least in the context of my foreword ☺).

CaaS means: ***C***onfusing ***a***ccumulation of ***a***cronyms in our ***S***ociety

Oracle has also jumped on the cloud train and has an impressive offering around cloud. One of the foundation and cornerstones for the JCS (Java Cloud Service) is the Oracle application server WebLogic. For many reasons WebLogic has been enhanced in version 12.2.x with a completely new administration and operation concept called partition – also referred to as microcontainers - that has a number of incredible benefits for cloud infrastructures but of course also for all other installations.

This book is all about multitenancy. It introduces the concepts and technologies behind it. The main focus of this book is to provide detailed understanding about the use-cases to which multitenancy provides real value. Therefore, this book is focused on real word scenarios and tries to provide technology details, including automation where this technology will bring you advantages.

> Note: Multitenancy and partitions have by nature **nothing** to with the cloud. But this concept offers a very good foundation for cloud offerings, therefore cloud terminology is also used and introduced in this book. Oracle is using the partition technology as one of the cornerstones of its own Java cloud offering.

As Oracle is advocating this new administration architecture as its new main model of operation and also as its main base concept for its own cloud offering, this book is not only targeted to administrators and deployers but to everybody using WebLogic. Especially architects and business decision makers can also benefit from the use-case discussions.

Understanding multitenancy and getting the most out of it can be a key factor for success in applying WebLogic in own infrastructure, own hosting services and also in understanding the Oracle WebLogic cloud offering.

May 2016
Martin Heinzl
WaaS_book@mh-enterpriseconsulting.de

Multitenancy in WebLogic Server

(Foreword by David Cabelus)

These are exciting times to be in the world of information technology, and specifically to be in the area of enterprise applications! Change is happening very rapidly. We are witnessing a transition from hosting applications in company-owned data centers to hosting them in public cloud data centers, and this transition is now happening even for the most sensitive and mission critical applications. We are seeing a huge adoption of DevOps and the rapid advance of DevOps tools and standards, such as Docker and the Open Container Initiative. We are also seeing huge interest in microservices. All of these changes are interrelated. That is, as we see adoption of public cloud infrastructure, with its simple, automated, and elastically available capacity, we need more automation built into the application management infrastructure and processes for applications (read: DevOps) to take advantage of this flexibility. And, as we now have this elasticity and automation, we are able to /we need to leverage that flexibility in a more fine-grained and efficient way through microservice architectures and with applications written to follow the 12 Factor App methodology. All of this means greater scalability, better efficiency and adaptability, and the opportunity to address business challenges that were difficult to tackle in the past.

I am just scratching the surface here, but you get the picture.

Amidst all of this activity, Oracle released Oracle WebLogic Server 12.2.1 with a new option called WebLogic Server Multitenant. This new option includes some innovative new capabilities that fit right into this swirling world of change. At the center of this set of features is the *domain partition*, which is really a *microcontainer* within the application server that encapsulates your application and the server services that it needs. These microcontainers enable:

Rapid and simple portability from environment to environment (think: easy cloud adoption), with flexible mutability/immutability, and fast startup and scale up.

Platform efficiency (read: cost savings) through consolidation of these microcontainers on a shared platform.

Business continuity through four flavors of isolation: runtime, security, administration, and data isolation.

Automation, DevOps, and elastic scalability with new features in WebLogic Server, such as automated rule-based elasticity for dynamic clusters, REST management APIs, WebLogic Diagnostics Framework, WebLogic Scripting Tool (WLST), Maven plugins, and certification on Docker containers.

This book brings together two things: Martin Heinzl, with his passion and expertise around all things WebLogic, and the new WebLogic Server Multitenant option, which I described above. I've known Martin for a number of years. Every time I talk with him,

I am struck by the level of enthusiasm he has for not only everything he does, but also for the ecosystem that he relies on. That ecosystem includes WebLogic Server as a chosen platform for Java applications. Martin is one of a few go-to guys that I rely on for feedback as we evolve WebLogic Server. And Martin is not shy with his ideas! He continually sends me suggestions for changes and new features that make WebLogic more useful to him in his consulting practice and ultimately for his customers.

When Martin approached me with the idea of writing this book, I was thrilled that he was up to the task. WebLogic Server Multitenant deserves the likes of Martin to deliver the essence of what is possible now with this new microcontainer platform. We are very lucky to have someone like Martin with extensive expertise, fervor, and zeal to deliver this body of work.

And deliver he did! This book starts with a high-level but thorough analysis of the state of the world for Platform as a Service (PaaS), and really "anything as a service," and then transitions through various levels of detail for how to apply WebLogic Server Multitenant to create a WebLogic as a Service platform. And, of course, Martin could not shy away from the thing that is central to his being – practicality. Throughout the book, Martin provides practical advice on what to do and what not to do, coupled with detailed instructions for using WLST and the WebLogic Server Administration Console to make everything work. I hope you enjoy the book as much as I did!

David Cabelus
Senior Principal Product Manager, Oracle WebLogic Server
ORACLE Corporation

Preface

Scope of this book

This book is all about the new multitenancy framework Oracle has added to WebLogic 12.2.1. Multitenancy support is based on the new WebLogic concept, which is called "partition". A partition – as it will be defined in the book – implements a new application bundling which I like to call "WebLogic application". This concept takes the J2EE archive model of an EAR and extends it in order to add infrastructure details like JDBC datasources, JMS configuration and many more. This concept can be seen as a foundation technology to implement a new service layer like WebLogic as a Service (WaaS). The complete book explains all the new concepts around multitenancy. Therefore, this book is based on WebLogic 12.2.1 or above.

The scripts and programs are specific to WebLogic and will only run on WebLogic 12.2.1 or above.

Prerequisites

In order to fully appreciate the contents book and all the scripts, a good working knowledge of WebLogic is required. For the more technical oriented reader it is recommended to read my books about WLST and WLDF first as both technologies will be used throughout this book.

How to read this book

This book is divided into seven main parts. After an introduction of the major technologies this book will describe the architecture behind the multitenancy implementation in WebLogic and show the main areas where these technologies can really help in common business use-cases. After that isolation level and technology discussions provide a comprehensive understanding of the underlying technology build into WebLogic. Equipped with that knowledge section five discusses a number of common use cases. The final part looks at some more advanced topics.

Part 1 is a very brief introduction to the main technologies. These are multitenancy and cloud fundamentals, WebLogic, Jython and JMX overviews and the general need for automation. Please refer to the appendix for suggestions on learning Jython, WLST, WLDF and JMX.

Part 2 is a general discussion about multitenancy in WebLogic and introduces the overall architecture. A second chapter discusses potential use cases when to use the new multitenancy features. It also provides example of use cases where multitenancy might not be a good idea.

Part 3 of the book discusses the different levels of isolation. Isolation is key for a correct multitenancy setup. Isolation has to be achieved on different levels and this sections divides the different levels into different chapter.

Part 4 of the book is a very technical oriented deep-dive section. This part introduces in detail the different technology building bricks Oracle has added to WebLogic.

Part 5 discusses – based on the knowledge of part 4 – a number of common use-cases and how to implement (or better improve) them using the new multitenancy model and the new WebLogic partitions. Note that all chapters in this section have two parts: A more business and architectural part and after that the technical implementation using an example.

Part 6 is a discussion about advanced concepts. This parts cover the extension of the multitenancy architecture into the load-balancer and caching layer. In addition, the new elastic services will be discussed. The last part ends with a comparison between the new partition technology and Docker container.

Part 7 summarizes all the technologies discussed in the book and puts them into the broader scope of cloud technologies.

Reading suggestion for technical audience

For everybody who really wants to dig into the new technology I recommend to read the book section by section. The book is written in a way that each section builds upon the previous. It is recommended to have a good working knowledge about WebLogic, WLST and WLDF.

Reading suggestion for Architects / Business audience

This book also wants to help everybody which is not interested in all the bits and details to understand the new multitenancy model and how it can be used. For all readers interested in the architecture and benefits it may bring for your business I suggest the following reading path:

1. Read the introduction.
2. Read section 2 of the book with the architecture and the user cases.
3. Read section 5 with the detailed discussion of each use case.
4. Read section 3 to understand the different isolation levels and where WebLogic has an offering.
5. Section 6 provides advanced topics and integration into other technology layers.

Source Code and Scripts

Every effort has been taken to provide ready-to-run scripts and examples. Some examples are not printed in full in the book, due to their length however, you will find the complete code for download online. Important note for all code examples: Please always make sure to change path names, server names, file locations and any other aspect which depends on your local machine prior to testing the scripts. This note applies to all code examples and there won't be a reminder at every code listing.

Acknowledgements

A special thank you to David Cabelus from the Oracle WebLogic Product Management Team who not only encouraged me to write this book but also helped with a review.

I would like thank the company Oracle for granting me the permission to quote or use a number of screenshots and some listings of the official documentation.

Also a big thank you to Thorsten Michels for his detailed review and help with information about Docker, Albert Barron for this Pizza example, Kunal Ashar for the permission to use parts of blog, Richard Seroter for his discussion about isolation levels, Fabrizio Marini and other contributors.

Finally thanks a lot to Pavan Bhavani Shekhar Devarakonda and Ralf Ernst for also helping me with the review.

Using the Online Code Depot

Purchase of this book provides complete access to the online code depot that contains sample code scripts. Any code depot scripts in this book are located at the following URL:

www.rampant.cc/WLMulti.htm

If technical assistance is needed with downloading or accessing the scripts, please contact Rampant TechPress at rampant@burleson.cc.

Part I

Introduction & Technology Overview

Multitenancy – What is it all about?

CHAPTER

What is Multitenancy?

Multitenancy is one of the buzzwords that is almost always used if a definition of cloud computing or cloud services is needed. So before digging deeper into the WebLogic concepts, let's have a look at the concept of Multitenancy first. Multitenancy can be views as "multi" and "tenant". It is one of the core technologies that can be used to share IT resources in a cost-efficiently way, without violating security or isolation. This concept allows internal (on premise) hosting or cloud providers to host multiple instances (tenants) with the ability to use the same software and interfaces to configure resources and isolate tenant specific traffic and isolate their data. Consider the following more detailed definitions:

Wikipedia uses the following definition of multitenancy:

> Software Multitenancy refers to a software architecture in which a single instance of a software runs on a server and serves multiple tenants. A tenant is a group of users who share a common access with specific privileges to the software instance. With a multitenant architecture, a software application is designed to provide every tenant a dedicated share of the instance including its data, configuration, user management, tenant individual functionality and non-functional properties. Multitenancy contrasts with multi-instance architectures, where separate software instances operate on behalf of different tenants. Multitenancy can be an important feature of cloud computing.
>
> *(c) http://en.wikipedia.org/wiki/Multitenancy*

Gartner also has a good definition:

> Multitenancy is a reference to the mode of operation of software where multiple independent instances of one or multiple applications operate in a shared environment. The instances (tenants) are logically isolated, but physically integrated. The degree of logical isolation must be complete, but the degree of

> physical integration will vary. The more physical integration, the harder it is to preserve the logical isolation. The tenants (application instances) can be representations of organizations that obtained access to the multitenant application (this is the scenario of an ISV offering services of an application to multiple customer organizations). The tenants may also be multiple applications competing for shared underlying resources (this is the scenario of a private or public cloud where multiple applications are offered in a common cloud environment).
> *(c) http://www.gartner.com/it-glossary/multitenancy*

Multitenancy does not only exist in software. It is a concept which we can find in different varieties in many parts of our life. Even though this book is all about enterprise software architecture let us try to also consider a non-software example:

The concept of multitenancy is actually applied in many areas of our daily live. As an example, let's take a call center. In a call center, a large number of agents are working. They basically share the main infrastructures like the building, floor and rooms. Some agents also share the same desk. But they also have dedicated resources like their own chair and phone. Now given as an example, let's assume that that the call center has 100 workplaces. For a specific time - say the summer months - 70 of them are used with agents for company A and 30 for agent working for company B.

During the winter company A has much less calls and therefore reduce the number of agents to 50. Company B - as a company selling winter articles - have a much higher demand of agents during winter. So the agents working for this call-center are sometimes working for company A, sometimes for B.

It would have been nonsense to use two different call center rooms, as this would have required much more resources (two rooms with 70 seats each = 140 seats and 40 of them are always empty). So the agents work independently, the amount of them can increased or decreased depending on the need but they share a common infrastructure. All of them are (of the type) agents but whenever they are actively working have a special company to answer calls for.

So this is all about sharing a common infrastructure between different, independent citizens – in this case agents - without sharing their secrets and knowledge (isolation).

Overview of Multitenancy

Multitenancy - now coming back to (enterprise) software - is commonly known as an architecture where multiple different customers can use the same software stack but without clashing into each other. This means that every customer has to a certain degree its private area. "To a certain degree" is not very concrete but this actually reflects the reality as every environment is different. Depending on the quality and architecture of the system, the amount of shared stack vs. the amount of private/dedicated stack can differ significantly (Figure 1-1):

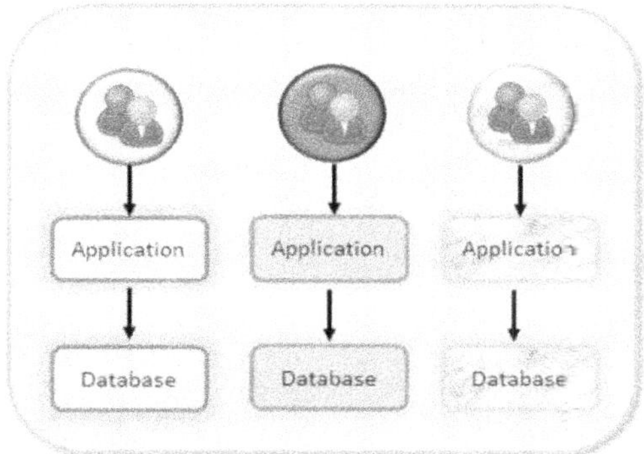

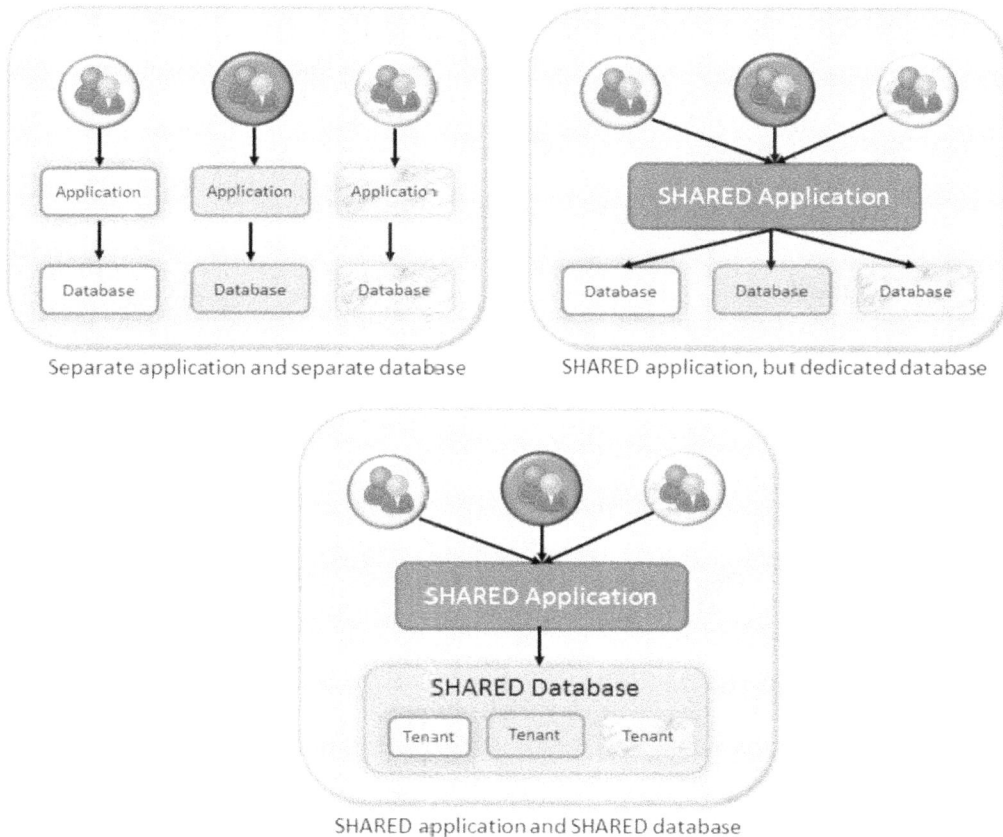

Separate application and separate database

SHARED application, but dedicated database

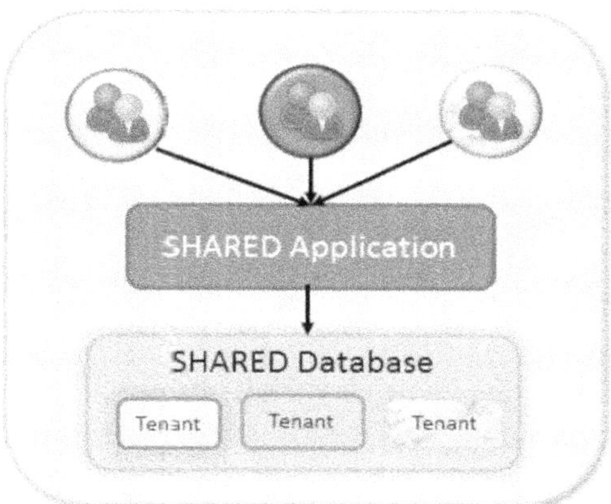

SHARED application and SHARED database

Figure 1-1: Levels of Multitenancy

In traditional systems, each software component runs in its own container, on its own virtual machine and maybe even on its own hardware. This depends on implementation and quality. Multitenancy is all about reducing footprint, increasing density, isolating resources and optimal usage of available resources. This helps a lot to reduce costs and to be more efficient. In these architectures the terminology software or component does not fully describe the setup, therefore a new terminology has been created, which is called "tenant". A tenant is the customized instance of the remaining parts of the system which is still dedicated to only one customer and not shared. A multitenancy system consists of a shared infrastructure which hosts specialized tenants.

A multi-tenant architecture is separating its resources to serve multiple installed, specialized components (tenants). We also call this a partitioned environment, as the system needs to create virtual partitions (like a hard drive) whereas each partition hosts data items and configuration items for one tenant. Due to isolation concepts, tenants can operate without consider the other tenants which may be hosted on the same infrastructure. Proper infrastructures offer resource and security isolation and more advanced features.

Isolation is key in Multitenancy

One of the key concepts in multitenancy is isolation. Isolation can happen on many different layers like network, operating system, process (like virtual machine), services, applications or user sessions. One part later in the book is dedicated to isolation.

Any service provider delivering a multi-tenant environment must adhere to these six commandments as nicely defined in the core principles (© Richard Seroter, centurylinkcloud)

1. Thou shalt isolate tenants within their own network. This one applies mainly to infrastructure-as-a-service (IaaS) providers who promise secure computing environments. Software-as-a-Service (SaaS) customers on a platform like Salesforce.com don't have this issue as customers do not have access to low level network traffic. When granting virtual machine access to users, the service provider has to ensure that there's no opportunity to intercept network traffic from other customers.

2. Thou shalt not allow tenants to see another tenant's metadata. Sometimes metadata can be just as sensitive as transactional data! Multi-tenant service providers must make sure that customers are logically or physically walled off from seeing the settings or user-defined customizations created by other customers.

3. Thou shalt encrypt data in transit AND at rest. Providers shouldn't let their guard down just because data is within their internal network. Rather, data should constantly be transferred over secure channels, and encrypted whenever it's stored on disk.

4. Thou shalt properly clean up deleted resources. In a multi-tenant IaaS environment, there is clearly reuse of resources. When a network is released by one customer, another can use it. When a storage volume is removed, that space on the SAN is now available for others. It's imperative that service providers reset and clear resources before allowing anyone else to acquire them.

5. Thou shalt prevent noisy neighbors from impacting others. This phenomenon is one of the hardest problems to address in multi-tenant environments. As a user, you have no say in who else is using the same environment. It's up to the service provider to make sure that one customer can't (intentionally or unintentionally) adversely impact the performance of other customers by overwhelming the shared compute, storage, or networking resources.

6. Thou shalt define and audit policies to ensure proper administration of shared environments. Let's be honest - using a multi-tenant environment involves a bit of trust. As a customer, you have to trust that the service provider has built a platform that properly isolates each customer, and that operational staff can't go off the reservation and compromise your business. However, to run mission-critical apps in someone's multi-tenant platform requires more than blind trust; you should also be able to demand to see 3rd party certifications and audits that prove that a mature organization is behind the platform.

Summary

Multitenancy is a very attractive concept with a number of benefits. It is not a silver bullet for all problems but if used properly it significantly improves the IT landscape. Furthermore, many people see multitenancy as the foundation for cloud hosting, especially in the PaaS (platform) and SaaS (services) level hosting offerings.

Multitenancy exists on many different level and this book will – after an introduction to understand cloud – into the areas where Oracle has recently added multitenancy features to WebLogic.

XaaS to WaaS - X-Ray through the cloud

CHAPTER

Introduction

In the last months and years, a new buzzword is getting more and more popular: Cloud and cloud infrastructure. Whenever cloud is mentioned, hundreds of new abbreviations are immediately shouted out e.g. IaaS, PaaS, SaaS, XaaS or many others.

For many of us these are all part of CaaS. If you know that CaaS only stands for "Cloud as a Service" then you are not fully right.

CaaS: ***C***onfusing ***a***ccumulation of ***a***cronyms in our ***S***ociety

Oracle has also jumped on the cloud train and has an impressive offering around cloud. Even though multitenancy – the topic of this book – has by nature nothing to do with cloud, it offers are very interesting foundation for cloud offerings. In order to understand the values offered by WLS multitenancy better, it is important to understand and differentiate all the buzzwords around the service offering.

This chapter will provide a very brief overview of PaaS, IaaS, SaaS, HPCaaS, DICaaS, HuaaS, MWaaS, MaaS and more. Throughout the rest of the book, the reader will get an understanding what WebLogic Multitenancy offers to this zoo and which of the XaaS services do benefit from WebLogic Multitenancy.

Pizza as a Service

What does Pizza has to do with SOA? Well, as technologists, we tend to live in a world of acronyms and terms that are quite common to those of us in the industry. But this abbreviated language can seem like a foreign language to those outside of it. For insiders, terms like SOA, PaaS, IaaS, REST or JEE are daily business, but when talking to others this might sound like a different language. Even though these cloud and SOA buzzwords can be seen everywhere these days – especially in sales PowerPoint presentations – it is wrong to assume that everybody knows the terminology and the technology.

How can SaaS, IaaS, PaaS, be explained without all those technology buzzwords and acronyms? Let's break down the basics of cloud computing and its associated service models by using the example of making a pizza (figure 2-1):

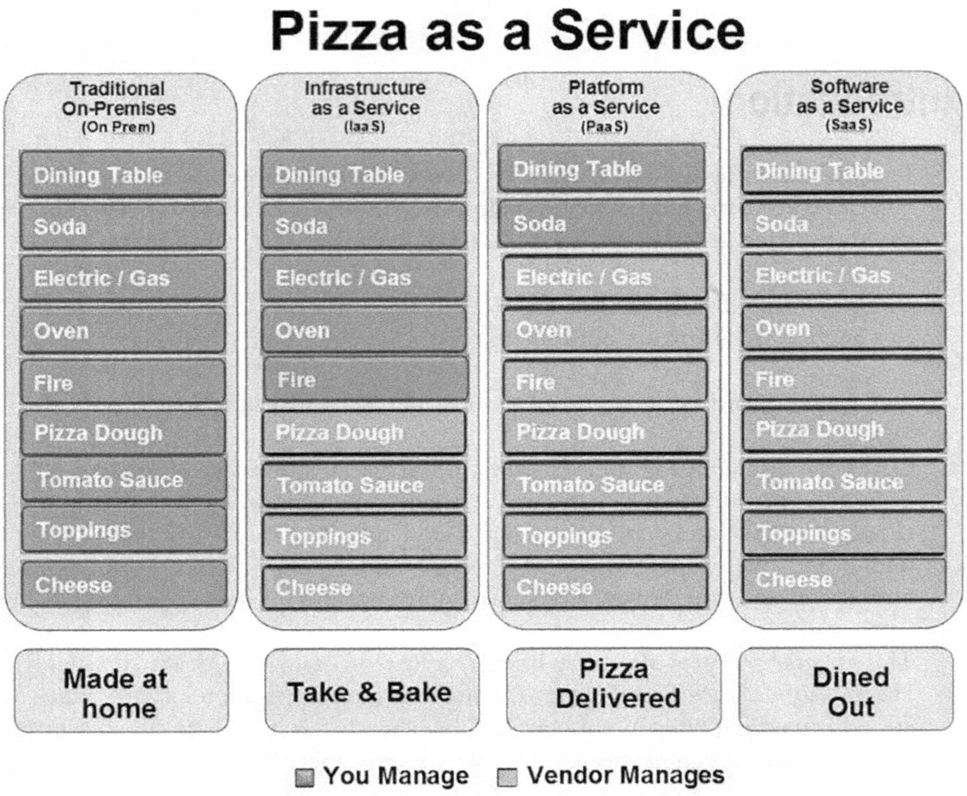

Pizza as a Service

Traditional On-Premises (On Prem)	Infrastructure as a Service (IaaS)	Platform as a Service (PaaS)	Software as a Service (SaaS)
Dining Table	Dining Table	Dining Table	Dining Table
Soda	Soda	Soda	Soda
Electric / Gas	Electric / Gas	Electric / Gas	Electric / Gas
Oven	Oven	Oven	Oven
Fire	Fire	Fire	Fire
Pizza Dough	Pizza Dough	Pizza Dough	Pizza Dough
Tomato Sauce	Tomato Sauce	Tomato Sauce	Tomato Sauce
Toppings	Toppings	Toppings	Toppings
Cheese	Cheese	Cheese	Cheese
Made at home	Take & Bake	Pizza Delivered	Dined Out

You Manage   Vendor Manages

Figure 2-1: Pizza as a Service (© Albert Barron – thanks for reprint permission)

The premise of the "Pizza as a Service" example is quite simple and can be explained as:

1. You can make a pizza at home where you're responsible for buying all of the ingredients including making the dough.
2. You can purchase some of the ingredients and buy pre-packaged dough.
3. You can have pizza delivered to your home.
4. You can simply load up the family and head out for pizza at your local dining establishment.

In each case you're still having pizza however in some cases you do all of the work and others where you have other people do the work for you.

It is easy to think about other similar examples which explain nicely the fundamental differences of IaaS, PaaS and SaaS.

The Next Generation Enterprise: Business as a Service in the Cloud

(Based on a blog of Kunal Ashar)

Businesses that see the cloud as the future of services are already living in the past. Cloud computing is no longer the future. It's the present. It's now. Companies began adopting and implementing cloud computing several years ago, and they've driven the Darwinian-like evolution of cloud computing from "What is the cloud?" to "How can we further extend and leverage the benefits of the cloud?" to "Can I run parts of or even my entire business in the cloud?"

The cloud is not just about technology - it is a paradigm shift. It presents new economic models that companies can use to provision IT and services. Today, most organizations have started at least one cloud project, with the promise of costs savings and faster time to realize tangible revenues.

More and more enterprises are turning to third-parties to reuse their solutions rather than lock-up their valuable capital by sourcing the hardware and software themselves. This model is allowing those enterprises to get more efficient, lower costs and achieve business agility across multiple channels, markets and customer segments (Figure 2-2).

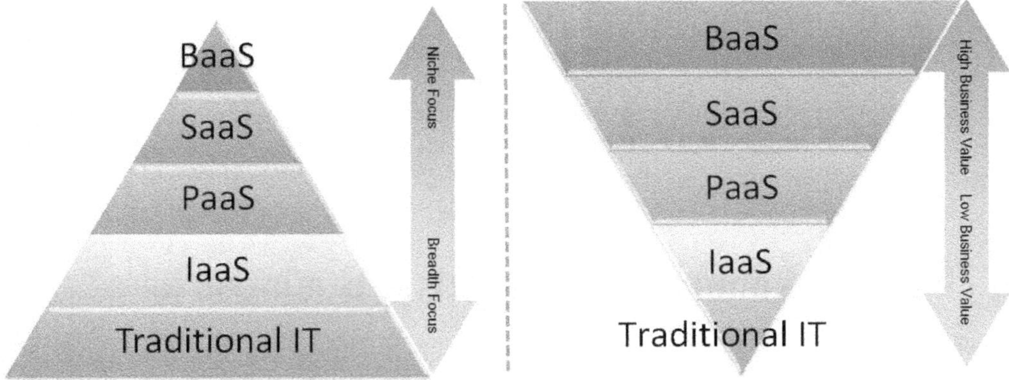

Figure 2-2: Traditional-IT to BaaS

What began as client-server, virtualization, service-oriented architecture (SOA), distributed computing and time sharing has rapidly evolved into various forms of cloud computing. It starts with Infrastructure-as-a-Service (IaaS), then progressing to Platform-as-a-Service (PaaS) and most recently, advancing to Software-as-a-Service (SaaS). There are several intermediate stages in this evolution, such as Management-as-a-Service (MaaS) and Business Process-as-a-Service (BPaaS) (Figure 2-3).

This "macroevolution" of the cloud begs the question, "What's next? What's the immediate future of the cloud, and where is it headed?"

- **MaaS** began by providing security, policy management, authentication, disaster recovery, billing, provisioning, capacity planning, monitoring, and systems management.
- **IaaS** provisioned hardware including processing, storage and networks to the consumer, while providing the consumer the capability to deploy and run both operating systems and applications on the provisioned resources.
- **PaaS** took the premise of IaaS a few steps further by provisioning hardware computing resources, operating systems and platforms or tools. It gives the consumer the capability to deploy and run self-created or acquired applications built using programming languages and the provisioned tools.
- **SaaS** extended PaaS by allowing consumers to provision their custom-built software business applications on top of hardware computing resources, operating systems and platforms/tools.

- **BPaaS** allowed providers to provision horizontal or vertical business process services on using SaaS, built on top of PaaS, IaaS and MaaS.

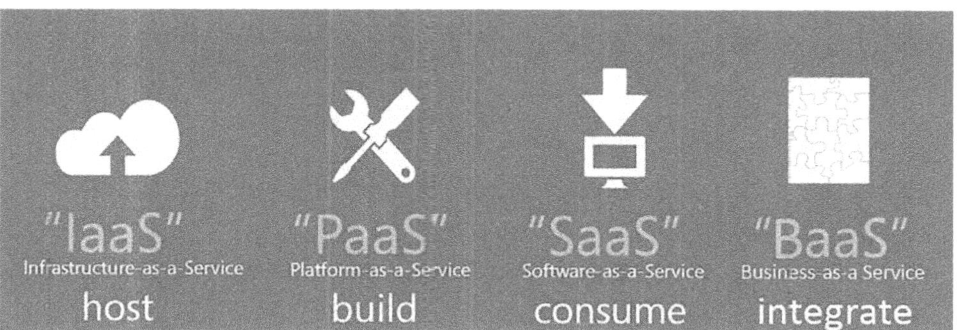

Figure 2-3: Major cloud service categories

The next step in this evolution is to move a business vertically or an entire business division into the cloud, in the form of Business-as-a-Service (BaaS). It's the service that will be provided to the consumer as an integrated set of transactional and collaborative activities to accomplish a specific organizational goal.

Comprehensive business services (offered as SaaS) will be orchestrated (as BPaaS), managed and monitored (as MaaS), run (as PaaS) and hosted (as IaaS) - all in a cloud. This concept of Business as a Service will allow end-users and partners to remotely run and monitor entire business verticals in the cloud, and allow CXOs to focus on their core businesses instead.

Using BaaS, vendors will not only host the software solution on their infrastructure on behalf of an organization but also take part in managing the business, to ensure goals are met. BaaS will bring together the architectural, modeling, technical, design, planning and monitoring templates and competencies necessary to allow an enterprise to quickly deliver low-cost, scalable and reliable business solutions to their customers.

Additionally, BaaS will allow CXOs to accomplish specific organizational goals and jumpstart their businesses by providing relevant tools, operating models, SLAs and integrated sets of transactional and collaborative activities (figure 2-4).

BaaS will bring to the table the following benefits:

- **Speed**: Business vendor experience and complex, knowledge-based work to deliver the best business results, fast

- **Adaptability/Agility:** Add on innovation from third parties to enterprise business processes
- **Scalability/Elasticity:** Service availability to other companies with shared costs and shared risk options
- **Reliability/Repeatability:** Process learning, improvement and automation internally and externally
- **Cost Flexibility:** No capital investment with a subscription pricing model
- **Analytics:** Performance, efficiency and cost improvement reports
- **Strategic Goal Focus:** Greater efficiencies and innovative business capabilities by combining platforms, applications, infrastructure and knowledge processes
- **Collaboration**: Improved communication between business and IT
- **Monitoring and Accountability**: Real-time monitoring and management of business processes

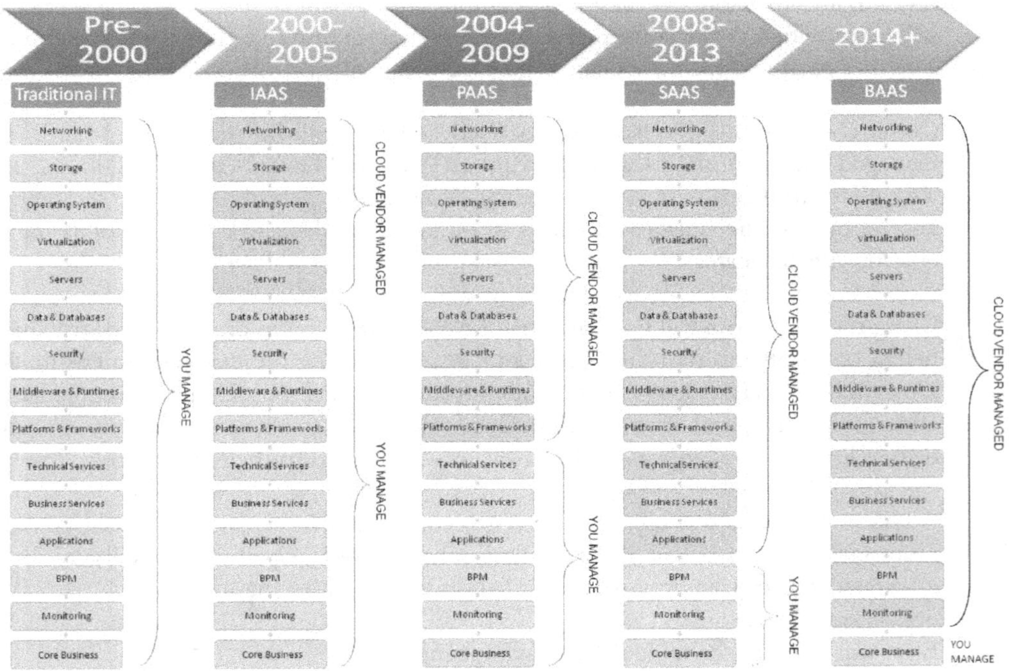

Figure 2-4: Different evolutions and stacked approaches of cloud services

BaaS isn't without some drawbacks, though most of them are arguably because of a lack of maturity. Without standards in place, the quality of service transparency and management will be questionable. Security of data, processes and applications will be another concern, because of the lack of maturity of cloud security policies and standards.

Finally, there is a lack of governance in cloud computing, with data consistency, integration, policy management and oversight are still in their infancy. However, none of these are insurmountable, and as BaaS comes into its own and matures, these problems will most probably vanish.

So where is cloud computing headed beyond BaaS? If VPNs, client-server and grid computing were classified as the pre-cloud era - version 0.1, then IaaS, PaaS and SaaS are the current mature standards in cloud computing - version 1.0. I foresee the next version of the cloud - version 2.0 - focused on businesses (BaaS), open standards, social media and mobile computing. Beyond that? XaaS - everything in the cloud, including Big Data.

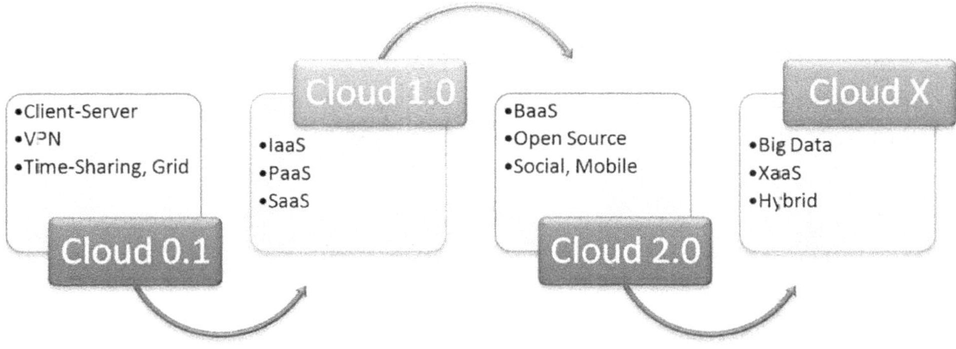

Cloud computing isn't a revolution. It isn't the "next big thing". It isn't the "silver bullet" to the problems of infrastructure costs, reliability and scalability. It is the slow but steady evolution of a thought process, a way of evolving business from one stage to the next. We're seeing the next stage of this evolution, as startups are being born in the cloud, and are shaping very future of the cloud itself.

Technical comparison of PaaS, IaaS and SaaS

Now after we enjoyed our pizza and looked at it from a more business perspective, let us look at those terminologies from a technical angle (figure 2-5).

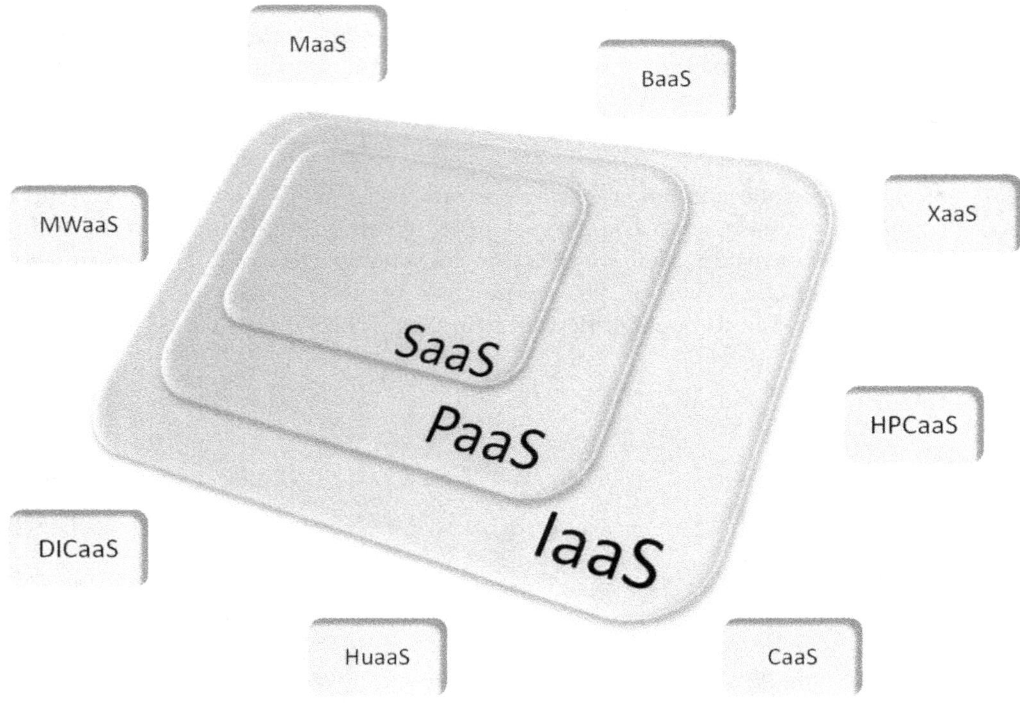

Figure 2-5: IaaS, PaaS and SaaS

IaaS, SaaS, and PaaS are all standing for different level of cloud solutions. It is important to understand the differences as explained in our Pizza example. You can either build all by yourself on premise or use ready-made service on different level (Infrastructure, Platform or even Software). Each level offers a number of services and all together these three main concepts offer a stack approach of services.

It is important to understand which services are offered on which level in order to choose the right level of service platform for your project. As depicted in the above graphic IaaS is the most basic, PaaS builds on IaaS and finally SaaS is being built on top of PaaS. So what do all these three acronym stand for?

IaaS (Infrastructure-as-a-service)

This is the most basic of the service offerings. Basically only the infrastructure (like network, operating system and storage) is created by the service provider. The project administrators then create their own platform and finally business systems based on this infrastructure. Also the responsibility of maintaining, patching, troubleshooting and updating is in the hand the project team. This kind of service offers a higher flexibility for the project but also demands deeper a higher amount of technical skills in different area.

Infrastructure as a Service (IaaS) means to use infrastructure services or most likely complete virtual machines on demand. The service provider has to take care of these devices or virtual machines including all their services they depend on, e.g. networking, hardware or operating system patches. This basic service is interesting for a number of use cases which includes special software that does not run on PaaS or even SaaS or software with special requirements which can be met by higher level offerings. The drawback is that for this service the user must have appropriate experts and skills for all lower level technologies like operating system and more.

Benefits include lower invest in hardware, better scalability, a better payment model (e.g. pay per usage) and more. In almost all cases this also offers a better independence from physical locations as service provider have usually more data center locations than the user itself.

PaaS (Platform-as-a-service)

PaaS is utilizing the infrastructure services and add software platform services to it. The basic idea is to relieve the application developer from dealing with the application hosting platform - like J2EE container, databases and others. It does not provide business applications, but all what is needed in order to host business applications. PaaS therefore operates on a lower level then SaaS. Throughout the rest of the book we will encounter WebLogic multitenancy to be located mainly in this area. The service provider is responsible for providing the infrastructure and the platform. PaaS service offerings abstract many of the usual non-business tasks which takes so much of typical application development. This includes for example, dealing with name services, security, persistency layers, connection to infrastructure and remote services and more.

Technically speaking, PaaS offers services which are required for your application to run in addition to the infrastructure. The most famous example is the database layer.

Almost all applications need a database, but not all projects have (or want to have) on own DBA which they need to pay. Also in this case they usually do not care if the database is running in multitenancy mode or standalone. Additionally, the patching and the maintenance of the database is the business of the service provider. Some for the operating system which usually is also considered to be part of PaaS whereas for IaaS you will just get the naked machine.

Benefits of this service offering includes especially the availability of service specialists on the provider side. The provider maintains services and also offers the support of those (like operating system, database, application container environment like J2EE environment, .NET or scripting environments)

SaaS (Software-as-a-service)

This is top level model of the aforementioned three. In many pictures IaaS, PaaS and SaaS are depicted as a pyramid whereas SaaS is the top part, sitting on top of PaaS which itself is sitting on top of IaaS. SaaS provides the infrastructure, the platform and even the software. Many software vendors today are offering SaaS versions of their products like Microsoft Office in the cloud, email services, social network services and so many more. This means SaaS comes with preinstalled business software.

Very often this goes hand-in-hand with multi-tenancy where these software instances will be tailored and configured differently for different tenants (e.g. customers). SaaS doesn't offer the flexibility of creating custom software like IaaS, it instead is targeting to users which would like to use ready-made enterprise software in a cloud based environment where they e.g. only need to pay per usage or order to timely restricted license. The big benefit for users of SaaS is that they do not need to worry about maintaining, patching or updating the underlying software. They can also switch to different versions or vendors more easily than users of PaaS or IaaS. A very popular example is Salesforce.

Special cloud offerings

Beside the very common IaaS (infrastructure), PaaS (platform) and SaaS (service) there are a number of others "*aaS" service offerings known in our industry. Some of them are still niche offerings and emerging others already better established.

This section only wants to name some of them as examples. There are more out there and new ones are appearing.

Monitoring as a Service (MaaS)

Every application, especially production environments - need a reliable monitoring and alerting. Many service provider - especially in the SaaS area but also in the PaaS area - offer this service to get business values, throughput values, non-functional requirement values for the applications and also to generate alerts on certain conditions

High Performance Computing as a Service (HPCaaS)

High Performance Computing as a Service is a service around high performance computing. This services basically offers a grid as a service for high performance and highly parallel computing requirements.

Database as a Service (DBaaS)

This basically only offers the database as a service. This could either be part of PaaS or PaaS provider can offer this as an additional services. In case of an application uses IaaS for whatever reasons but would like to service out the database to a provider DBaaS could be a nice offering as well. But customers should take into in account, that there will be a noticeable network latency. This limits the possible scenarios, but does not always make them impossible.

Backup as a Service (BaaS)

A very important service for all applications. Which application or platform nowadays could live without backups? Backup and restore based on certain SLA's (service level agreements) are vital services for all applications. Instead of building an own service it would be better to use available services. It also is a huge advantage, if you store backups away from your servers. In case of any disaster, you have a reasonable chance not losing your business critical data completely. It is recommended to practice disaster recoveries on a regular bases.

Communication as a Service (CaaS)

Not the CaaS definition used at the beginning of the chapter is meant here. Communication as a service means outsourcing infrastructure like VoIP or even emails or social networking to a standard service.

Data Intensive Computing as a Service (DICaaS)

This is a special service for dealing with very large amount of data. This is very common for scientific institutes.

Other possible special services

- Humans as a Service (HuaaS)
- Business Process as a Service
- Container as a Service
- Data as a Service
- Desktop as a Service
- Identity as a Service
- Network as a Service
- Security as a Service
- Storage as a Service

XaaS – Anything as a Service

So finally… what does XaaS mean?

XaaS or in other words "anything as a service" is basically a model where everything is offered and can be used usually through a hybrid cloud computing model. It is usually a combination of different services or a mix of everything.

XaaS is quickly becoming a definition of integrated services which emerged from former separate services being now possibly hosted in hybrid clouds.

Summary

Even though this book does not have cloud as its main topic, it is important to understand and differentiate the different main terminologies around cloud. With the new multitenancy features added to WebLogic, Oracle also provides a foundation for WebLogic in the cloud.

Please note that the WebLogic multitenancy features are NOT a requirement to run WebLogic in the cloud but it makes a PaaS offering of WebLogic much easier and much more powerful.

I prefer to name this **WaaS - WebLogic as a Service** - and will use this acronym throughout the book when appropriate.

Introduction to WebLogic

CHAPTER

Introduction to WebLogic

As this book is not a WebLogic tutorial or beginners guide, this chapter only provides a very brief overview over the WebLogic concepts. This book will not introduce WebLogic in detail. Please refer to the extensive WebLogic documentation from Oracle, all the different (administration) books or all the other websites and blogs which are available

What is WebLogic?

WebLogic is a complex, professional application server environment with a complex and powerful security environment. WebLogic server at its core implements the J2EE specification stack and its main purpose is to offer a hosting environment for J2EE applications. But WebLogic is much more than just J2EE.

Like most professional J2EE servers, WebLogic also offers a large number of extended features like very comprehensive management, clustering and failover functionality on different levels, and a number of extended enterprise features that are not required by J2EE but very useful in the enterprise world and required by many companies.

What is a Domain?

A domain is the basic administration unit for WebLogic. This administration unit consists of one or more server instances and is managed by one of the server with a special role, the so called administration server (=AdminServer). This server hosts the management console and manages none or more managed servers which may be hosted local to the AdminServer or remotely on different physical or virtual machines.

Managed servers may be grouped into clusters. If managed servers are located on remote machines, separate NodeManager instances can be used for lifecycle operations (start, stop, and monitor). You can define multiple domains based on different system administrators' responsibilities. You may also (although this is definitely not recommended) use a single domain to manage and monitor all WebLogic Server instances. The central configuration file is called *config.xml* and it will play a major role in our further understanding of the scripts and management tasks. This *config.xml* file is stored on the Administration Server together with other files such as database configuration files and security files.

Each AdminServer manages exactly ONE domain and all changes or activities will only apply to this domain. All the scripts and source code in this book runs against one AdminServer (unless states otherwise) and therefore targets one domain. For more information on domains, see e.g. the Oracle Documentation

Every domain must contain at least one the administration server. For development and testing this might be sufficient as this server can also host applications but this setup is strongly discouraged in production and production like systems.

The next diagrams show the most typical WebLogic domain configurations

Typical development domain

This is the most basic setup. This shows a WebLogic domain with just one server - the administration server.

This is a typical development setup or setup on a private machine. The administration server here also hosts all the application components

Local WebLogic domain

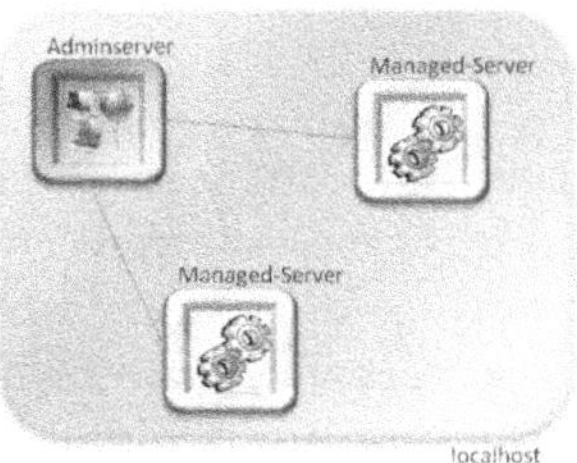

This is a more complex but still local domain. This domain includes an administration server for administration tasks and two manages servers which host the application components.
Note that in this setup the managed server cannot be started by the AdminServer. The managed servers

need to be started using the generated start scripts.

Domain managed by Nodemanager

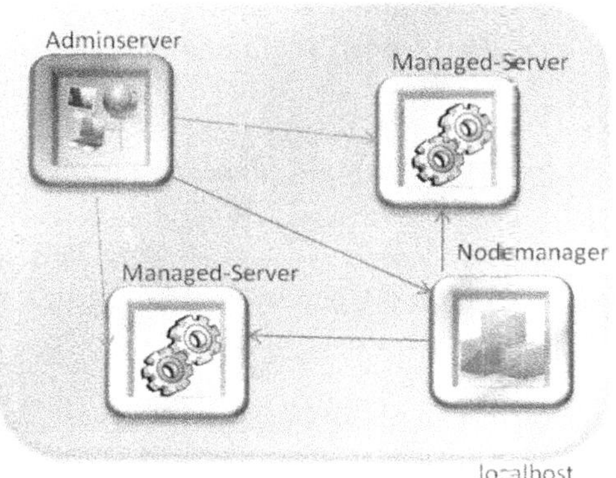

Now we are moving to the first complex but fully managed domain.

In this setup we introduce the nodemanager as local control instance which is able to start (on the request from the AdminServer) the managed servers on its own machine.

The AdminServer will request a server to be started and the NodeManager will do the job.

The NodeManager is also responsible to restart a crashed managed server (if configured to do so!)

Unmanaged distributed domain

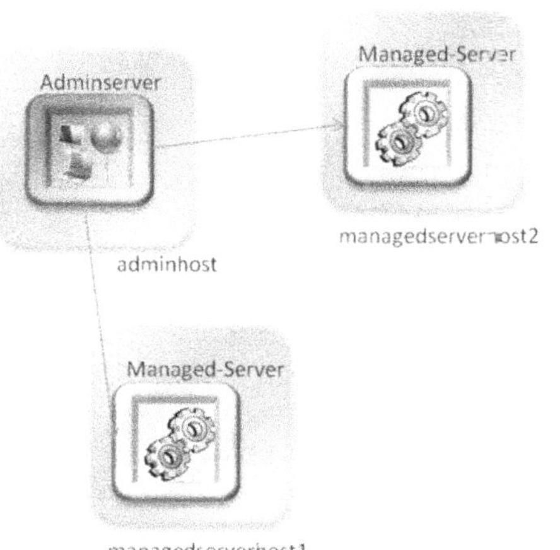

Now we are moving to a truly distributed domain which spans multiple physical machines. The AdminServer may of course also be collocated with one or many managed server but it is advisable to separate it from the managed servers.

In this example also the managed server must be started using the generated scripts. This is a rather rare setup as it involves a number of manual steps on different machines to start/restart a domain.

Standard remote domain, managed by NodeManager

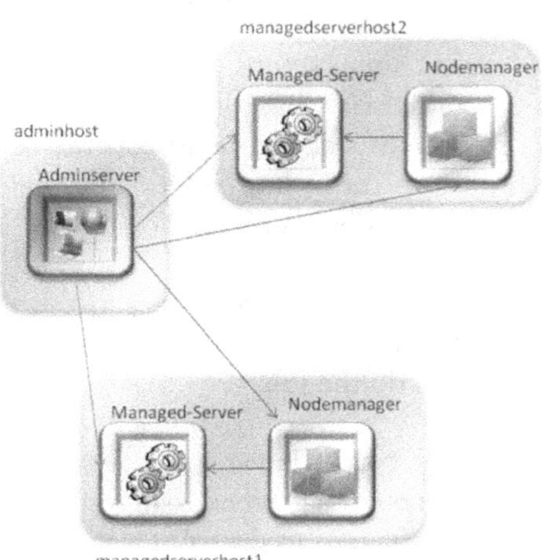

The last example is the most common setup for production and production-like systems. Here we have a fully managed distributed domain.

Each machine must be equipped with its own NodeManager in order to start the managed server on demand. Of course it is necessary to start at the NodeManager already during system boot (init.d on Linux)

The NodeManager is also responsible to restart a crashed managed server (if configured to do so!)

Deployment, configurations and monitoring is all done through the NodeManager which will delegate appropriate actions to the managed servers.

Note: In the above diagrams: Blue lines are AdminServer<->managed server communications and red lines are NodeManager communications

WebLogic Cluster

Every WebLogic domain can be composed of a number of managed servers. Beside the administration server, managed servers can be grouped into clusters. Every WebLogic domain can host multiple clusters, but each managed server can only be a member of one cluster (if at all).

A cluster hides the complexity of a potential distributed group of servers and offers a single interface to the client that can be used for communication and deployment. Furthermore, a cluster offers a wide range of features with regards to scalability, load-balancing, replication, failover and migration.

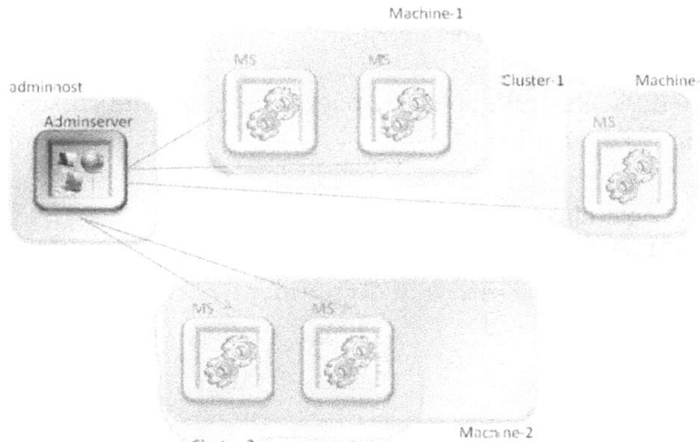

WebLogic domain with multiple clusters

Every domain can have multiple clusters. Every cluster can (but does not need to) include managed server hosted on different machines

From many years of working with clusters in different companies and environments the following rule of thumb has been proven to be a good general approach (but this does not mean that it can be applied to all environments!):

> For development and testing it has been proven to be beneficial to create domains hosting one cluster only as these domains - including the admin - need to restarted, reconfigured and redeployed quite often.

Furthermore, those domains are usually under the control of the developers or test teams. Small domains with a small number of managed servers form much better isolated environments and also do reduce the start/restart time. Production and production like system (like load and performance test, final integration test or similar) have a different character. Those domains are owned by system administrators and are usually stable.

For those types of domains, it is advisable to create domains hosting many different clusters as this makes the life of system admins much easier. It is a nightmare for all system administrators if they need to do administration server hoping all the time. As we will see in this book automation should be used for most activities. Nevertheless, the admin console is still a very valuable tool for controlling and error searching.

Otherwise it is frustrating, wastes a lot of time and makes the monitoring and management much more complex. It's good advice to group applications with similar functionality together, like, for example all human resource applications or applications for a specific region in the world, or all application with the same patching/lifecycle requirements. For WebLogic it is often required to group applications with the same security (provider) requirements as we will see later.

What can be clustered?

A clustered service or component is available on all managed server of the cluster. For those failover and load balancing is available.

For the following objects WebLogic clustering is available: Servlets, JSPs, EJBs, RMI objects, JMS destinations, and JDBC connections. We will see during the upcoming chapters which options are available for the different components.

What cannot be clustered?

The following options cannot be clustered: File services including file shares and time services.

Cluster communication

Since WebLogic 10 a cluster offers two different ways for the internal communication: Unicast and Multicast

Prior to WebLogic 10 only multicast was supported. Multicast is based on UDP broadcast for sending announcements out to all cluster members who are listening on a specific multicast address and port. There is a defined range for valid Multicast addresses (224.0.0.1 to 239.255.255.255). Everyone listening on the given address gets the announcement. Multicast has a number of issues as it must be supported by routers, subnet, and firewalls.

Unicast uses a point to point UDP protocol to send the packet to a specific member and not everyone. In order to realize cluster communication using unicast, one server in the cluster (not the administration server) has the role of the cluster master. In big clusters WebLogic also divides the cluster in different groups with one "group"-master for each group. In the case of WebLogic, the oldest manages server in the cluster/group has the role of the cluster master. If this server dies, the next-oldest takes over its role. Unicast is also the preferred option of network administrators.

Older environments are sometimes still using multicast.

A useful tool provided by WebLogic to monitor multicast traffic is the Multicast-Monitor. This is a command line tool which can be used on the shell. It takes the multicast address, the port and the domain and cluster information as input:

```
weblogic.cluster.MulticastMonitor <address> <port> <domain-name> c name-of-
```

The WebLogic Nodemanager

Especially in production systems, almost every WebLogic domain will contain managed server running on different physical nodes. In order to separate administration from application, it is highly recommended to run the administration server on own physical machines. But then we ask:

- Who is in charge of starting/stopping the managed servers?
- Who can take of failed managed-server and can try to restart them on the remote boxes?

Remember, these are the primary tasks of the nodemanager.

The nodemanager is a small process that can communicate (secure or unsecure) with the administration server. Also, the administration server can issue commands like start/stop/restart/status or others to the nodemanager. The communication between administration server and nodemanager is pure TCP, and it can be secured using a secure SSL protocol. Thus, every machine which hosts managed servers has to have a nodemanager so that the administration server can also be used for lifecycle operations of these managed-servers. The alternative to the nodemanager is to do it yourself.

Resource

As we know, WebLogic is a full blown J2EE server. One of the main tasks of every J2EE server is to control and coordinate resources and provide them to the applications - normally via JNDI. The developers of a J2EE application should never care about resources. The resources must be provided and maintained by the application environment - the J2EE server.

Many tasks around WebLogic have to be done by the administrators (in an automated way) to configure, maintain and control resources. The most important resources are:

Transactions

Nearly everything in a J2EE server is based on transactions. So different transaction requirements must be fulfilled depending on the applications. JTA (Java Transaction API) is the top-level API in charge of transactions. Settings include e.g. transaction timeouts, amount of transactions …

JDBC based databases

Can you imagine a modern server based J2EE system without a database? Well there are some but not too many. Databases very often host critical and confidential data and are therefore very important and critical resources which must be secured and controlled

Java messaging (JMS)

Messaging provides the means for asynchronous communication. JMS (Java Messaging System) is the most common API which must be supported by all J2EE servers

Java mail

Sending emails as notifications is an often used feature. JavaMail provides this capability.

Threads / Connections

Threads and connections are very valuable resources and overload protection is key for most server systems, especially if the number of parallel users varies over time.

Any other (proprietary) resources

WebLogic offers a number of other resources like Tuxedo access, COM access, network access points …

WebLogic Security

Due to its complex nature and the potential usage in many different environments, including DMZ, real-time, high risk financial system, confidential/secret data handling and many other usages, WebLogic has a comprehensive security environment spanning all areas of security. Please refer to the detailed Oracle documentation (including several book dedicated only to security).

WebLogic Security stack overview

WebLogic has a comprehensive security stack which covers all areas of security. Later in this book we will look at different ways to configure the various security aspects using WLST and later JMX. Therefore a brief summary of the different security areas is provided here and will be referenced later.

Security can be divided into a number of areas and technologies/specifications:

- **Auditing:** means collecting security relevant information about operating requests and their results. The collected information are stored and distributed for the purposes of non-repudiation. Auditing is very helpful in critical environments where the company has to make sure that they know and can prove who did what and when. In WebLogic auditing providers are used to provide auditing services and collect the information. If provided, every call in WLS will go through to the auditing before and after security operations have been performed, when changes to the domain configuration are made, or when management operations on any resources in the domain are invoked.

- **Authentication:** means that the systems needs to find out who is the caller and to verify that the caller's credentials are valid (e.g. correct password, username is valid, certificate has not yet expired). Authentication providers are used for this purpose and remember, transport, and make identity information available to various components using the JAAS (Java authentication authorization service) subject.

- **Security Assertion Markup Language (SAML):** The SAML standard defines a common XML framework for creating, requesting, and exchanging security assertions between software artifacts
- **Authorization:** This includes all actions which have to take place before the real application/resource is called in order to verify if the user credentials which are provided with the incoming call do have the permission to access to requested resource. An authorization provider or even a chain of providers have to be passed. These providers are using security policies or access control lists (ACLs) and answer the question "Who has access to the WebLogic resource?" By default, the XACML Authorization provider is configured in a domain, and security policies are stored in the embedded LDAP server.
- **Identity and Trust:** Establishing trust is a very important aspect of security. Artifacts used and supported in WebLogic are private keys, digital certificates, and trusted CA's (certificate authorities). This is not only needed for establishing trust, but also for verifying identity. The public key is embedded into a digital certificate. A private key and digital certificate provide identity and the trusted certificate authority (CA) certificate establishes trust for a certificate. Certificates and certificate chains need to be validated before a trust relationship is established.
-
- **Secure Sockets Layer (SSL):** WebLogic supports SSL communication, which enables secure communication between applications. SSL can be used standard client communication with the flavors of SSL over t3 (t3s) or SSL over iiop (iiops). For web applications WebLogic supports https.

Security Realms

All security mechanism for protecting WebLogic resources are grouped into a security realm. WebLogic does support the definition of multiple realms but unfortunately WebLogic only allows one realm active at any given time. The default name of this security realm is *myrealm*. Due to the fact that only one realm can be active at any time, it usually does not make sense to define own realms. The only reason for defining own realms might be if you need to exchange default security providers with own implementations (e.g. if you have special security requirements like own security or back-ends)

A realm contains a set of configured security providers, users, groups, security roles, and security policies. Users must exist in this realm and granted the correct rights in order to access WebLogic resources.

The following security provider types do exist. This does not mean that all of them are always needed or used. Available types: Authentication Providers, Identity Assertion Providers, Principal Validation Providers, Authorization Providers, Adjudication Providers, Role Mapping Providers, Auditing Providers, Credential Mapping Providers, Certificate Lookup and Validation Providers, Keystore Providers, Realm Adapter Providers

Extended security services

- **RDBMS Security Store:** It is possible to setup a WebLogic domain to use an external RDBMS as a data store which is beside the user/groups directory used by different providers to store security information

- **OPSS (Oracle Platform Security Services):** OPSS is the Oracle implementation of a security framework which provides a standards-based, portable, integrated, enterprise-grade security framework. OPSS is used in many products in the Oracle Fusion Middleware family including WebLogic, ESB, SOA Suite, OWSM ADF and other. This framework provides APIs and an abstraction layer in order to unify and ease security configurations.

- **OWSM:** The Oracle Webservice Security Manager is an advanced concept which outsources web service security aspects to an external server. The idea is to have a central repository for web service security policies which can be used by many different servers from potentially many different domains. This is substantially reduce security configurations for each domain, but adds administration, management and monitoring pain for the administrators. A whole chapter in this book is dedicated to OWSM

Benefits of WebLogic Automation

WebLogic environments normally grow quickly, and I have been working with production environment with hundreds of WebLogic domains with altogether several thousands of managed servers. It is impossible to manage (bigger) WebLogic environments manually. Especially for production and production like systems this is close to impossible. For legal and audit guidelines it is normally always required to use automated environments which will document what has been done, when, where and from whom. Please see next chapter for details

Summary

WebLogic is a comprehensive J2EE hosting environment with a wealth of additional features. The core concept of WebLogic is the WebLogic domain. WebLogic server instances can have the role of an administration server for a domain and/or a managed server for hosting J2EE applications.

The Need for Automation

CHAPTER

Introduction

Have you ever tried to configure dozens or even hundreds of domains using the WebConsole? Have you ever setup a larger number of domains by using the wizard which ships with WLS? Albeit these are very good tools for testing and private installations, they are very inefficient for large - and especially production - installations.

For whatever tasks that need be done in daily business operation, automation is the key and WLS offers a number of different technologies to achieve this goal. As the rest of this book will make use of these technologies, this chapter provides a brief introduction to automation. In the appendix readers will find references and links to books and resources for further information about these technologies.

Automation and multitenancy are by nature two very distinct topics. With the new partition model (which will be explained in detail in this book), there is even a higher need to settings up resources and repeat configurations. Therefore automations – especially for configurations – are important technologies in order to utilize these new WLS features.

Scripts and automations are essential for every (infrastructure) architect, administrator, deployer, operator but also for every developer. Only with automated processes it is possible to create actions which are audit save, can be reviewed, can run at any time, can run frequently (monitoring!) and can be scheduled with automated scheduler. And only automated processes can be replayed in the exact same way, they have been performed before. Especially if one needs to roll-back or just replay the installation, it won't be possible to do the same things again.

Complex environments may consist of hundreds of domains and thousands of managed servers. It is impossible for an administrator group to maintain all those servers with manual tasks or even with the web console. The web console is a very useful tool for development and also up to production for human eye checking and verification, but from my experience the web console should never be used in higher integration or even production environments for changing tasks of any kind.

Therefore WebLogic offers a comprehensive and powerful automation API which can be used either via WLST (Jython based) or via JMX.

The following is just a list of examples (far from complete) what can be automated using WebLogic APIs.

Examples for automation which is possible with the WebLogic API

- Creation of domains
- Using WebLogic templates, extending WebLogic templates, using own WebLogic templates
- Extending domains with cluster, machines, node managers, managed-servers
- Configure all kinds of resources
- Configure data sources
- Configure JMS / JNDI resources
- Deploy applications to cluster or individual servers
- Start/stop/restart domains, clusters or managed servers
- Start/stop/restart data sources, deployments, …
- Settings on-the-fly debug configurations
- Setting log configurations
- Monitor ALL parts of the server, including data sources, JTA pools, thread/connection pools
- Monitor java heap and other VM settings
- Monitor server/domain/cluster state
- Configuring all aspects of the security layer including SSL, keystores, SSL-NodeManager communications, web service security, security provider, authentication/authorization provider
- Configure user, groups and user access roles
- Monitor http access counts, EJB access counts, transaction values
- Monitor application state

Especially with production systems, we should never use the WebLogic GUI console for configurations or administrative tasks. The console is still very useful for control activities, but all actions should always be done in a documented and reproducible way. This is not only useful for administrators and save their time but is also very often a "must have" requirement to fulfill audit requirements.

Therefore WLST and/or JMX are very common technologies to achieve this goal in a sensible and cost-effective way.

There is also another technology which WebLogic is making use of which can help to create even more flexible setups. WebLogic supports templating for different components within WebLogic. Templates can be used for dynamic clusters and also in the JMS area.

Jython and WebLogic

The WebLogic Scripting Tool (WLST) is a toolkit that administrators and operators can use to monitor and manage WebLogic domains. It is based on the Java scripting interpreter Jython. In addition to WebLogic scripting functions, you can use common features of interpreted languages, including local variables, conditional variables, and flow control statements. Administrators can extend WLST for their own needs by providing features, functions, or classes based on the Jython language syntax. Three different forms of executions are available: scripting, interactive, and embedded. WLST can be enabled for online and offline connection modes and can act as a JMX client (figure 4-1).

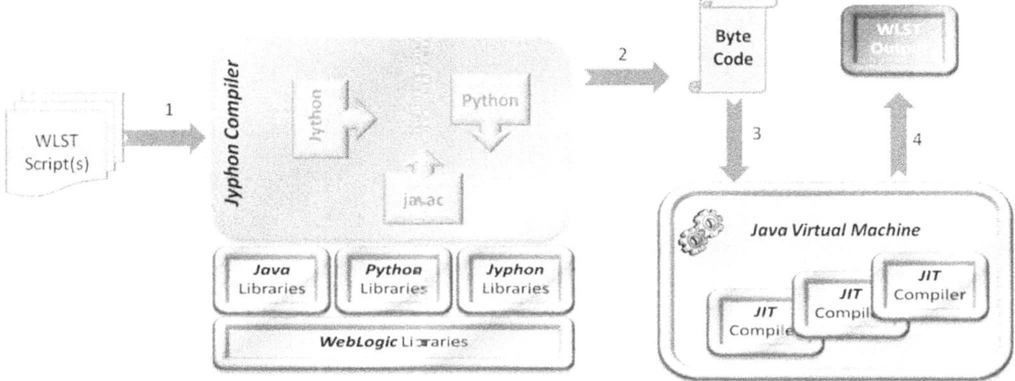

Figure 4-1: Depiction of the Jython/WebLogic compilation process

The source code for the WLST script is written as a Jython script. It is recommended that the WLST program file should have the file extension ".py" which is the default extension for Jython/Python source code files.
This source code is going to use a JVM machine when it is instructed to RUN the script; its invocation internally generates Java byte code to interpret with the JVM to produce the desired output.

JMX and WebLogic

WebLogic makes heavily use of JMX. In fact everything is organized in a different MBean server and different MBean trees. The WLST (WebLogic scripting environment) is just a Jython interface to the complex MBean structure (beside the other WLST features of course).

In order to understand the administration and monitoring, it is essential to understand the WLS MBean structures. It is essential to understand the differences between Runtime- and Edit-MBeanServer and the concepts WebLogic is using for their JMX layer (figure 4-2).

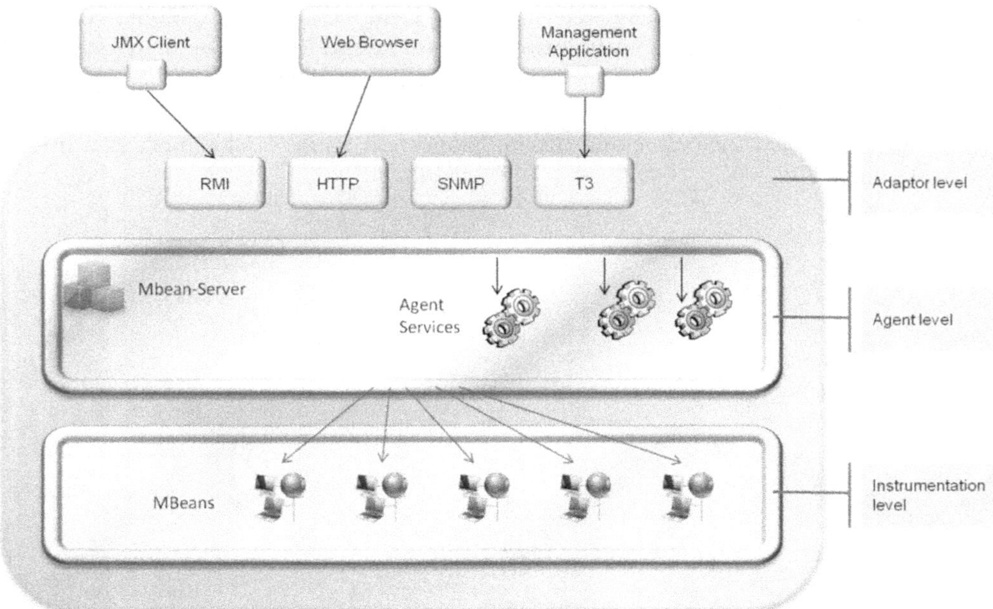

Figure 4-2: Different levels of JMX

REST and WebLogic

WebLogic has introduced a new management and automation API based on REST web services.

To the zoo of WLST and JMX, Oracle has added a new management animal - management via RESTful services. With this addition Oracle moves away from the traditional java management via JMX (pure java) or Jython (WLST).

REST was introduced in WLS 12.1.2 and starting with WLS 12.1.3 the management offering via REST has been extended and offers another - albeit proprietary - management capability.

So what is the benefit of using RESTful management instead of JMX/WLST ?

First of all the easier way of communication in protected systems areas like a DMZ. It is quite cumbersome to manage WLS domains remotely via JMX or WLST when you need to open (sometimes complicated) firewall paths. Firewall holes always introduces risks to environments.

Furthermore, most firewalls cannot inspect java/JMX calls. As REST is based on HTTP, it will become much easier to reach those kind of domains. Second major benefit is that Oracle opens up WLS management to basically any language. The only requirement is to use the http protocol and REST and maybe some JSON data on top of it.

So, what is the catch? The only real disadvantage is that Oracle introduces a proprietary way of management here. JMX is defined in a standard, Jython is a programming language. The definition of the WLS REST calls are Oracle specific though.

WLDF and WebLogic

WLDF (WebLogic Diagnostic Framework) is an integrated framework in WebLogic in order to collect, save and analyze runtime data for monitoring or troubleshooting. It provides a number of services which will be executed within the WebLogic server VM. Using these services, you will be able to gather information which will help you to get a detailed view into the runtime performance of our server instances and also inside the deployed applications. It is a very valuable tool for error location and diagnostic operations.

WLDF offers a set of features and configurations can be composed out of a number of components. One of them is the integration with Mission Control (which has been added to the Hotspot JVM 1.7.0_40 and above) which means that WLDF can add information to the JRockit Flight Recording file. Capture Diagnostic Image allows the administrator to record a live snapshot which can later be used to analyze problems.

The archive feature capture and archives information. Code instrumentation allow the user to collect data at specific operations. The harvester feature allow the data collection from standard and custom MBeans. There is also a feature to send out notifications when certain events occur.

WLDF consists of the following:

- Data creators
- Data collectors for the logger and the harvester components
- Archive component
- Accessor component
- Instrumentation component
- Watch and Notification component
- Image Capture component
- Monitoring Dashboard

Data creators collect diagnostic data which is then passed to the components "*Logger*" and the "*Harvester*". The main server state can also be captured using the image capture component. The logger and also the harvester will use the archive feature in order to persist the collected information. In case there are notifications or watches configured, these components will also inform these parts of WLDF. In order to query and use the data, the accessor subsystem will be used.

The WebLogic Diagnostics Framework (WLDF) is provided by Oracle as an integrated set of components which offer powerful features for analysis and monitoring.

WLDF is a powerful subsystem of WebLogic. It is neither a separate product nor has to be installed separately. WLDF is completely integrated in WebLogic, runs in each WebLogic server instance and provides components and APIs which enables the user to access runtime information from WebLogic's MBeanServer.

Note that it does not provide access to the ConfigurationMBeans, only to the runtime MBeans. WLDF is not meant to be a tool for creating reports about the configuration. WLDF is targeted to work with runtime information. WLDF can be used to collect

data from different MBeans or create state snapshots. Other WLDF components can perform certain analysis or actions based on the collected data. The data can be access via external tools or displayed using the integrated dashboard. Main goal of WLDF is it to provide access to insight information into the runtime state of servers and applications in order to monitor health or detect and analyze problem situations.
One very important aspect of WLDF is that the data collection can be started/stopped at any time without restarting the WebLogic instance. Furthermore the amount of data (collector definitions) can be changed at any time without restarting the WebLogic instance.

WLDF Components

WLDF provides a very powerful framework. The side effect is that its structure and component dependencies are quite complicated. The following simplified and higher level overview shows the main artifacts and components of WLDF (figure 4-3).

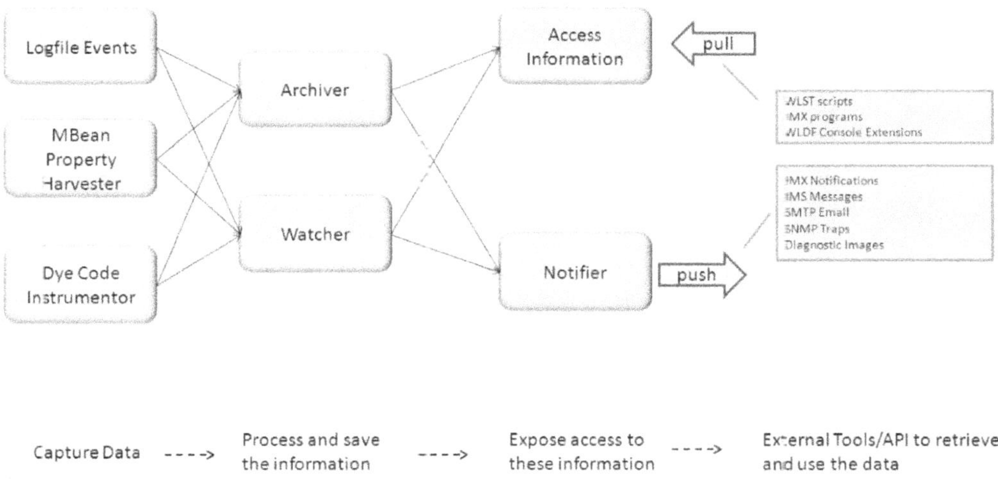

Figure 4-3: Simplified view on WLDF

(Based on the blog of Paul Done http://pauldone.blogspot.com/feeds/posts/default)

WLDF consists of the following components:

- Data creators (basically the standard and custom MBeans available in WLS)
- Data collectors (the Logger and the Harvester components)
- Image Capture component

- Archive component
- Accessor component
- Instrumentation component
- Watch and Notification component
- Monitoring Dashboard

Logger, Harvester (and also the image capture feature) collect and consume runtime information which is created by the different data creators. Normally data creators are the different runtime MBeans inside the runtime MBeanServer of the WebLogic instances. Its collected data is used by the "*Archive*" component for persistence and by the "*Watch*" and "*Notification*" components for monitoring and analysis. The data access subsystem communicates with the harvester and the logger for getting real time information and with the archive for historical data.

Summary

WebLogic is the technology stack used for hosting J2EE applications. WebLogic consists of many different APIs and features for developers, but also a rich set of features for administrators, which includes WLST based on Jython and JMX.

WLDF (WebLogic Diagnostic framework) is an integrated part of WebLogic. WLDF is a complex framework that offers a lot of components for collecting data, analyzing data, creating notifications based on conditions and much more. It can be configured and used by using either the WebLogic console or WLST scripting or JMX.

Automation based on different technologies like WLST (Jython), JMX or REST are key to handle any size of a complex environment.

Part II

Multitenancy & WaaS - WebLogic as a Service

Interesting couple: Multitenancy and WebLogic

CHAPTER

Introduction

After looking at Multitenancy in general in the first chapter and its broader scope with cloud services, this chapter provides an architectural overview of the new partitioning and multitenancy features of WebLogic 12.2.x

Middleware as part of the entire stack

As we have seen in the introduction (for example with the nice pizza example) multitenancy and isolation are concepts which can be implemented on many different levels. In addition, typical applications include a number of technology stacks, therefore is a logic – albeit big –move made by Oracle to re-architecture WebLogic to also support multitenancy natively.

In this section I do not want to look at a technology stack like platform->OS->JVM->e.t.c. Instead I would like to focus at different Oracle technologies working together. Having support for a concept like multi-tenancy only in the middleware but not in the database for example is by itself definitely an improvement but not a complete story.

Oracle is completing its multitenancy story step-by-step. After having support in the Oracle database and also in the Oracle caching infrastructure called Coherence the next step is now done by adding similar support for the middleware technology.

The following graphic shows an infrastructure based on the WebLogic 12.2.x codebase, which implements multitenancy from the entry point (load balancer) all way though into the database (figure 5-1).

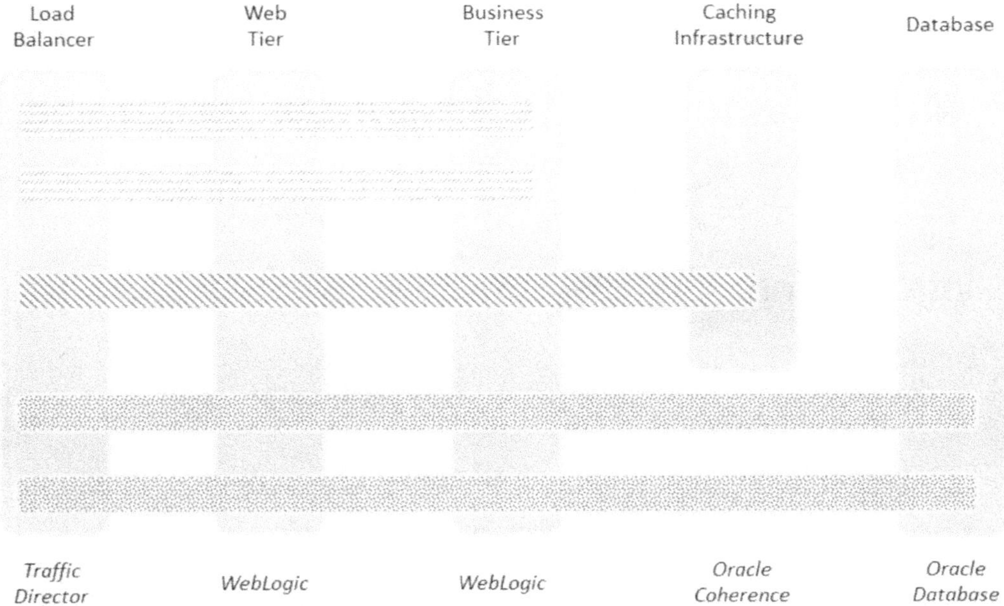

Figure 5-1: Example multi-tenancy setup

In the example above two tenants of the same type (first two rows) have a multi-tenant setup from the load balancer (e.g. different DNS names like myshop1.xyz.de and myshop2.abc.de or different URL prefix like shops.de/xyz and shops.de/abc) to a webapp running in a tenant setup and finally to the core business running as a tenant setup. This could very well be a cloud setup service.

The second example (row 3) goes a step further and also uses a tenant specific cache and the last example (last 2 rows) also utilized multitenant features up to the database.

This picture demonstrates well that with the new multitenancy feature WebLogic can move down the chain from pure application level to be part of the platform. Service providers – like cloud service providers – can feature this by offering WebLogic as a platform and allow you to order your proper share of that WebLogic platform. I like to call this "WebLogic as a Service" or just WaaS.

Multitenancy in WebLogic or WaaS

With the introduction of WebLogic 12.2.x, a completely new concept was introduced into WebLogic in order to support multitenancy setups and concepts. The new administrative and organizational concept is called a partition. A partition is – similar to a filesystem partition – meant to be a well-defined area of WebLogic, with some new and powerful features.

Other than the standard J2EE bundling units like EAR, WAR or RAR archives, the partition goes beyond that and allows a bundling of applications (J2EE units) and required resources like JDBC, JMS and many others.

Therefore for the scope of this book (note this is not an official Oracle terminology) I will define a "WebLogic application" which combines application and resources. It is up to the designer or administrator to define, which service should be part of which partition. So these services are isolated and dedicated to just one partition. In opposite to that, there are services that will be shared among all or at least some partitions. This depends on the demands and the decisions been made by the designer or administrator (figure 5-2).

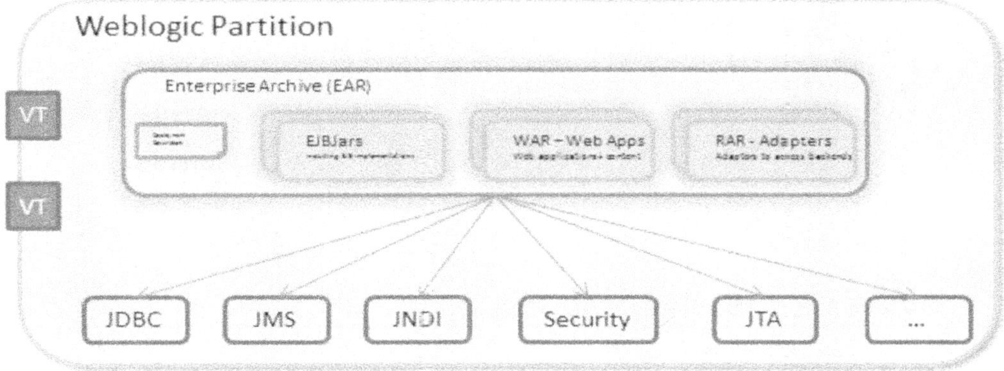

Figure 5-2: Partition as new "WebLogic application" which combines applications and resources

The traditional WebLogic setup always required the full stack starting from the JVM up to the application (unless it was agreed to co-deploy applications). This also means two JVM instances on the machine, a full WebLogic including all internal resources for each JVM and no chance to share resources. Furthermore JEE applications were always separated from their resources as all resources were defined on WebLogic level (figure 5-3).

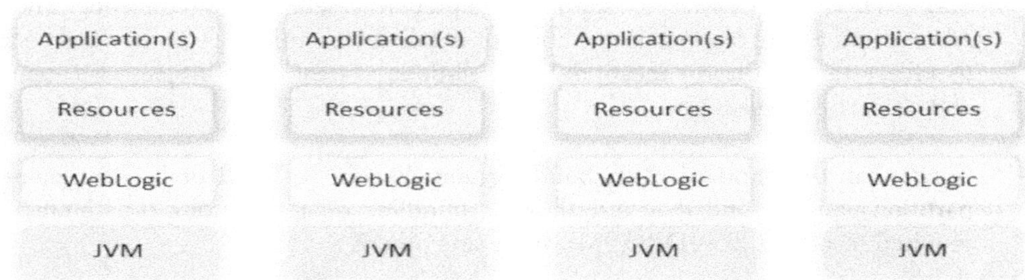

Figure 5-3: Traditional WebLogic setup

The new model actually basically implements a number of ideas from cloud based systems, albeit it has by nature nothing to do with a cloud (figure 5-4).

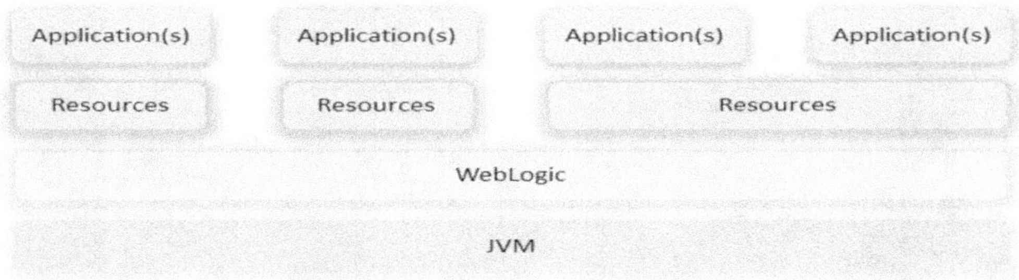

Figure 5-4: Example of a new WebLogic setup

The new model share the same virtual machine, even though (see the next section of the book) the JVM resources can be separated for different applications. Also the WebLogic kernel will we shared. On top of WebLogic it is then possible to define resources (JDBC, JMS or others) in the traditional style and share them between applications (right part of the example) or to form a new atomic unit between application and resources whereas resources are only visible and usable for one application. These new units are called partitions.

This has a number of benefits which are explained in detail later in the book. Benefits include a reduced number of domains, a reduced footprint on the filesystem, reduced costs as hardware can be more effectively utilized via a higher density of applications on the machines. This supports PaaS or SaaS like cloud models to be implemented on top of WebLogic. WebLogic also implements more features like security isolation and resource isolations.

Despite of features like higher density and others, this concept supports multi-tenancy. The terminology "tenant" in this context is basically an instance of such a "WebLogic-Application" running as partition in WebLogic. Based on a common resource template it is possible to create multiple instances for different purposes or customers. This is the core concept of multitenancy to host different instances of the same applications whereas every instance has its proper purpose.

WebLogic support these concepts with a number of new technologies which have been implemented into WebLogic. Resource templates can be created in order to form administrative units of resources and to target all of these resources to the same target. Instances of these templates can either run in the core WebLogic in order to share resources or can be assigned to be part of a partition. Whenever a partition is created based on a shared resource template, it is possible to adapt the template to partition needs using resource overrides.

A new target mechanism has also been added to WebLogic. It allows an abstraction layer between real targeting and resource/partition targeting. This is called "virtual targets" (figure 5-5).

Key Concepts

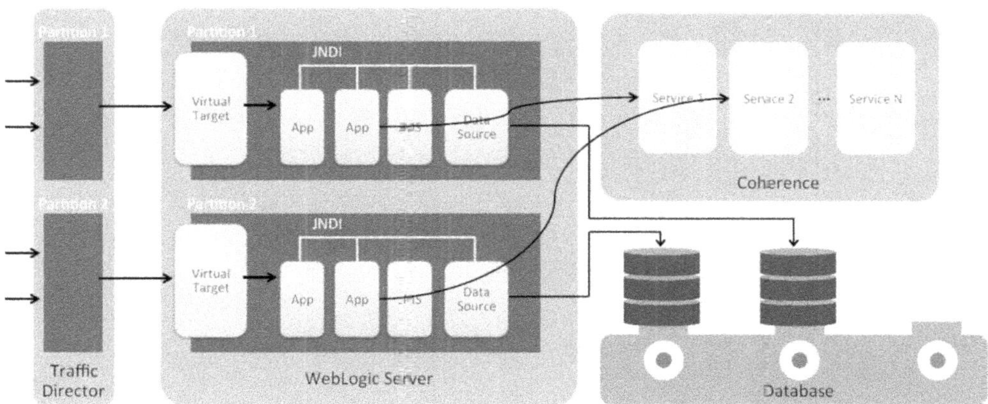

Figure 5-5: Key concepts © Oracle

Resource Targeting

Up to WebLogic 12.1.3, all resources (like datasource or JMS servers) were created on WebLogic level, which means that they were globally available for this domain. The administrator only had the option to target them to a specific managed server (or servers) or to a cluster, which would reduce their visibility to those WebLogic instances.

In the new partition model, which is based on the concept of "WebLogic applications", the old model of targeting resources to WebLogic server or cluster is no longer sufficient. As stated above resources either belong to WebLogic core (old style) or are part of a resource group.

For example, a traditional setup of a datasource would define a datasource on domain level. All applications can make use of the same datasource. With the new partition model, the datasource can be defined to only be accessible for this partition only. This also means that the datasource becomes a part of this partition.
If the same type of resources should be reused for multiple tenants then a resource can also be part of a resource group template.

Putting this all together requires WebLogic to support different targeting or resources. As this targeting influences the visible scope, WebLogic is calling this resource scoping (figure 5-6_.

Figure 5-6: Example: Scoping of a new datasource

Based on the new features, WebLogic supports four different scopes. A scope is a fundamental configuration decision and cannot be changed later. The scope influences the location and also the name of the associated MBeans in the configuration tree.

WebLogic supports the following 4 levels of scoping:

- **Global:** This is the default and implements the old style WebLogic core resource services. These resources or applications are not part of a resource group or a partition

- **Resource group template:** Note that each resource group template will be named in the scope list as each template is an own potential scope by itself. Resource group templates are always on domain level and cannot be targeted. The real availability of the resource or application depends on the instance of this template and weather this instance is created on domain or partition level.

- **Partition based resource group:** The resource/application is limited to this partition only. Only this scope allow an administrator to create a resource or deploy an application which is only visible within a specific partition. As this is not a template, only one instance of this resource will be available at a time.

- **Global resource group:** Resources are bundled into the global resource group and are not scoped to a specific partition.

How does WebLogic implement multitenancy?

The basic idea behind the concepts implemented in WebLogic is not new, but it is the first time they have been implemented in a J2EE server infrastructure.

Let us draw a "big picture" of the partition and multitenancy support of WebLogic. WebLogic has basically implemented two new concepts: Resource isolation and resource + application bundling. In addition WebLogic provides some interesting lifecycle and management features around it.

One of the fundamental new concept is the concept of resource groups. Resources like JDBC datasources or JMS are grouped together into a resource group. The complete group – means all resources of that group – can be started/stopped together. For flexible resource isolation these resource groups can either be scoped globally or for a specific partition. In order to create "WebLogic applications" the new concept of a partition has been created, it can combine applications and resources into a new unit. This new unit can be targeted using an abstraction layer called virtual target, so that administrators can assign units to real infrastructure without changing the internal partition or resource group targeting.

Multitenancy means that the same application (JEE applications and resources) can be instantiated multiple times with tenant specific characteristics. It does not make much sense that in this case resource groups must be created multiple times for each tenant as this is unnecessary work and pretty error prone. The answer to this problem are so called resource group templates which allow the administrator to create resources only once and scope them to a resource group template.

The template itself is not a real group, therefore it cannot be started or stopped. But it is possible to instantiate global or even partition scoped resource groups based on this template. For each real resource group based on the same template, an own set of resources will be created, which also raises the question that this might be not optimal as it does not allow tenant specific configurations like JDBC schema users. Again, WebLogic has implemented an answer to this problem which is called resource overrides. These overrides allow the administrator to tailor the instance of a resource group template to the tenants needs.

As partitions form their own unit, WebLogic also allows administrators to create an own – partition scoped – security realm which makes security configuration much easier. In addition it allows WebLogic to export the partition security together which the partition.

As partitions form units, WebLogic has already implemented export and import features which enables an administrator to export a partition from one environment and import it to another (e.g. move it from UAT and production).

The following key technologies are part of the multitenancy offering

- **Resource Groups:** Resources can be grouped together under a common name – the group name. As this implements a new abstraction layer, WebLogic also offers lifecycle operations like start and stop for the whole group, which means these will be then executed for each resource in that group.

- **Resource Group Templates:** Blueprints for resource groups. Everything deployed to such a template will not be instantiated but will kept in the configuration MBean tree. As soon as concrete resource groups are created based on this template, the resources get instantiated in the scope of the real group. The resource group template can contain one or more elements of the following list:

  - Application Deployments
  - Library Deployments
  - JDBC System Resources
  - JMS System Resources
  - Coherence System Resources
  - File Stores
  - JMS Servers
  - Messaging Bridges
  - Path Services
  - Persistent Stores
  - SAF Agents
  - Foreign JNDI Providers
  - Mail Sessions
  - WLDF Modules

- **Partitions:** Partitions are the core administrative concept in WebLogic which implements the concept of "WebLogic applications". The partition is THE unit in

WebLogic which can combine applications and resources and which can provide different levels of isolation – down from the JVM up to WebLogic services, security and more.

- **Tenants:** Tenants are not configuration concepts of WebLogic. Tenants are instances of the same application but tailored to different customers, which is the principal concept of multitenancy. Tenants are technically also implemented as partitions

- **Resource Overrides:** Adapting instances of resource groups to tenant specific needs. Overrides allow the administrator to change certain settings of the resources defined in the template like database user/password

- **Resource Isolation:** Isolation is key of the multitenancy implementation of WebLogic. There are different levels of isolation which will be explained in more details in a following section of this book.
- **Virtual Targets:** Virtual targets provide an abstraction layer which can be used to target partitions and resource group. On WebLogic level these virtual targets have a concrete configuration based on hostname mapping, port mapping or URL prefix. As the same virtual target can be configured differently in different WLS domains, migrating partitions to other domains (like UAT -> PROD) is much easier and straightforward.

Different layers of multitenancy

(© by Oracle WLS 12.2.1 documentation)

Understanding SaaS Multitenancy

In a SaaS environment, if an application cannot internally provide a per-tenant view or the necessary per-tenant isolation, you might instead deploy separate instances of the application and its related server-side resources for each tenant. Each tenant might get its own stack that includes hardware capacity or Java virtual machines, WebLogic Server domains, Administration Servers, Managed Servers, clusters, and other related resources, such as web servers, data grids, networking, and storage. At the very least, this is inefficient.

The WebLogic Server MT (MT=Multitenancy) SaaS model provides a way to get the most efficient use from server resources while still providing resource isolation. Each tenant gets an application instance plus resource instances on the targeted servers and clusters. The same application or applications run concurrently and independently on multiple domain partitions. No code changes to the applications are needed: WebLogic Server manages the domain partition identification and isolation.

In the SaaS model, you typically define one or more applications and the resources they depend on in a resource group template. You then reference this template from every domain partition in which you want to use the same applications. You make any domain partition-specific changes by editing the values of the associated resource group.

Understanding PaaS Multitenancy

The WebLogic Server MT PaaS model is synonymous with consolidation. Consolidation means that you can deploy different applications from many tenants into the same WebLogic infrastructure. WebLogic Server MT shares the infrastructure and underlying resources including the domain, clusters, Managed Servers, hardware, and network. In the SaaS use case, the WebLogic Server system administrator typically manages all the domain partitions and their resource instances. However, in the PaaS use case, partition administrators are more likely to administer their respective domain partitions and the resources within them, including configuring resources and deploying applications.

Summary

After looking at Multitenancy in general and it broader scope with cloud services in the first chapters, this chapter discussed an architectural overview of the new partition and multitenancy features of WebLogic 12.2.x

On the overall picture Oracle has closed a gap in its technology stack by also adding multitenancy features to its WebLogic middleware product after similar features are also available to the database and Coherence caching.

These new features provide a fundamental architectural change in WebLogic administration as WebLogic provides solutions for a number of use cases which were unsatisfied up to now. The next chapter will discuss the major uses cases which benefits from this new architecture.

Please note that multi-tenancy is an offer but NOT a must. WebLogic can be used in the same way as before in case you do not want to use partitions but it is definitely advisable to move to partitions, even if you only plan to host one.

When, where and how to use Multitenancy

CHAPTER

Multitenancy is not the golden source for everything

Multitenancy is for Oracle a very big step forward in the evolution of WebLogic. Albeit not required, multitenancy offers a very interesting and powerful foundation for WaaS (WebLogic as a service) and WebLogic cloud services.

The last chapters provide an overview what multitenancy is all about and what WebLogic multitenancy has to offer. Nevertheless, multitenancy is not a silver bullet for everything. It is important to understand its value and use cases where this approach adds real benefit.

One of the main sections later in this book explain a number of use-cases in detail including technical configuration and usages. This chapter already lists those use-cases which are discussed later, but we also discuss the benefits and disadvantages. It is also important to understand where to not use this approach, this chapter also includes a section about possible scenarios and use cases where the traditional approach has more benefits than multitenancy.

The following use-cases will be reviewed from a WebLogic perspective. This means that the benefits and disadvantages discussed should be understood as benefits and disadvantages for your WebLogic setup.

The concept of multitenancy exists in many different technologies like databases, virtual machines (like VMWare) and others. Looking at the following use-cases with a focus on other technologies might have a different result with regards to benefits and disadvantages.

Use-Cases for multitenancy

The following list includes some use cases where (WebLogic) multitenancy features and technologies definitely add advantages. Note that all these use cases will be explained in detail later in the book. Please refer to section five of the book.

Optimized usage of memory by co-locating different test/integration/uat environments

One of the major technical advantages is a much higher density of resource utilization. A very popular example are test environments. It is often necessary for a project to have multiple test environments for different development teams or for different versions of a product. In the traditional approach all of them would be installed, use their space on the file system and as they are usually up and running using memory and so on. With multitenancy this could become a one installation environment with the different test environment being different tenants.

Optimized usage of resources (density)

Applications hosted as multiple tenants can share resources. In case of WebLogic resource sharing is a flexible and configurable process which allow applications to either share resources like JMS, JDBC or JNDI or use (part of them) exclusively. In addition sharing means that there is no network overhead like t3 calls or http calls involved as all tenants are co-located in the same address space. Multitenancy concepts of course already exist for resource systems like databases or caches (e.g. coherence).

Reducing platform footprint

Installation of application servers need a significant amount of disk space. Even if done right and the binaries are separated from the WebLogic domain so that these are not duplicated, still domain structures and all sorts of standard files need space. In a multitenancy environment this can be reduces to a small number of real application server installations which reduces the amount of disc space (and also backup, tape space and so on) necessary.

A new way of looking at applications by including their resources

The biggest packaging format defined in the J2EE standard is the EAR file. An EAR file contains all deployments for the different application server container. It can contain standard archives (like EJBs, WARs, and RARs) but also vendor specific ones.

All these components together form a deployable application. But it does not contain the resources and resource definitions needed by this application like JDBC pools, JMS destinations, JNDI trees or network endpoint to name a few. WebLogic multitenancy changes this by defining a new application container (called partition) which combines all these.

Optimized usage of CPU power by co-locating apps with different resource footprint

This is a day-to -day business nightmare for many companies running global applications. For example, an application which serves Europe has high CPU requirements during European day time. Another application which serves the US has CPU requirements during US time and applications for Asia need system resources for the Asian day time. But as all applications are installed and reserve their resources they usually are installed on different hardware. This also means that the hardware is basically idle for 66% of the day. By hosting them as different tenants on the same infrastructure, companies can reduce their installation of hardware and have a much better CPU utilization

Improved long-term migration between application versions

This scenarios is also a well-known nightmare. Given that an application "A" has to be replaced by "A_v2" but users have a grace period (days or even weeks) to migrate from "A" to "A_v2". This means that the company has to run both in parallel for the same time. The user load will stay all the time the same but will be shifted from "A" to "A_v2". Hosting them on the same hardware/middleware as multiple tenants has a significant benefit that no additional hardware/middleware is needed.

Shared app server/domain = Reduced administrative costs

Have you ever administered environments with thousands or hundreds of domains? Well this is really no fun without proper automation. A reduction of domains by combining applications as multiple tenants into fewer domains reduces the administrative overhead a lot.

Technical benefits by using the new isolation stack (one partition model)

Another technical benefit of using the new multitenancy (partition) model in WebLogic is the fact that Oracle has improved the lower level stack – the Java VM in this case – to support resource isolation. Even with only a single tenant, which is equal to the traditional hosting, the new lower level stack features – especially the resource managers - can be used.

Application Update/Versioning

How does updates usually work? Well a second server environment is build, configured and tested. Then during a downtime the connectivity and real traffic is redirected to this new environment. Or in a downtime like a bet and pray approach all configuration will be done on the live system. The first is resource consuming and the second gambling. With multitenancy a new tenant can be setup on the production system and when finished the traffic can be redirected. Afterwards the old tenant is archived. This is much more efficient and less error prone

Lightweight application transitioning and migration

An application is usually configured and tested in "integration". After that this application has to be installed in the "UAT (user acceptance test)" environments in order to test non-functional requirements and very often production like setups, e.g. end-to-end connectivity. By using the new partition model, application together with their resources can be copied from one environment to the next without the need of updating/re-installing a WLS server environment. This makes the transition much faster and easier. Similar benefits exist for the migration between different servers or even migration to new WLS versions.

Improved/Optimized (production like) testing and troubleshooting

Even more important than the previous use case is the problem of re-creating production issues. Typically a reference environment exist which can be used to reproduce production issues. But both need to be setup and maintained. Using the WebLogic multitenancy model it is possible to take a snapshot of the production model (with WebLogic 12.2.1 onwards only an offline snapshot but maybe in the future even a hot snapshot with production states) and moves it to the reference system.

This guarantees that application and resources are really identical to the production which had the issue. Furthermore this allows that the reference system can be used to reproduce issues from different production systems and versions which is a bit benefit w.r.t. to time, cost and resources and most probably will lead to short times until a fix can be provided.

Where multitenancy cannot be used

WebLogic's concept of multitenancy offers a flexible way decide which part of the server resources should be shared and which not. Even though there are a number of scenarios where I would not recommend to use multitenancy or multitenancy is even not possible at all.

Special (real-time) load requirements

Multitenancy certainly offers a lot of benefits for resource and density usage. But there also exist systems which are really designed to utilize all CPU cycle by itself and it would cause business impacts and damage if these applications could not reserve all the resources for themselves. Examples may include real-time-trading applications, medical systems and others.

Special hardware integrations

Standard WebLogic applications can virtually run everywhere. But there are systems which require special hardware integration or special (expensive) hardware components. It would be contra productive to spend a lot more money for more of these special hardware only to co-locate applications onto it.

Special software requirements

WebLogic exists in many different versions and patch level. Albeit you always should run the latest versions, this is often not possible. Furthermore there are cases where special custom patches or libraries are needed which need to be applied to the middleware layer (WebLogic installation). In this case these modifications would affect all tenants as they all share the same WebLogic middleware layer. If this is not possible or not wanted then it is better to stay away from multitenancy and run these applications on their special platform.

Special security requirements

WebLogic offers separated security realm per partition (tenant) or a shared security model. Nevertheless all tenants are running in the same WebLogic instance and therefore in the same process and therefore using the same operating system user. In case it is required that different applications are also separated by operating system users in order to shield access to files/information from each other, then this cannot be implemented using WebLogic multitenancy. It is still a kind of IaaS multitenancy on operating system level but no longer on WebLogic level.

Legal requirements

International companies often face the issue that some countries require that their data must not leave the country. Countries like Poland, Saudi Arabia, Turkey and many others insist that the servers running the business logic must be located in their countries. In this case it is not possible to use the aforementioned benefits like better density or resource sharing due to forced geographical restrictions.

Summary

Multitenancy has a number of benefits. This chapter has named a number of concrete use cases where WebLogic multitenancy can be very beneficial. Later in the book all these use cases will be explained in greater detail with examples and configurations.

Part III

Isolation on different levels

Technology and Tenant Isolation

CHAPTER

Importance of Isolation

In the last chapter, the term "isolation" was mentioned a number of times. Isolation is actually key for multitenancy and therefore this part of the book discusses the most important levels of isolation and depicts which levels are of importance for WebLogic and the WebLogic multitenancy offering.

Multitenancy's key element is the sharing vs. isolation of resources for multiple tenants. Sharing can happen on different levels, which means that multiple tenants can share the same resources.

The more important concern is isolation. What happens if one tenant requires too many resources (like too many threads or too much CPU) of if one tenant causes a deadlock on resources? Isolation is a key concept to ensure that tenants which live together and share common resources cannot harm each other by "stealing" the resources reserved for the other tenants. Another important area is separation of tenants.

Any service provider delivering a multi-tenant environment must adhere to these six commandments as nicely defined in the core principles (© Richard Seroter)

1. **Thou shalt isolate tenants within their own network**. This one applies mainly to infrastructure-as-a-service (IaaS) providers who promise secure computing environments. Software-as-a-Service (SaaS) customers on a platform like Salesforce.com don't have this issue as customers do not have access to low level network traffic. When granting virtual machine access to users, the service provider has to ensure that there's no opportunity to intercept network traffic from other customers.

2. **Thou shalt not allow tenants to see another tenant's metadata**. Sometimes metadata can be just as sensitive as transactional data! Multi-tenant service providers must make sure that customers are logically or physically walled off from seeing the settings or user-defined customizations created by other customers.

3. **Thou shalt encrypt data in transit AND at rest**. Providers shouldn't let their guard down just because data is within their internal network. Rather, data should constantly be transferred over secure channels, and encrypted whenever it's stored on disk.

4. **Thou shalt properly clean up deleted resources**. In a multi-tenant IaaS environment, there is clearly reuse. When a network is released by one customer, another can use it. When a storage volume is removed, that space on the SAN is now available for others. It's imperative that service providers reset and clear resources before allowing anyone else to acquire them.

5. **Thou shalt prevent noisy neighbors from impacting others**. This phenomenon is one of the hardest problems to address in multi-tenant environments. As a user, you have no say in who else is using the same environment. It's up to the service provider to make sure that one customer can't (intentionally or unintentionally) adversely impact the performance of other customers by overwhelming the shared compute, storage, or networking resources.

6. **Thou shalt define and audit policies to ensure proper administration of shared environments**. Let's be honest - using a multi-tenant environment involves a bit of trust. As a customer, you have to trust that the service provider has built a platform that properly isolates each customer, and that operational staff can't go off the reservation and compromise your business. However, to run mission-critical apps in someone's multi-tenant platform requires more than blind trust; you should also be able to demand to see 3rd party certifications and audits that prove that a mature organization is behind the platform.

Technology Isolation

This part of the book discusses technical isolation levels and especially discusses in which area WebLogic and the WebLogic multitenancy can be used to achieve isolation. There are a lot of different technology levels and technical isolation areas. In some of them WebLogic offers new features. It is key for administrators to understand where WebLogic own features can be used and where other technologies must be added to achieve the desired isolation. Note that isolation is very often a useful addition, sometimes even required due to legal or physical restrictions but also in many cases just not necessary. A case by case analysis is required when and what level of isolation is necessary (figure 7-1).

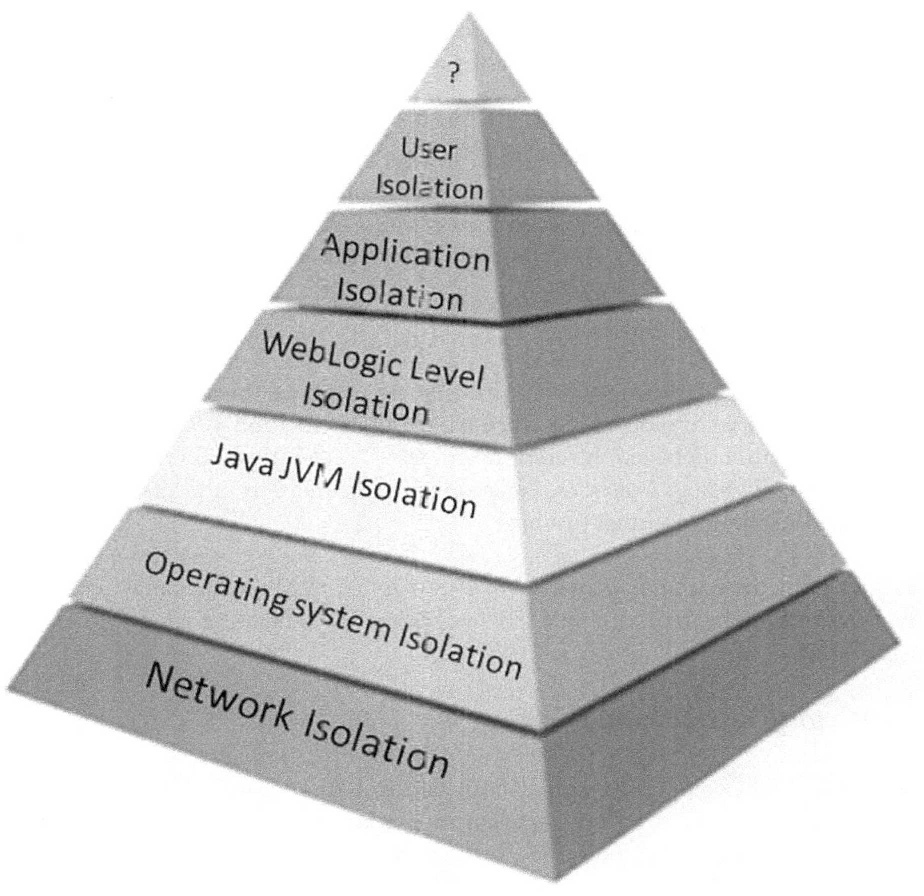

Figure 7-1: Technology levels of isolation

Technical isolation levels

The following levels of isolation can be distinguished.

Network isolation

This isolation means that different tenants or in general technical components cannot be reached using the same network. Examples include DMZ, dedicated database LANs, special LAN segments and more.

Operating system isolation

This isolation can actually be divided into two different topics. The more "coarse grained" means that each technical component is running using its own operating system. Very common example are virtualized machines like VMWare or VirtualBox.

Another interpretation which falls into this category is an isolation on a single operating system using operating system features. This mainly means separating processes by system users/group such that different processes cannot utilize disk space from other processes and cannot access files/directories from other processes (tenants).

Java JVM isolation

As Java is our base platform we will be looking especially on this virtual machine. There are a number of technologies out there which allow isolation WITHIN a Java virtual machine. Isolation between different machines => see operating system isolation Especially for WebLogic, resource isolation (threads, memory, and file descriptors) has been added to the Java virtual machine.

Another implementation is provided by the Waratek JVM multitenancy feature where a hypervisor layer protects multiple tenants whereas each tenant is running in a specially forked JVM.

(WebLogic) Service level isolation

Coming to WebLogic as the application platform running on top of the base JVM system. WebLogic offers with the new partition concept a way to isolate system services like JNDI, security, JDBC and more for the different partitions. In a flexible way it can be configured which services shall be shared and which shall be isolated.

Application isolation

The partition concept of WebLogic is the key to run multiple, isolated tenants. Each tenant is usually an own application. All can (if wanted) run in the same JVM address space but are isolated from each other. This is called throughout the book a WebLogic application in order to distinguish it from a traditional J2EE application which is packed as EAR (Enterprise Archive) deployment unit.

User isolation

It is possible to implement even more fine grained isolation whereas each user gets an isolated address space for a user session or even each business call. This is not possible with standard WebLogic features but mentioned for the sake of completeness.

Isolation provided and used by WebLogic

With WebLogic features it is possible to implement or configure isolation in different of the aforementioned areas.

Network isolation

WebLogic can of course provide nothing for real hardware separation of networks. But it is possible to simulate network isolation by using different network channels inside the different partitions which are configured to listen on different network adapter. The hardware itself is in this case a multi-homed host but each partition can only be reached using a different network adapter.

Operating system isolation

There is nothing WebLogic provides for this category.

Java JVM isolation

Especially for WebLogic, resource isolation (threads, memory, and file descriptors) has been added to the Java virtual machine.

(WebLogic) Service level isolation

The new partition feature – which is the core topic of the whole book – is the new key concept which has been added to WebLogic to implement service and application level isolation.

Application isolation

Applications as defined by J2EE, which are provided as enterprise archives were always isolated in WebLogic (unless explicitly not wanted) as they are loaded in own class loaders and they also had own environmental naming context areas.

This books also defines the terminology "WebLogic-Applications" which are basically the classic J2EE-applications together with their resources. This new broader application is also isolated between other WebLogic-applications. This is supported by WebLogic through the new partition model.

Summary

Isolation is a very important factor for multi-tenancy systems and cloud hosting. Many different levels of isolation are possible and it must be considered on a case by case analysis which level(s) of isolation are required.

Operating System Isolation

CHAPTER

Description

Even WebLogic has no OS isolation features in this category, but this level is so important that we will discuss potential solutions in this chapter.

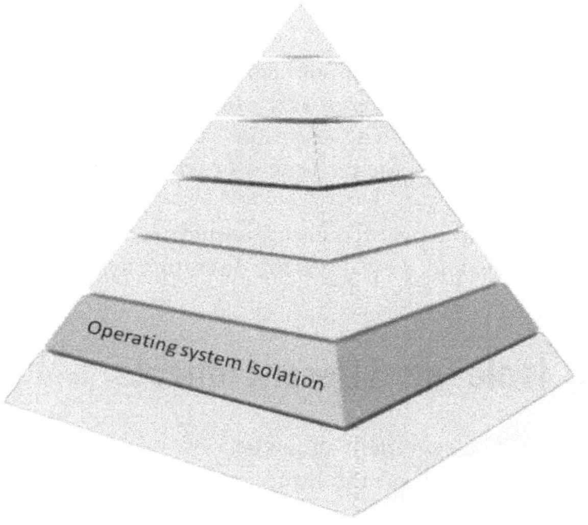

Operating system isolation can actually be divided into two different topics. The more coarse grained means that each technical component is running using its own operating system. Very common example are virtualized machines like VMWare or VirtualBox.

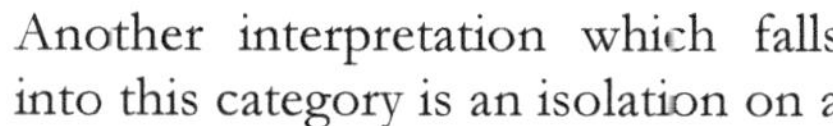

Another interpretation which falls into this category is an isolation on a single operating system using operating system features. This mainly means separating processes by system users/group such that different processes cannot utilize disk space from other processes and cannot access files/directories from other processes (tenants).

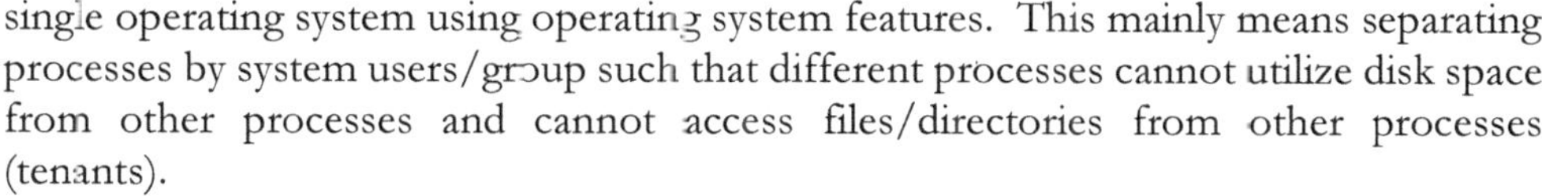

This section will focus on process isolation within one operating system using system security features like distinct users/groups.

Protecting the platform

A common security vulnerability is code injection. Using WebLogic, there is a simple way of achieving code injection. For example, imagine an application that is writing a special library to server/lib which replaces a WebLogic library. As soon as the server restarts, the new code gets loaded and the server is hacked. And this is only one example out of many ways that. code injection can be used.

Therefore, one very important aspect of every WebLogic installation should be to isolate the WebLogic platform – basically all files provided by Oracle and all installation directories like domain/lib and others in a way that the WebLogic process cannot write or change files in these areas.

This can easily be achieved by using different operating system users. One user for installation files and one runtime user which is used to start the WebLogic server instance. The "runtime" user gets read-only permission to the installation files. This prevents the runtime user from changing or hacking the WebLogic platform.

This type of security is the prerequisite for running multiple – isolated – WebLogic instances on the same operating system.

Isolating different tenants

The statement above becomes even more important if multiple WebLogic instances are running on the same machine. In this case it is important to isolate them from each other so that they cannot disturb each other, but also for privacy and security cannot access files and data from each other (not even read only).

- **Memory isolation:** Memory isolation is given automatically as every WebLogic instance is running in a different java virtual machine and there has its own junk of memory.
- **CPU isolation:** This idea of CPU fencing is quite difficult but possible. There are technologies out there which allows to restrict the amount of CPU a single process can consume. This can be used to prevent one instance eating up the complete CPUs of the machine.
- **Resource isolation:** Resources like file descriptors are controlled by the operating system and usually can be configured for each process

- **File system access:** This is a bit trickier. The requirements in case of WebLogic can be summarized as such:

    1) The WebLogic platform (installation) shall be shared by all WebLogic instances but none is allowed to make changes to the platform
    2) Each WebLogic can only read some special domain directories like <domain>/lib but cannot write to it. It must not be possible that one WebLogic instance can read domain specific files from any other WebLogic instance
    3) Each WebLogic instance is started with a dedicated runtime user which has write permission only to certain directories in its local domain folder

This can be achieved by one user for the platform installation and for each WebLogic another user for the deployment and domain files and one user to start the WebLogic instance.

Summary

Albeit WebLogic itself does not offer any features in this area, it is important to think about isolation on operating system level in order to lay out the foundation for higher level multi-tenancy isolation configurations and features.

Isolation on Java JVM Level

CHAPTER

Description

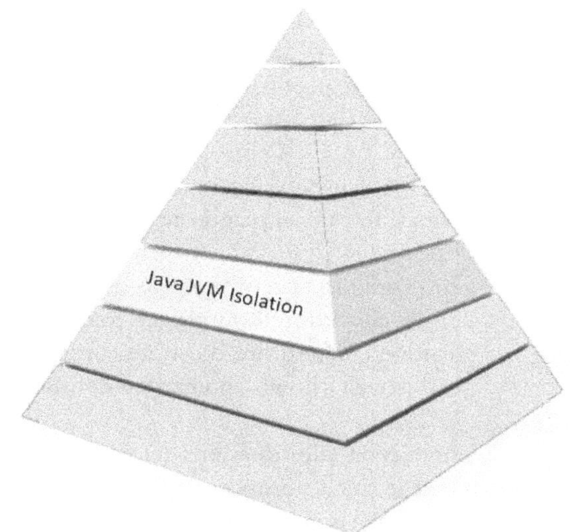

Isolation on the virtual machine level has a special priority. All system resources like threads, CPU, memory and file descriptors are controlled on this level

There are a number of technologies out there which allow isolation WITHIN a Java virtual machine. Isolation between different machines => see operating system isolation
Especially for WebLogic, resource isolation (threads, memory, and file descriptors) has been added to the Java virtual machine. Another implementation is provided by the Waratek JVM multitenancy feature where a hypervisor layer protects multiple tenants whereas each tenant is running in a specially forked JVM.

Starting with Java 1.8.40 isolation features have been added for cooperation with WebLogic on the virtual machine level in order to provide isolation down to physical resources, especially threads, memory, file descriptors and more.

This chapter is dedicated to the resource isolation capabilities within the Java JVM. Please note that these feature can only be used in combination with WebLogic partitions.

Resource Manager

The technology behind this isolation feature is called Resource Manager. Even though the configuration is part of the WebLogic configuration, this is all done within the JVM. The Java virtual machines does not know about partitions, it only knows about consumers – resource consumers to be precise. The resource which can be controlled are mainly file descriptors, CPU and memory.

Resource Managers are similar to WebLogic work managers, but configured and operated far below on the java virtual machine level. They are used to manage the operating system and JVM resources. Speaking in WebLogic terminology, this would mean that resources are tracked at virtual machine level PER partition and therefore the virtual machine is acting on behalf of WebLogic. For customer convenience runtime information is made available using standard JMX MBeans which can be accessed through the WebLogic standard runtime MBean server. Further integration into WebLogic is available for data collecting and metrics. WebLogic offers a subsystem called WLDF (WebLogic diagnostic framework). Metrics of these resource manager MBeans can be collected using WLDF harvesters and in addition watch rules can be defined for alerting and other reactions.

The configuration of these resource managers is usually static. They allow customers to define allocation boundaries and limit the resource consumption of the different partitions. Therefore these resource restrictions are mainly suitable when the resource need is well known and can be defined in numbers and shares of the overall JVM.

There is an additional model which is called "Fair Share". This is more flexible model albeit it has a number of uncertainties. Given for example a configuration where one partition has peak resource consumption during the night where the other partitions are more or less idle and normal requirements during the day. Using this model the partition with the peak requirement can "borrow" resources which are actually reserved for other partitions if its "partition mates" do not need them. As soon as the others also needs their resources fairness will be established again.

In order to make use of the new resource management it is required to run JDK 1.8 patch level 40 or later. In addition the G1 garbage collector must be used.

This new feature must be activated (Note that it is not activated by default on new domains!) by adding the following JVM arguments:

```
-XX:+UnlockCommercialFeatures -XX:+ResourceManagement -XX:+UseG1GC
```

Exhausted Resources?!

Managing resources while all parties are happy is an easy job. But what can be done if resources of some kind for a specific consumer – WebLogic partition in our case – are exhausted?

For this case a number of possible actions have been implemented. The available actions depend on the resource type. Not all actions are available for all types of resources.

The following actions – also called triggers - could be possible:

Ignore
Pseudo recourse which informs WebLogic to track the particular resource without triggering any related actions

Notify
Inform administrator that a threshold has been surpassed.

Slow
Reduce the ability of the partition to consume resources, predominantly through manipulation of work manager settings. This behavior should help the system to self-correct.

Fail
Reject requests for the resource, i.e. throw an exception. This action is in 12.2.1 only supported for file descriptors. Support for other resources may be added in the future.

Stop
This will cause the partition which requests too much resources to be shutdown. The internal shutdown process of this partition will be called. Note that other partitions and the core server are not affected. **Warning**: Do not configure this in production until you are really sure that you want this severe action as all requests and states of this partition will be lost. It is most likely to happen, that important data will get lost! Furthermore you do not know if there are other partitions which can take over the load so that you may cause a complete outage of your application.

Creating and scoping a resource manager

As always in WebLogic, resource manager can be created using different management technologies like web console, WLST, JMX or even REST.

During the creation of a resource manager it is a very important decision which scope and visibility this resource manager should have. It is possible to scope it globally or locally to a partition. "Global" scope does not mean that it applies to the complete WebLogic server. This means that these resource managers are defined on domain level and can be shared/used by multiple partitions. Each partition will be able to reference such a global resource manager (figure 9-1).

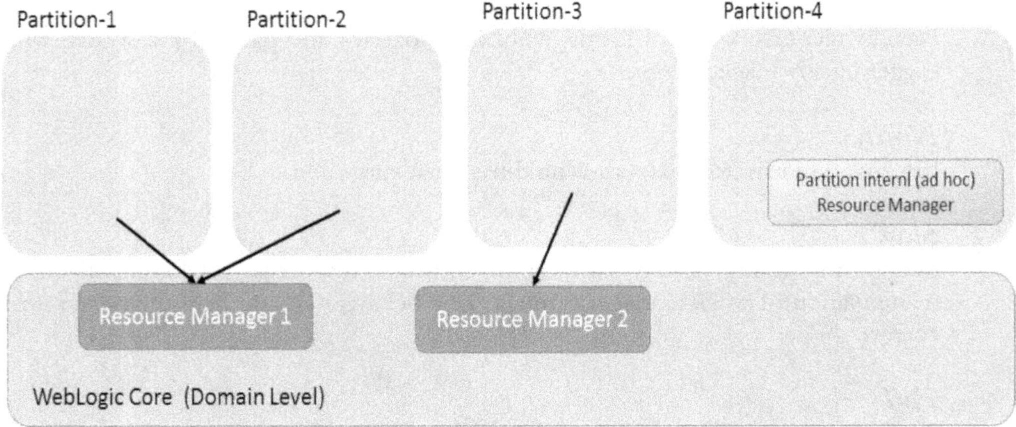

Figure 9-1: Scoping of resource managers

Different use cases exist for the two different types of resource managers. The WebLogic platform admins who are managing a WebLogic domain are meant to host domain partitions, and they would know the general capacity of the clusters in that domain. For this domain they would create a set of reusable Resource Managers. When they need to create a new partition, they would choose a Resource Manager already available in the domain. They may have high, medium, and low resource managers to reflect typical resource usage patterns. Each of these Resource Managers would be in the domain – also called "global to a domain"

Another pattern is to define the Resource Manager attributes inside a single partition. This would be useful for a more ad-hoc pattern of creating partitions - the admin would ask what the partition needs, and then define the Resource Manager attributes for the partition. This should be part of the partition configuration itself, and not something separate. Another difference is that this resource manager will also be exported/imported with the partition whereas the "global" ones will not.

In order to create a resource manager using the web console, you need to navigate to the "Resource Management" section underneath "Environments" (figure 9-2).

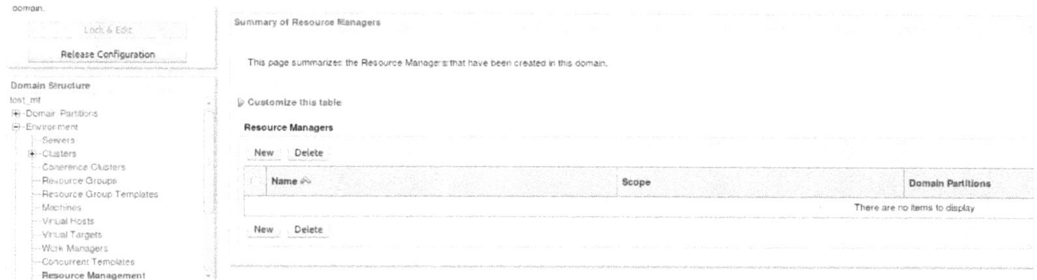

Figure 9-2: Section to create resource managers

By clicking on "New" the user will be guided to create a new resource manager. Beside the name it is important to specify the scope of the new resource manager (figure 9-3).

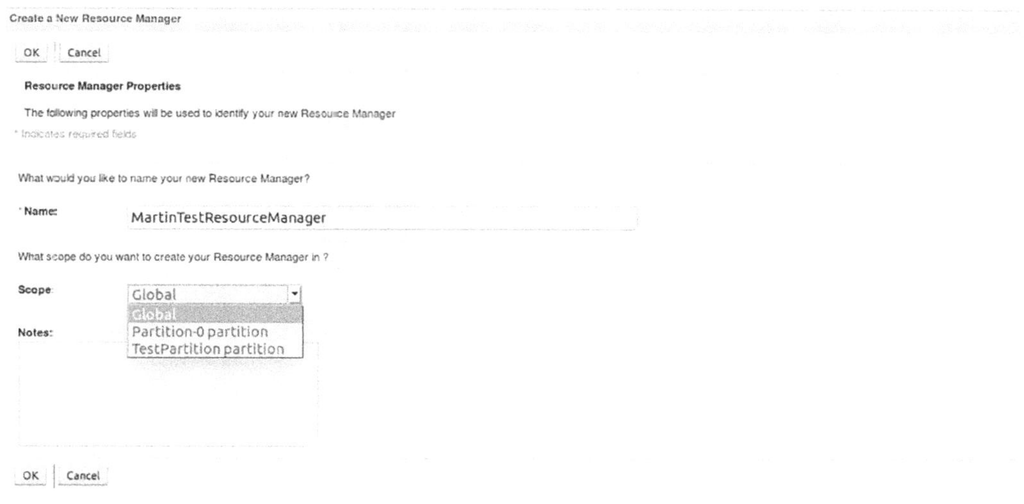

Figure 9-3: Scoping a resource manager

Depending on its scope the resource manager will be created on different levels in the configuration MBean tree –either global level or partition level.

Example: Creating two resource managers (figure 9-5)

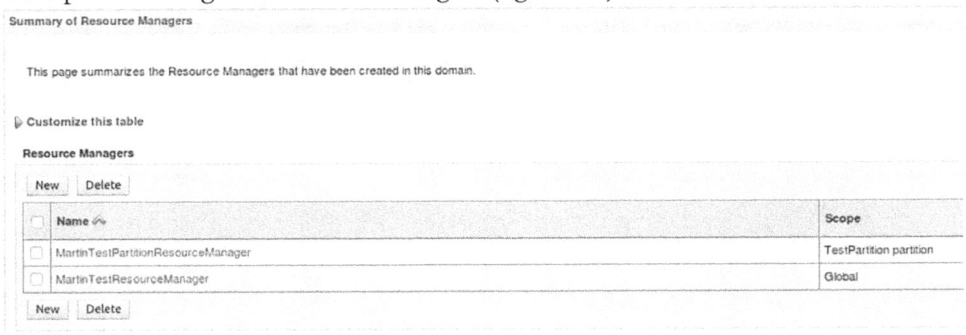

Summary of Resource Managers

This page summarizes the Resource Managers that have been created in this domain.

Customize this table

Resource Managers

New Delete

	Name	Scope
	MartinTestPartitionResourceManager	TestPartition partition
	MartinTestResourceManager	Global

New Delete

Figure 9-5: Creating two different resource manager

First of all we will create a global scoped resource manager – in this example called MartinTestResourceManager. It can either be created using the web console (see second last screenshot) or using WLST.

WLST to create this resource manager (note that "test_domain" is the name of the WebLogic domain):

```
cd('/ResourceManagement/test_domain')
cmo.createResourceManager('MartinTestResourceManager')
```

As you can see, this will result in a resource manager added to the global MBean "ResourceManagement". In the config.xml this will look like:

```
<resource-manager>
  <name>MartinTestResourceManager</name>
  ...
</resource-manager>
```

Now as a second example let us create a resource manager with partition scope – in this example called MartinTestPartitionResourceManager. As you can see in the screenshot above, this resource manager is scoped to a partition and therefore in the config.xml also configured as part of the partition.

Using WLST this resource manager can be configured like this:

```
cd('/Partitions/TestPartition')
```

```
cmo.createResourceManager('MartinTestPartitionResourceManager')
```

Now examine the config.xml of your domain. You will not find it as part of the global resource-management. You will find it defined as part of the partition!

```
    <name>TestPartition</name>
    <resource-group>
      <name>default</name>
    </resource-group>
    <available-target>VirtualTarget-0</available-target>
    <partition-id>8389f682-1961-4c0e-875c-dd12b44957f4</partition-id>
     <resource-manager>
       <name>MartinTestPartitionResourceManager</name>
     </resource-manager>
    <system-file-system>

<root>/opt/development/wls_beta/12_2_1/user_projects/domains/test_mt/partitions/TestPartition/system<
/root>
      <create-on-demand>true</create-on-demand>
      <preserved>true</preserved>
    </system-file-system>
```

Now we have created the resource managers. The domain defined resource managers are pretty much useless yet without partitions referencing them. The partition configuration section offer a way for a partition to reference to resource manager (figure 9-6).

Figure 9-6: Referencing a resource manager

This can of course also be done using WLST

```
cd('/Partitions/Partition-0')
cmo.setResourceManagerRef(getMBean('/ResourceManagement/test_mt/ResourceManagers/MartinTestResourceMa
nager'))
```

After the reference has been created, this is also reflected in the config.xml through an additional XML tag called <resource-manager-ref>

```
<name>MyTestPartitionWithGlobalResourceManager</name>
<resource-group>
  <name>ResourceTemplate-0_group</name>
  <resource-group-template>ResourceTemplate-0</resource-group-template>
</resource-group>
<available-target></available-target>
<partition-id>afe830fd-fa98-4756-beba-d995602657ac</partition-id>
<resource-manager-ref>MartinTestResourceManager</resource-manager-ref>
<system-file-system>
  <root>/opt/development/wls_beta/12_2_1/user_projects/domains/test_mt/partitions/Partition-
0/system</root>
  <create-on-demand>true</create-on-demand>
  <preserved>true</preserved>
</system-file-system>
```

Unfortunately WebLogic 12.2.1 does not support both types of resource managers for the same partition. If a partition has a partition scoped resource manager and the administrator adds a reference to a domain wide resource manager, the partition scoped resource manager has to be destroyed first.

Example in WLST:

```
cd('/Partitions/TestPartition')
cmo.destroyResourceManager(getMBean('/Partitions/TestPartition/ResourceManagers/MartinTestPartitionRe
sourceManager'))
cmo.setResourceManagerRef(getMBean('/ResourceManagement/test_mt/ResourceManagers/MartinTestResourceMa
nager'))
```

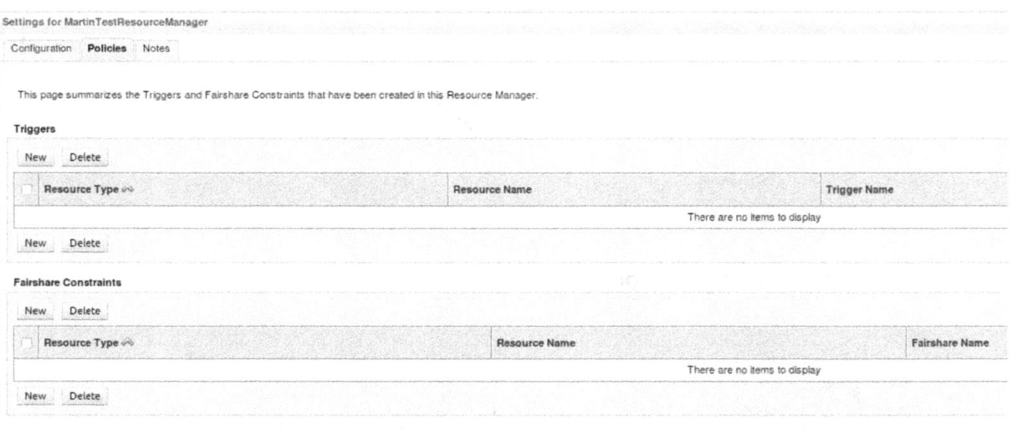

File descriptors resource management

One important resource a resource manager can control is the amount of file descriptors. Each process running on an operating system is allowed to open only a limited amount of file descriptors – and file descriptors are NOT only needed for reading/writing files!

At least under Linux/Unix also resources like connections need file descriptors.

Real word example:

> Have you ever seen the following strange behavior? A number of concurrent users can work with a system. Suddenly as load increases new clients do not get a connection and running into timeouts while older clients can work without problems or timeouts. Sometimes new clients are waiting long for a connection and then can work, sometimes running into a timeout. This example describes in almost all cases that the file descriptor limit has been reached.

Configuration

Within resource managers, so called triggers need to be configured. First step in creating a trigger is to select the type of resource (in this case file descriptors) (figure 9-7)

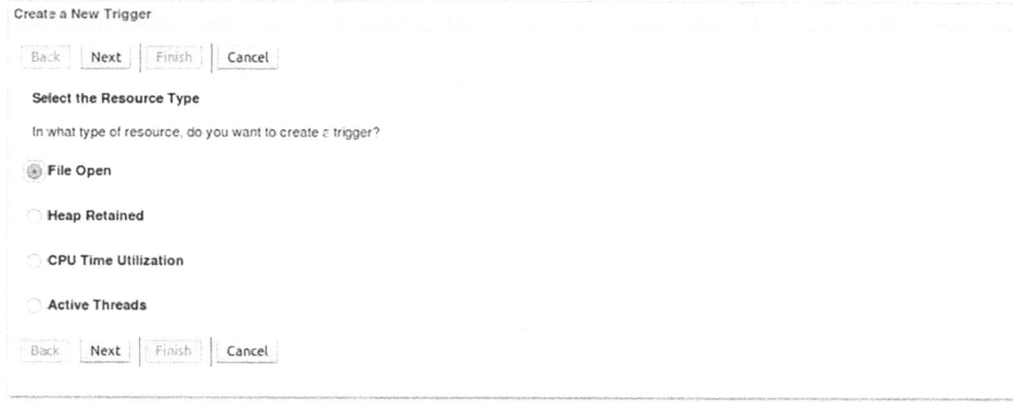

Figure 9-7: Create a file descriptor trigger inside a resource manager

As you can create multiple triggers of the same type, you need to give the trigger a unique name (figure 9-8):

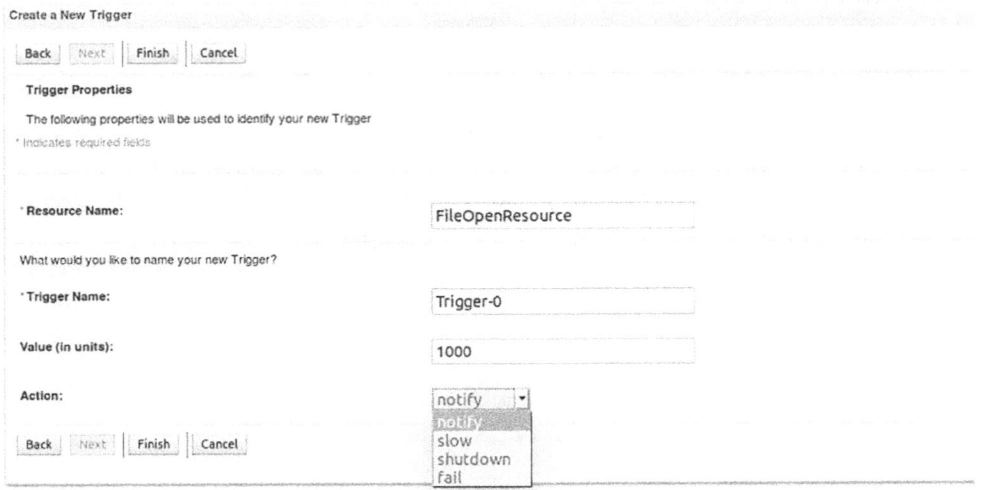

Figure 9-8: Select the desired action for this trigger

For each trigger you need to select the action you want to be performed. Note that not all action types are available for all trigger types.

Example:

It is possible to create multiple triggers of the same type. In the following example three triggers will be created. At the level of 1000 open descriptors a notification will be issued (it is e.g. possible to react using WLDF). At the level of 5000 the resource provisioning will be slowed down and finally at the level of 10000 no more resources will be granted (fail action) (figure 9-9).

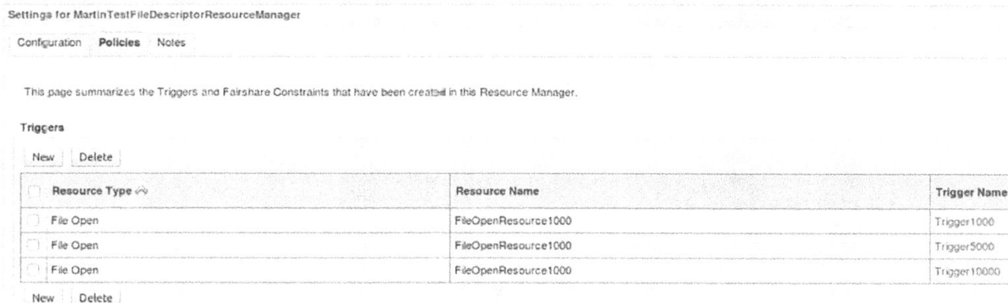

Figure 9-9: Create 3 triggers using the WebLogic console

The same can be of course automated using WLST or JMX. The following WLST script will create the same triggers:

```
cmo.createResourceManager('MartinTestFileDescriptorResourceManager')

cd('/ResourceManagement/test_mt/ResourceManagers/MartinTestFileDescriptorResourceManager')
cmo.createFileOpen('FileOpenResource1000')

cd('/ResourceManagement/test_mt/ResourceManagers/MartinTestFileDescriptorResourceManager/FileOpen/Fil
eOpenResource1000')
cmo.createTrigger('Trigger1000', 1000, 'notify')
cmo.createTrigger('Trigger5000', 5000, 'slow')
```

And finally the result will be persisted into the config.xml like this:

```
      <name>MartinTestFileDescriptorResourceManager</name>
      <file-open>
        <name>FileOpenResource1000</name>
        <trigger>
          <name>Trigger1000</name>
          <value>1000</value>
          <action>notify</action>
        </trigger>
        <trigger>
          <name>Trigger5000</name>
          <value>5000</value>
          <action>slow</action>
        </trigger>
        <trigger>
          <name>Trigger10000</name>
          <value>10000</value>
          <action>fail</action>
        </trigger>
      </file-open>
```

As you can see, multiple trigger of the same resource can be very useful at different levels of actions starting from pure notification until failing or even partition shutdown.

As discussed earlier, resource managers can also be partition scoped (local to a partition and embedded – not referenced). In this case an example with one trigger can look like:

```
    <name>Partition-0</name>
    <resource-group>
      <name>ResourceTemplate-0_group</name>
      <resource-group-template>ResourceTemplate-0</resource-group-template>
    </resource-group>
    <available-target></available-target>
    <partition-id>afe830fd-fa98-4756-beba-d995602657ac</partition-id>
    <resource-manager>
      <name>PartitionInternalResourceManager</name>
      <file-open>
        <name>FileOpenResourceInternal1000</name>
        <trigger>
          <name>Trigger1000</name>
          <value>1000</value>
          <action>notify</action>
        </trigger>
      </file-open>
    </resource-manager>
    <system-file-system>
      <root>/opt/development/wls_beta/12_2_1/user_projects/domains/test_mt/partitions/Partition-
0/system</root>
      <create-on-demand>true</create-on-demand>
      <preserved>true</preserved>
    </system-file-system>
```

CPU resource management

The next resource which can be controlled using ResourceManager is the actual CPU usage. CPU usage is something the manager can detect but it cannot recover. This means that the system can react as soon as a violation of the configured rules is detected. Possible recourses here include

- "**Notify**" : only notification but no action
- "**Slow**": Slow down the partition which uses too much CPU
- "**Stop**": Stop the partition. This is *quite dangerous* as the partition will no longer work afterwards
- "**Fair Share**": Apply the fair share model where the manager allows the partition to "over utilize" the CPU, if the other partitions do not require their CPU cycles at the moment

Configuration

After creating a resource manager using the WebLogic console, it is possible to create a CPU trigger. CPU trigger means to define a threshold of CPU usage in "%".

In order to create a trigger, "CPU Time Utilization" must be selected from the trigger menu. (figure 9-10)

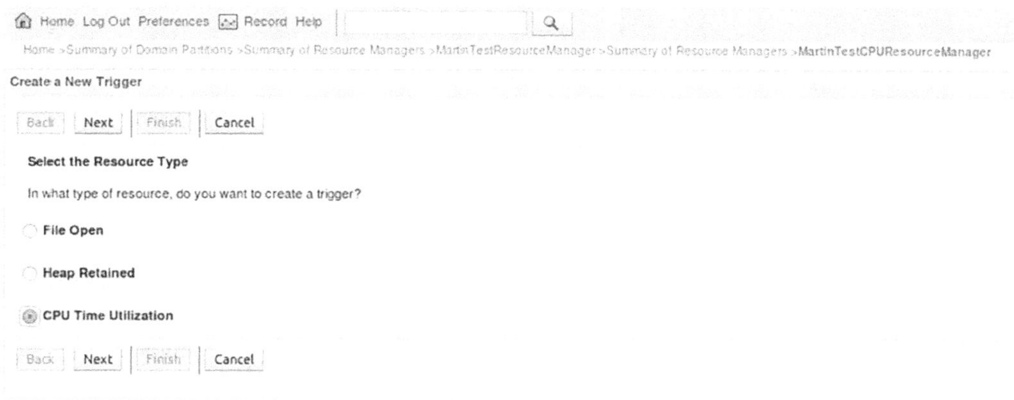

Figure 9-10: Select CPU Time Utilization in order to create a CPU trigger

After this selection has been made, the following dialog allows the user to specify the value (in percentage) and also the action which should be triggered by the resource manager (figure 9-11).

Figure 9-11: Specify CPU trigger details

The same can of course also be configured using WLST or JMX

WLST Example (note: "martin_1221" is the name of the domain in this example):

```
cmo.createResourceManager('MartinTestCPUResourceManager')
```

```
cd('/ResourceManagement/martin_1221/ResourceManagers/MartinTestCPUResourceManager')
cmo.createCpuUtilization('CpuTimeResource')

cd('/ResourceManagement/martin_1221/ResourceManagers/MartinTestCPUResourceManager/CpuUtilization/CpuT
imeResource')
```

In the config XML this would look like:

```
<name>MartinTestCPUResourceManager</name>
<cpu-utilization>
  <name>CpuTimeResource</name>
  <trigger>
    <name>CPUTrigger</name>
    <value>80</value>
    <action>slow</action>
  </trigger>
</cpu-utilization>
```

Note that you cannot define slow trigger together with fair-share trigger

Example

The following example will define three CPU triggers. One to notify the administrator, then the second to slow down the partition and finally, if the partition still tries to get more CPU to shutdown the partition.

WLST Example:

```
cmo.createResourceManager('MartinCPUResourcesManager')

cd('/ResourceManagement/martin_1221/ResourceManagers/MartinCPUResourcesManager')
cmo.createCpuUtilization('CpuTimeResource')

cd('/ResourceManagement/martin_1221/ResourceManagers/MartinCPUResourcesManager/CpuUtilization/CpuTime
Resource')
cmo.createTrigger('NotifyTrigger', 50, 'notify')
cmo.createTrigger('SlowTrigger', 75, 'slow')
```

You can also see the triggers in the WebLogic console (figure 9-12).

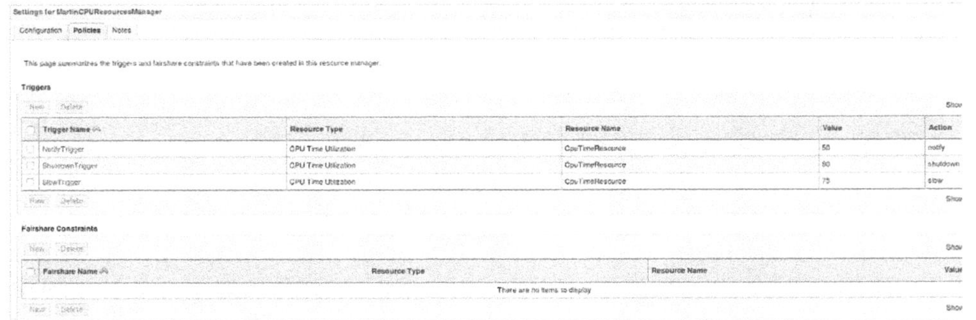

Figure 9-12: Trigger view in the WebLogic console

Heap space resource management

Heap space management is a more problematic trigger as it has a number of restrictions. Overconsumption can only be detected in cooperation with the garbage collector. Detection relies on the outcome of the garbage collector analysis.

In comparison to the CPU trigger, heap consumption is a great challenge for all administrators. The main problem is that heap which is consumed by one partition is gone and cannot be revoked immediately. CPU trigger can be easily used to influence how much CPU will be granted from now on to a partition. But as soon as heap has been consumed it is allocated and no longer available. Therefore it is very advisable to not define limits without leaving some headroom so that the manager can react on time and the system will still be stable even the partition may has consumed more heap than it should.

Possible recourses here include

- "**Notify**" : only notification but no action
- "**Slow**": Slow down the partition which means that heap will not be granted as fast as it will be granted to others
- "**Stop**": Stop the partition. This is *quite dangerous* as the partition will no longer work afterwards
- "**Fair Share**": Apply the fair share model where the manager allows the partition to "over utilize" the heap if the other partitions do not consume all their heap at the moment

Configuration

Similar to the other triggers, the administrator has to create a resource manager (unless the trigger should be added to an existing one) and then create a new trigger and configure it (figure 9-13).

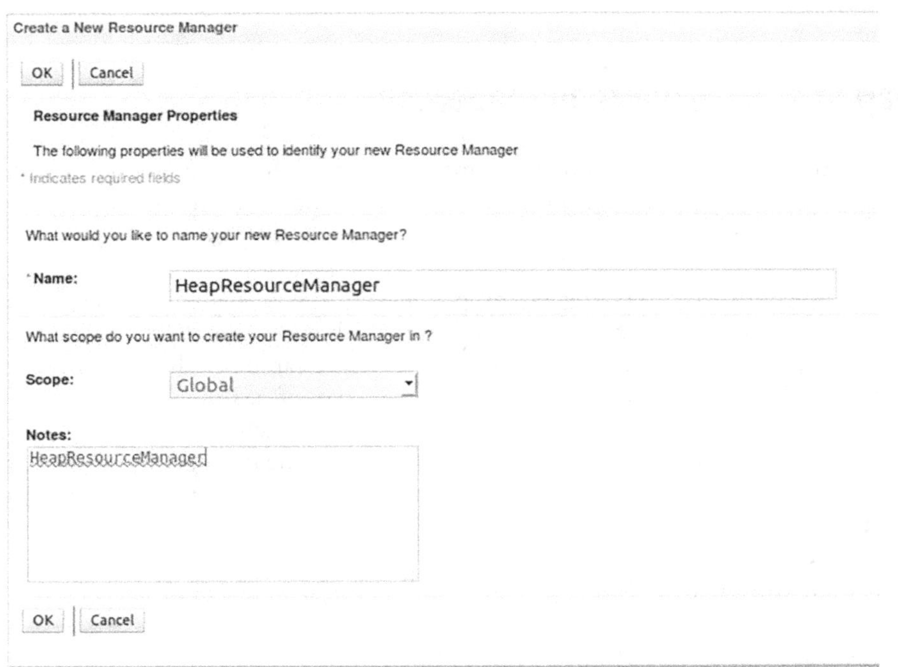

Figure 9-13: Create a new resource manager

After that, a new trigger can be added to this resource manager (figure 9-14).

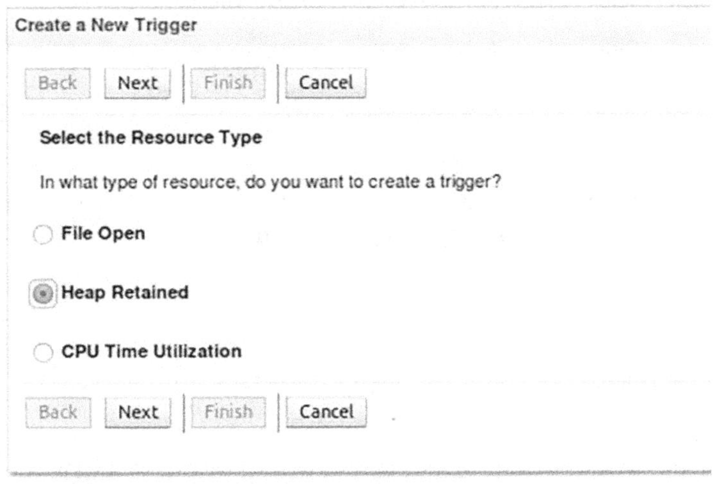

Figure 9-14: Add a new heap trigger

Finally, the new trigger can be configured. The administrator has to choose between the available actions. This defines what the resource manager has to do if this trigger is reached. And the administrator also needs to define the threshold in MB (figure 9-15).

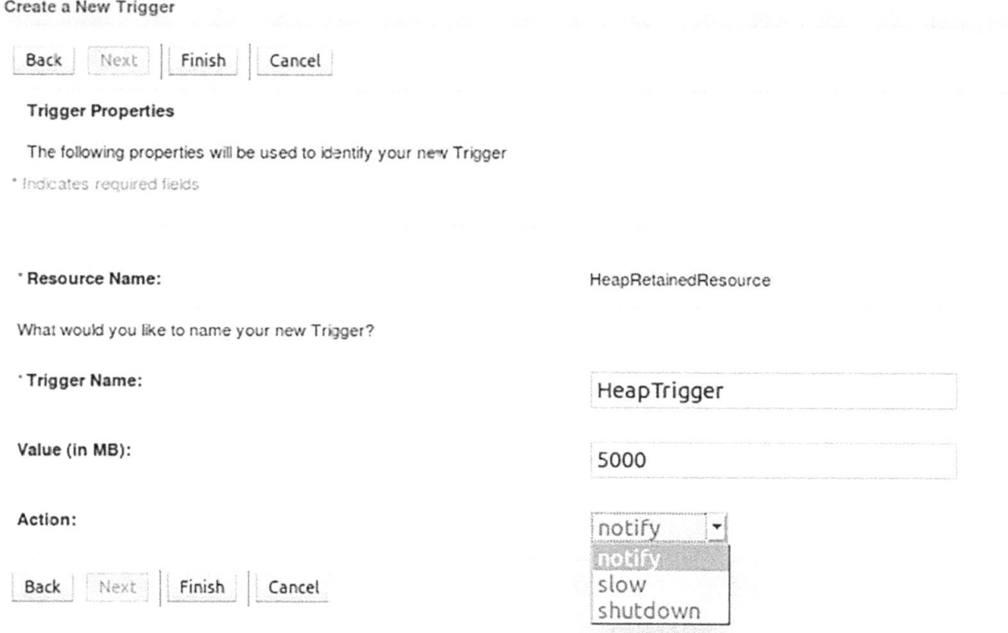

Figure 9-15: Configure the trigger

Example

Based on different triggers the resource manager can react in certain situations. Given the following example with 4 partitions and 3 defined triggers. Depending on the amount of heap a partition is requesting from the JVM, the resource manager gets triggered and can react according to the action defined in the trigger (figure 9-16).

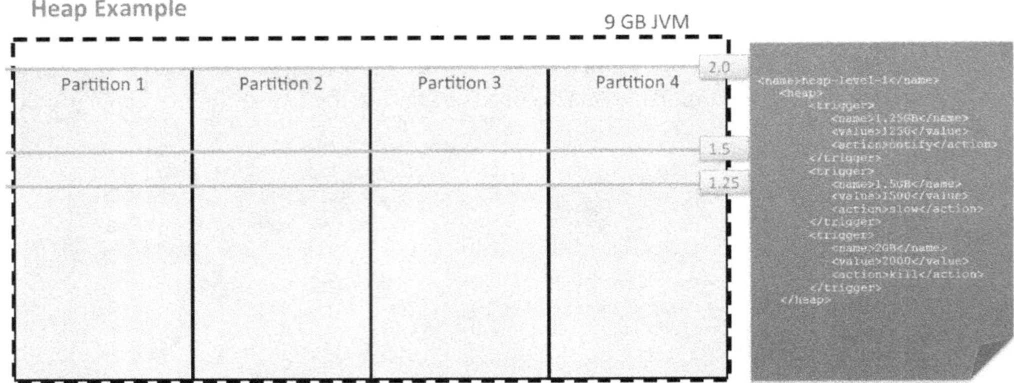

Figure 9-16: Baseline example: 4 partitions and a resource manager with 3 triggers

During normal operation (as long as no partition reaches on of the trigger thresholds) everything is fine and the resource manager has nothing to do (figure 9-17)

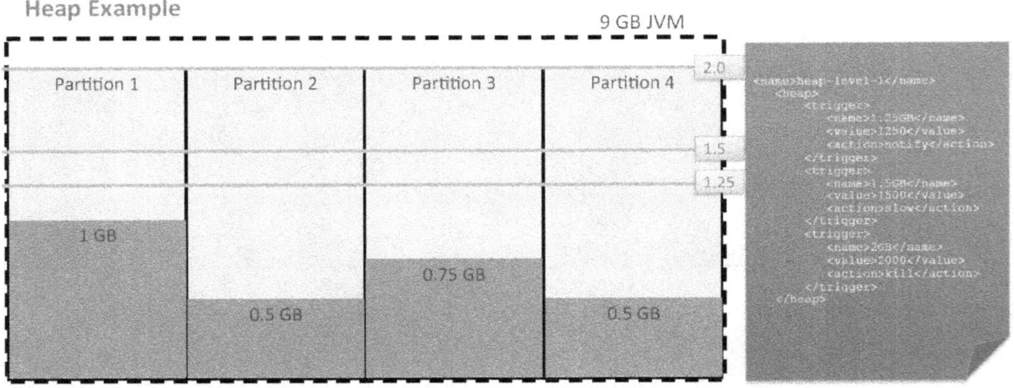

Figure 9-17: Normal operation

If one partition reaches the first threshold (notify trigger), a notification will be raised but the partition can continue to operate normally. It is expected that an administrator will look into this (figure 9-18).

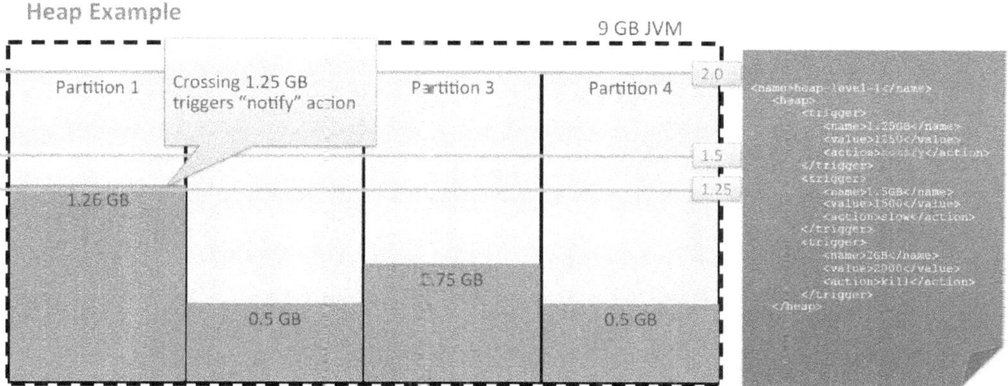

Figure 9-18: "Partition_1" reached the notify trigger threshold

In this example, "partition_1" requests more and more resources and after a while it also hits the level of the second trigger. During the higher resource consumption, the resource manager will react and slow down the partition. To slow down means in this case, that the partition will not get heap as fast as it was used too. This, of course, may have an impact on the overall performance of the partition (figure 9-19).

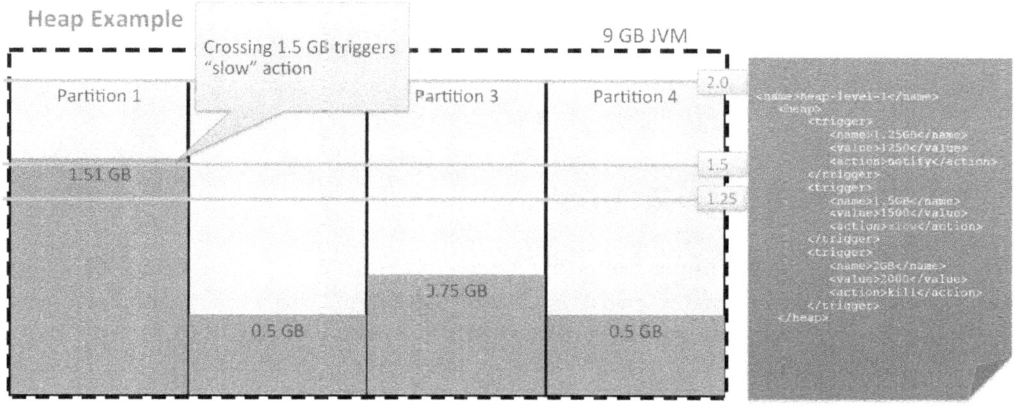

Figure 9-19: Partition hitting the slow trigger

Now let's assume, that heap of partition one keeps growing and finally hits the level of the last trigger. Now the resource manager has to take the worst action possible and will trigger the shutdown of the partition. The resource manager will ask WebLogic to shutdown this partition in order to protect all the other co-hosted partitions. Be aware, that this may lead to the loss of important data!! (figure 9-20)

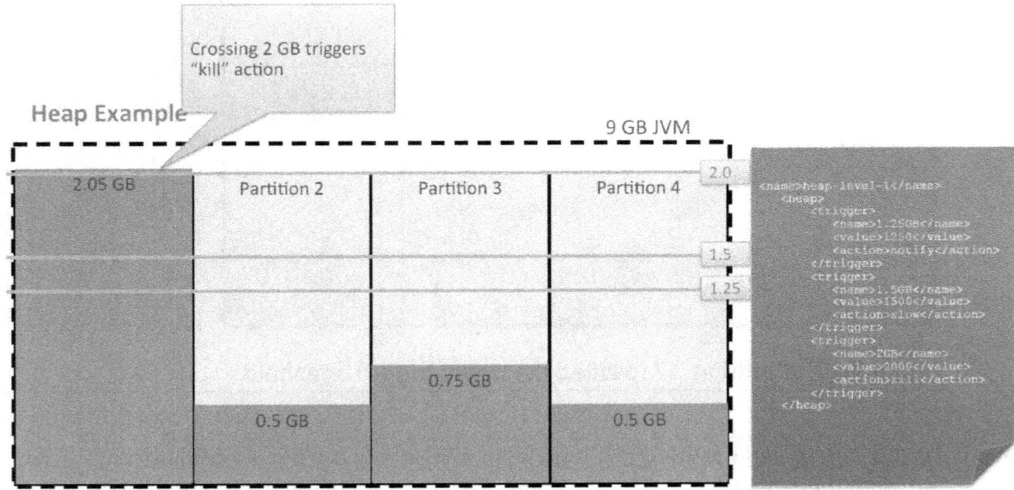

Figure 9-20: Partition hitting the last trigger level

Please note that this action is a dangerous action as the partition will be shutdown. This really affects operation as this partition can of course no longer serve any business request. A shutdown action should definitely NOT be configured unless there is a real need for it.

Fair share configurations

Another extension implemented by Oracle is the so called "fair share" policy. This basically describes that all partitions, which are sharing the same resource manager are supposed to get (almost) the same share of the resources (CPU or heap).

In case the resources are not fully requested, a partition is allowed to utilize more than its share. As soon as the other partitions request their "share" of the resources, the resource manager must try to regain the over-used resources and grant them to the partition(s) these resource resources actually belong to.

Two types of resources can be configured as fair share – CPU or heap.

Configuration

It is possible to configure fair share constraints for each resource manager alongside with the different triggers. It is not possible to combine fair share constraints with "slow" triggers (figure 9-21).

Figure 9-21: Fair share constraints can be configured for each resource manager

Two different types of fair share constraints are available – Heap and CPU (figure 9-22).

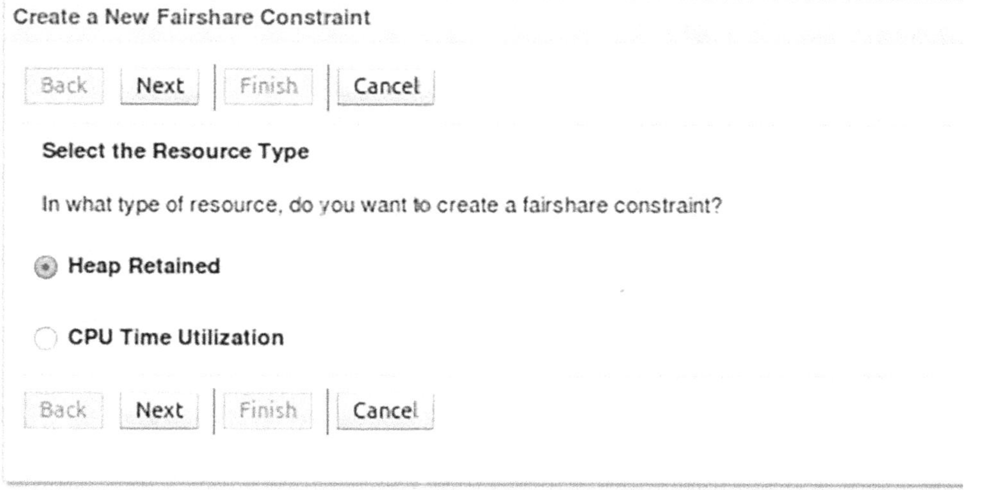

Figure 9-22: Selection of Heap or CPU

After the decision has been made which kind of constraint should be configured, it is required to define the optimal value in percent how much resources are considered to be a fair share (figure 9-23).

Figure 9-23: Configure size of fair share

The following code depicts how a fair share constraint for heap resource manager looks like in the config.xml file:

```
      <name>TestFairShareHeapResourceManager</name>
      <heap-retained>
        <name>HeapRetainedResource</name>
        <fair-share-constraint>
          <name>HeapFairshare</name>
          <value>25</value>
        </fair-share-constraint>
      </heap-retained>
```

Instead of using the WebLogic console, this can also be configured using WLST.

```
edit()
startEdit()

cd('/ResourceManagement/martin_1221')
cmo.createResourceManager('TestFairShareHeapResourceManager')

cd('/ResourceManagement/martin_1221/ResourceManagers/TestFairShareHeapResourceManager')
cmo.setNotes('TestFairShareHeapResourceManager')
cmo.createHeapRetained('HeapRetainedResource')
```

```
cd('/ResourceManagement/martin_1221/ResourceManagers/TestFairShareHeapResourceManager/HeapRetained/He
apRetainedResource')
cmo.createFairShareConstraint('HeapFairshare', 25)

save()
```

Very similar a fair share constraint for CPU can be created and this will look in the config.xml like this:

```
<name>TestFairShareCPUResourceManager</name>
<notes>TestFairShareCPUResourceManager</notes>
<cpu-utilization>
  <name>CpuTimeResource</name>
  <fair-share-constraint>
    <name>CPUFairshare</name>
    <value>25</value>
  </fair-share-constraint>
</cpu-utilization>
```

And also a CPU constraint can be configured using WLST

```
edit()
startEdit()

cd('/ResourceManagement/martin_1221')
cmo.createResourceManager('TestFairShareCPUResourceManager')

cd('/ResourceManagement/martin_1221/ResourceManagers/TestFairShareCPUResourceManager')
cmo.setNotes('TestFairShareCPUResourceManager')
cmo.createCpuUtilization('CpuTimeResource')

cd('/ResourceManagement/martin_1221/ResourceManagers/TestFairShareCPUResourceManager/CpuUtilization/C
puTimeResource')
cmo.createFairShareConstraint('CPUFairshare', 25)

save()
```

Example

Based on different triggers the resource manager can react. Given the following example where 4 partitions are hosted in a WLS server and all four do share the same resource manager. This resource manager has defined two heap triggers and a fair share policy.

The first picture does show the state where each partition does have its fair share (25% each) of the heap. But there is still room in the heap, so that more can be allocated (figure 9-24).

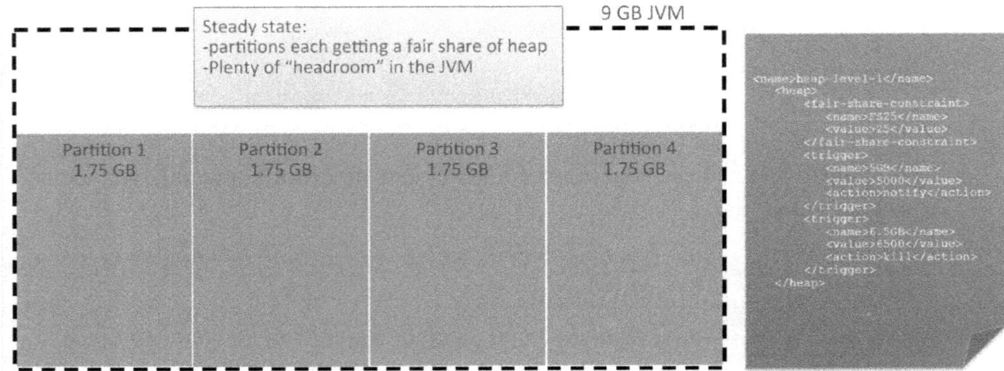

Figure 9-24: Steady state

The following diagram shows another state where 3 partitions are only using a fraction of their share. This allows partition 1 to request more heap, as it is usually allowed by its share.

Note that with the 4GB, this partition is still below the defined triggers, so that everything is fine (figure 9-25).

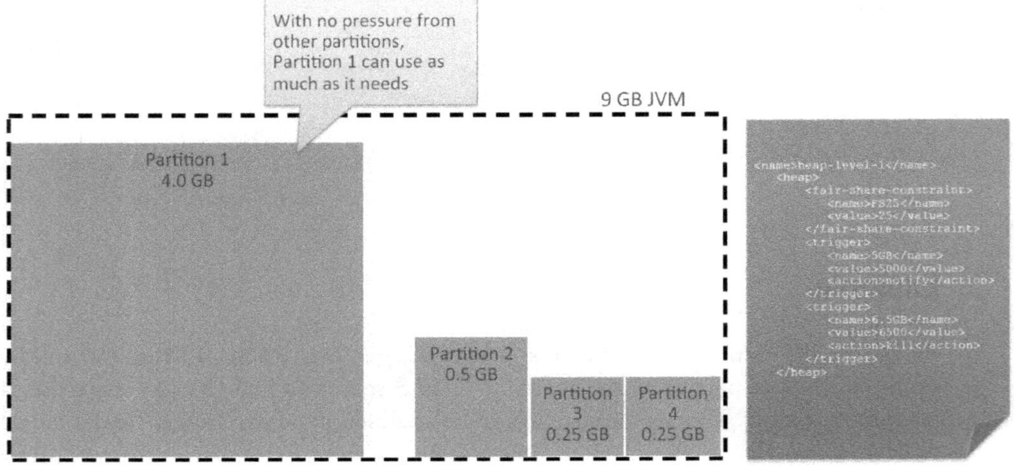

Figure 9-25: "Partition_1" uses more as its share as the other partitions do not fully need their share

But of course it is not allowed for "partition_1" to use all available heap due to the defined triggers. After reaching 5GB only a notification is issued.

In this example "partition_1" also reached the absolute maximum it is allowed to use – 6.5GB so the resource manager is forced to kill (shutdown) this partition in order to protect the other partitions in this server (figure 9-26).

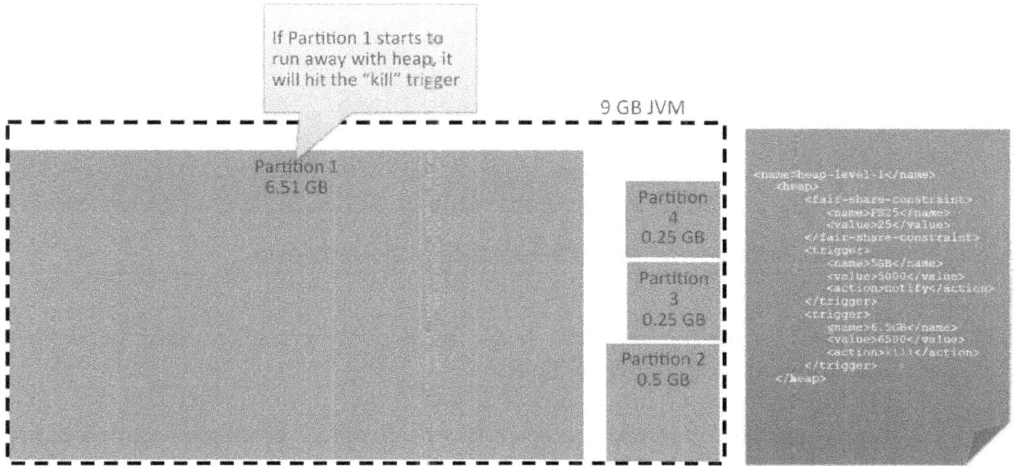

Figure 9-26: Partition reaches critical value and will be killed

Now looking at the second scenario. Given that partition one uses 4GB and all others using 1.3GB. Now the other partitions request more heap and the resource manager needs to slow down new request for heap from partition one, because partition one already used more than its share (figure 9-27).

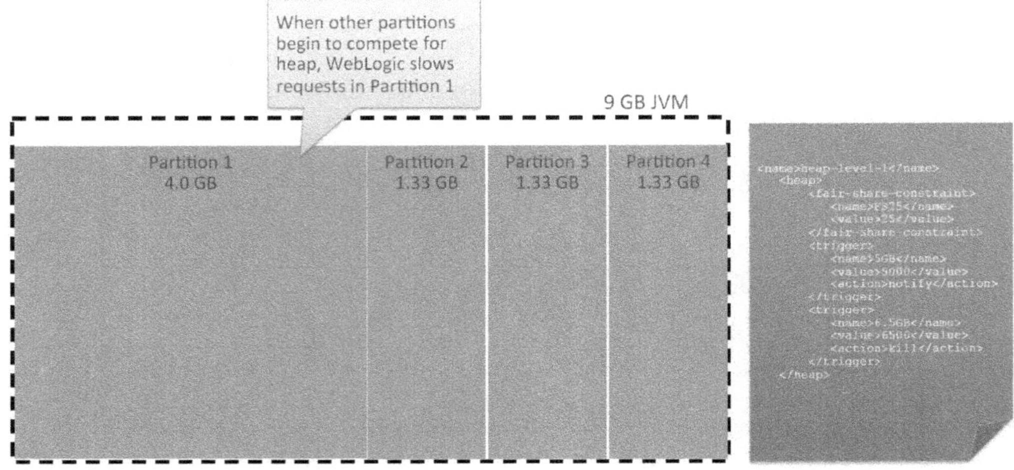

Figure 9-27: Partition one will be automatically slowed down

This is also the reason why the heap trigger slow actions cannot be defined in combination with heap fair share policies.

As soon as partition one releases heap, this heap will be given to the other partitions until all reaching their share (figure 9-28).

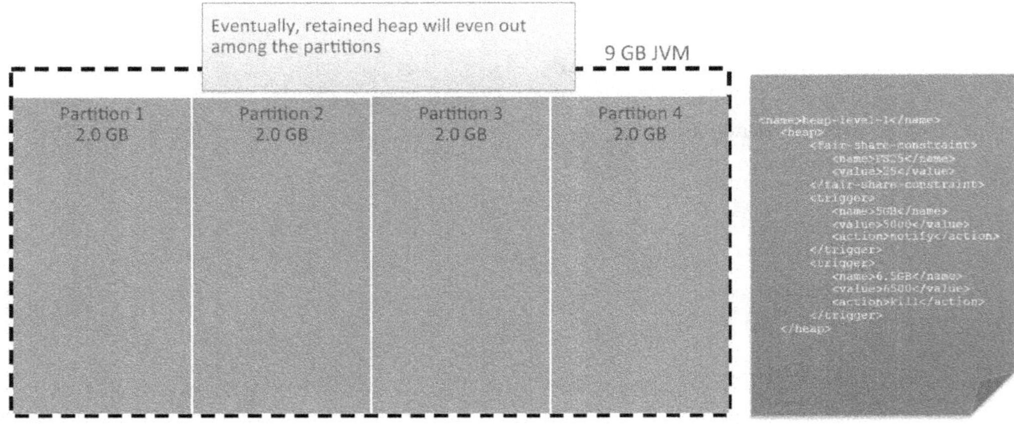

Figure 9-28: Released heap will be given to the other partitions

Comprehensive examples

The last section shows a number of more complex examples.

The first examples defines one complex resource manager which controls all sorts of resources. It also defines triggers for all available actions (figure 9-29).

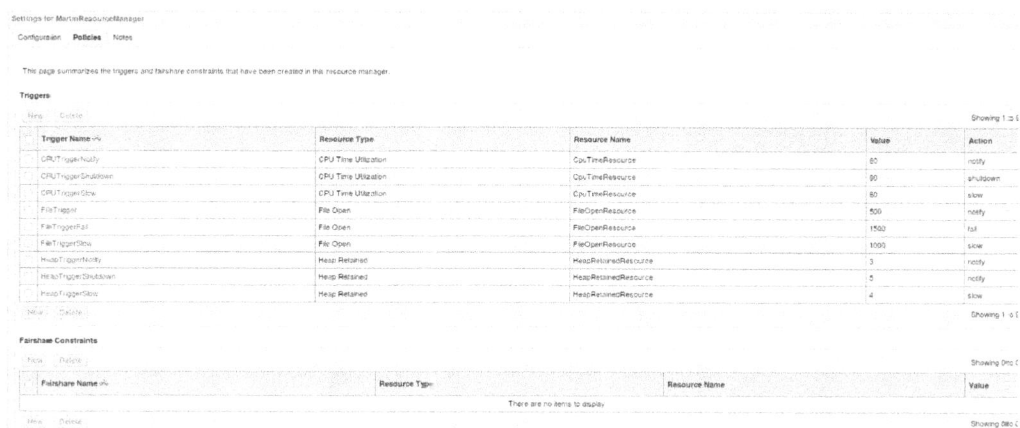
Settings for MartinResourceManager
Configuration
Policies
Notes
This page summarizes the triggers and fairshare constraints that have been created in this resource manager.
Triggers

Trigger Name	Resource Type	Resource Name	Value	Action
CPUTriggerNotify	CPU Time Utilization	CpuTimeResource	80	notify
CPUTriggerShutdown	CPU Time Utilization	CpuTimeResource	90	shutdown
CPUTriggerSlow	CPU Time Utilization	CpuTimeResource	60	slow
FileTrigger	File Open	FileOpenResource	500	notify
FileTriggerFail	File Open	FileOpenResource	1500	fail
FileTriggerSlow	File Open	FileOpenResource	1000	slow
HeapTriggerNotify	Heap Retained	HeapRetainedResource	3	notify
HeapTriggerShutdown	Heap Retained	HeapRetainedResource	5	notify
HeapTriggerSlow	Heap Retained	HeapRetainedResource	4	slow

Fairshare Constraints

Fairshare Name	Resource Type	Resource Name	Value
There are no items to display			

Figure 9-29: WebLogic view

The resource manager above needs to be defined in the WebLogic config.xml in the following way

```
<resource-manager>
  <name>MartinResourceManager</name>
  <notes>A conprehensive resource manager</notes>
  <file-open>
    <name>FileOpenResource</name>
    <trigger>
      <name>FIleTrigger</name>
      <value>500</value>
      <action>notify</action>
    </trigger>
    <trigger>
      <name>FileTriggerSlow</name>
      <value>1000</value>
      <action>slow</action>
    </trigger>
    <trigger>
      <name>FileTriggerFail</name>
      <value>1500</value>
      <action>fail</action>
    </trigger>
  </file-open>
  <heap-retained>
    <name>HeapRetainedResource</name>
    <trigger>
      <name>HeapTriggerNotify</name>
      <value>3</value>
      <action>notify</action>
```

```
      </trigger>
      <trigger>
        <name>HeapTriggerSlow</name>
        <value>4</value>
        <action>slow</action>
      </trigger>
      <trigger>
        <name>HeapTriggerShutdown</name>
        <value>5</value>
        <action>notify</action>
      </trigger>
    </heap-retained>
    <cpu-utilization>
      <name>CpuTimeResource</name>
      <trigger>
        <name>CPUTriggerNotify</name>
        <value>60</value>
        <action>notify</action>
      </trigger>
      <trigger>
        <name>CPUTriggerSlow</name>
        <value>80</value>
        <action>slow</action>
      </trigger>
      <trigger>
        <name>CPUTriggerShutdown</name>
        <value>90</value>
        <action>shutdown</action>
      </trigger>
    </cpu-utilization>
  </resource-manager>
```

And the above defined resource manager and of course also be configured using automated WLST scripts:

```
cmo.createResourceManager('MartinResourceManager')

cd('/ResourceManagement/martin_1221/ResourceManagers/MartinResourceManager')
cmo.setNotes('A conprehensive resource manager')
cmo.createFileOpen('FileOpenResource')

cd('/ResourceManagement/martin_1221/ResourceManagers/MartinResourceManager/FileOpen/FileOpenResource'
)
cmo.createTrigger('FIleTrigger', 500, 'notify')
cmo.createTrigger('FileTriggerSlow', 1000, 'slow')
cmo.createTrigger('FileTriggerFail', 1500, 'fail')

cd('/ResourceManagement/martin_1221/ResourceManagers/MartinResourceManager')
cmo.createCpuUtilization('CpuTimeResource')

cd('/ResourceManagement/martin_1221/ResourceManagers/MartinResourceManager/CpuUtilization/CpuTimeReso
urce')
cmo.createTrigger('CPUTriggerNotify', 60, 'notify')
cmo.createTrigger('CPUTriggerSlow', 80, 'slow')
cmo.createTrigger('CPUTriggerShutdown', 90, 'shutdown')

cd('/ResourceManagement/martin_1221/ResourceManagers/MartinResourceManager')
cmo.createHeapRetained('HeapRetainedResource')

cd('/ResourceManagement/martin_1221/ResourceManagers/MartinResourceManager/HeapRetained/HeapRetainedR
esource')
cmo.createTrigger('HeapTriggerNotify', 3, 'notify')
cmo.createTrigger('HeapTriggerSlow', 4, 'slow')
```

The second example is similar to the first one. The main difference is that it does not define explicit “slow” actions. It defines fair share constraints instead (figure 9-30).

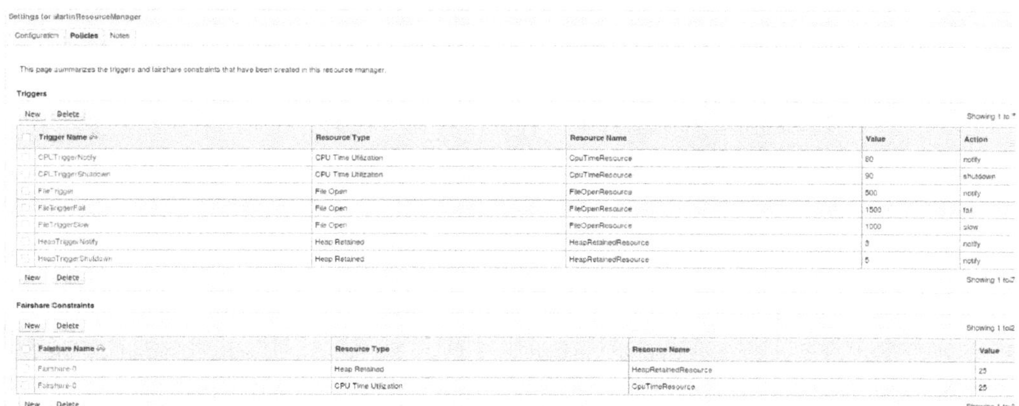

Figure 9-30: WebLogic view

In the WebLogic config.xml this looks like:

```
<resource-manager>
  <name>MartinResourceManager</name>
  <notes>A conprehensive resource manager</notes>
  <file-open>
    <name>FileOpenResource</name>
    <trigger>
      <name>FIleTrigger</name>
      <value>500</value>
      <action>notify</action>
    </trigger>
    <trigger>
      <name>FileTriggerSlow</name>
      <value>1000</value>
      <action>slow</action>
    </trigger>
    <trigger>
      <name>FileTriggerFail</name>
      <value>1500</value>
      <action>fail</action>
    </trigger>
  </file-open>
  <heap-retained>
    <name>HeapRetainedResource</name>
    <trigger>
      <name>HeapTriggerNotify</name>
      <value>3</value>
      <action>notify</action>
    </trigger>
    <trigger>
      <name>HeapTriggerShutdown</name>
      <value>5</value>
      <action>notify</action>
    </trigger>
    <fair-share-constraint>
      <name>Fairshare-0</name>
      <value>25</value>
    </fair-share-constraint>
  </heap-retained>
  <cpu-utilization>
    <name>CpuTimeResource</name>
    <trigger>
```

```
        <name>CPUTriggerNotify</name>
        <value>60</value>
        <action>notify</action>
      </trigger>
      <trigger>
        <name>CPUTriggerShutdown</name>
        <value>90</value>
        <action>shutdown</action>
      </trigger>
      <fair-share-constraint>
        <name>Fairshare-0</name>
        <value>25</value>
      </fair-share-constraint>
    </cpu-utilization>
```

Also the WLST script looks similar to example one, only that the fair share constraints will be created.

```
cmo.createResourceManager('MartinResourceManager')

cd('/ResourceManagement/martin_1221/ResourceManagers/MartinResourceManager')
cmo.setNotes('A conprehensive resource manager')
cmo.createFileOpen('FileOpenResource')

cd('/ResourceManagement/martin_1221/ResourceManagers/MartinResourceManager/FileOpen/FileOpenResource'
)
cmo.createTrigger('FIleTrigger', 500, 'notify')
cmo.createTrigger('FileTriggerSlow', 1000, 'slow')
cmo.createTrigger('FileTriggerFail', 1500, 'fail')

cd('/ResourceManagement/martin_1221/ResourceManagers/MartinResourceManager')
cmo.createCpuUtilization('CpuTimeResource')

cd('/ResourceManagement/martin_1221/ResourceManagers/MartinResourceManager/CpuUtilization/CpuTimeReso
urce')
cmo.createTrigger('CPUTriggerNotify', 60, 'notify')
cmo.createTrigger('CPUTriggerShutdown', 90, 'shutdown')

cd('/ResourceManagement/martin_1221/ResourceManagers/MartinResourceManager')
cmo.createHeapRetained('HeapRetainedResource')

cd('/ResourceManagement/martin_1221/ResourceManagers/MartinResourceManager/HeapRetained/HeapRetainedR
esource')
cmo.createTrigger('HeapTriggerNotify', 3, 'notify')
cmo.createTrigger('HeapTriggerShutdown', 5, 'notify')

# create fair share
# -------------------
cd('/ResourceManagement/martin_1221/ResourceManagers/MartinResourceManager/HeapRetained/HeapRetainedR
esource')
cmo.createFairShareConstraint('Fairshare-0', 25)

cd('/ResourceManagement/martin_1221/ResourceManagers/MartinResourceManager/CpuUtilization/CpuTimeReso
urce')
```

ResourceManager and JMX

WebLogic is based on MBeans. It is therefore also possible to use JMX in order to create, configure or delete ResourceManager, Trigger or FairShare policies.

MBeans used to work with ResourceManagers

The central domain MBean has one child called "ResourceManagement" which manages all the resource managers. Resource managers can be globally scoped or partition scoped. Each resource manager can have three child MBeans for the different trigger and policy types. Each of these three child MBeans manage a list of triggers and/or a fairshare policy (figure 9-31)

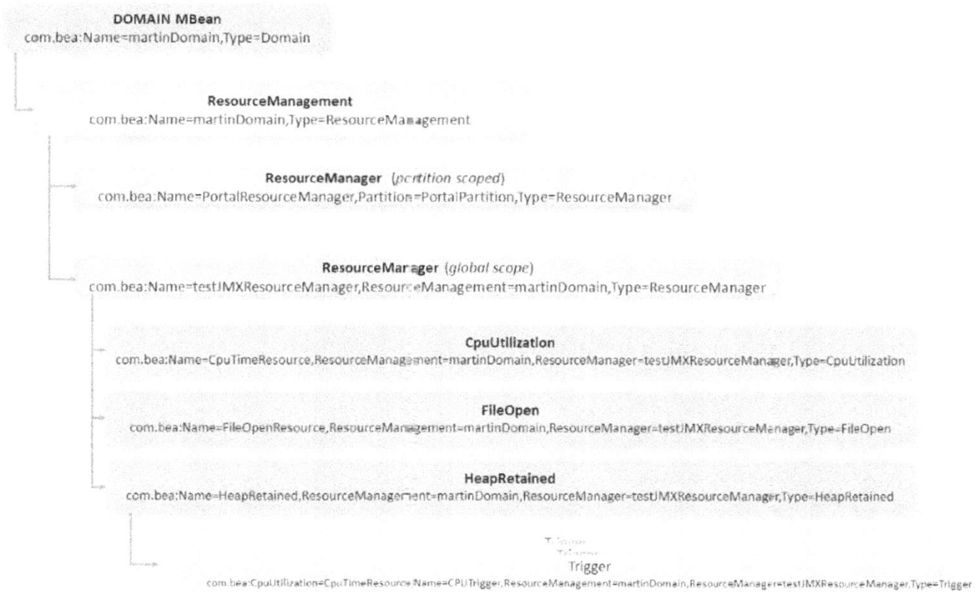

Figure 9-31: MBean hierarchy for ResourceManagers

The domain MBean only has an attribute:

```
....
Attribute: ResourceManagement   of Type : javax.management.ObjectName
```

The ResourceManagement MBean has the operations for creation, lookup and destroy for the all the resource managers managed by this MBean

```
  Attribute: DynamicallyCreated   of Type : java.lang.Boolean
  Attribute: Id   of Type : java.lang.Long
  Attribute: Name   of Type : java.lang.String
  Attribute: Notes   of Type : java.lang.String
  Attribute: Parent   of Type : javax.management.ObjectName
  Attribute: ResourceManagers   of Type : [Ljavax.management.ObjectName;
  Attribute: Tags   of Type : [Ljava.lang.String;
  Attribute: Type   of Type : java.lang.String
  Operation: java.lang.Boolean  isSet(propertyName:java.lang.String  )
  Operation: java.lang.Boolean  addTag(tag:java.lang.String  )
  Operation: java.lang.Void  restoreDefaultValue(attributeName:java.lang.String  )
  Operation: javax.management.ObjectName  lookupResourceManager(name:java.lang.String  )
  Operation: javax.management.ObjectName  createResourceManager(name:java.lang.String  )
  Operation: [Ljava.lang.String;  getInheritedProperties(propertyNames:[Ljava.lang.String;  )
  Operation: java.lang.Boolean  removeTag(tag:java.lang.String  )
  Operation: java.lang.Void  freezeCurrentValue(attributeName:java.lang.String  )
  Operation: java.lang.Boolean  isInherited(propertyName:java.lang.String  )
  Operation: java.lang.Void  destroyResourceManager(resMgrMBean:javax.management.ObjectName  )
```

The resource manager maintains three child MBeans. Each of if ("CpuUtilization", "FileOpen" and "HeapRetained") represents a different type of triggers or policies.

```
  Attribute: CpuUtilization   of Type : javax.management.ObjectName
  Attribute: DynamicallyCreated   of Type : java.lang.Boolean
  Attribute: FileOpen   of Type : javax.management.ObjectName
  Attribute: HeapRetained   of Type : javax.management.ObjectName
  Attribute: Name   of Type : java.lang.String
  ...
  Operation: javax.management.ObjectName  createHeapRetained(name:java.lang.String  )
  Operation: javax.management.ObjectName  createCpuUtilization(name:java.lang.String  )
  Operation: java.lang.Void  freezeCurrentValue(attributeName:java.lang.String  )
  Operation: javax.management.ObjectName  createFileOpen(name:java.lang.String  )
  Operation: java.lang.Void  destroyHeapRetained(heapRetainedMBean:javax.management.ObjectName  )
  Operation: java.lang.Void  destroyCpuUtilization(cpuUtilizationMBean: ObjectName  )
```

Each of the category MBeans maintains a list of triggers and maximum one "FairShare" policy.

```
e=HeapRetained
  Attribute: FairShareConstraint   of Type : javax.management.ObjectName
  Attribute: Name   of Type : java.lang.String
  Attribute: Triggers   of Type : [Ljavax.management.ObjectName;
  ...
  Operation: javax.management.ObjectName  lookupTrigger(name:java.lang.String  )
  Operation: java.lang.Void  freezeCurrentValue(attributeName:java.lang.String  )
  Operation: java.lang.Void  destroyTrigger(triggerMBean:javax.management.ObjectName  )
  Operation: java.lang.Void  destroyFairShareConstraint(fairShareConstraintMBean: ObjectName  )
  Operation: javax.management.ObjectName  createTrigger(name: String  value: Long  action: String  )
```

Each trigger maintains its name, action ("notify", "slow" or "shutdown") and the trigger value.

```
2GB,Partition=PortalPartition,ResourceManager=PortalResourceManager,Type=Trigger
  Attribute: Action   of Type : java.lang.String
  Attribute: Name   of Type : java.lang.String
  Attribute: Value   of Type : java.lang.Long
```

Working with ResourceManager

The first code example explains how a reference to a ResourceManager can be obtained. This is done by looking up the "ResourceManagement" MBean from the domain first and query it for the desired ResourceManager.

```
{
    try
    {
        // e.g.: com.bea:Name=TestDomain,Type=Domain
        ObjectName myDomainMBean = myJMXWrapper.getDomainConfigRoot();

         // get resource management
        ObjectName myResourceManagementMBean =
                   (ObjectName)myJMXWrapper.getAttribute(myDomainMBean, "ResourceManagement");

        // test if resource manager already exist
        return(ObjectName)myJMXWrapper.invoke(myResourceManagementMBean,
                  "lookupResourceManager",
                  new Object[]{new String(resourceManagerName)},
                  new String[]{String.class.getName()});
    }
    catch(Exception ex)
    {
      throw new WLSAutomationException(ex);
    }
  }
```

The next examples creates a new resource manager. In order to avoid exceptions, the code will do a check first if a ResourceManager with the desired name already exists. In this case the reference to the existing MBean will be returned.

```
{
   try
   {
      // e.g.: com.bea:Name=TestDomain,Type=Domain
      ObjectName myDomainMBean = myJMXWrapper.getDomainConfigRoot();

      // get resource management
     ObjectName myResourceManagementMBean =
                (ObjectName)myJMXWrapper.getAttribute(myDomainMBean, "ResourceManagement");

     // test if resource manager already exist
     ObjectName myResourceManagerMBean = (ObjectName)myJMXWrapper.invoke(myResourceManagementMBean,
                  "lookupResourceManager",
                  new Object[]{new String(resourceManagerName)},
                  new String[]{String.class.getName()});

     if (myResourceManagerMBean==null)
     {
        // create the resource manager
        myResourceManagerMBean = (ObjectName)myJMXWrapper.invoke(myResourceManagementMBean,
                  "createResourceManager",
                  new Object[]{new String(resourceManagerName)},
                  new String[]{String.class.getName()});
     }

     return myResourceManagerMBean;

  }
```

```
    catch(Exception ex) {
        throw new WLSAutomationException(ex);
    }
}
```

The last code example shows how to delete a ResourceManager.

```
{
   try
   {
      // e.g.: com.bea:Name=TestDomain,Type=Domain
      ObjectName myDomainMBean = myJMXWrapper.getDomainConfigRoot();

      // get resource management
      ObjectName myResourceManagementMBean =
               (ObjectName)myJMXWrapper.getAttribute(myDomainMBean, "ResourceManagement");

      // test if resource manager already exist
      ObjectName myResourceManagerMBean = (ObjectName)myJMXWrapper.invoke(myResourceManagementMBean,
                  "lookupResourceManager",
                  new Object[]{new String(resourceManagerName)},
                  new String[]{String.class.getName()});

      if (myResourceManagerMBean!=null)
      {
         // delete
         myJMXWrapper.invoke(myResourceManagementMBean, "destroyResourceManager",
              new Object[]{new String(resourceManagerName)},
              new String[]{String.class.getName()});
      }
   }
   catch(Exception ex)
   {
        throw new WLSAutomationException(ex);
   }
```

Working with Triggers

This section provides the corresponding JMX code which can create or update a trigger. The source code for the three trigger types are very similar so that only one is shown. The full source code is part of the code download.

```
public ObjectName createOrUpdateHeapTrigger(String resourceManagerName, String triggerName,
                  Long value, String action)  throws WLSAutomationException
{
     return createOrUpdateHeapTrigger(lookupResourceManager(resourceManagerName),
                                      triggerName,value,action);
}


// the method accepts the object-name of the resource manager
public ObjectName createOrUpdateHeapTrigger(ObjectName myResourceManagerMBean,
                  String triggerName,Long value, String action)  throws WLSAutomationException
{
   try {
       ObjectName myTrigger = null;

       // can only procees if the reference to the resource manager is not null
       if (myResourceManagerMBean!=null)
       {
          // get the category mbean and if null, create a new
```

```
        ObjectName myHeapRetainedMBean =
                  (ObjectName)myJMXWrapper.getAttribute(myResourceManagerMBean, "HeapRetained");

        if (myHeapRetainedMBean==null)
        {
          myHeapRetainedMBean = (ObjectName)myJMXWrapper.invoke(myResourceManagerMBean,
                  "createHeapRetained",
                  new Object[]{new String("HeapRetained")},
                  new String[]{String.class.getName()});
        }

        // check if trigger already exist
        myTrigger = (ObjectName)myJMXWrapper.invoke(myHeapRetainedMBean,
                 "lookupTrigger",
                 new Object[]{new String(triggerName)},
                 new String[]{String.class.getName()});

        // if trigger does not exist then create , otherwise update
        if (myTrigger==null)
        {
           // createTrigger
           myTrigger = (ObjectName)myJMXWrapper.invoke(myHeapRetainedMBean,
              "createTrigger",
              new Object[]{new String(triggerName), value, action},
              new String[]{String.class.getName(), Long.class.getName(), String.class.getName()});

           System.out.println("Heap Trigger: "+triggerName+" created !");
        }
        else //update
        {
           myJMXWrapper.setAttribute(myTrigger,new Attribute("Action",new String(action)));
           myJMXWrapper.setAttribute(myTrigger,new Attribute("Value",value));

           System.out.println("Heap Trigger: "+triggerName+" updated !");
        }
      }
      return myTrigger;
    }
    catch(Exception ex)
    {
      throw new WLSAutomationException(ex);
    }
```

The other trigger types and the fairshare policy code is very similar. The important aspect is to understand the MBean hierarchy.

Summary

Resource managers are a very important new element in WebLogic as they fill a gap in the isolation hierarchy. Without them, partitions would be able to influence each other more than they may should. They could fight against each other for the resources of the WebLogic server they are running on.

With resource managers, administrators have a utility to control the resources used and guarantee that all partitions running on this WebLogic server have at least their share of the system resources. The most important aspect here is that no single partition can eat up the complete resources and would therefore knock out all other partitions.

Different triggers are available for different resources. All of them have a defined set of recourses whereas possible reactions depend on the nature of the resource.

WebLogic Services Isolation

Description

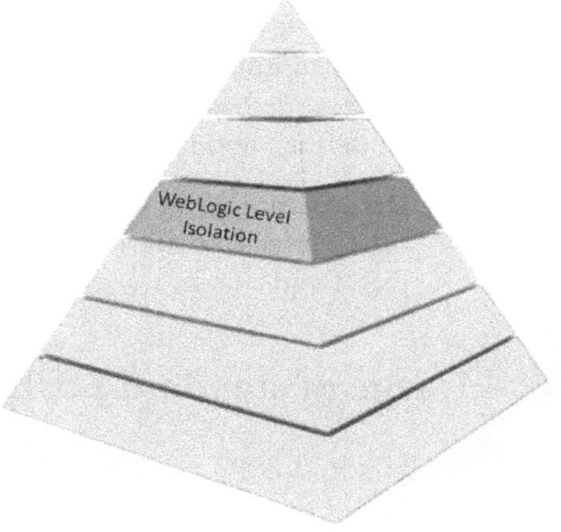

Coming to WebLogic as the application platform running on top of the base JVM system. WebLogic offers (with the new partition concept) a way to isolate system services like JNDI, security, JDBC and more for the different partitions. In a flexible way, it can be configured which services shall be shared and which shall be isolated.

Before we dive deeper in to WebLogic service and applications, it is important to understand the scoping of applications and to understand what is meant by the word "application". As always in our industry, many people or companies do define the same words with different meanings. In order to clearly separate "application" within this book I would like to introduce two different specializations of applications.

JEE applications

In the JEE world, an application is usually known as a deployable and packed unit. In most cases this is packed into a standard archive structure called an EAR file (Enterprise archive). It is also possible for less complex applications to use WAR (web archives) or EJBJar (enterprise bean archives) or others. The benefit of an EAR is, that it provides one archive for all the different application parts (figure 10-1).

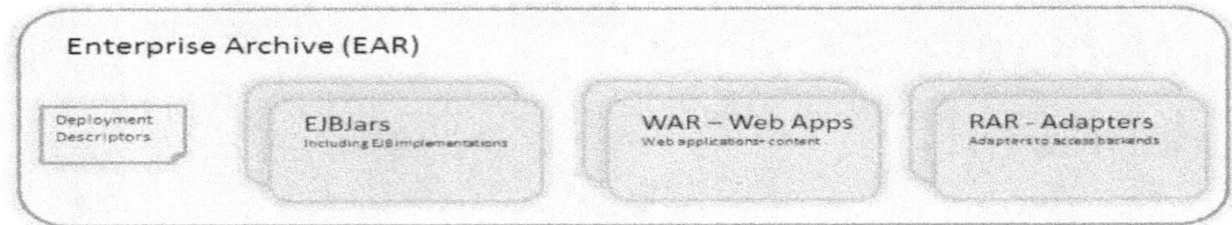

Figure 10-1: EAR structure

- **Advantage:** Standard format and standard structure as defined in the JEE specifications. This application is well understood by all compliant application servers. It has its own environmental naming context and required resources can be defined application locally using resource references.
- **Disadvantage:** This packaging only includes the application code and references to resources. It does not include resources. Resources like databases, JMS, JTA, JNDI and others are shared between all applications.

Usage of standard J2EE applications

By default, WebLogic (like other application servers) have the ability to deploy multiple JEE applications into the same server. The applications are separated from each other using different technologies like classloaders, environmental naming context (ENC) or others. But the datasources, JMS and more are defined on WebLogic level, and therefore all applications have shared access to these resources. Even though a datasource most likely is defined only for one JEE application, it is considered as a shared resource as it is – for this WLS server – globally available (figure 10-2).

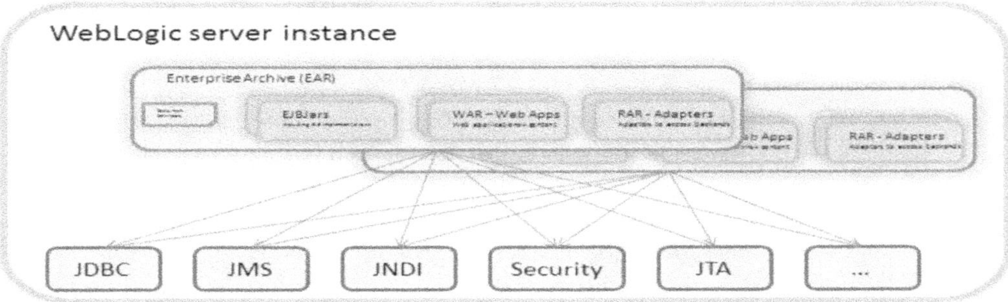

Figure 10-2: Shared WebLogic services

Furthermore resources are not attached to applications. They are working together but they do not build a closed unit (like a black-box).

WebLogic applications

As the JEE standards do not define such a combination of application(s) and real resources, WebLogic has introduced in the 12.2.x product line a new container concept called "partition", which was introduced earlier in this book. This concept allows administrators to define complete applications as units. These units can then contain JEE archives like EAR, WAR, and RAR or other files and also resource definitions like JDBC datasources, JMS or JNDI. In addition WebLogic own services like security and other can also be added to this unit.

That is why we will define (please note, this is not an official Oracle terminology) a "WebLogic application" which combines applications and resources (figure 10-3).

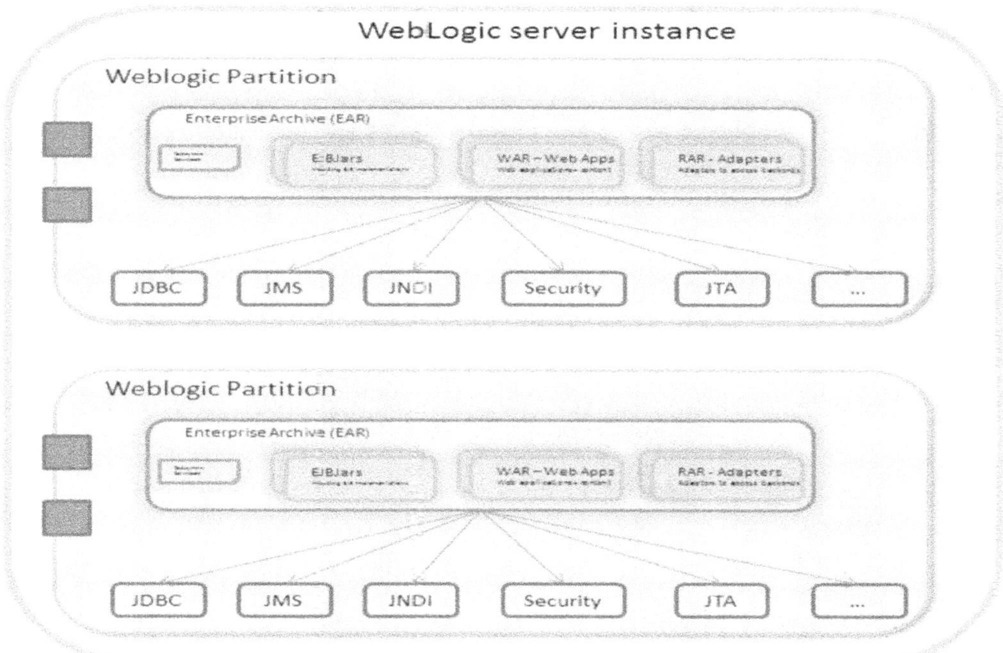

Figure 10-3: WebLogic server with 2 partitions and only dedicated services

In opposite to the last scenario where all services have been dedicated to their partition, it is often required or wanted to also have shared services (figure 10-4).

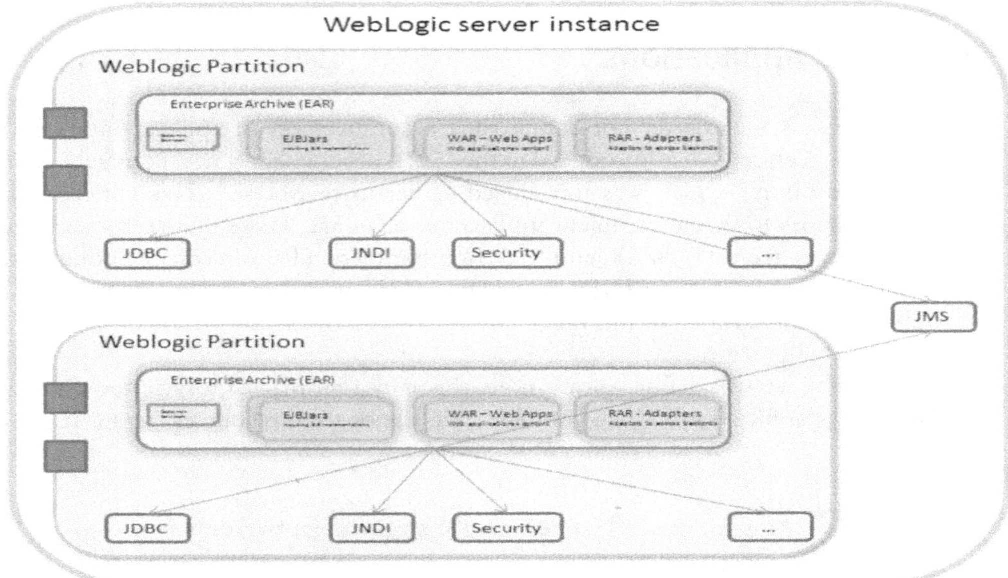

Figure 10-4: WebLogic server with mixed – shared and dedicated - services

Areas of Isolation

The concept of bundling applications and services to a unit can be applied to a number of areas in WebLogic. The most important areas are:

1) **Runtime isolation** (see previous chapter)
2) **Traffic and Data Isolation**
   This is the most visible area of an isolation for customers and customer applications as this includes the data flow into WebLogic (see virtual targets in the next section of the book) and also the access to data by using isolated data services like JDBC datasources , JMS, Mail or Coherence caches or more.
3) **Security Identity Isolation**
   WebLogic allows all partitions to have their own security realm and their own set of users which creates isolated security setups per "WebLogic application".
4) **Administrative Isolation**

WebLogic offers a range of administrative features which can operate on the partition level, like named edit sessions, separated lifecycles for partitions, separated logging information, separated administrative users and roles (e.g. partition admins) and more.

Shared vs. Isolated Services

The following section discusses the different services of WebLogic and provides general information and guidelines when to use what. Please note that every application and domain setup is different so that the following discussion can only be taken as a guideline.

JNDI

Moving the JNDI service from "shared" to "isolated" (dedicated) has a number of implications. First of all this means that applications hosted in different partitions can no longer easily lookup references from each other. If applications in different partitions use the same JNDI name (very likely in multi-tenancy applications) then these JNDI entries are no longer considered as alternative destinations as each partition has its own naming service.

Example: A WLS domain is hosting an application "MyShop" for different tenants. In this example lets imagine a MyShop instance for "PetFood Inc." and one MyShop instance for "CoolSchool Utilities Inc.". Of course, each tenant requires a cluster with multiple instances of its application. All MyShop instances though use the same codebase and hence the same JNDI names. If the JNDI naming service would be running in shared mode, then all tenants would register their objects in the same naming service. This would lead to the unwanted behavior, that a lookup for "/jndi/myshop/products" will provide in a round-robin manner a list of MyShop. Sometimes the request will be answered with a list of "CoolSchool Utils" and sometimes with a list of "PetFood". And this can be some kind of surprising to the customer. One may wonder, if this is the desired behavior (figure 10-5).

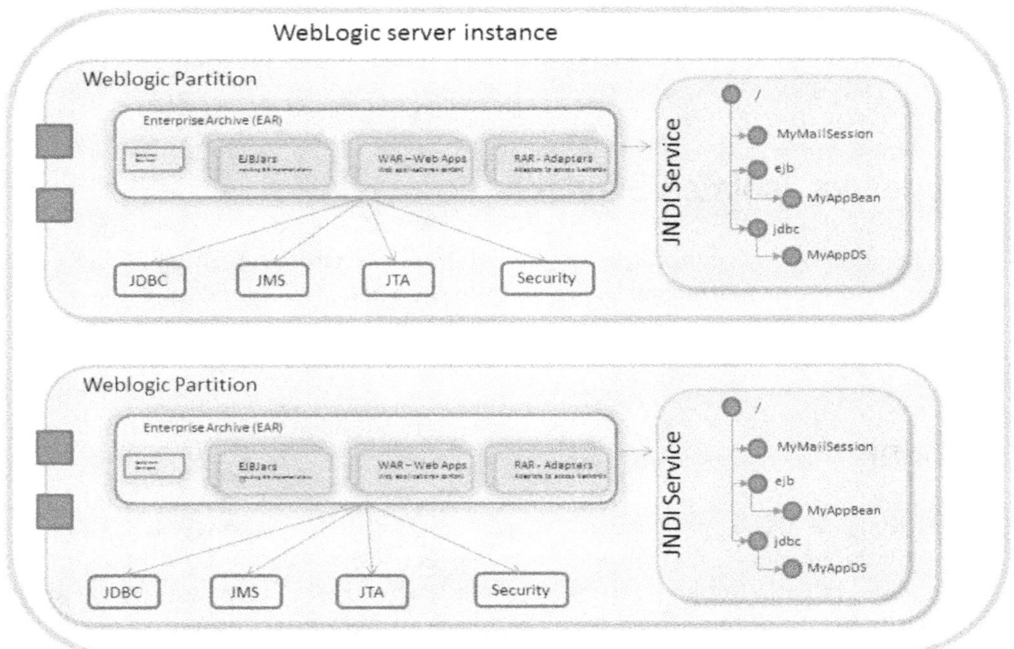

Figure 10-5: Isolated JNDI trees

Using a JNDI which resides **within** the partition would solve this problem. All partitions of MyShop ("Petfood") would have one naming service and all instances of MyShop ("CoolSchool Utils") would share another JNDI service. This is a reliable way to keep these instances independent from each other.

JDBC

Now all applications, hosted in different partitions, do no longer need to share a common connection pool. This has several advantages: The pool size and other datasource parameters (e.g. timeouts) do no longer apply to the whole WebLogic instance. They apply for any partition individually as the JDBC pool is not dedicated to a partition.

It is most likely, that all tenants which host the same software, will be usually configured to use the same lookup name and so the same JDBC pool. By moving the JDBC pool into the partition it will not only become a part of this partition but it is now also dedicated with all its resources to this partition. Datasource configurations like user, password, URL, timeouts, ONS or others can be set different for each partition while, for example, the JNDI lookup and datasource name can stay the same if the applications in the different partitions requires this approach (figure 10-6).

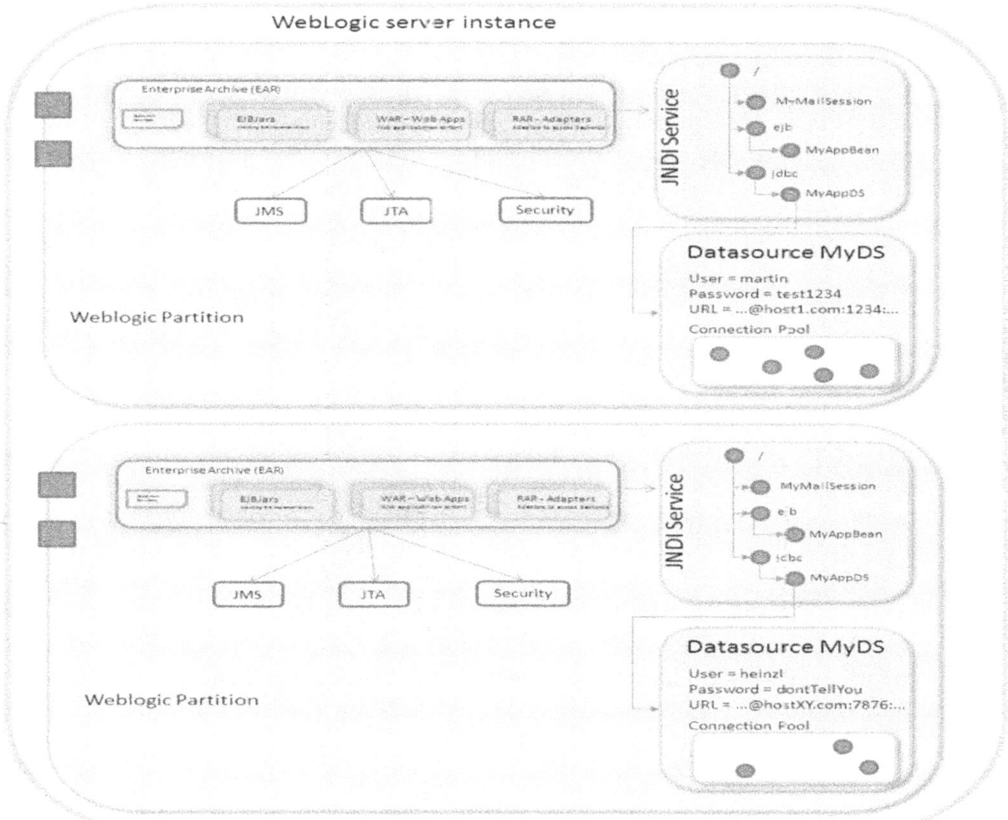

Figure 10-6: Isolated JDBC service

As you can see in the example above, both applications are using an identical JNDI tree, but not the same. In this case both partitions have a separated JNDI tree. Pay especially attention to the JNDI branch "/jdbc/MyAppDS" which points to a datasource.

Even though both partitions are using the same JNDI lookup, they are in fact using different datasources as the datasource lives within its individual partition. And as the picture also reveals, both datasources – albeit having the same name and JNDI lookup - are pointing to different databases and having different credentials. In addition each datasource has its own connection pool and limitations in the pool only affect the local partition.

JMS

JMS in WebLogic is a quite challenging topic, most likely the most complex topic in WebLogic. JMS supports many different setup and configuration combinations. This includes managed-server or cluster based JMS servers, system/application modules with many different elements like Queue, Topic, uniformed elements, SAF, elements, bridge elements, integration to foreign messaging systems like IBM-MQ or Tibco using foreign server configurations and much more. Most of the JMS elements can now also be part of the resource group or partition configuration so that it can be scoped to a partition.

JavaMail

Mail sessions are another very common example. Mail sessions based on JavaMail do provide a resource which can be used to send out and to receive emails. By revisiting the MyShop example it becomes quite obvious that emails send to the instance for "PetFood" should not be received by the instance for "CoolSchool Utils". Also it is quite natural that each instance wants to send email out with a different sender name.

Therefore – similar to JDBC and JMS - it must be possible to provide mail session instances for each tenant. This must have a different configuration like mail account, signature and so on. This can be achieved by isolating a JavaMail session to a partition and therefore having a partition specific, independent instance for mail access.

WebLogic Security

Another area is security. Since its infancy, WebLogic uses security realms and security providers to deal with authentication, authorization and other security aspects. It was always one of the biggest weaknesses of WebLogic that only one realm per WebLogic server instance was allowed to be active.

Since 12.2.1 WebLogic has changed this model and allows beside the global security realm a dedicated security realm per partition, if this is wanted. Partitions can share the global WebLogic server realm or can have their own partition security realm.

WebLogic always suffered from this one security realm model. All possible security models had to be fit into one complex list of security providers with the correct order and with the appropriate control flags. Usually it was very difficult to do this right if multiple applications were deployed into the same server. Also the maintenance was quite a challenge, if applications were exchanged.

With 12.2.1 this has been significantly improved in multiple ways. Security aspects can be defined isolated for each partition and without the need to consider aspects of other partitions. Security provider configurations and also user/groups/policies can now be bundled with a WebLogic application.

As an example, users only need to be known to the dedicated (partition) security realms where they have the right to do something. Other partitions do not even need to know about these users so that even the first authentication will fail and these users cannot even enter the partition.

This concept has also be extended to partition management. A set of users like "partition admin" or "partition monitor" form the administrative part of a partition realm so that each partition can be managed separately from different administrators.

Incoming Data Traffic

With multiple partitions hosted in the same WebLogic server, it is vital for WebLogic to distinguish incoming traffic according to the different partitions. WebLogic has invented so called "virtual targets" which describe an entry point into a partition. This concept can be compared to the "virtual host" feature in WebLogic. Also Webservers like Apache have a similar concept.

The main idea is that the virtual target will be used as deployment target for the partition resources. If a partition is deployed into a WebLogic, the virtual target will be mapped to a physical target. Now incoming requests will be routed to this particular virtual target. In order to avoid clashes with other partitions, each virtual target has internally its own HTTP server.

WebLogic has invented a new MBean called "VirtualTargetMBean". Mapping to physical targets can be achieved using the "addTarget" functionality of that MBean.

One major aspect is the matching of incoming traffic to partitions Virtual targets support different possible settings in order to allow WebLogic to match incoming traffic to partitions. "Hostname matching" will match the target of the incoming traffic to the hostname used by the client. This of course requires a proper DNS setup and routing. If no hostname separation is possible or if this is not wanted, it is possible to specify an URL prefix so that all clients can use the same hostname, will prefix the URL like

- http://myserver.xyz.com/shop1/index.html
- http://myserver.xyz.com/shop2/index.html

But what about older clients which can't change their URL? In this case it is possible to use different ports. Explicit ports and also port offsets are available for virtual targets. In case of explicit port numbers WebLogic will even support this by creating dedicated channels for this virtual target.

Resource Management – Work Manager

The main WebLogic work-engine for dealing with threads are WorkManagers. WebLogic offers system wide WorkManagers whereas the default one is also called "default" and also deployment specific WorkManagers (also called application WorkManager). This can be specified in the WebLogic specific deployment descriptor of an EAR file.

With the support of partitions WebLogic also introduces the same concept on partition level. (Please note: DO NOT (!) confuse WorkManagers with the formerly introduced ResourceManagers!)

WorkManagers provide resource – especially threads – management. Partition based WorkManagers can be defined in different ways. It is either possible to define them on WebLogic server level so that one partition WorkManager can be shared between multiple partitions, or it can also be embedded into the partition itself. There is a one to many relationship: A partition WorkManager (if defined on WebLogic level) can be shared between multiple partitions but each partition can be associated with ONLY one WorkManager.

Classloading

WebLogic always had different levels of class loading (system, core, and application (EAR, WAR) so on). Therefore every partition also has its own classloader.

Now the question arises: "Hmm they are talking about reducing footprint, higher density and so on – but now we still need to load application classes multiple times in case of multiple tenants?" In general this is the best thing you can do as you never know if all tenants are really running the same patch level, the same versions, etc.

The implementation in WebLogic even goes one step beyond and consider the case where you DO have the same application version hosted in multiple tenants and you want to even optimize your memory footprint further.

For this special case WebLogic has implemented a new shared application classloader. This new feature is only relevant if an application is deployed to a resource group template. To be clear: This only affects applications with this special setting deployed to partitions. Applications deployed to WebLogic directly – if they are the same applications – are not considered.

This feature is surprisingly NOT configured on partition level, NOR via MBeans. It must be configured in the **weblogic-application.xml** of the EAR file itself.

Three different locations for libraries can be defined as "shareable". This means that specific libs from these locations can be shared across partitions in order to load their content only once. This includes the JEE specific "lib" folder and/or the WebLogic specific "APP-INF/classes" or "APP-INF/lib" of the same EAR where this classloader policy is defined. Restrictions on the directory content can be done via include and exclude definitions.

The following logic is implemented in WebLogic: If no restriction is defined then all is sharable, if an "include" restriction is defined then only the content in "include" is shareable and if an exclude is defined all is shareable except the restrictions defined in "exclude".

Example for a definition in a weblogic-application.xml file:

```
<!—share all in classes -->
<shareable dir="APP-INF-CLASSES"/>
</shareable>

<!—share only 2 jars in LIB -->
<shareable dir="APP-INF-LIB">
  <include>my_application.jar</include>
  <include>app_resources.jar</include>
</shareable>


<!—share all except one in JEE-LIB -->
<shareable dir="LIB-DIR">
  <exclude>partition_non_shareable.jar</exclude>
</shareable>
```

Configuration

As explained earlier, the fundamental new concept is the concept of resource groups. Resources like JDBC datasources or JMS are grouped together into a resource group. So in order to configure the setups discussed above the following steps are needed:

- Create a new resource group template in your domain (in case you only need one instance of the partition this may be skipped)
- Create a new partition and base it on the just created resource group template. Alternatively you can also create a partition with a new empty resource group
- Now create your resources like datasources
    - Create them as usual in your WLS domain BUT scope them to your partition resource group (or resource group template)
    - Repeat the step above for all resources required
- Revisit your resource group (or resource group template) and you will see that it is now filled with your resources.

Example

The subsequent section of the book will look at all the technology aspects in more detail, so let's consider the following as a first example.

For the following example, we define a resource group template which shall be a blueprint for a shop. A JDBC datasource and a JMS server are created and scoped to the resource group template. In addition to that, a new tenant for a "Construction Shop" will be created. This partition is based on our resource group template.

As you can see in the following screenshot, our partition "MyConstructionShop" as a JDBC service which is scoped to the ShopResourceTemplate (figure 10-7).

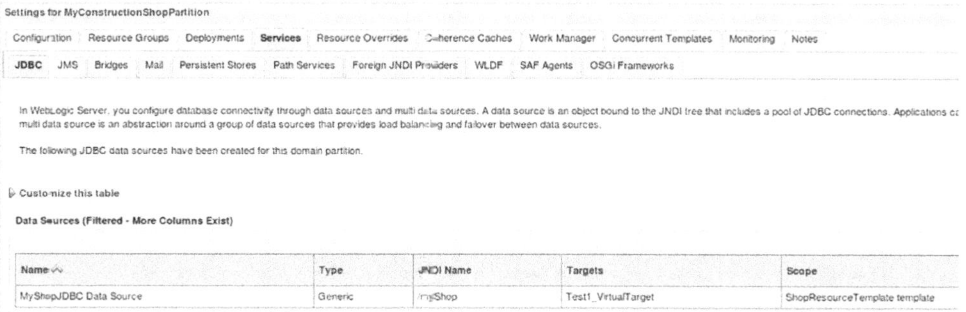

Figure 10-7: Partition scoped JDBC service

The complete setup can be done using a WLST script. The script does all the setup of the resource group template, the partition, the services and all the scoping.

Create the resource group template

```
cmo.createResourceGroupTemplate('ShopResourceTemplate')

cd('/ResourceGroupTemplates/ShopResourceTemplate')
```

Create the partition

```
cmo.createPartition('MyConstructionShopPartition')

cd('/Partitions/MyConstructionShopPartition/SystemFileSystem/MyConstructionShopPartition')
cmo.setRoot('/opt/development/wls/wls1221/user_domains/martin_1221/partitions/MyConstructionShopParti
tion/system')
cmo.setCreateOnDemand(true)
cmo.setPreserved(true)

cd('/Partitions/MyConstructionShopPartition')
```

Configure the partition to be based on our resource group template

```
cd('/Partitions/MyConstructionShopPartition/ResourceGroups/ShopResourceTemplate_group')
```

Target the partition

```
set('AvailableTargets',jarray.array([ObjectName('com.bea:Name=Test1_VirtualTarget,Type=VirtualTarget'
)], ObjectName))
set('DefaultTargets',jarray.array([ObjectName('com.bea:Name=Test1_VirtualTarget,Type=VirtualTarget')]
```

Create the JDBC datasource and scope (not target) it to the resource group template

```
cmo.createJDBCSystemResource('MyShopJDBC Data Source')

cd('/ResourceGroupTemplates/ShopResourceTemplate/JDBCSystemResources/MyShopJDBC Data
Source/JDBCResource/MyShopJDBC Data Source')
cmo.setName('MyShopJDBC Data Source')

cd('/ResourceGroupTemplates/ShopResourceTemplate/JDBCSystemResources/MyShopJDBC Data
Source/JDBCResource/MyShopJDBC Data Source/JDBCDataSourceParams/MyShopJDBC Data Source')
set('JNDINames',jarray.array([String('/myShop')], String))

cd('/ResourceGroupTemplates/ShopResourceTemplate/JDBCSystemResources/MyShopJDBC Data
Source/JDBCResource/MyShopJDBC Data Source')
cmo.setDatasourceType('GENERIC')

cd('/ResourceGroupTemplates/ShopResourceTemplate/JDBCSystemResources/MyShopJDBC Data
Source/JDBCResource/MyShopJDBC Data Source/JDBCDriverParams/MyShopJDBC Data Source')
cmo.setUrl('jdbc:oracle:thin:@//mydb.com:1521/ORCL')
cmo.setDriverName('oracle.jdbc.OracleDriver')
setEncrypted('Password', 'Password_1449701182266',
'/opt/development/wls/wls1221/user_domains/martin_1221/Script1449700907598Config',
'/opt/development/wls/wls1221/user_domains/martin_1221/Script1449700907598Secret')

cd('/ResourceGroupTemplates/ShopResourceTemplate/JDBCSystemResources/MyShopJDBC Data
Source/JDBCResource/MyShopJDBC Data Source/JDBCConnectionPoolParams/MyShopJDBC Data Source')
cmo.setTestTableName('SQL ISVALID\r\n')

cd('/ResourceGroupTemplates/ShopResourceTemplate/JDBCSystemResources/MyShopJDBC Data
Source/JDBCResource/MyShopJDBC Data Source/JDBCDriverParams/MyShopJDBC Data
Source/Properties/MyShopJDBC Data Source')
cmo.createProperty('user')

cd('/ResourceGroupTemplates/ShopResourceTemplate/JDBCSystemResources/MyShopJDBC Data
Source/JDBCResource/MyShopJDBC Data Source/JDBCDriverParams/MyShopJDBC Data
Source/Properties/MyShopJDBC Data Source/Properties/user')
cmo.setValue('martin')

cd('/ResourceGroupTemplates/ShopResourceTemplate/JDBCSystemResources/MyShopJDBC Data
Source/JDBCResource/MyShopJDBC Data Source/JDBCDataSourceParams/MyShopJDBC Data Source')
cmo.setGlobalTransactionsProtocol('OnePhaseCommit')

cd('/Partitions/MyConstructionShopPartition/ResourceGroups/ShopResourceTemplate group')
```

Create a JMS filestore and a JMS server and also scope (do not target) it to the resource group template.

```
cmo.createFileStore('MyShopFileStore')

cd('/ResourceGroupTemplates/ShopResourceTemplate/FileStores/MyShopFileStore')
cmo.setDirectory('/filestore')

cd('/ResourceGroupTemplates/ShopResourceTemplate')
cmo.createJMSServer('MyShopJMSServer')

cd('/ResourceGroupTemplates/ShopResourceTemplate/JMSServers/MyShopJMSServer')
cmo.setPersistentStore(getMBean('/ResourceGroupTemplates/ShopResourceTemplate/FileStores/MyShopFileSt
ore'))

cd('/Partitions/MyConstructionShopPartition/ResourceGroups/ShopResourceTemplate group')
```

NOTE:
Instead of using a resource group template I could have also scoped the JDBC and JMS service directly the partition internal resource group.

The configuration discussed above will we configured in the config.xml:

```
    <name>MyConstructionShopPartition</name>
    <resource-group>
      <name>ShopResourceTemplate_group</name>
      <resource-group-template>ShopResourceTemplate</resource-group-template>
    </resource-group>
    <default-target>Test1_VirtualTarget</default-target>
    <available-target>Test1_VirtualTarget</available-target>
    <realm>myrealm</realm>
    <partition-id>cbf8e187-dfc4-4253-a08d-a731ab974b72</partition-id>
    <system-file-system>

<root>/opt/development/wls/wls1221/user_domains/martin_1221/partitions/MyConstructionShopPartition/sy
stem</root>
      <create-on-demand>true</create-on-demand>
      <preserved>true</preserved>
    </system-file-system>
  </partition>
  <resource-group-template>
    <name>ShopResourceTemplate</name>
    <notes>My ShopResourceTemplate</notes>
    <jms-server>
      <name>MyShopJMSServer</name>
      <persistent-store>MyShopFileStore</persistent-store>
    </jms-server>
    <file-store>
      <name>MyShopFileStore</name>
      <directory>/filestore</directory>
    </file-store>
    <jdbc-system-resource>
      <name>MyShopJDBC Data Source</name>
      <descriptor-file-name>resource-group-
templates/ShopResourceTemplate/jdbc/MyShopJDBC_Data_Source-5838-jdbc.xml</descriptor-file-name>
    </jdbc-system-resource>
```

As a special note, pay attention to the "<descriptor-file-name>resource-group-templates/ShopResourceTemplate/jdbc/MyShopJDBC_Data_Source-5838-jdbc.xml</descriptor-file-name>". The JDBC definition is not saved – as administrators are used to – under "<domain>/config/jdbc" but instead as part of the resource group template.

The JDBC definition itself does not have anything special. The scope is defined in the config.xml as this datasource is part of the resource group template.

```
<jdbc-data-source ...>
  <name>MyShopJDBC Data Source</name>
  <datasource-type>GENERIC</datasource-type>
  <jdbc-driver-params>
    <url>jdbc:oracle:thin:@//mydb.com:1521/ORCL</url>
    <driver-name>oracle.jdbc.OracleDriver</driver-name>
    <properties>
      <property>
        <name>user</name>
        <value>martin</value>
      </property>
    </properties>
    <password-encrypted>{AES}9BLVDxNTRfWxoBmNe6DK1UDX6LFrC9mA2ItubXOz08=</password-encrypted>
  </jdbc-driver-params>
  <jdbc-connection-pool-params>
    <test-table-name>SQL ISVALID</test-table-name>
  </jdbc-connection-pool-params>
  <jdbc-data-source-params>
    <jndi-name>/myShop</jndi-name>
    <global-transactions-protocol>OnePhaseCommit</global-transactions-protocol>
  </jdbc-data-source-params>
```

Summary

With WebLogic services isolation it is possible to share a service between different tenants or applications or to use services dedicated to a partition (tenant). In many cases dedicated services are very important (see JNDI example) in order to truly implement multi-tenancy.

Isolation in this chapter does NOT mean to isolate a service into its own JVM process. Isolation of services in this chapter means, restrict its usage and accessibility to tenant (partition) level.

WebLogic offers the flexibility to you to decide if services should be shared or dedicated.

Application Isolation

CHAPTER

Description

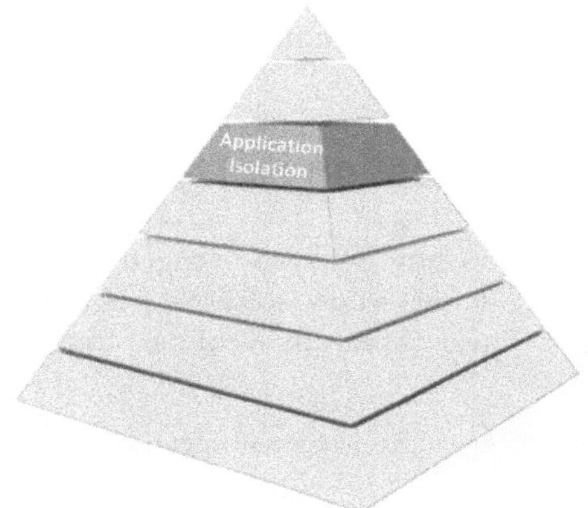

Note that this section does NOT talk about the "WebLogic-Applications" as it has been defined in previous chapters, because these are handled by the WebLogic partitions. This section discusses isolation in traditional J2EE applications.

Coming to the application level,. Application isolation is basically nothing new for the J2EE world.

The J2EE specification defines the applications bundled as WAR files, EJB-Jar files or better as EAR files as independent applications. All of them have their own deployment descriptor.

WebLogic – similar to most other application servers – provides application level isolation based on own classloader and the environmental naming context.

Therefore this level is a well-known way to isolate application deployments.

Technology used

This isolation level is NOT another partition style method for doing isolation. Applications in WebLogic are based on deployments. The best possible way to package an application is the EAR file format specified by the JEE specification.

Each deployment is usually loaded in its own classloader in order to provide independent lifecycles (start/stop/deploy/undeploy), and even more important, it is done to allow each application to utilize different versions of the same libraries or classes without clashing into each other.

In addition to the classloading, each application as its own area in the naming service called "ENC" which means environmental naming context.

The JEE specification also defines a concept of resource references which allow an application to rely on resource definitions made in their own deployment descriptors. This allows an administrator to have an additional layer which completely separates the references in the code from the real resources used in the application server.

Application isolation and partitions?

So, how does this fit together with the aforementioned concept of partitions? Partitions defines a new isolation option in WebLogic which can define resources and applications as new units in WebLogic (figure 11-1).

- EACH partition can contain resources and multiple applications (like EARs)
- ALL applications within a partitions share the same partition resources and also the same JVM resources as these are partition based
- EACH application (e.g. EAR) within the partition though is in addition isolated using the above mentioned technologies from each other

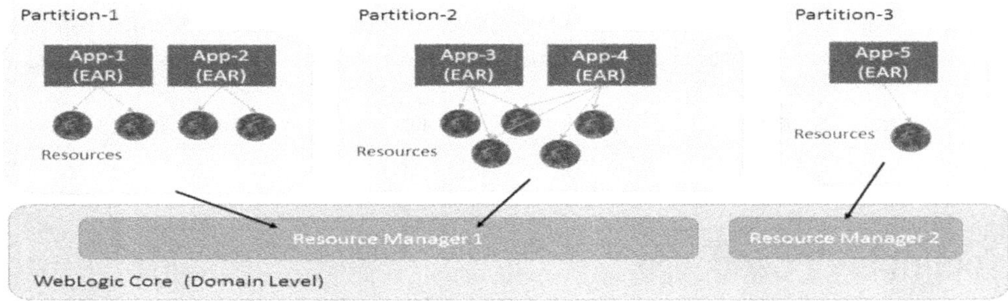

Figure 11-1: Applications – Resources - Partitions

The picture above explains the relationship between these different artifacts. A WebLogic server can host multiple partitions, and each partition can have multiple resources which belong only to its own partition. Each partition can also host multiple applications (e.g.: EAR, WAR). Resources within a partition can be shared between the different applications of this partition.

It is NOT possible though that for example "App-1" from partition-1 can access resources from partition-2

Summary

Application isolation in the context of WebLogic does only mean that each application has some kind of isolation. This is based on classloading, resource references and environmental naming context. This cannot be compared to the isolation capabilities partition offers.

Each partition can have multiple applications. Each application is to a certain degree isolated but these applications share all the resources defined in the partition.

In order to really isolate the complete stack – application and resources – there must not be more than one application hosted in each partition.

User Isolation

CHAPTER 12

Description

User isolation is a very uncommon request nowadays. This actually means that every user (session) gets its own isolated tenant. Modern enterprise systems based on J2EE do not have this requirement. This requirement for isolation was more common in the older days of mainframe applications or cases where applications which are never designed to be multithreaded needed to be made available over common middleware like CORBA.

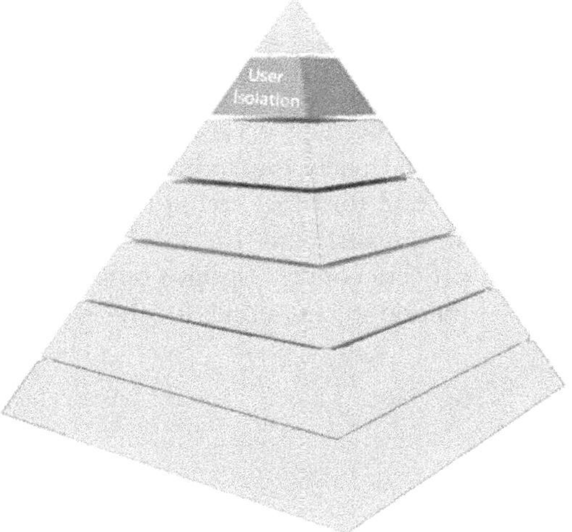

Technology Challenges

CORBA is a good example where the isolation protocol can be used – together with ORB specific daemons to achieve even this kind of isolation. VisiBroker ORB as an example has a daemon called OAD (object activation daemon) which could be configured in a way that this daemon would start a new application for each new user or even request.

WebLogic does not support this kind of isolation. Given that multitenancy should be used to provide more condensed infrastructure it would be contra-productive to create partitions and virtual targets only for one particular user. Therefore, the rest of this book will not consider this level of isolation as it cannot be achieved with standard WebLogic technology components.

Do **NOT** confuse User isolation with user sessions. Like shopping portals, where each user has its own shopping basket, there are a great number of applications which needs to provide user specific context information. This is not meant with user isolation as those users do not have their own application instance and their own resources like for example JDBC. They only have the possibility to keep personal data separated from each other which is usually implemented with sessions. Famous examples are http sessions (servlet container) or stateful session beans (EJB container).

Summary

WebLogic does not offer straightforward features for isolating users or business requests. This is far too fine grained. Frankly speaking, everybody having this request should really think about a redesign / re-implementation of the application (or shop around for other technologies like CORBA). But even other technologies treat this as an unusual case. In all cases, this level of granularity brings a lot of other issues like process count, response time or more and therefore should definitely be avoided. It is mentioned here only for the sake of completeness.

Part IV

WebLogic technology building blocks for multitenancy

WebLogic Technology for Multitenancy and Cloud Support

CHAPTER

Architecture

This part of the book discusses in detail the new technology additions which have been added to WebLogic in order to implement the multitenancy features.

WebLogic has basically implemented two new concepts: Resource isolation and resource + application bundling. In addition, WebLogic provides some interesting lifecycle and management features around it.

One of the fundamental new concept is the concept of resource groups. Resources like JDBC data sources or JMS are grouped together into a resource group. The complete group – means all resources of that group – can be started/stopped together. For flexible resource isolation these resource groups can either be scoped globally or for a specific partition. In order to create "WebLogic applications" the new concept of a partition has been created to combine applications and resources into a new unit. This new unit can be targeted using an abstraction layer called "virtual target", so that administrators can assign units to real infrastructure without changing the internal partition or resource group targeting.

Multitenancy means that different applications can be operated in the same environment but without conflicting each other or competing for the same resources. This also includes the user-case that the same application (JEE applications and resources) can be instantiated multiple times with tenant specific characteristics. It does not make much sense that in this case resource groups must be created multiple times for each tenant as this is unnecessary work and pretty error prone.

The answer to this problem are so called "resource group templates" which allow the administrator to create resources only once and scope them to a resource group template. The template itself is not a real group, therefore it cannot be started or stopped. But it is possible to instantiate global or even partition scoped resource groups, based on this template. For each real resource group based on the same template, an own set of resources will be created, which also raises the question that this might be not optimal as it does not allow tenant specific configurations like JDBC schema users. Again WebLogic has implemented an answer to this problem which is called "resource overrides". These overrides allow the administrator to tailor the instance of a resource group template to the tenants needs.

As partitions form their own unit, WebLogic also allows administrators to create an own – partition scoped – security realm which makes security configuration much easier. In addition, it allows WebLogic to export the partition security together which the partition. Security cannot yet be exported as part of the exported partition archive, but WLST scripts can be used to export the partition security realm.

Partitions can be seen as **microcontainers**. Oracle often refers to partitions as microcontainers as these containers only contain whatever is need for the apps deployed to it. It is somehow similar to Docker (see advanced section of the book).

The following could be seen as an analogy (albeit technically not really correct):

- WebLogic is like a virtual machine (VirtualBox, VMWare, …)
- Partition is like a Docker image running in a virtual machine

As partitions form units, WebLogic has already implemented export and import features which enables an administrator to export a partition from one environment and import it to another (e.g. move it from UAT and production), as shown in figure 13-1.

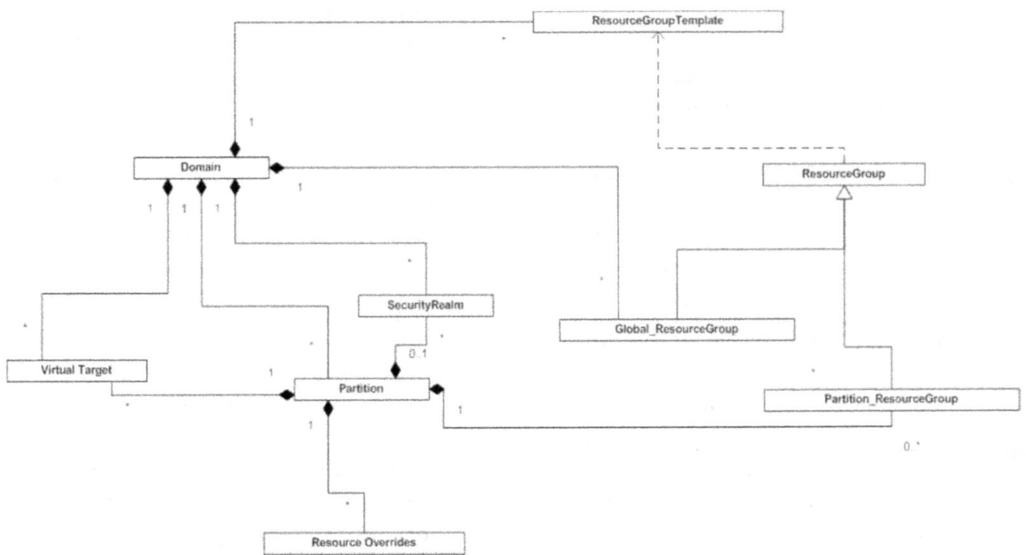

Figure 13-1: Dependencies between elements

As described above the support for multitenancy consists of different components which form a complex set of dependency rules between them.

In the center – as usual in WebLogic – is the domain. Also in the multitenancy world nothing outmatches the domain. Resource scoping is one of the key concepts. There are different types of resource groups available. Global resource groups which are defined on domain level (note that there is no link in the diagram between a global resource group and a partition) and partition scoped resource groups which exists in the context and scope of a partition. The later has no direct link to the domain, but to the partition.

Resource group templates are defined as a pure abstract resource container. It is defined on domain level as it does not have a concrete target. Resource groups can either have own resources scoped to them or can be instances of a specific resource group.

Understanding the different elements and their relationship is key in doing multitenancy setups right. The following chapter provide deep dives into the different elements.

Summary

WebLogic 12.2.1 has been re-architected to support a new way to bundle applications, services and resources. This offers a solution for many problems in the J2EE world and was especially designed as a foundation for cloud-based services or a cloud-based WebLogic infrastructure. The terminology WaaS (WebLogic as a Service) used in this book is unfortunately not an official Oracle terminology but in my opinion describes the intention of this new architecture quite well.

WebLogic offers now a service model (PaaS or even SaaS based approach) which offers a platform for many applications including proper isolation without relying on potential unknown factors like operating system, OS user isolation and many others. WebLogic can now be used to offer its own platform. In order to fulfill this, WebLogic has been extended with a number of new technologies and concepts which all work hand-in-hand to implement this new model.

The following chapters will discuss the different new technologies in detail before subsequent book parts will discuss how these technologies can be used to solve a number of very well-known issues which WebLogic alone could not have solved before.

Resource Grouping – Foundation for Isolation

CHAPTER

Overview

Resource isolation and resource grouping is one of the fundamental concepts which have been added to WebLogic in order to implement the necessary isolation concepts but also to provide all the flexibility for WebLogic administrators to configure different requirements of different applications.

Resources like JDBC datasources or JMS are grouped together into a global or partition local resource group. The complete group – means all resources of that group – can be started/stopped together.

WebLogic provide two different configuration artifacts, which we will discuss in this chapter. WebLogic either offers a concrete resource group, which is a single instance with a concrete target or a template that defines a blueprint to be used for many concrete group instances.

Templates as Group Blueprints

Resource group templates have been defined as a powerful concept in order to define resource group blueprints. Especially for a multitenancy setup which runs the same software but for multiple tenants this is the only efficient way to setup your configuration. As in this case all partitions have a very similar if not equal setup (except for some configuration items like database schema). It would be a duplication of work to define all resource multiple times (once for each tenant). Templates define an abstract blueprint which on its own does not create any resource instances. But it is possible to create multiple instances of a resource bundle based on this blueprint.

Resource groups are always defined on domain level (in order to create reusable artifacts). They must have a unique name. The resources of that group only create configuration MBeans, but no runtime MBeans. There I prefer to call them abstract groups or group blueprints as they do not work with generic resource types but contain concrete resource definitions. The main difference to resource groups is that they do not have resource instances or – in WebLogic terminology – runtime components (figure 14-1).

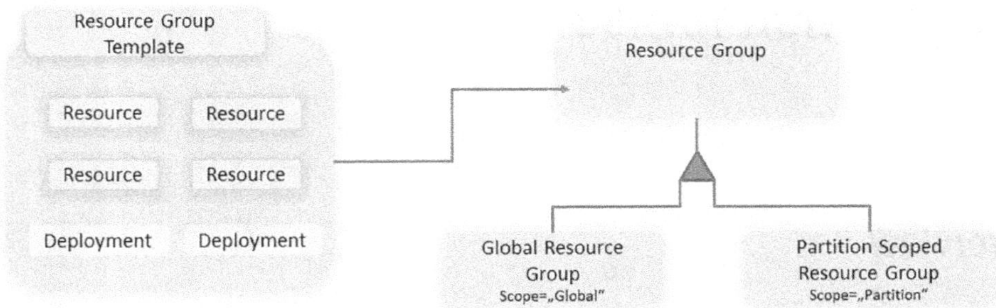

Figure 14-1: Idea behind resource group templates

As you can see in the above diagram, when a resource group template is used, the resources and also deployments are added to the blueprint only. Resource groups (normally) do not have own resources but create instances of the resources defined in the blueprint.

Creating a resource group template is easy because the group itself does not have many options. Group templates can be created in different ways. They can be created using the WLS admin console, using WLST or also using JMX.

It is possible to create a new empty group or to clone an existing group (figure 14-2).

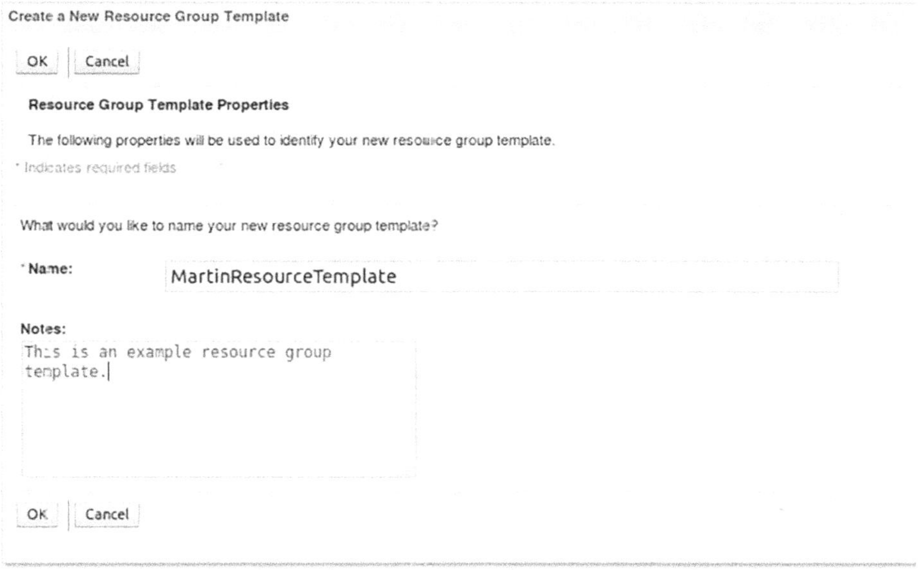

Figure 14-2: Creating a new resource group template using the admin console

After a new blueprint has been created, it is empty. No deployments or services are defined. Note in the screenshot below, that there is NO way to add services or deployments to the resource group template from this wizard. This is done using scoping (see next chapter), see figure 14-3.

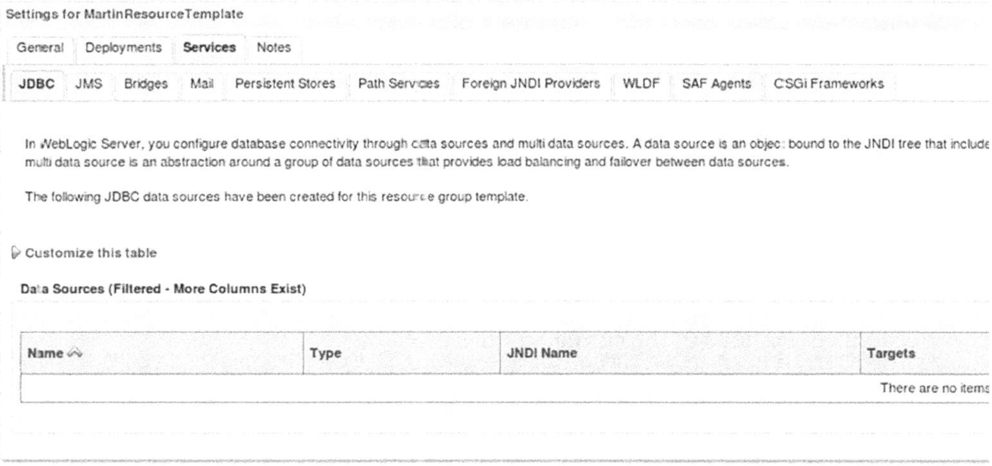

Figure 14-3: After creation resource group templates are empty containers

Resource group templates can also be created using a simple WLST script:

```
cmo.createResourceGroupTemplate('MartinResourceTemplate')

cd('/ResourceGroupTemplates/MartinResourceTemplate')
```

After creating the resource group, an empty subfolder will be created underneath the "config" folder in the domain directory. <domain>/config/<name of resource-group-template>, see figure 14-4:

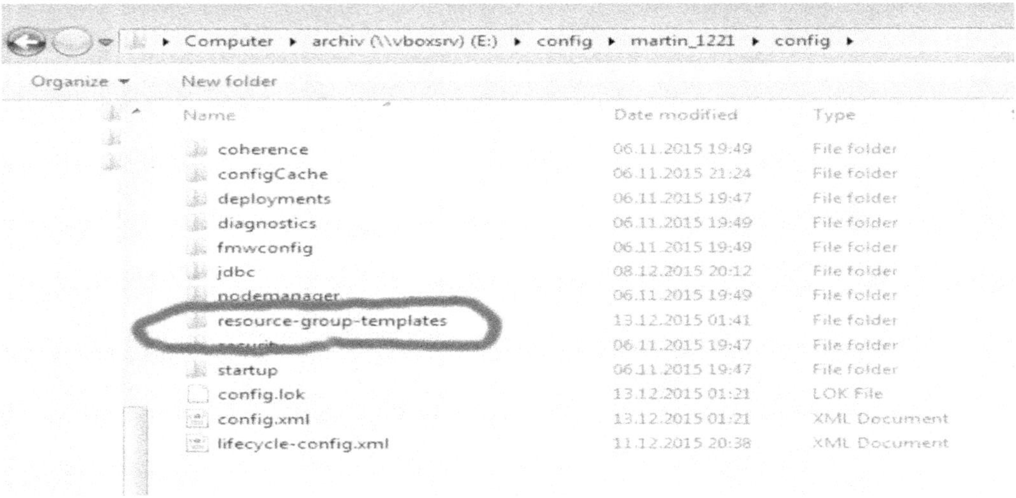

Figure 14-4: Base folder of the resource group template

After adding resources to the template, appropriate subfolders will be created like "jdbc" or "jms". This is one of the most visible changes, that the resource definitions are no longer stored directly underneath the "config" folder.

Resource group templates are of course also configured in the configuration MBean tree and therefore part of the config.xml file.

Example definitions in the config.xml file:

```
<name>ShopResourceTemplate</name>
<notes>My ShopResourceTemplate</notes>
<jms-server>
  <name>MyShopJMSServer</name>
  <persistent-store>MyShopFileStore</persistent-store>
</jms-server>
<file-store>
  <name>MyShopFileStore</name>
  <directory>/filestore</directory>
```

```
    </file-store>
    <jdbc-system-resource>
      <name>MyShopJDBC Data Source</name>
      <descriptor-file-name>resource-group-
templates/ShopResourceTemplate/jdbc/MyShopJDBC_Data_Source-5838-jdbc.xml</descriptor-file-name>
    </jdbc-system-resource>
  </resource-group-template>
  <resource-group-template>
    <name>MartinResourceTemplate</name>
    <notes>This is an example resource group template.</notes>
```

As mentioned earlier, resource group templates can also be created by cloning existing blueprints. This is supported as a functionality in the admin console (figure 14-5).

Clone a Resource Group Template

OK | Cancel

Resource Group Template Properties

The following properties will be used to identify your new resource group template.

* Indicates required fields

What would you like to name your new resource group template?

* **Name:** MartinClonedResourceTemplate

OK | Cancel

Figure 14-5: Cloning of resource group templates

Deleting a Resource Group Template

Especially resource group templates are a vital and fundamental resource. Deleting resource group templates means that all the services defined in this template will no longer be available. It is not easy to delete them once they are in use. These templates – once created – will be referenced in potentially many resource groups. If you want to delete such a template, it is therefore necessary to shut down and delete all resource groups which references this template first (figure 14-6).

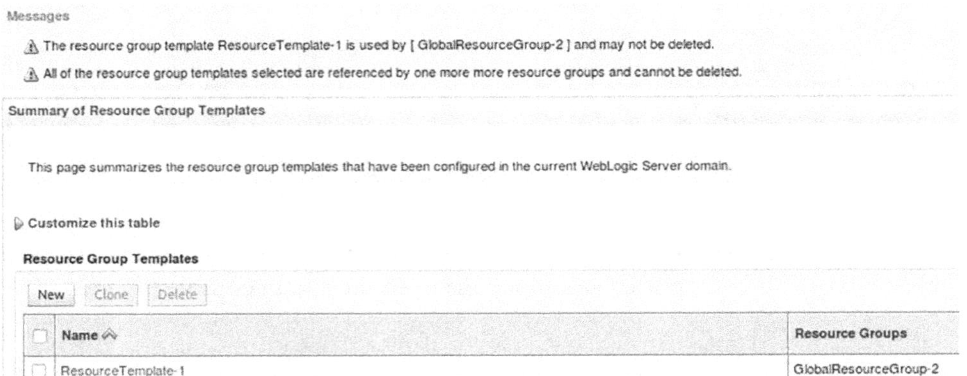
Messages
The resource group template ResourceTemplate-1 is used by [GlobalResourceGroup-2] and may not be deleted.
All of the resource group templates selected are referenced by one more more resource groups and cannot be deleted.
Summary of Resource Group Templates
This page summarizes the resource group templates that have been configured in the current WebLogic Server domain.
Customize this table
Resource Group Templates
New
Clone
Delete
Name
Resource Groups
ResourceTemplate-1
GlobalResourceGroup-2

Figure 14-6: Error while trying to delete a template which is still referenced

In case you try to delete a template which has still references in a resource group (regardless if this group is started or not), you will get an error as WebLogic does not allow you to delete this template.

Concrete resource group Instances

WebLogic has a new way of grouping resources. The templates are one way to define generic blueprints for resource bundling. But blueprints are not real runtime resource instances. Only resource groups have a real target and therefore create runtime resource instances. Resource groups can be created based on blueprints or – as the next screenshot demonstrates – can have their own collection of resources and deployments (figure 14-7).

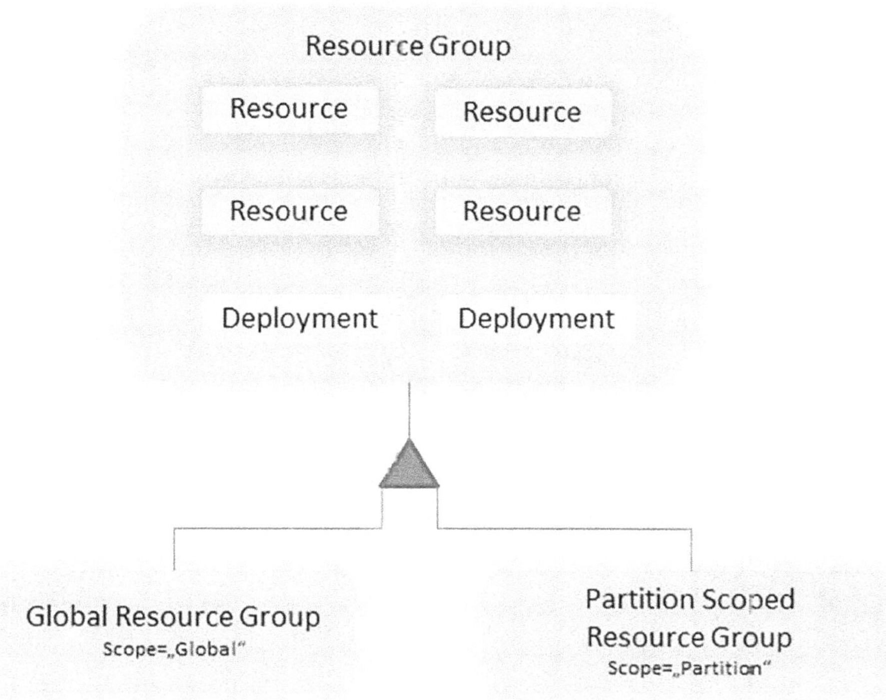

Figure 14-7: Resource group with individual resources not based on a template

Resource groups are also configuration items and therefore represented by an MBean called "ResourceGroupMBean". This MBean forms the container which can contain deployments and/or the different services. Services includes: JDBC, JMS, Mail sessions, persistent stores, WLDF diagnostics and more.

Creating domain level resource groups

Creating a resource group is quite different from creating a resource group template. A group can be created on domain level or on partition level. Furthermore a group can be based on a template or not (figure 14-8).

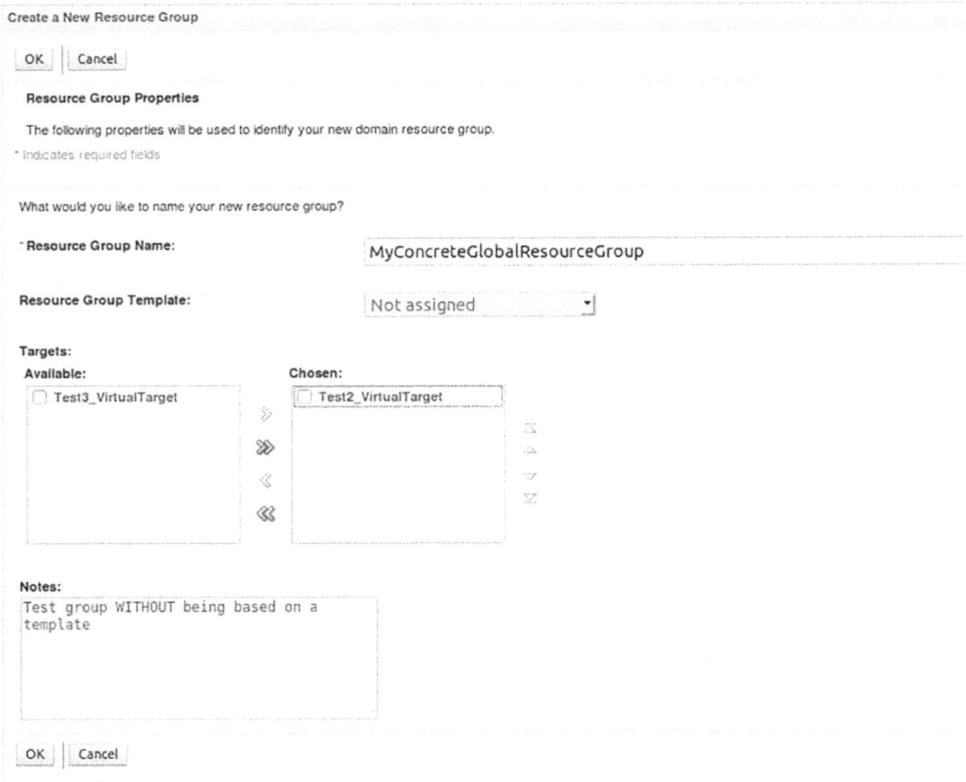

Create a New Resource Group

OK | Cancel

Resource Group Properties

The following properties will be used to identify your new domain resource group.

* Indicates required fields

What would you like to name your new resource group?

* Resource Group Name: MyConcreteGlobalResourceGroup

Resource Group Template: Not assigned

Targets:

Available: Test3_VirtualTarget

Chosen: Test2_VirtualTarget

Notes:

Test group WITHOUT being based on a template

OK | Cancel

Figure 14-8: Create an independent resource group on domain level

The screenshot above shows how to create an independent resource group on domain level. This group has a unique name but is NOT (!) based on a resource group template. During the creation process it is also possible to target the group to one or more virtual targets.

Appropriate WLST script to create this group:

```
cmo.createResourceGroup('MyConcreteGlobalResourceGroup')

cd('/ResourceGroups/MyConcreteGlobalResourceGroup')
set('Targets',jarray.array([ObjectName('com.bea:Name=Test2_VirtualTarget,Type=VirtualTarget')],
ObjectName))
cmo.setNotes('Test group WITHOUT being based on a template')
```

The other option is to create a group which is based on a resource group template (figure 14-9)

Create a New Resource Group

OK | Cancel

Resource Group Properties

The following properties will be used to identify your new domain resource group.

* Indicates required fields

What would you like to name your new resource group?

* **Resource Group Name:** MyConcreteGlobalResourceGroup2

Resource Group Template: MartinResourceTemplate

Targets:

Available:

Chosen: Test3_VirtualTarget

Notes

Test group WHICH IS based on a template

OK | Cancel

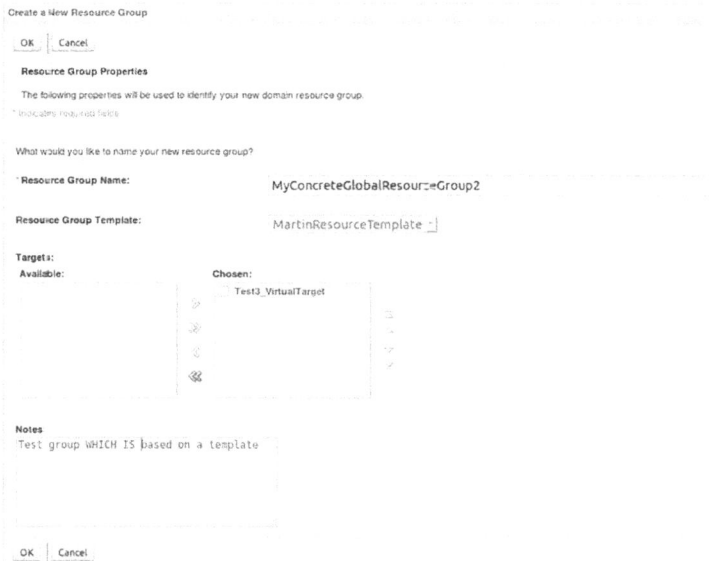

Figure 14-9: Resource group which is based on a template

Example of a WLST script

```
cmo.createResourceGroup('MyConcreteGlobalResourceGroup')

cd('/ResourceGroups/MyConcreteGlobalResourceGroup')
set('Targets',jarray.array([ObjectName('com.bea:Name=Test2_VirtualTarget,Type=VirtualTarget')],
ObjectName))
cmo.setNotes('Test group WITHOUT being based on a template')
```

After these two groups have been created, they are visible in the WLS console under resource groups (figure 14-10).

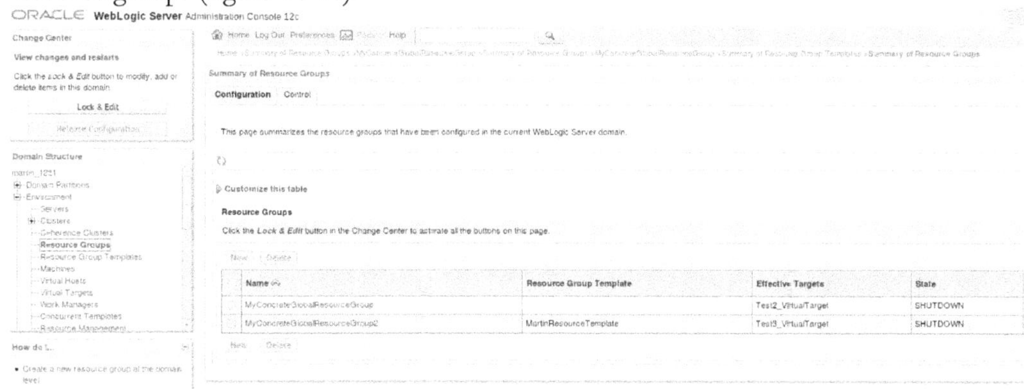

Figure 14-10: Visibility of global resource groups in the WLS console

Two interesting observations can be made in the above screenshot. First the list of targets. This is the indication that these are groups with runtime MBeans and second the "State". Resource groups – other than resource group templates – have a state and associated control actions which allow the administrator to start or stop them. Start or stop means starting all resources or deployments which are part of this resource group.

The console tab of the resource group overview provide the administrator access to the control actions (figure 14-11).

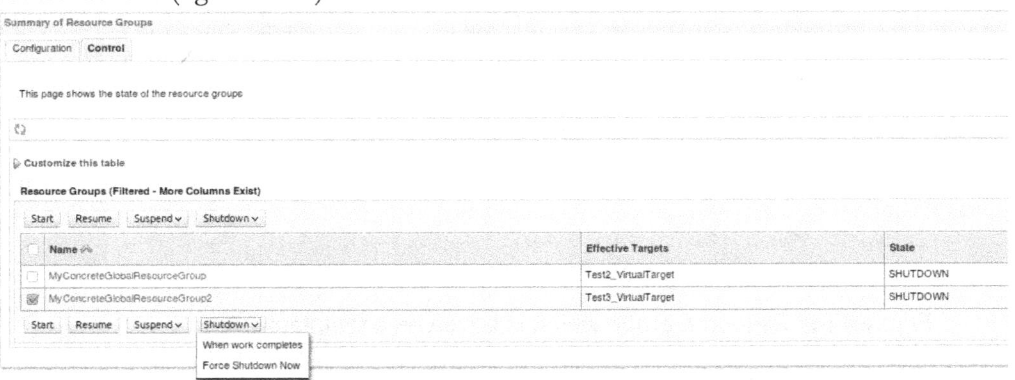

Figure 14-11: Control actions of resource groups

Creating partition level resource groups

Creating a partition scoped resource is quite different from creating a global resource group even though both are resource groups.

Creating a new partition with a default resource group:

When a new partition gets created, the administrator can select a resource group template (note: not a resource group). If a template is selected then the partition creation process will automatically create a partition with a default resource group which is based on the selected template (figure 14-12).

Figure 14-12: Create a partition with a default resource group

After the partition has been created the created resource group shows up in the "Resource Groups" tab. By default it is also automatically targeted to the targets selected for the partition (if any). Albeit the lifecycle of these resource groups will most likely be always bound to the partition lifecycle, the partition internal resource groups also have their own control actions and can be started and stopped (figure 14-13).

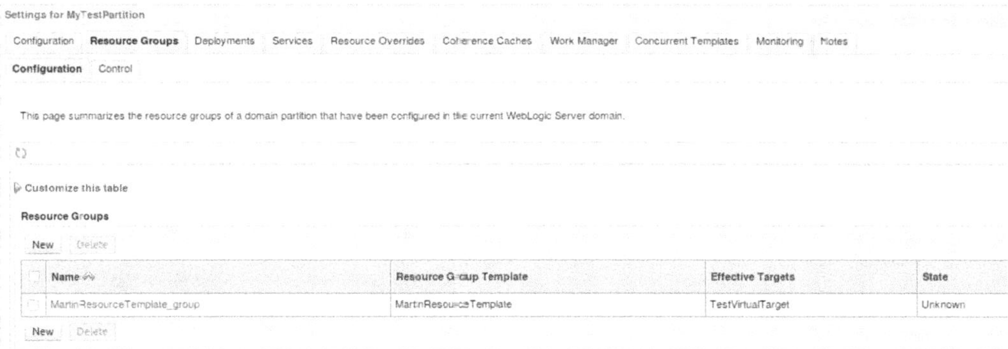

Figure 14-13: Default resource group after partition creation

This can of course also be done using WLST. An interesting side effect is that with WLST the administrator has even more flexibility as he can also influence the name of the default resource group. This cannot be done when using the portal.

Example WLST script:

```
cmo.createPartition('MyTestPartition')

cd('/Partitions/MyTestPartition/SystemFileSystem/MyTestPartition')
```

```
cmo.setRoot('/opt/development/wls/wls1221/user_domains/martin_1221/partitions/MyTestPartition/system'
)
cmo.setCreateOnDemand(true)
cmo.setPreserved(true)

cd('/Partitions/MyTestPartition')
cmo.setRealm(getMBean('/SecurityConfiguration/martin_1221/Realms/myrealm'))
cmo.createResourceGroup('MartinResourceTemplate_group')

cd('/Partitions/MyTestPartition/ResourceGroups/MartinResourceTemplate_group')
cmo.setResourceGroupTemplate(getMBean('/ResourceGroupTemplates/MartinResourceTemplate'))

cd('/Partitions/MyTestPartition')
set('AvailableTargets',jarray.array([ObjectName('com.bea:Name=TestVirtualTarget,Type=VirtualTarget')]
, ObjectName))
set('DefaultTargets',jarray.array([ObjectName('com.bea:Name=TestVirtualTarget,Type=VirtualTarget')],
ObjectName))

cd('/Partitions/MyTestPartition/ResourceGroups/MartinResourceTemplate_group')
```

Besides creating a default resource group during partition creation, which could be based on a template, it is possible to create any number of additional resource groups for this partition after the creation was done. These additional groups may also be placed on other resource group templates or may not be based on a template (figure 14-14):

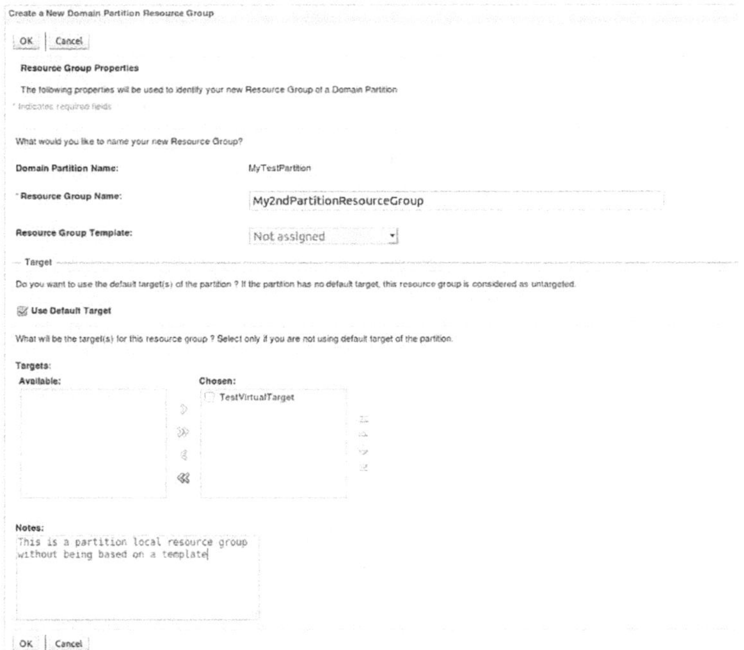

Figure 14-14: Creating additional resource groups for a partition

All resource groups of the partition will show up in the list of resource groups.

The following script shows how WLST can be used in order to add a partition scoped resource group.

```
cmo.createResourceGroup('My2ndPartitionResourceGroup')

cd('/Partitions/MyTestPartition/ResourceGroups/My2ndPartitionResourceGroup')
cmo.setUseDefaultTarget(true)
cmo.setTargets(None)
cmo.setNotes('This is a partition local resource group without being based on a template\r\n')

cd('/Partitions/MyTestPartition/ResourceGroups/My2ndPartitionResourceGroup')
```

Note that this script uses default targeting of the additional group. If ,for example the group has different virtual targets, then it might be needed to select a different targeting for the resource group, which is possible.

If a resource group specific targeting is needed, the following WLST script can be used:

```
cmo.createResourceGroup('My3rdPartitionResourceGroup')

cd('/Partitions/MyTestPartition/ResourceGroups/My3rdPartitionResourceGroup')
cmo.setResourceGroupTemplate(getMBean('/ResourceGroupTemplates/ShopResourceTemplate'))
cmo.setUseDefaultTarget(false)
set('Targets',jarray.array([ObjectName('com.bea:Name=TestVirtualTarget,Type=VirtualTarget')],
ObjectName))
cmo.setNotes('3rd example group')

cd('/Partitions/MyTestPartition/ResourceGroups/My3rdPartitionResourceGroup')
```

All resource groups of the partition can be visited by selecting the "resource group" tab (figure 14-15).

Settings for MyTestPartition

Configuration | Resource Groups | Deployments | Services | Resource Overrides | Coherence Caches | Work Manager | Concurrent Templates | Monitoring | Notes

Configuration | Control

This page summarizes the resource groups of a domain partition that have been configured in the current WebLogic Server domain.

Customize this table

Resource Groups

New | Delete

	Name	Resource Group Template	Effective Targets	State
	MartinResourceTemplate_group	MartinResourceTemplate	TestVirtualTarget	Unknown
	My2ndPartitionResourceGroup		TestVirtualTarget	Unknown

New | Delete

Figure 14-15: Partition resource group list

Deleting a Resource Group

Resource groups and even more resource group templates are a vital and fundamental concept. It is not easy to delete them once they are in use. This is intended to prevent accidentally deletion.

Deleting resource groups means that all the services defined in this group will no longer be available. If the resource group was already started – which means that WebLogic has created life instances – then the resource group you want to delete must be stopped first. This applies to globally and partition scoped resource groups (figure 14-16).

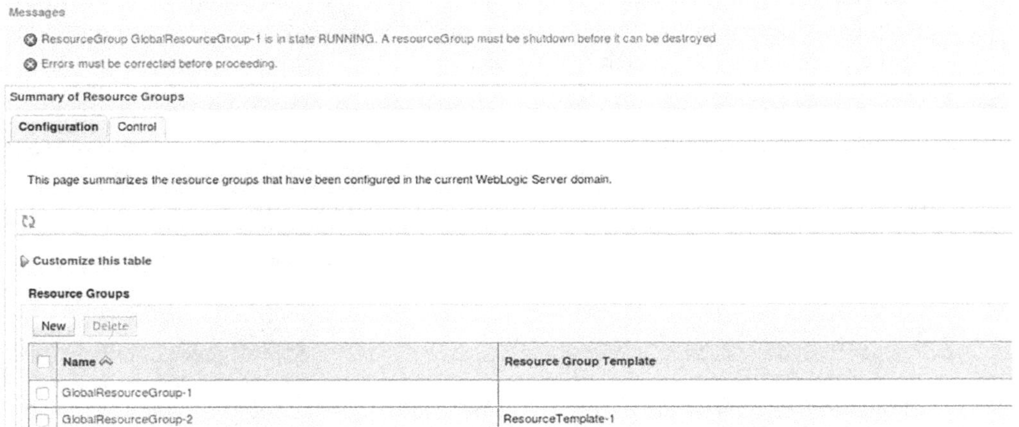
Messages
ResourceGroup GlobalResourceGroup-1 is in state RUNNING. A resourceGroup must be shutdown before it can be destroyed
Errors must be corrected before proceeding.
Summary of Resource Groups
Configuration
Control
This page summarizes the resource groups that have been configured in the current WebLogic Server domain.
Customize this table
Resource Groups
New
Delete
Name
Resource Group Template
GlobalResourceGroup-1
GlobalResourceGroup-2
ResourceTemplate-1

Figure 14-16: Started resource groups cannot be deleted

As you can see in the above screenshot, a resource group which has been started cannot be deleted. You need to shutdown the group first.

Using WLST it is easy to delete a resource group after it has been shutdown:

```
startEdit()
cd('/')
cmo.destroyResourceGroup(getMBean('/ResourceGroups/GlobalResourceGroup-1'))
```

Browsing Resource Group MBeans

Each resource group has MBeans – runtime and configuration MBeans. According to the usual structure of WLST the new MBeans have been organized in new subcategories within the configuration and the runtime MBean servers.

Browsing configuration MBeans for Resource Group TEMPLATES

Resource group templates have an own subtree underneath the main domain configuration MBean.

```
...
dr--   ResourceGroupTemplates
dr--   ResourceGroups
dr--   ResourceManagement
...

wls:/martin_1221/domainConfig/> ls ('ResourceGroupTemplates')
dr--   MartinResourceTemplate
dr--   ShopResourceTemplate

wls:/martin_1221/domainConfig/> ls ('ResourceGroups')
dr--   MyConcreteGlobalResourceGroup
dr--   MyConcreteGlobalResourceGroup2

wls:/martin_1221/domainConfig/> ls ('ResourceGroupTemplates/ShopResourceTemplate')
dr--   AppDeployments
dr--   CoherenceClusterSystemResources
dr--   FileStores
dr--   ForeignJNDIProviders
dr--   JDBCStores
dr--   JDBCSystemResources
dr--   JMSBridgeDestinations
dr--   JMSServers
dr--   JMSSystemResources
dr--   Libraries
dr--   MailSessions
dr--   ManagedExecutorServices
dr--   ManagedScheduledExecutorServices
dr--   ManagedThreadFactories
dr--   MessagingBridges
dr--   OsgiFrameworks
dr--   SAFAgents
dr--   WLDFSystemResources

-r--   DynamicallyCreated                            false
-r--   Id                                            0
-r--   Name                                          ShopResourceTemplate
-r--   Notes                                         My ShopResourceTemplate
-r--   Tags                                          null
-r--   Type                                          ResourceGroupTemplate
-r--   UploadDirectoryName                           ./servers/AdminServer/upload/resource-group-
templates/ShopResourceTemplate/

-r-x   freezeCurrentValue                            Void : String(attributeName)
-r-x   getInheritedProperties                        String[] : String[](propertyNames)
-r-x   isInherited                                   Boolean : String(propertyName)
-r-x   isSet                                         Boolean : String(propertyName)
-r-x   unSet                                         Void : String(propertyName)

wls:/martin_1221/domainConfig/> ls
('ResourceGroupTemplates/ShopResourceTemplate/JDBCSystemResources')
dr--   MyShopJDBC Data Source

wls:/martin_1221/domainConfig/> ls
('ResourceGroupTemplates/ShopResourceTemplate/JDBCSystemResources/MyShopJDBC Data Source')
```

```
dr--   JDBCResource
dr--   Resource
dr--   SubDeployments
dr--   Targets

-r--   CompatibilityName                             null
-r--   DeploymentOrder                               100
-r--   DeploymentPrincipalName                       null
-r--   DescriptorFileName                            resource-group-
templates/ShopResourceTemplate/jdbc/MyShopJDBC_Data_Source-5838-jdbc.xml
-r--   DynamicallyCreated                            false
-r--   Id                                            0
-r--   ModuleType                                    null
-r--   Name                                          MyShopJDBC Data Source
-r--   Notes                                         null
-r--   SourcePath                                    ./config/resource-group-
templates/ShopResourceTemplate/jdbc/MyShopJDBC_Data_Source-5838-jdbc.xml
-r--   Tags                                          null
-r--   Type                                          JDBCSystemResource

-r-x   freezeCurrentValue                            Void : String(attributeName)
-r-x   getInheritedProperties                        String[] : String[](propertyNames)
-r-x   isInherited                                   Boolean : String(propertyName)
-r-x   isSet                                         Boolean : String(propertyName)
-r-x   unSet                                         Void : String(propertyName)

wls:/martin_1221/domainConfig/> ls ('ResourceGroupTemplates/ShopResourceTemplate/JMSServers')
dr--   MyShopJMSServer

wls:/martin_1221/domainConfig/> ls
('ResourceGroupTemplates/ShopResourceTemplate/JMSServers/MyShopJMSServer')
dr--   JMSMessageLogFile
dr--   JMSSessionPools
dr--   PersistentStore
dr--   SessionPools
dr--   Targets

-r--   AllowsPersistentDowngrade                     false
-r--   BlockingSendPolicy                            FIFO
-r--   BytesMaximum                                  -1
-r--   BytesPagingEnabled                            false
-r--   BytesThresholdHigh                            -1
-r--   BytesThresholdLow                             -1
-r--   ConsumptionPausedAtStartup                    default
-r--   DeploymentOrder                               1000
-r--   DynamicallyCreated                            false
-r--   ExpirationScanInterval                        30
-r--   HostingTemporaryDestinations                  true
-r--   Id                                            0
-r--   InsertionPausedAtStartup                      default
-r--   MaximumMessageSize                            2147483647
-r--   MessageBufferSize                             -1
-r--   MessageCompressionOptions                     GZIP_DEFAULT_COMPRESSION
-r--   MessagesMaximum                               -1
-r--   MessagesPagingEnabled                         false
-r--   MessagesThresholdHigh                         -1
-r--   MessagesThresholdLow                          -1
-r--   Name                                          MyShopJMSServer
-r--   Notes                                         null
-r--   PagingBlockSize                               -1
-r--   PagingDirectory                               null
-r--   PagingFileLockingEnabled                      true
-r--   PagingIoBufferSize                            -1
-r--   PagingMaxFileSize                             1342177280
-r--   PagingMaxWindowBufferSize                     -1
-r--   PagingMessageCompressionEnabled               false
-r--   PagingMinWindowBufferSize                     -1
-r--   ProductionPausedAtStartup                     default
-r--   StoreEnabled                                  true
-r--   StoreMessageCompressionEnabled                false
-r--   Tags                                          null
-r--   TemporaryTemplateName                         null
-r--   TemporaryTemplateResource                     null
```

Browsing configuration MBeans for Resource Groups

Resource groups represent real resource groups and therefore the main difference is that the groups have targets.

```
dr--   MyConcreteGlobalResourceGroup
dr--   MyConcreteGlobalResourceGroup2

wls:/martin_1221/domainConfig/> ls('ResourceGroups/MyConcreteGlobalResourceGroup')
dr--   AppDeployments
dr--   CoherenceClusterSystemResources
dr--   FileStores
dr--   ForeignJNDIProviders
dr--   JDBCStores
dr--   JDBCSystemResources
dr--   JMSBridgeDestinations
dr--   JMSServers
dr--   JMSSystemResources
dr--   Libraries
dr--   MailSessions
dr--   ManagedExecutorServices
dr--   ManagedScheduledExecutorServices
dr--   ManagedThreadFactories
dr--   MessagingBridges
dr--   OsgiFrameworks
dr--   ResourceGroupTemplate
dr--   SAFAgents
dr--   Targets
dr--   WLDFSystemResources

-r--   DynamicallyCreated                           false
-r--   Id                                           0
-r--   Name                                         MyConcreteGlobalResourceGroup
-r--   Notes                                        Test group WITHOUT being based on a template
-r--   ResourceGroupTemplate                        null
-r--   Tags                                         null
-r--   Type                                         ResourceGroup
-r--   UploadDirectoryName                          ./servers/AdminServer/upload/
-r--   UseDefaultTarget                             true

-r-x   findEffectiveTargets                         WebLogicMBean[] :
-r-x   freezeCurrentValue                           Void : String(attributeName)
-r-x   getInheritedProperties                       String[] : String[](propertyNames)
-r-x   isInherited                                  Boolean : String(propertyName)
-r-x   isSet                                        Boolean : String(propertyName)
-r-x   unSet                                        Void : String(propertyName)

wls:/martin_1221/domainConfig/> ls('ResourceGroups/MyConcreteGlobalResourceGroup/Targets')
dr--   Test2_VirtualTarget

wls:/martin_1221/domainConfig/>
ls('ResourceGroups/MyConcreteGlobalResourceGroup/Targets/Test2_VirtualTarget')
dr--   Targets
dr--   WebServer

-r--   DeploymentOrder                              1000
-r--   DynamicallyCreated                           false
-r--   ExplicitPort                                 0
-r--   HostNames                                    java.lang.String[second.test.host.com]
-r--   Id                                           0
-r--   Name                                         Test2_VirtualTarget
-r--   Notes                                        null
-r--   PartitionChannel                             PartitionChannel
-r--   PortOffset                                   0
-r--   Tags                                         null
-r--   Type                                         VirtualTarget
-r--   UriPrefix                                    /

-r-x   freezeCurrentValue                           Void : String(attributeName)
-r-x   getInheritedProperties                       String[] : String[](propertyNames)
-r-x   isInherited                                  Boolean : String(propertyName)
-r-x   isSet                                        Boolean : String(propertyName)
```

Browsing runtime MBeans

Remember that only resource groups and not resource group templates have runtime MBeans as resource group templates are only blueprints for resource group instances.

```
dr--   AppRuntimeStateRuntime
dr--   BatchJobRepositoryRuntime
dr--   CoherenceServerLifeCycleRuntimes
dr--   ConsoleRuntime
dr--   CurrentDomainPartitionRuntime
dr--   DeployerRuntime
dr--   DeploymentManager
dr--   DomainPartitionRuntimes
dr--   DomainServices
dr--   EditSessionConfigurationManager
dr--   ElasticServiceManagerRuntime
dr--   LogRuntime
dr--   MessageDrivenControlEJBRuntime
dr--   MigratableServiceCoordinatorRuntime
dr--   MigrationDataRuntimes
dr--   NodeManagerRuntimes
dr--   PolicySubjectManagerRuntime
dr--   ResourceGroupLifeCycleRuntimes
dr--   RolloutService
dr--   SNMPAgentRuntime
dr--   ServerLifeCycleRuntimes
dr--   ServerRuntimes
dr--   ServerServices
dr--   ServiceMigrationDataRuntimes
dr--   SystemComponentLifeCycleRuntimes

-r--   ActivationTime                               Fri Dec 18 22:29:26 CET 2015
-r--   CurrentDomainPartitionRuntime                null
-r--   MigrationDataRuntimes                        null
-r--   Name                                         martin_1221
-rw-   Parent                                       null
-r--   ServiceMigrationDataRuntimes                 null
-r--   Type                                         DomainRuntime

-r-x   forceShutdownPartitionWait                   WebLogicMBean :
WebLogicMBean(partitionMBean),Integer(timeout)
-r-x   restartSystemResource                        Void : WebLogicMBean(resource)
-r-x   startPartitionWait                           WebLogicMBean :
WebLogicMBean(partitionMBean),String(initialState),Integer(timeOut)

wls:/martin_1221/domainRuntime/> ls ('ServerRuntimes')
dr--   AdminServer
```

On the WebLogic server level a number of new subcategories and operations designed to work with resource groups and partitions have been added to the main runtime MBeans

```
...
dr--   PartitionRuntimes
dr--   PathServiceRuntime
dr--   PathServiceRuntimes
...
...

-r-x   forceShutdownResourceGroup                   Void : String(resourceGroupName)
-r-x   forceSuspendResourceGroup                    Void : String(resourceGroupName)
```

```
-r-x   resumeResourceGroup                          Void : String(resourceGroupName)
-r-x   shutdownResourceGroup                        Void : String(resourceGroupName)
-r-x   shutdownResourceGroup                        Void :
String(resourceGroupName),Integer(timeout),Boolean(ignoreSessions)
-r-x   shutdownResourceGroup                        Void :
String(resourceGroupName),Integer(timeout),Boolean(ignoreSessions),Boolean(waitForAllSessions)
-r-x   startPartition                               Void : String(partitionName)
-r-x   startPartitionInAdmin                        Void : String(partitionName)
-r-x   startResourceGroup                           Void : String(resourceGroupName)
-r-x   startResourceGroupInAdmin                    Void : String(resourceGroupName)
-r-x   suspendResourceGroup                         Void : String(resourceGroupName)
-r-x   suspendResourceGroup                         Void :
String(resourceGroupName),Integer(timeout),Boolean(ignoreSessions)
...

wls:/martin_1221/domainRuntime/> ls ('ResourceGroupLifeCycleRuntimes')
dr--   MyConcreteGlobalResourceGroup
dr--   MyConcreteGlobalResourceGroup2

wls:/martin_1221/domainRuntime/> ls ('ResourceGroupLifeCycleRuntimes/MyConcreteGlobalResourceGroup')
dr--   Tasks

-r--   Name                                         MyConcreteGlobalResourceGroup
-r--   State                                        SHUTDOWN
-r--   Type                                         ResourceGroupLifeCycleRuntime

-r-x   forceShutdown                                WebLogicMBean :
-r-x   forceShutdown                                WebLogicMBean : WebLogicMBean[](targets)
-r-x   forceSuspend                                 WebLogicMBean :
-r-x   forceSuspend                                 WebLogicMBean : WebLogicMBean[](targets)
-r-x   getState                                     String : WebLogicMBean(serverMBean)
-r-x   purgeTasks                                   Void :
-r-x   resume                                       WebLogicMBean :
-r-x   resume                                       WebLogicMBean : WebLogicMBean[](targets)
-r-x   shutdown                                     WebLogicMBean :
-r-x   shutdown                                     WebLogicMBean :
Integer(timeout),Boolean(ignoreSessions)
-r-x   shutdown                                     WebLogicMBean :
Integer(timeout),Boolean(ignoreSessions),Boolean(waitForAllSessions)
-r-x   shutdown                                     WebLogicMBean :
Integer(timeout),Boolean(ignoreSessions),Boolean(waitForAllSessions),WebLogicMBean[](targets)
-r-x   shutdown                                     WebLogicMBean :
Integer(timeout),Boolean(ignoreSessions),WebLogicMBean[](targets)
-r-x   shutdown                                     WebLogicMBean : WebLogicMBean[](targets)
-r-x   start                                        WebLogicMBean :
-r-x   start                                        WebLogicMBean : WebLogicMBean[](targets)
-r-x   startInAdmin                                 WebLogicMBean :
```

As you can see from the above examples, all settings and also all runtime lifecycle operations are exposed through appropriate MBeans.

Putting it all together

The section above discussed resource templates, resource groups and partition scoped groups are all configured in a different way in WebLogic. The following part of the config.xml shows the configuration structure of the above examples.

```
    <name>MyTestPartition</name>
    <resource-group>
      <name>MartinResourceTemplate_group</name>
      <resource-group-template>MartinResourceTemplate</resource-group-template>
    </resource-group>
    <resource-group>
      <name>My2ndPartitionResourceGroup</name>
      <notes>This is a partition local resource group without being based on a template</notes>
      <target></target>
```

```
      <use-default-target>true</use-default-target>
    </resource-group>
    <resource-group>
      <name>My3rdPartitionResourceGroup</name>
      <notes>3rd example group</notes>
      <resource-group-template>ShopResourceTemplate</resource-group-template>
      <target>TestVirtualTarget</target>
      <use-default-target>false</use-default-target>
    </resource-group>
    <default-target>TestVirtualTarget</default-target>
    <available-target>TestVirtualTarget</available-target>
    <realm>myrealm</realm>
    <partition-id>0b63de1a-8ad0-490b-aa9a-000f12127534</partition-id>
    <system-file-system>
      <root>/opt/wls1221/user_domains/martin_1221/partitions/MyTestPartition/system</root>
      <create-on-demand>true</create-on-demand>
      <preserved>true</preserved>
    </system-file-system>
  </partition>


  <resource-group>
    <name>MyConcreteGlobalResourceGroup</name>
    <notes>Test group WITHOUT being based on a template</notes>
    <target>Test2_VirtualTarget</target>
  </resource-group>

  <resource-group>
    <name>MyConcreteGlobalResourceGroup2</name>
    <notes>Test group WHICH IS based on a template</notes>
    <resource-group-template>MartinResourceTemplate</resource-group-template>
    <target>Test3_VirtualTarget</target>
  </resource-group>


  <resource-group-template>
    <name>ShopResourceTemplate</name>
    <notes>My ShopResourceTemplate</notes>
    <jms-server>
      <name>MyShopJMSServer</name>
      <persistent-store>MyShopFileStore</persistent-store>
    </jms-server>
    <file-store>
      <name>MyShopFileStore</name>
      <directory>/filestore</directory>
    </file-store>
    <jdbc-system-resource>
      <name>MyShopJDBC Data Source</name>
      <descriptor-file-name>resource-group-
templates/ShopResourceTemplate/jdbc/MyShopJDBC_Data_Source-5838-jdbc.xml</descriptor-file-name>
    </jdbc-system-resource>
  </resource-group-template>

  <resource-group-template>
    <name>MartinResourceTemplate</name>
    <notes>This is an example resource group template.</notes>
```

Configurations items which are not directly stored in the config.xml are stored in different (new) locations on the WebLogic domain filesystem structure.

There are a number of new subdirectories underneath the well-known "config" directory of the WebLogic domain.

Every resource group template and every partition get their own subdirectory underneath "config" (figure 14-17).

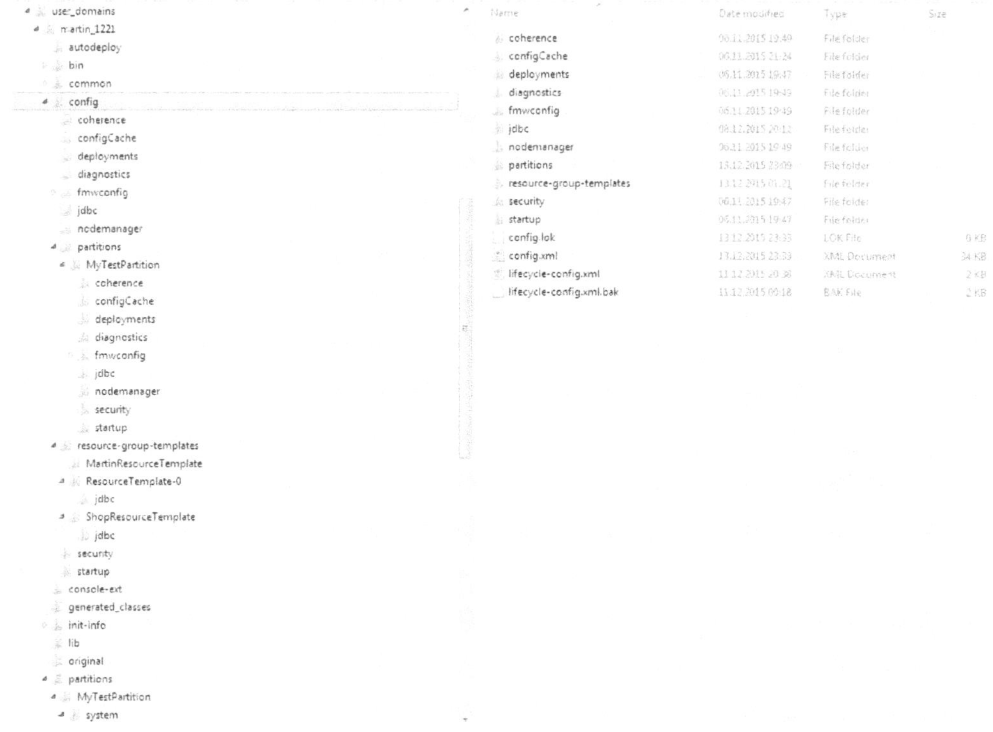

Figure 14-17: Resource group partition subdirectories

Resource Group Templates and JMX

The central domain MBean has a list of children of the type "ResourceGroupTemplate". As resource group templates can only be created on the domain level, this is the only available list (figure 14-18).

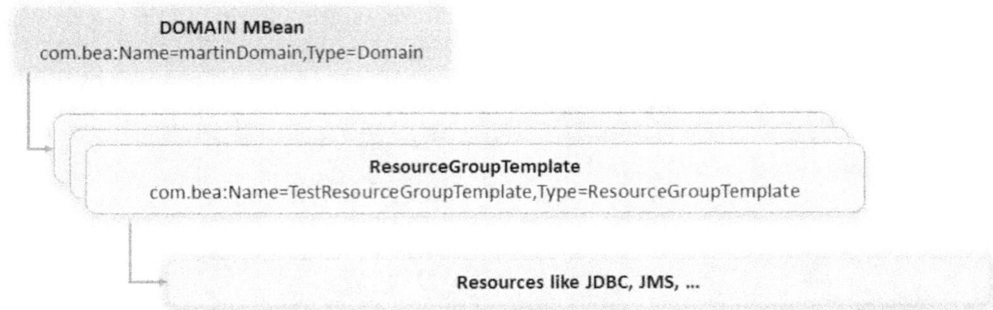

Figure 14-18: MBean hierarchy for resource group templates

The main domain MBean supports lookup, create and destroy operations for resource group templates.

```
Attribute: ResourceGroupTemplates   of Type : [Ljavax.management.ObjectName;
...
Operation: javax.management.ObjectName  createResourceGroupTemplate(name:java.lang.String  )
Operation: javax.management.ObjectName  lookupResourceGroupTemplate(name:java.lang.String  )
```

Each MBean of the type ResourceGroupTemplate has the following structure:

```
Attribute: AppDeployments   of Type : [Ljavax.management.ObjectName;
Attribute: CoherenceClusterSystemResources   of Type : [Ljavax.management.ObjectName;
Attribute: DynamicallyCreated   of Type : java.lang.Boolean
Attribute: FileStores   of Type : [Ljavax.management.ObjectName;
Attribute: ForeignJNDIProviders   of Type : [Ljavax.management.ObjectName;
Attribute: Id   of Type : java.lang.Long
Attribute: JDBCStores   of Type : [Ljavax.management.ObjectName;
Attribute: JDBCSystemResources   of Type : [Ljavax.management.ObjectName;
Attribute: JMSBridgeDestinations   of Type : [Ljavax.management.ObjectName;
Attribute: JMSServers   of Type : [Ljavax.management.ObjectName;
Attribute: JMSSystemResources   of Type : [Ljavax.management.ObjectName;
Attribute: Libraries   of Type : [Ljavax.management.ObjectName;
Attribute: MailSessions   of Type : [Ljavax.management.ObjectName;
Attribute: ManagedExecutorServices   of Type : [Ljavax.management.ObjectName;
Attribute: ManagedScheduledExecutorServices   of Type : [Ljavax.management.ObjectName;
Attribute: ManagedThreadFactories   of Type : [Ljavax.management.ObjectName;
Attribute: MessagingBridges   of Type : [Ljavax.management.ObjectName;
Attribute: Name   of Type : java.lang.String
Attribute: Notes   of Type : java.lang.String
Attribute: OsgiFrameworks   of Type : [Ljavax.management.ObjectName;
Attribute: Parent   of Type : javax.management.ObjectName
Attribute: PathServices   of Type : [Ljavax.management.ObjectName;
Attribute: SAFAgents   of Type : [Ljavax.management.ObjectName;
Attribute: Tags   of Type : [Ljava.lang.String;
Attribute: Type   of Type : java.lang.String
Attribute: UploadDirectoryName   of Type : java.lang.String
Attribute: WLDFSystemResources   of Type : [Ljavax.management.ObjectName;
...
```

Based on this MBean a number of basic functionalities can be implemented easily using JMX.

List all available resource group templates. This method will return a list of ObjectNames:

```
{
  ArrayList<ObjectName> result = new ArrayList<ObjectName>();

  try {
      // e.g.: com.bea:Name=TestDomain,Type=Domain
      ObjectName myDomainMBean = myJMXWrapper.getDomainConfigRoot();

      ObjectName[] resGroups = (ObjectName[]) myJMXWrapper.getAttribute(
                  myDomainMBean, "ResourceGroupTemplates");

      for (int i=0;i<resGroups.length;i++)
       result.add(resGroups[i]);

      return result;
  }
  catch(Exception ex) {
   throw new WLSAutomationException(ex);
  }
```

The next method is very similar but will return a list of resource group template names

```
{
  ArrayList<String> result = new ArrayList<String>();

  try {
      // e.g.: com.bea:Name=TestDomain,Type=Domain
      ObjectName myDomainMBean = myJMXWrapper.getDomainConfigRoot();

      ObjectName[] resGroups = (ObjectName[]) myJMXWrapper.getAttribute(
                  myDomainMBean, "ResourceGroupTemplates");

      for (int i=0;i<resGroups.length;i++)
       result.add(resGroups[i].getKeyProperty("Name"));

      return result;
  }
  catch(Exception ex) {
   throw new WLSAutomationException(ex);
  }
```

For subsequent examples if will often be necessary to lookup the object reference. The following method takes a name and – if exist – returns the object name reference for that resource group template

```
{
  try {
      // e.g.: com.bea:Name=TestDomain,Type=Domain
      ObjectName myDomainMBean = myJMXWrapper.getDomainConfigRoot();

      // test if resource manager already exist
      return(ObjectName)myJMXWrapper.invoke(myDomainMBean, "lookupResourceGroupTemplate",
              new Object[]{new String(resGTName)}, new String[]{String.class.getName()});
  }
  catch(Exception ex) {
     throw new WLSAutomationException(ex);
  }
```

The next method finally creates a new resource group template. For code safety reasons the method does a check first if this resource group template already exist

```
{
  try {
   ObjectName root = myJMXWrapper.getDomainConfigRoot();

      // test if resource manager already exist
      ObjectName myResourceGroupMBean = (ObjectName)myJMXWrapper.invoke(root,
                 "lookupResourceGroupTemplate",
                 new Object[]{new String(resGTName)}, new String[]{String.class.getName()});

       if (myResourceGroupMBean==null) {
            myResourceGroupMBean = (ObjectName)myJMXWrapper.invoke(root,
                 "createResourceGroupTemplate",
                 new Object[]{new String(resGTName)}, new String[]{String.class.getName()});
       }

       return myResourceGroupMBean;

  }
  catch(Exception ex) {
      throw new WLSAutomationException(ex);
  }
```

Also, a cleanup is possible by removing resource group templates. Note that the following code simplifies the process. It is recommended to check first if the resource group template still does contain resources.

```
{
  try {
      ObjectName root = myJMXWrapper.getDomainConfigRoot();

      // test if resource manager already exist
      ObjectName myResourceGroupTemplateMBean = (ObjectName)myJMXWrapper.invoke(root,
                                "lookupResourceGroupTemplate",
                                new Object[]{new String(resGTName)},
                                new String[]{String.class.getName()});
       if (myResourceGroupTemplateMBean!=null) {
              myJMXWrapper.invoke(root, "destroyResourceGroupTemplate",
                 new Object[]{myResourceGroupTemplateMBean},
                 new String[]{ObjectName.class.getName()});
       }
  }
  catch(Exception ex) {
     throw new WLSAutomationException(ex);
  }
```

Resource Groups and JMX

Resource groups more difficult to handle. Remember that resource groups can have different scopes. Actually, the MBeans are the same but based on the scope that they different parent MBeans. Resource groups can have the main domain MBean as its root or any of the partition MBeans (figure 14-19).

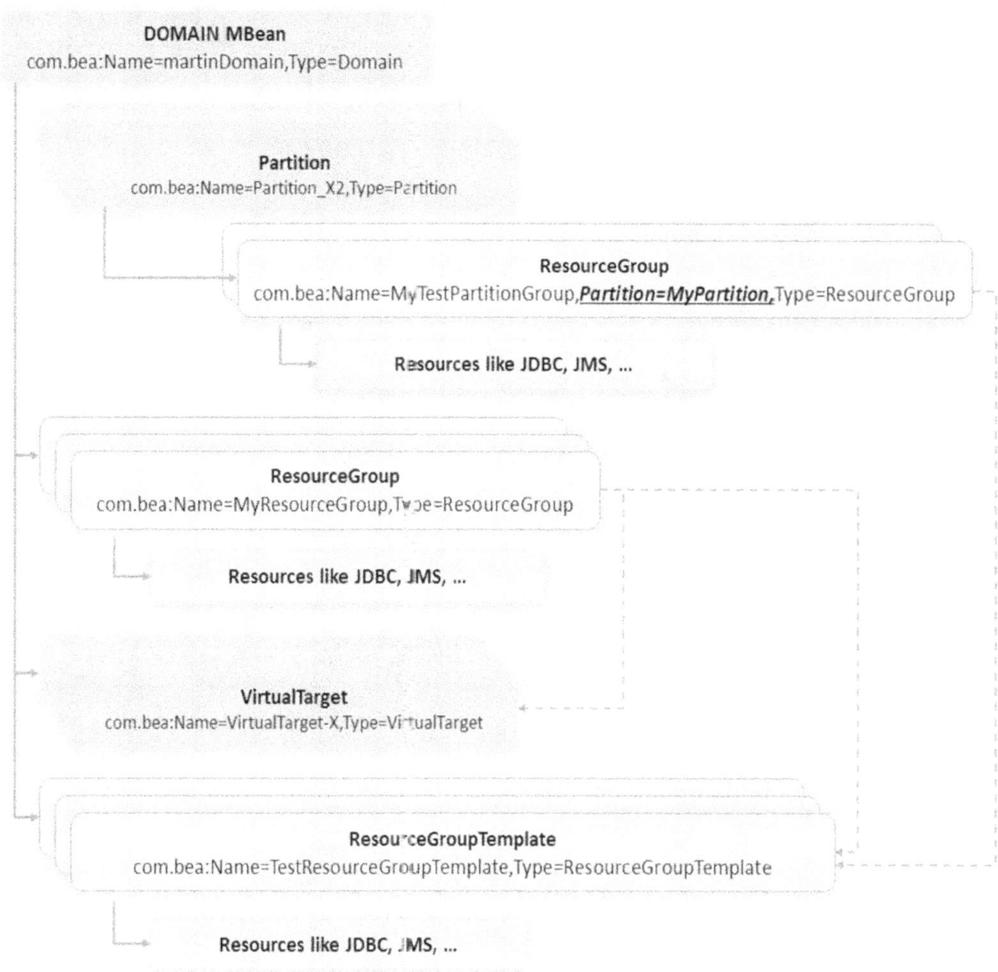

Figure 14-19: Resource Group MBeans

The main MBeans have the following attributes and operations:

Elements of the main domain MBean with regards to resource groups:

```
Attribute: ResourceGroups    of Type : [Ljavax.management.ObjectName;
...
Operation: javax.management.ObjectName  createResourceGroup(name:java.lang.String  )
Operation: javax.management.ObjectName  lookupResourceGroup(name:java.lang.String  )
```

The interesting that you will find exactly the same content in each partition MBean. From an implementation aspect this makes sense, as a partition is just another scope for a resource group.

```
Attribute: ResourceGroups    of Type : [Ljavax.management.ObjectName;
...
Operation: javax.management.ObjectName  createResourceGroup(name:java.lang.String  )
Operation: javax.management.ObjectName  lookupResourceGroup(name:java.lang.String  )
```

The resource group itself looks similar to the resource group template with the main difference that it may have targets and a reference to a resource group template. Both are optional as discussed in this chapter.

```
Attribute: AppDeployments    of Type : [Ljavax.management.ObjectName;
Attribute: CoherenceClusterSystemResources    of Type : [Ljavax.management.ObjectName;
Attribute: DynamicallyCreated    of Type : java.lang.Boolean
Attribute: FileStores    of Type : [Ljavax.management.ObjectName;
Attribute: ForeignJNDIProviders    of Type : [Ljavax.management.ObjectName;
Attribute: Id    of Type : java.lang.Long
Attribute: JDBCStores    of Type : [Ljavax.management.ObjectName;
Attribute: JDBCSystemResources    of Type : [Ljavax.management.ObjectName;
Attribute: JMSBridgeDestinations    of Type : [Ljavax.management.ObjectName;
Attribute: JMSServers    of Type : [Ljavax.management.ObjectName;
Attribute: JMSSystemResources    of Type : [Ljavax.management.ObjectName;
Attribute: Libraries    of Type : [Ljavax.management.ObjectName;
Attribute: MailSessions    of Type : [Ljavax.management.ObjectName;
Attribute: ManagedExecutorServices    of Type : [Ljavax.management.ObjectName;
Attribute: ManagedScheduledExecutorServices    of Type : [Ljavax.management.ObjectName;
Attribute: ManagedThreadFactories    of Type : [Ljavax.management.ObjectName;
Attribute: MessagingBridges    of Type : [Ljavax.management.ObjectName;
Attribute: Name    of Type : java.lang.String
Attribute: Notes    of Type : java.lang.String
Attribute: OsgiFrameworks    of Type : [Ljavax.management.ObjectName;
Attribute: Parent    of Type : javax.management.ObjectName
Attribute: PathServices    of Type : [Ljavax.management.ObjectName;
Attribute: ResourceGroupTemplate    of Type : javax.management.ObjectName
Attribute: SAFAgents    of Type : [Ljavax.management.ObjectName;
Attribute: Tags    of Type : [Ljava.lang.String;
Attribute: Targets    of Type : [Ljavax.management.ObjectName;
Attribute: Type    of Type : java.lang.String
Attribute: UploadDirectoryName    of Type : java.lang.String
Attribute: UseDefaultTarget    of Type : java.lang.Boolean
Attribute: WLDFSystemResources    of Type : [Ljavax.management.ObjectName;
...
```

Summary

All of the configuration options discussed in this chapter have different strengths and weaknesses so that it is up to the administrator and the application requirements to choose the possible option.

Resource groups and group blueprints – officially names resource group templates – are – beside the partition - the major new concepts in WebLogic 12.2.x. They allow administrators to group resources together, provide a common target for these resources and execute control actions on the complete group.

Groups can have global or partition scope, which implement to isolation requirements discussed in the previous book section.

Generic Targeting as new Target Model

CHAPTER

Overview

Virtual targets provide an abstraction layer that can be used to target partitions and resource groups too. On WebLogic level these virtual targets have a configuration based on hostname mapping, port mapping or URL prefix. As the same virtual target can be configured differently in different WLS domains, migrating partitions to other domains (like UAT -> PROD) is much easier and straightforward (figure 15-1).

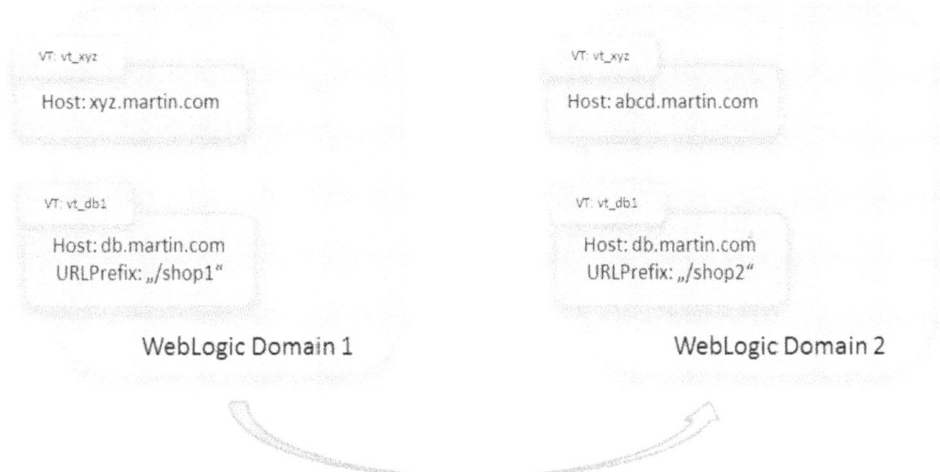

Figure 15-1: Concept behind virtual targets

The diagram above demonstrates the basic idea behind virtual targets. Virtual targets defined in different domains can have the same name. These names are being used to target partitions or resource groups. This means targeting is no longer done using WebLogic channel with an IP and port but on a higher – virtual – level based. Key here is that a virtual target with the same name exists in both WebLogic domains. If partitions are being migrated to another domain they just get targeted to the name they were used to, regardless of its configuration.

Virtual targets have two different functions. They provide an abstraction layer and hide where a partition or resource group is really targeted and they define how incoming traffic is routed. Routing especially means that only the traffic which a partition is allowed to get will arrive at this partition. Content of a virtual target includes host names or IP addresses, protocol settings, optional URL prefix and targeting. Virtual targets therefore provide an isolation layer between physical WebLogic resources and partitions or resource groups.

Create a Virtual Target

Creating a virtual target must be done BEFORE the partitions or resource groups are created or imported. Even though partitions and resource groups are target to virtual targets, virtual targets are NOT included in a partition (figure 15-2).

Figure 15-2: Creating a new virtual target

A virtual target can either be itself targeted to one WebLogic server instance or to a whole cluster. The available targets can be selected (if the WLS console is used) from a drop-down list as shown above.

In addition, all characteristics of this new virtual target like URL prefix or hostname have to be configured during the creation of the virtual target (figure 15-3).

Figure 15-3: Virtual target screen

The same virtual target can also be created using WLST.

```
startEdit()

cd('/')
cmo.createVirtualTarget('MyShopVirtualTarget')

cd('/VirtualTargets/MyShopVirtualTarget')
set('HostNames',jarray.array([String('testshop.nowhere.com')], String))
set('Targets',jarray.array([ObjectName('com.bea:Name=Cluster1,Type=Cluster')], ObjectName))
```

Virtual targets – like many other configuration artifacts which are based on MBeans – can also be created using JMX or even REST management calls.

In order to isolate http web traffic, WebLogic has added an own http webserver for each virtual target.

Features and Restrictions with for Virtual Targets

Virtual targets are the base targeting model for partition scoped and global scoped resource groups. As such, there are a number of architecture and deployment guidelines that must be taken into account when designing virtual targets.

Take the following just as general guideline, but be aware that every domain setup has its own requirements and restrictions.

- In order to instantiate a resource group - which means to create real runtime resource instances - a resource group needs at least one virtual target.
- A resource group can also have more than one virtual target.
- Virtual targets can either be used on domain (global) level or on partition level.
- Consider the following target restriction: A resource group, defined as global resource group can be targeted to any virtual target that is not assigned to a partition.
- Partitions get one or more virtual targets assigned to it. For resource groups which are scoped to partition level you can select only virtual targets which are assigned to this partition
- Any virtual target can be either used globally (domain level) or by one - and only one - partition.
- Virtual targets cannot be shared. It is not possible that more than one partition can be targeted to the same virtual target. Take this into account when partitions are designed. In case you want to migrate partitions to other domains, it is therefore advisable to use appropriate names. As a suggestion, the author recommends to uses names like VT_<partiton_name> where VT stands for "virtual target".
- It is also not possible to use the same virtual target for global and partition scoped resource groups.
- But it is possible to share a resource group within the same scope. This means, multiple resource groups within the same partition or on domain level are allowed to be targeted to the same virtual target
- There is also a restriction to where virtual targets can be targeted to. It is either possible to assign a virtual target to a cluster or to a single managed server. Be aware that it is not possible to assign a virtual target to a number of managed-servers
- Virtual targets with the same configuration - e.g. URL prefix - must have different physical targets.

Browsing Virtual Targets

WLST can be used to browse virtual targets. All virtual targets are organized in the structure that follows the well-known WLST model of hierarchies. This model allows administrators to browse virtual target configuration MBeans using WLST.

List all virtual targets

```
dr--   MyShopVirtualTarget
dr--   Test1_VirtualTarget
dr--   Test2_VirtualTarget
dr--   Test3_VirtualTarget
dr--   TestVirtualTarget
```

Inspect content of a virtual target

```
wls:/martin_1221/domainConfig/VirtualTargets/MyShopVirtualTarget> ls()
dr--   Targets
dr--   WebServer

-r--   DeploymentOrder                              1000
-r--   DynamicallyCreated                           false
-r--   ExplicitPort                                 0
-r--   HostNames                                    java.lang.String[testshop.nowhere.com]
-r--   Id                                           0
-r--   Name                                         MyShopVirtualTarget
-r--   Notes                                        null
-r--   PartitionChannel                             PartitionChannel
-r--   PortOffset                                   0
-r--   Tags                                         null
-r--   Type                                         VirtualTarget
-r--   UriPrefix                                    /

-r-x   freezeCurrentValue                           Void : String(attributeName)
-r-x   getInheritedProperties                       String[] : String[](propertyNames)
-r-x   isInherited                                  Boolean : String(propertyName)
-r-x   isSet                                        Boolean : String(propertyName)
-r-x   unSet                                        Void : String(propertyName)

wls:/martin_1221/domainConfig/VirtualTargets/MyShopVirtualTarget> ls('Targets')
dr--   Cluster1


wls:/martin_1221/domainConfig/> ls ('VirtualTargets/Test1_VirtualTarget')
dr--   Targets
dr--   WebServer

-r--   DeploymentOrder                              1000
-r--   DynamicallyCreated                           false
-r--   ExplicitPort                                 0
-r--   HostNames                                    java.lang.String[mytest1.martin.com]
-r--   Id                                           0
-r--   Name                                         Test1_VirtualTarget
-r--   Notes                                        null
-r--   PartitionChannel                             PartitionChannel
-r--   PortOffset                                   0
-r--   Tags                                         null
-r--   Type                                         VirtualTarget
-r--   UriPrefix                                    /

-r-x   freezeCurrentValue                           Void : String(attributeName)
-r-x   getInheritedProperties                       String[] : String[](propertyNames)
-r-x   isInherited                                  Boolean : String(propertyName)
-r-x   isSet                                        Boolean : String(propertyName)
```

```
-r-x   unSet                                       Void : String(propertyName)

wls:/martin_1221/domainConfig/> ls ('VirtualTargets/Test1_VirtualTarget/Targets')
dr--   Cluster1
```

Inspect the webserver configuration of a virtual target

```
dr--   Test1_VirtualTarget

wls:/martin_1221/domainConfig/> ls
('VirtualTargets/Test1_VirtualTarget/WebServer/Test1_VirtualTarget')
dr--   Targets
dr--   WebServerLog

-r--   AcceptContextPathInGetRealPath              false
-r--   AuthCookieEnabled                           true
-r--   Charsets                                    null
-r--   ChunkedTransferDisabled                     false
-r--   ClientIpHeader                              null
-r--   DefaultWebAppContextRoot                    null
-r--   DeploymentOrder                             1000
-r--   DynamicallyCreated                          false
-r--   FrontendHTTPPort                            0
-r--   FrontendHTTPSPort                           0
-r--   FrontendHost                                null
-r--   HttpsKeepAliveSecs                          60
-r--   Id                                          0
-r--   KeepAliveEnabled                            true
-r--   KeepAliveSecs                               30
-r--   MaxPostSize                                 -1
-r--   MaxPostTimeSecs                             -1
-r--   MaxRequestParameterCount                    10000
-r--   Name                                        Test1_VirtualTarget
-r--   Notes                                       null
-r--   OverloadResponseCode                        503
-r--   PostTimeoutSecs                             30
-r--   SendServerHeaderEnabled                     false
-r--   SingleSignonDisabled                        false
-r--   Tags                                        null
-r--   Type                                        WebServer
-r--   URLResource                                 null
-r--   UseHeaderEncoding                           false
-r--   UseHighestCompatibleHTTPVersion             true
-r--   WAPEnabled                                  false
```

Virtual Targets and Partition Channels

Virtual targets are targeted by themselves either to a cluster or to a managed-server. WebLogic also supports the concept of communication channels. Channels configure additional network legs with different hostname, port or protocols. Partitions by nature will be targeted to virtual targets and virtual targets to the WebLogic default channels.

Starting with version 12.2.1 WebLogic also supports a new concept which allows a partition not only to be based on a virtual target, but also for that virtual target to use a specific WebLogic channel. When the partition gets started, WebLogic creates, under the cover a new partition network channel. This new channel can reference the original channel (same port) or an additional listener can be created if the administrator defines a port offset or an explicit port. Explicit ports are useful if the application must listen on a well-defined port. Port offsets can help that the new port will always be – regardless in which domain the partition get imported – in an assigned range (figure 15-4).

Create a new virtual target based on an existing channel.

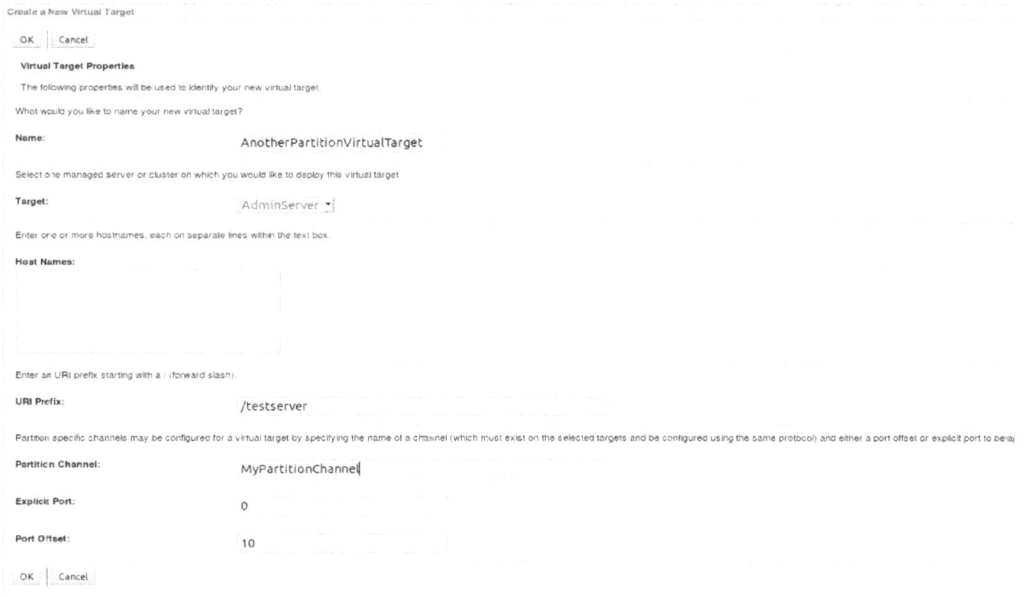

Figure 15-4: Create a new virtual target

In the above example, we have created a new virtual target that is based on an existing WebLogic channel. For partition channels we want to have an offset of 10 (means channel port + 10). Please note that in case multiple virtual targets shall be based on the same network channel, it is important to have either the same port as the channel, or different port / different offsets or target them to different WebLogic servers.

Example using WLST:

```
cmo.createNetworkAccessPoint('MyPartitionChannel')

cd('/Servers/AdminServer/NetworkAccessPoints/MyPartitionChannel')
cmo.setProtocol('t3')
cmo.setListenPort(12030)
cmo.setEnabled(true)
cmo.setHttpEnabledForThisProtocol(true)
cmo.setTunnelingEnabled(false)
cmo.setOutboundEnabled(false)
cmo.setTwoWaySSLEnabled(false)
cmo.setClientCertificateEnforced(false)

cd('/')
cmo.createVirtualTarget('AnotherPartitionVirtualTarget')

cd('/VirtualTargets/AnotherPartitionVirtualTarget')
cmo.setUriPrefix('/testserver')
cmo.setPartitionChannel('MyPartitionChannel')
cmo.setPortOffset(10)
set('Targets',jarray.array([ObjectName('com.bea:Name=AdminServer,Type=Server')], ObjectName))

cd('/')
cmo.createPartition('TestServerPartition')

cd('/Partitions/TestServerPartition/SystemFileSystem/TestServerPartition')
cmo.setRoot('/opt/development/wls/wls1221/user_domains/martin_1221/partitions/TestServerPartition/sys
tem')
cmo.setCreateOnDemand(true)
cmo.setPreserved(true)

cd('/Partitions/TestServerPartition')
cmo.setRealm(getMBean('/SecurityConfiguration/martin_1221/Realms/myrealm'))
cmo.createResourceGroup('ShopResourceTemplate_group')

cd('/Partitions/TestServerPartition/ResourceGroups/ShopResourceTemplate_group')
cmo.setResourceGroupTemplate(getMBean('/ResourceGroupTemplates/ShopResourceTemplate'))

cd('/Partitions/TestServerPartition')
set('AvailableTargets',jarray.array([ObjectName('com.bea:Name=AnotherPartitionVirtualTarget,Type=Virt
ualTarget')], ObjectName))
set('DefaultTargets',jarray.array([ObjectName('com.bea:Name=AnotherPartitionVirtualTarget,Type=Virtua
```

The example above creates a network channel, then it creates a virtual target and finally a partition which uses that virtual target.

Please note that the network channel has port 12030 and the virtual target an offset of 10. After the partition has been started, the following can be seen on the server:

```
Active Internet connections (servers and established)
Proto Recv-Q Send-Q Local Address           Foreign Address         State
tcp6       0      0 127.0.0.1:12030         :::*                    LISTEN
tcp6       0      0 127.0.0.1:12001         :::*                    LISTEN
tcp6       0      0 127.0.0.1:12002         :::*                    LISTEN
```

You can see different listeners for the network channel and the partition network channel (partition: 12030+10 (offset) = 12040)

The configuration – including the channel and the port offset - can be seen in the configuration MBean tree:

```
wls:/martin_1221/domainConfig/Partitions/TestServerPartition/DefaultTargets> ls()
dr--   AnotherPartitionVirtualTarget

wls:/martin_1221/domainConfig/Partitions/TestServerPartition/DefaultTargets> cd
('AnotherPartitionVirtualTarget')
wls:/martin_1221/domainConfig/Partitions/TestServerPartition/DefaultTargets/AnotherPartitionVirtualTa
rget> ls()
dr--   Targets
dr--   WebServer

-r--   DeploymentOrder                              1000
-r--   DynamicallyCreated                           false
-r--   ExplicitPort                                 0
-r--   HostNames                                    null
-r--   Id                                           0
-r--   Name                                         AnotherPartitionVirtualTarget
-r--   Notes                                        null
-r--   PartitionChannel                             MyPartitionChannel
-r--   PortOffset                                   10
-r--   Tags                                         null
-r--   Type                                         VirtualTarget
-r--   UriPrefix                                    /testserver

-r-x   freezeCurrentValue                           Void : String(attributeName)
-r-x   getInheritedProperties                       String[] : String[](propertyNames)
-r-x   isInherited                                  Boolean : String(propertyName)
-r-x   isSet                                        Boolean : String(propertyName)
```

On the runtime MBean tree you can see the newly created partition channel and its configuration:

```
wls:/martin_1221/domainRuntime> cd ('ServerRuntimes/AdminServer/ServerChannelRuntimes')

wls:/martin_1221/domainRuntime> ls()
dr--   DefaultSecure[https]
dr--   DefaultSecure[iiops]
dr--   DefaultSecure[ldaps]
dr--   DefaultSecure[t3s]
dr--   Default[http]
dr--   Default[iiop]
dr--   Default[ldap]
dr--   Default[snmp]
dr--   Default[t3]
dr--   MyNewPartitionChannel
dr--   MyNewPartitionChannel[http]
dr--   TestServerPartition-AnotherPartitionVirtualTarget[http]
dr--   TestServerPartition-AnotherPartitionVirtualTarget[iiop]
dr--   TestServerPartition-AnotherPartitionVirtualTarget[t3]

wls:/martin_1221/domainRuntime/ServerRuntimes/AdminServer/ServerChannelRuntimes> ls
('MyNewPartitionChannel')

-r--   AcceptCount                                  0
-r--   AssociatedVirtualTargetName                  null
-r--   BytesReceivedCount                           0
-r--   BytesSentCount                               0
-r--   ChannelName                                  MyNewPartitionChannel
-r--   ConnectionsCount                             0
-r--   MessagesReceivedCount                        0
-r--   MessagesSentCount                            0
-r--   Name                                         MyNewPartitionChannel
-r--   PublicURL                                    t3://localhost:12030
-r--   ServerConnectionRuntimes                     null
-r--   Type                                         ServerChannelRuntime
```

```
wls:/martin_1221/domainRuntime/ServerRuntimes/AdminServer/ServerChannelRuntimes> ls
('TestServerPartition-AnotherPartitionVirtualTarget[t3]')

-r--   AcceptCount                                 0
-r--   AssociatedVirtualTargetName                 AnotherPartitionVirtualTarget
-r--   BytesReceivedCount                          0
-r--   BytesSentCount                              0
-r--   ChannelName                                 TestServerPartition-
AnotherPartitionVirtualTarget[t3]
-r--   ConnectionsCount                            0
-r--   MessagesReceivedCount                       0
-r--   MessagesSentCount                           0
-r--   Name                                        TestServerPartition-
AnotherPartitionVirtualTarget[t3]
-r--   PublicURL                                   t3://localhost:12040
-r--   ServerConnectionRuntimes                    null
```

Delete Virtual Targets

A virtual target is a strategic resource for a partition and especially for all resource groups - global or partition scoped. As soon as a resource group or a partition is started, the virtual target is in use. Being the necessary base resource for real instances this also means that deleting a virtual target may not work as most WebLogic administrators expect. If a virtual target is in use by a partition or by a global resource group, it cannot be deleted.

In order to delete a virtual target you must first disburden it from all its current customers. In case of a global resource group, you need to stop the resource group first, then you need to remove this virtual target from the list of resource group targets. After you have done this for ALL resource groups that have this virtual target in its target list, you can now finally delete the virtual target.

In case the virtual target is used by a partition, the process is very similar albeit a bit more complicated. You need to stop the partition first. Then depending on the targeting model you either need to remove the virtual target from the different resource groups of that partition and then you also need to remove it from the partition targets as well. Or in case that default targeting is used within the partition you only need to remove this virtual target from the partition targets.

In the following example, we want to delete the virtual target "Test3_VirtualTarget". But note that this virtual target is still used within a global resource group.

First, we try to delete it using the WebLogic console. This will result in the following error (figure 15-5):

Summary of Virtual Targets

Messages

Errors must be corrected before proceeding.

Summary of Virtual Targets

A virtual target represents a target for a resource group in a partition. It defines access points to resources, such as hostname, port, and partition URI path.

This page summarizes the virtual target instances that have been configured for the current domain.

Figure 15-5: Error while deleting the virtual target

The following WLST script would have tried the same and would have run into the same error:

```
startEdit()
cd('/')
cmo.destroyVirtualTarget(getMBean('/VirtualTargets/Test3_VirtualTarget'))
```

In order to delete the virtual target it is necessary to remove it first from all resource group or partition target lists. In our example this virtual target is still used as a target in the resource group called: MyConcreteGlobalResourceGroup

The complete working script for our example looks like:

```
startEdit()

cd('/ResourceGroups/MyConcreteGlobalResourceGroup')
cmo.findEffectiveTargets()

cd('/ResourceGroups/MyConcreteGlobalResourceGroup2')
cmo.findEffectiveTargets()

cd('/ResourceGroups/MyConcreteGlobalResourceGroup')
cmo.findEffectiveTargets()

cd('/ResourceGroups/MyConcreteGlobalResourceGroup2')
cmo.findEffectiveTargets()
cmo.setUseDefaultTarget(false)
cmo.setTargets(None)
cmo.setResourceGroupTemplate(getMBean('/ResourceGroupTemplates/MartinResourceTemplate'))

cd('/')
cmo.destroyVirtualTarget(getMBean('/VirtualTargets/Test3_VirtualTarget'))
```

The script will first execute the "untarget" operation and finally destroy the virtual target itself.

Summary

Virtual targets are one of the fundamental new concepts in WebLogic 12.2.x in order to support a kind of abstract targeting. This allows partitions and/or resource groups to be targeted to something virtual that by itself does not have any real target. Hidden inside the virtual target it is then necessary to wire this target up with a physical target or describe how a new physical target for this virtual target can be derived (e.g. port offset).

Only with the concept of virtual targeting WebLogic can offer a flexible and encapsulated resource group and partition model. The catch here is that when partitions should be migrated to different domains the destination domain also must have a virtual target with the same name.

Virtual targets therefore enable WebLogic to decouple the new partition and multitenancy layer from the real domain resources in a way that these resources do not even know where they get targeted at the end as all they need to know is the name of the virtual, abstract target.

Extended Security with WebLogic Partitions

CHAPTER

Relaxing WebLogic Security Restriction

Since ever, one of the major weaknesses of WebLogic was its complicated support of different security constellations. WebLogic has the powerful notion of security realms but unfortunately up to WLS 12.1.3 only ONE active security realm was supported. This always led to a complicated setup where the different authentication providers needed to be ordered well, so that all necessary security rules could be achieved without introducing backdoors. With the advent of partitions, the situation got worse with regards to security. One central security domain actually violates the isolation principles. Therefore, Oracle finally added restricted support for multiple security realms.

To offer the flexibility and the choice of isolation, an own security realm for every partition is optional. In addition, WebLogic has been extended with a number of additional concepts, like identity domains, direct partition security realm logins and more.

The most significant extensions to the WebLogic security model are

- Support of multiple active realms. Unfortunately, this is restricted to one additional active security realm per partition (if wanted) and one global security realm. There is still no concept of an "administrative realm" in order to separate administration and business security. It is the choice of the administrator, if partitions will be equipped with an own security realm or not. In case they get their own realm, the partition can have its own users and groups, security providers, roles and policies. In case the partition does not have an own security realm, it will share the default realm and there won't be any security isolation.
- A new concept has been added which is called *Identity domain*. An identity domain is a logical namespace for users and groups and their task is to identify the users associated with a partition.
- Due to these new additions also WLST - or in general the administration connectivity - has been extended. It is now possible to connect directly to the partition using WLST or JMX (figure 16-1).

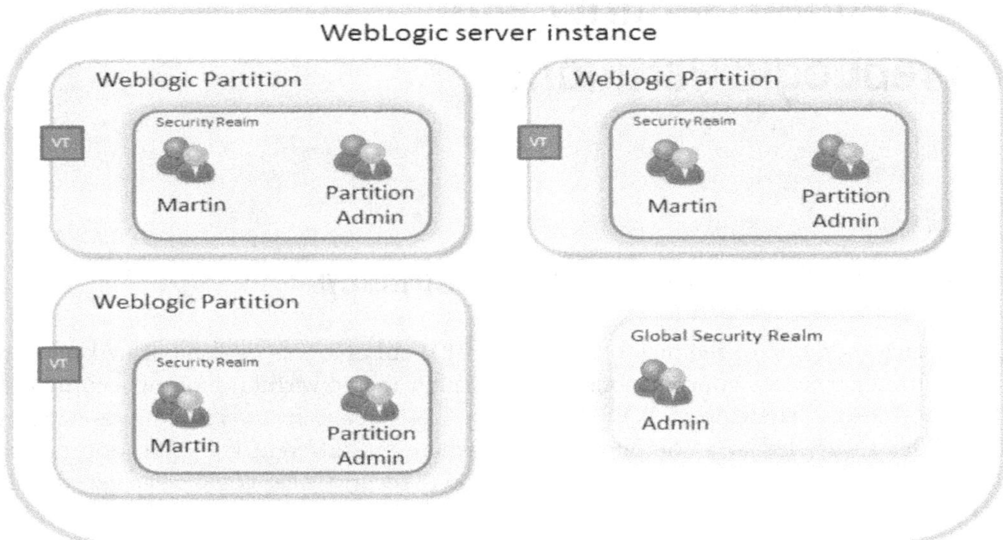

Figure 16-1: New WebLogic feature: One active security realm per partition

Beside the global – default – security realm, it is possible that each partition can have its own active realm in the partition. This security realm will then be partition scoped. One caveat of the current implementation is that the partition scoped security realm will not exported or imported. The partition security realm is not part of the partition export.

Identity Domains

Revisit the above diagram. As an example, all three partitions have the same setup, as they may be based on the same partition (e.g. same base partition imported multiple time but with a different partition deployment plan). All three partitions have the same set of users, the same groups and policies. If a user (e.g. the user "martin") wants to access some partition external resource, then WebLogic cannot really distinguish the three different users as all have the same name and the realms are WebLogic internally only logical groups of providers and security services.

In the following example two partitions should be able to access an external resource, but the third partition (see red flash) must not (figure 16-2).

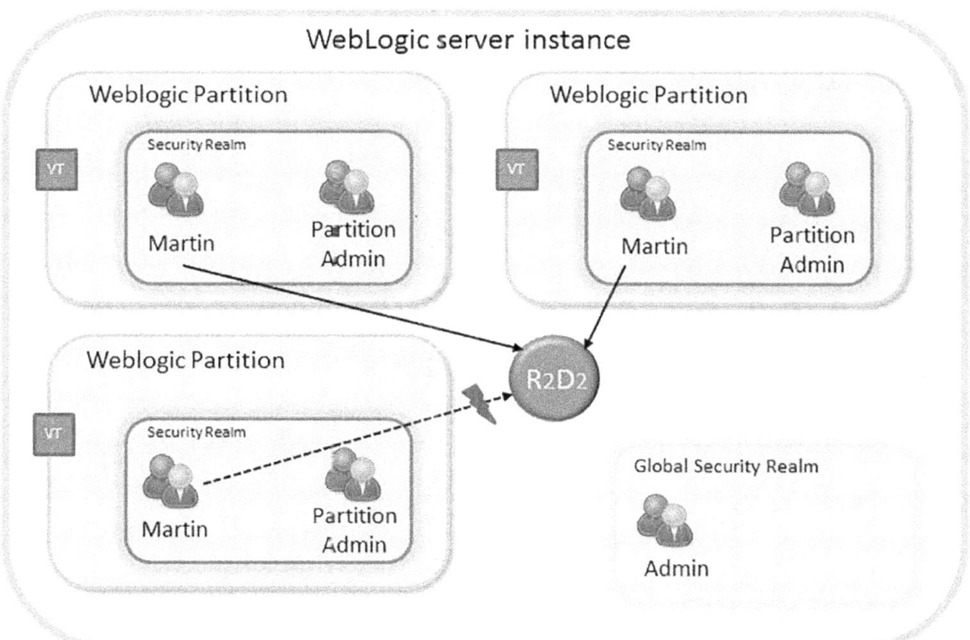

Figure 16-2: Example access

In the standard setup it is not possible for WebLogic to distinguish between the three different users called "martin".

In order to distinguish users from different domains, WebLogic has added the concept of an Identity Domain (short IDD). This is an optional feature as it must be supported in the user backend, e.g. as separate table or field. This also means that the way this support is implemented or managed is not known to WebLogic and must be done on the backend itself.

Let us revisit the example above and add identity domains to all three partitions (figure 16-3).

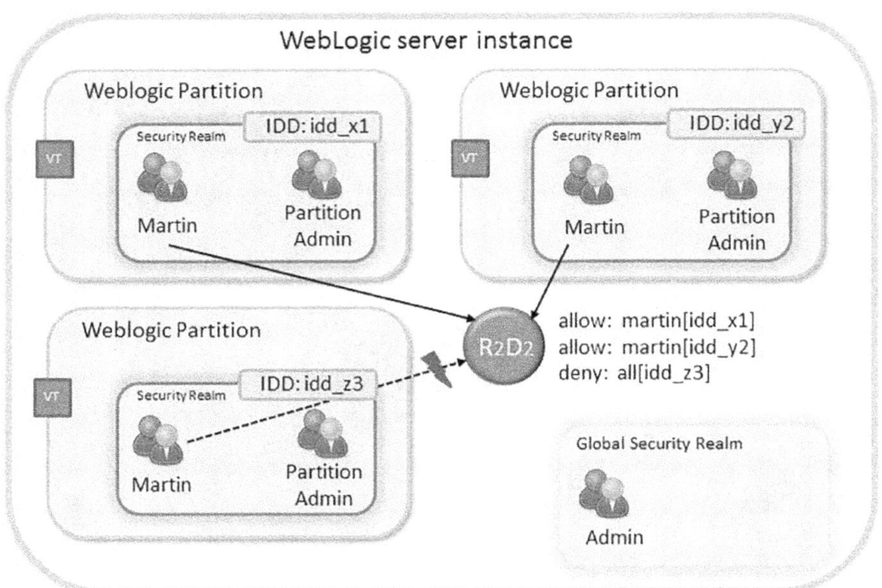

Figure 16-3: Same example with support for identity domains

After identity domains have been added to the partitions, access to the central resource can be configured as requested. Usually every security domain gets mapped to its own identity domain "1:1 mapping", but it is also possible that multiple domains share the same identity domain (figure 16-4).

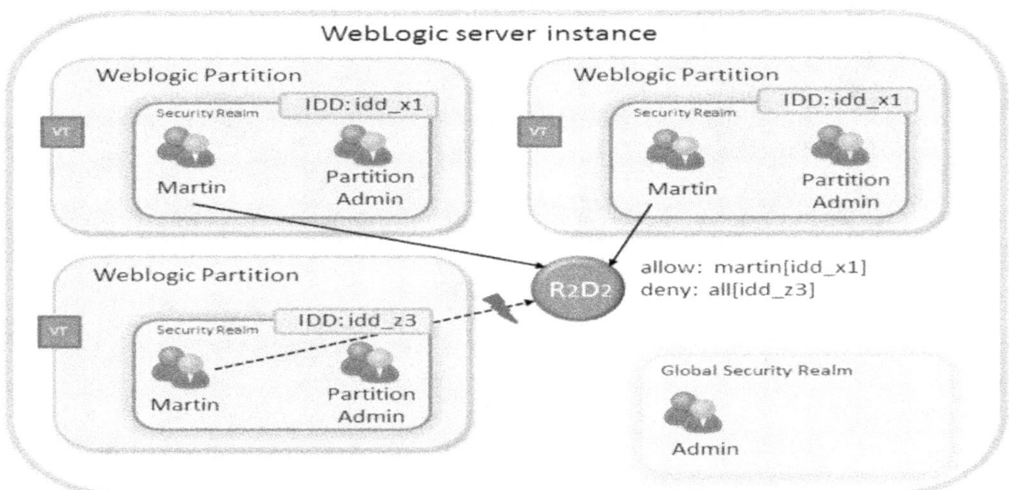

Figure 16-4: Multiple domains sharing the same identity domain

So far the example assumed that each partition has its own identity domain and also its own security realm. But an identity domain is not based on the security realm. There is no 1:1 relationship between security realm and identity domain (figure 16-5).

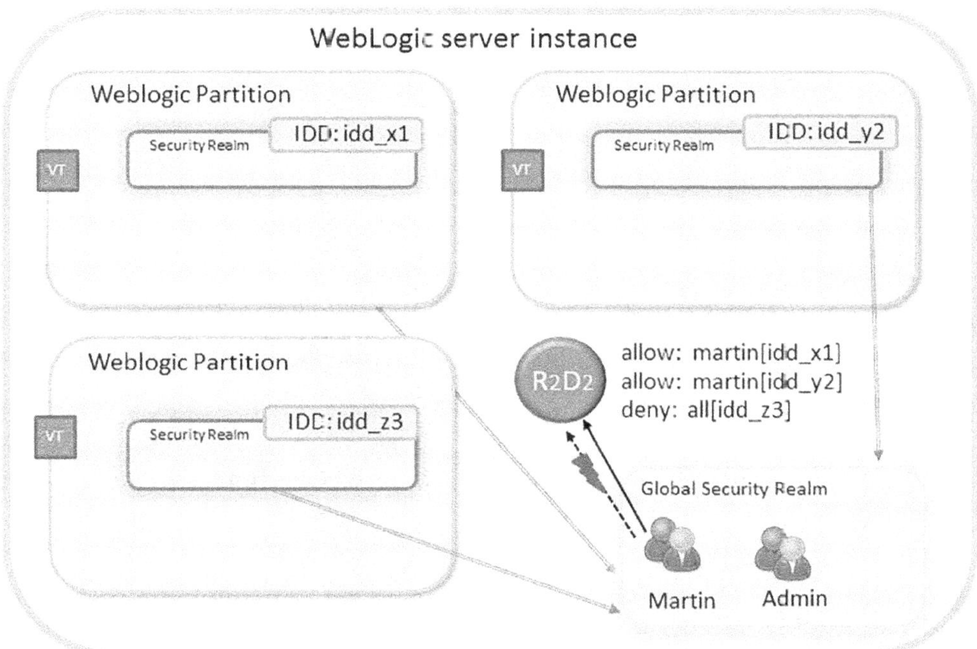

Figure 16-5: All partitions using the default realm but different identity domains

WebLogic distinguishes between two different types of identity domains. The distinction is based on the scope.

The first type is called "Administrative Identity Domain", as this identity domain is used for the global scoped default realm on domain level. This security realm has a special task as it will distinguish between users of the default (domain level) security realm and users which are defined on partition scope in the partition security realm. WebLogic by default created an administrative identity domain called "idd_DOMAIN" for the default realm (figure 16-6).

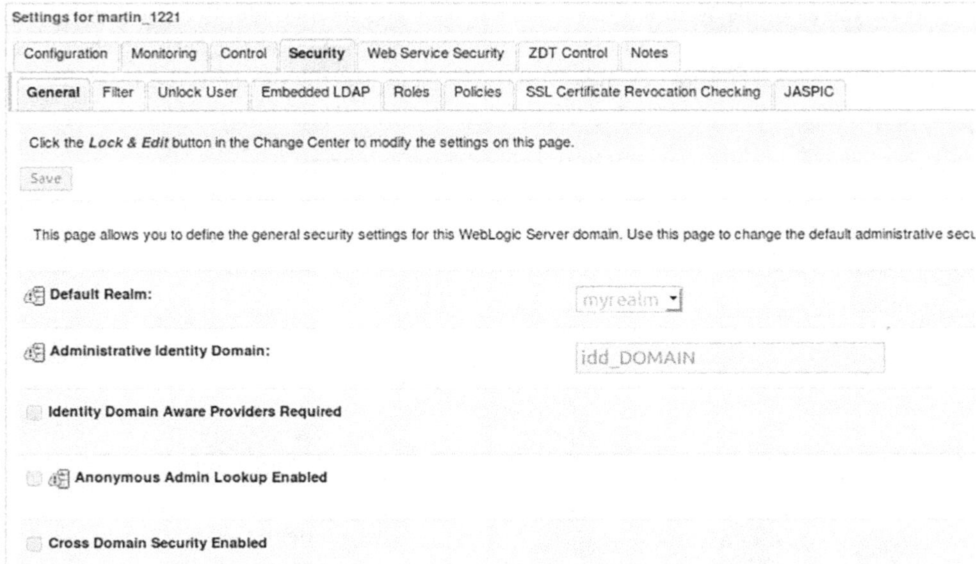

Figure 16-6: The administrative security realm can be found under the domain security settings

In addition, the identity domain must be set on the "DefaultAuthenticator" in the default security realm (figure 16-7).

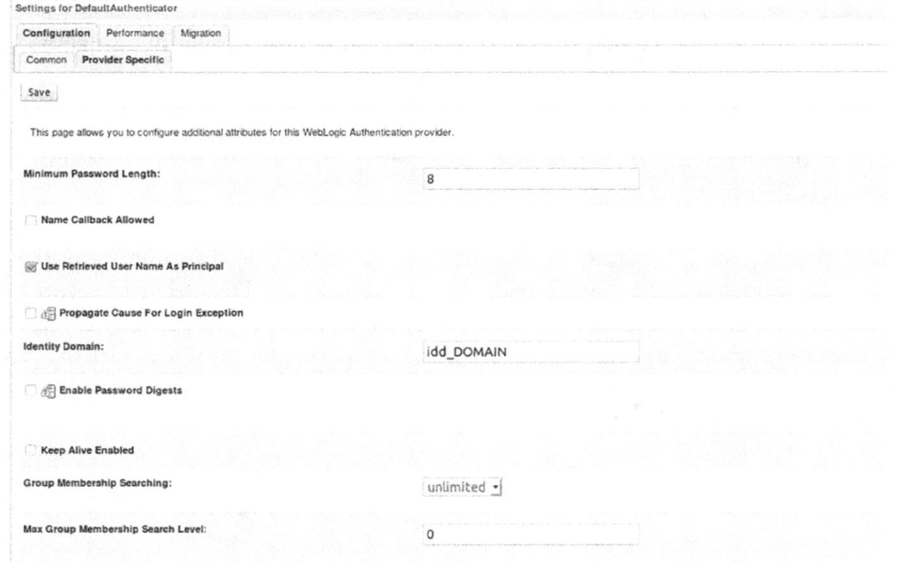

Figure 16-7: Set the identity domain in the authenticator provider

In order to change the administrative identity domain the following script can be used:

```
startEdit()

cd('/SecurityConfiguration/martin_1221')
cmo.setAdministrativeIdentityDomain('idd_DOMAIN_MARTIN_ADMIN')
cmo.setCrossDomainSecurityEnabled(false)
cmo.setAnonymousAdminLookupEnabled(false)
cmo.setIdentityDomainAwareProvidersRequired(false)
cmo.setDefaultRealm(getMBean('/SecurityConfiguration/martin_1221/Realms/myrealm'))

# set in security realm
cd('/SecurityConfiguration/martin_1221/Realms/myrealm/AuthenticationProviders/DefaultAuthenticator')
cmo.setIdentityDomain('idd_DOMAIN_MARTIN_ADMIN')
```

The second type of identity domain is called "Primary Identity Domain". Other than the "Administrative Identity Domain" type there may exist multiple identity domains of the second type as this type is defined on partition level. For each partition, WebLogic will create - unless specified otherwise - an identity domain which is called "idd_"+<name of partition>.

At the partition level, it is similar to the domain level. The identity domain is part of the partition configuration and not part of the security realm. This is also the pre-requisite for having different identity domains even if the partitions may all use the default realm (figure 16-8).

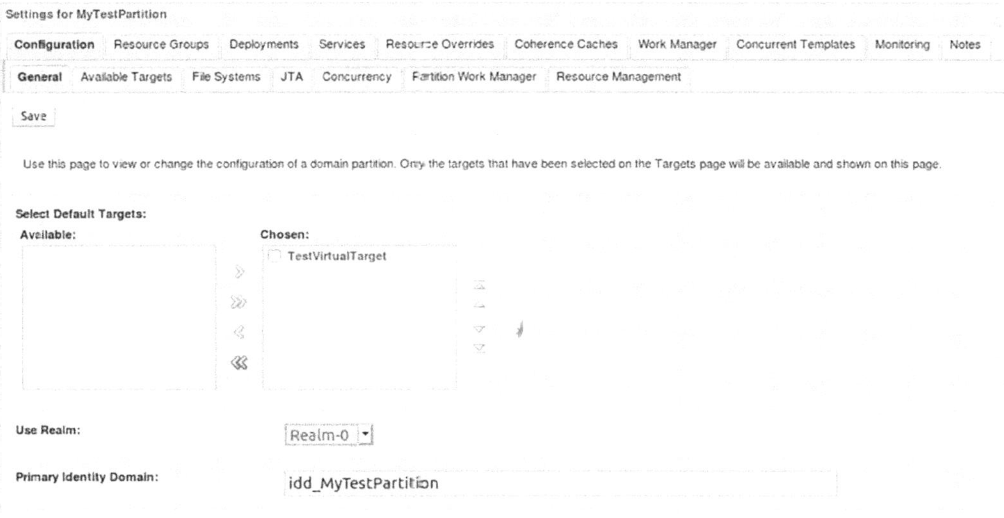

Figure 16-8: Identity domain at partition level

The following script can be used to set realm and identity domain on partition level:

```
startEdit()


cd('/Partitions/MyTestPartition')
set('DefaultTargets',jarray.array([ObjectName('com.bea:Name=TestVirtualTarget,Type=VirtualTarget')],
ObjectName))
cmo.setRealm(getMBean('/SecurityConfiguration/martin_1221/Realms/Realm-0'))
cmo.setDataSourceForJobScheduler(None)
cmo.setPrimaryIdentityDomain('idd_MyTestPartition_x1')

# set in security realm
cd('/SecurityConfiguration/martin_1221/Realms/Realm-0/AuthenticationProviders/DefaultAuthenticator')
cmo.setIdentityDomain('idd_MyTestPartition_x1')
```

Putting it all together

Identity domains are a new concept of WebLogic which provides an additional bit of information so that the traditional user/group information pair will be extended with a new concept – the identity domain. So different identity domains can make use of the same security realm. In this case there must be a separate authentication provider defined in the security realm for EACH identity domain.

Let us revisit the previous example (figure 16-9).

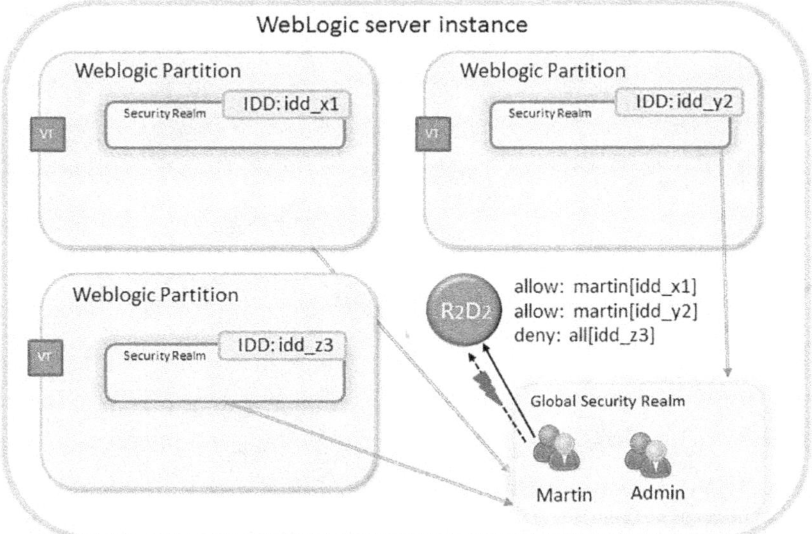

Figure 16-9: Shared security domain for multiple identity domains

First, we need to setup the default security realm with the additional providers. Alternatively, this can be done during partition deployment. The only caveat is that creating new authentication provider requires a domain restart, therefore this is not recommended to be done during partition creation or import.

Let us assume the following setup of the default security realm with 4 authentication providers (figure 16-10).

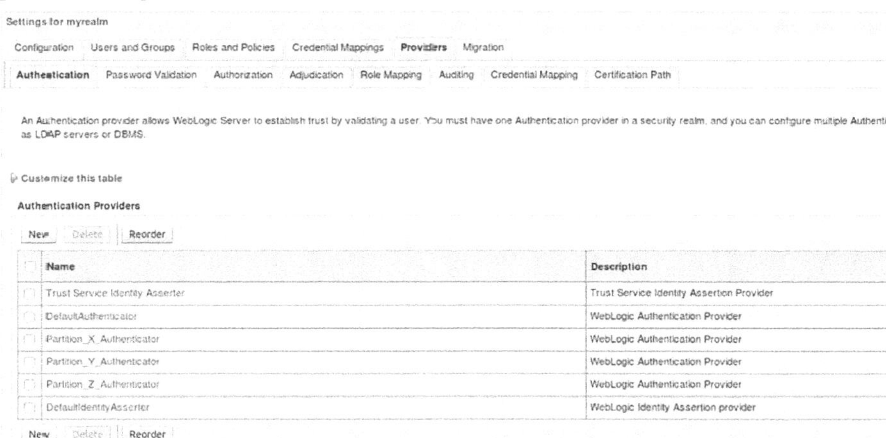

Figure 16-10: Default security realm setup

Albeit this can also be done during domain creation or import, the different authenticators are configured as described below. Note that the authentication providers are identical except for the identity domain (figure 16-11).

Settings for DefaultAuthenticator

Configuration Performance Migration

Common Provider Specific

Save

This page allows you to configure additional attributes for this WebLogic Authentication provider.

Minimum Password Length: 8

Name Callback Allowed

Use Retrieved User Name As Principal

Propagate Cause For Login Exception

Identity Domain: idd_DOMAIN

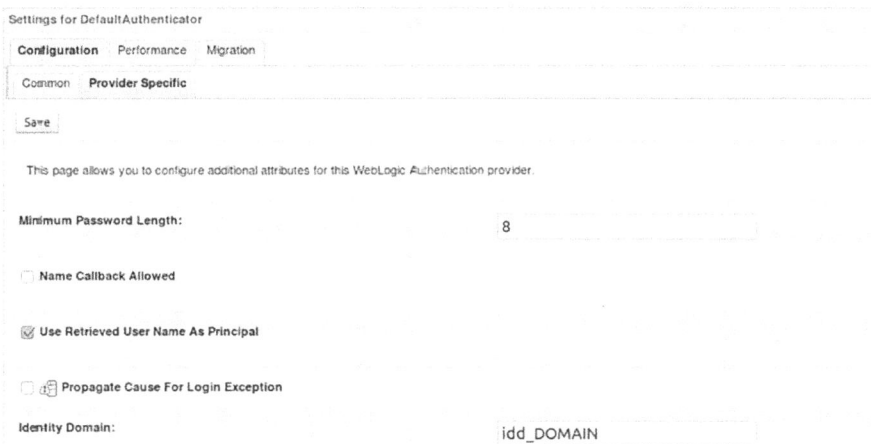

Figure 16-11: Administrative IDD

The default authenticator is configured for the global, administrative identity domain (figure 16-12).

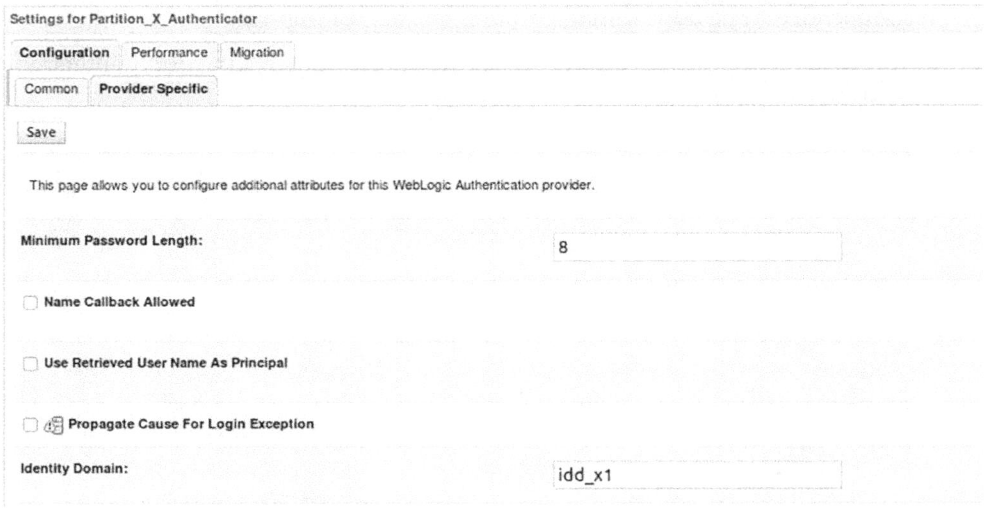

Settings for Partition_X_Authenticator
Configuration
Performance
Migration
Common
Provider Specific
Save
This page allows you to configure additional attributes for this WebLogic Authentication provider.
Minimum Password Length:
8
Name Callback Allowed
Use Retrieved User Name As Principal
Propagate Cause For Login Exception
Identity Domain:
idd_x1

Figure 16-12: Partition_X_Authenticator

The second authenticator has been configured for the identity domain idd_x1 (figure 16-13).

Settings for Partition_Y_Authenticator
Configuration
Performance
Migration
Common
Provider Specific
Save
This page allows you to configure additional attributes for this WebLogic Authentication provider.
Minimum Password Length:
8
Name Callback Allowed
Use Retrieved User Name As Principal
Propagate Cause For Login Exception
Identity Domain:
idd_y2

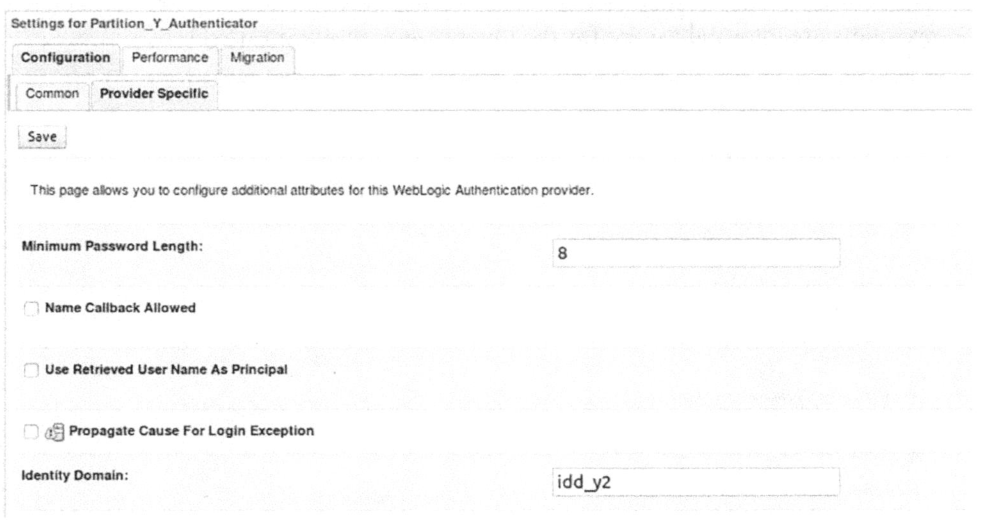

Figure 16-13: Partition_Y_Authenticator

The third authenticator has been configured for the identity domain idd_y2 and the last one for the identity domain idd_z3

After this has been done, the following WLST script can be used in order to setup the three different partitions.

```
startEdit()

cd('/')
cmo.createPartition('Partition-X')

cd('/Partitions/Partition-X/SystemFileSystem/Partition-X')
cmo.setRoot('/opt/development/wls/wls1221/user_domains/martin_1221/partitions/Partition-X/system')
cmo.setCreateOnDemand(true)
cmo.setPreserved(true)

cd('/Partitions/Partition-X')
cmo.setRealm(getMBean('/SecurityConfiguration/martin_1221/Realms/myrealm'))
cmo.createResourceGroup('default')
set('AvailableTargets',jarray.array([], ObjectName))
cmo.setDefaultTargets(None)
cmo.setRealm(getMBean('/SecurityConfiguration/martin_1221/Realms/myrealm'))
cmo.setPrimaryIdentityDomain('idd_x1')

# set idd in special authenticator in security realm
cd('/SecurityConfiguration/martin_1221/Realms/myrealm/AuthenticationProviders/Partition-X-
Authenticator')
cmo.setIdentityDomain('idd_x1')

cd('/')
cmo.createPartition('Partition-Y')

cd('/Partitions/Partition-Y/SystemFileSystem/Partition-Y')
cmo.setRoot('/opt/development/wls/wls1221/user_domains/martin_1221/partitions/Partition-Y/system')
cmo.setCreateOnDemand(true)
cmo.setPreserved(true)

cd('/Partitions/Partition-Y')
cmo.setRealm(getMBean('/SecurityConfiguration/martin_1221/Realms/myrealm'))
cmo.createResourceGroup('default')
set('AvailableTargets',jarray.array([], ObjectName))
cmo.setDefaultTargets(None)
cmo.setRealm(getMBean('/SecurityConfiguration/martin_1221/Realms/myrealm'))
cmo.setPrimaryIdentityDomain('idd_y2')

# set idd in special authenticator in security realm
cd('/SecurityConfiguration/martin_1221/Realms/myrealm/AuthenticationProviders/Partition-Y-
Authenticator')
cmo.setIdentityDomain('idd_y2')

cd('/')
cmo.createPartition('Partition-Z')

cd('/Partitions/Partition-Z/SystemFileSystem/Partition-Z')
cmo.setRoot('/opt/development/wls/wls1221/user_domains/martin_1221/partitions/Partition-Z/system')
cmo.setCreateOnDemand(true)
cmo.setPreserved(true)

cd('/Partitions/Partition-Z')
cmo.setRealm(getMBean('/SecurityConfiguration/martin_1221/Realms/myrealm'))
cmo.createResourceGroup('default')
set('AvailableTargets',jarray.array([], ObjectName))
cmo.setDefaultTargets(None)
cmo.setRealm(getMBean('/SecurityConfiguration/martin_1221/Realms/myrealm'))
cmo.setPrimaryIdentityDomain('idd_z3')

# set idd in special authenticator in security realm
cd('/SecurityConfiguration/martin_1221/Realms/myrealm/AuthenticationProviders/Partition-Z-
Authenticator')
cmo.setIdentityDomain('idd_z3')
```

After this has been done the WebLogic setup in the default security realm shows an interesting list of default users. The interesting aspect is users of the same name are part of different providers. In the list below, users with the same name are different and most likely have different passwords (figure 16-14).

Figure 16-14: Default users in the default realm

Each of the "weblogic" users is in the "Administrators" group, but with different providers (figure 16-15).

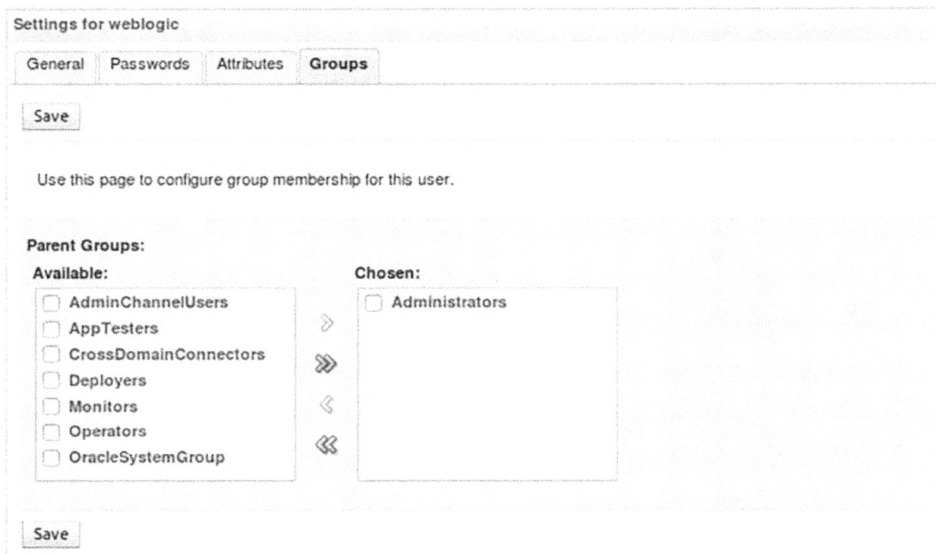

Figure 16-15: Setup of the "weblogic" user

Creating Partitions with own Security Realms

Finally, WebLogic has added support for multiple active realms. Unfortunately, with the restriction that still only one global security realm can be active. All other active security realms must be scoped to partitions. In addition, there can be only one active security realm per partition. This now also raises the need to create new security realms. This was not necessary prior to WebLogic 12.2.x. WebLogic also does not support automatic creation of new realms during partition creation, which would be a nice feature.

Creating a new security realm in WebLogic is a quite complicated action. A security realm consists of many different elements like providers, users and groups, roles, policies and more. All these elements are complex by themselves and each needs to be taken care of. A complete discussion of creating security realms are out of scope for this book, therefore this chapter will provide some common examples. See also my WLST book that provides much more details about scripting security.

First, let us create a new standard security realm with the standard providers. This includes authentication providers, authorization providers and more.

```
startEdit()

cd('/SecurityConfiguration/martin_1221')
cmo.createRealm('MyPartitionXRealm')

cd('/SecurityConfiguration/martin_1221/Realms/MyPartitionXRealm')
cmo.setDeployCredentialMappingIgnored(false)
cmo.createAuthenticationProvider('DefaultAuthenticator',
                                 'weblogic.security.providers.authentication.DefaultAuthenticator')
cmo.createAuthenticationProvider('DefaultIdentityAsserter',
                                'weblogic.security.providers.authentication.DefaultIdentityAsserter')
cmo.createAuthorizer('XACMLAuthorizer',
                     'weblogic.security.providers.xacml.authorization.XACMLAuthorizer')
cmo.createRoleMapper('XACMLRoleMapper',
                     'weblogic.security.providers.xacml.authorization.XACMLRoleMapper')
cmo.createAdjudicator('DefaultAdjudicator',
                      'weblogic.security.providers.authorization.DefaultAdjudicator')
cmo.createCredentialMapper('DefaultCredentialMapper',
                           'weblogic.security.providers.credentials.DefaultCredentialMapper')
cmo.createCertPathProvider('WebLogicCertPathProvider',
                           'weblogic.security.providers.pk.WebLogicCertPathProvider')
cmo.setCertPathBuilder(getMBean('/SecurityConfiguration/martin_1221/Realms/MyPartitionXRealm/CertPath
Providers/WebLogicCertPathProvider'))

cmo.createPasswordValidator('SystemPasswordValidator',
'com.bea.security.providers.authentication.passwordvalidator.SystemPasswordValidator')

cd('/SecurityConfiguration/martin_1221/Realms/MyPartitionXRealm/PasswordValidators/SystemPasswordVali
dator')
cmo.setMinPasswordLength(8)
cmo.setMinNumericOrSpecialCharacters(1)
```

If the partition is not using an external user/group database which is already setup (like an external LDAP) users, groups and more can be added to the security realm.

Using Automation to add or change security elements to realms

This section provides a few most common use-cases. Note that the **MAIN** difference between traditional WLST scripts and multitenancy WLST scripts in the security area is that the default name "myrealm" cannot longer be assumed as security realm name. It will most likely still be the name of the global security realm but all scripts now need to be enabled to work with different realms. Therefore all WLST methods below have the "realmName" parameter.

One very common task is to add a new user to the domain. The user will be added to the default authenticator, the internal LDAP. It is advisable to test if the user already exists, before you try to create it. Using this check you will avoid unnecessary exceptions or script exists.

```
def createUser(realmName, newUserName, newUserPassword, newUserDescription, deleteUserFirstIfExists):
    try:
        cd('/SecurityConfiguration/'+domainName+'/Realms/'+ realmName
           +'/AuthenticationProviders/DefaultAuthenticator')

        if (cmo.userExists(newUserName)):
            if (deleteUserFirstIfExists):
                     print 'User '+newUserName+' already exists - removing old user first !'
                     cmo.removeUser(newUserName)
            else:
                     # cannot create !!
                     print 'User '+newUserName+' already exists - CANNOT create !'
                     return

        # create user
        cmo.createUser(newUserName, newUserPassword, newUserDescription)
          print 'User '+newUserName+' has been created !'
    except:
```

Add a new group to the domain. A group here is nothing else but a list of users. Grouping helps the administrator to keep security rule-set small and stable by defining rules and permissions on group level. Also for groups it is advisable to test if the group exists before you try to create it.

```
def createGroup(realmName,newGroupName, newGroupDescription, deleteGroupFirstIfExists):
    try:
        cd('/SecurityConfiguration/'+domainName+'/Realms/'+ realmName
           +'/AuthenticationProviders/DefaultAuthenticator')

        if (cmo.groupExists(newGroupName)):
            if (deleteGroupFirstIfExists):
                     print 'Group '+newGroupName+' already exists - removing old group first !'
                     cmo.removeGroup(newGroupName)
            else:
                     # cannot create !!
                     print 'Group '+newGroupName+' already exists - CANNOT create !'
```

```
                return

        # create group
        cmo.createGroup(newGroupName, newGroupDescription)

          print 'Group '+newGroupName+' has been created !'
    except:
```

Groups and users cannot exist independent from each other. In order to use them efficiently, users must be added to one or more groups. One user can of course be a member of different groups. In that case you have to do this assignment multiple times - once for each group. Again proper testing if both - group and user - exist or at least proper exception handling should always be added to production ready scripts.

```
def addUserToGroup(realmName, userName, groupName):
    try:
        cd('/SecurityConfiguration/'+domainName+'/Realms/'+realmName+
           '/AuthenticationProviders/DefaultAuthenticator')

        # check if user exists
        if (cmo.userExists(userName)==0):
            print 'User '+userName+' does not exist - CANNOT add '+
                   userName+' to group '+groupName+' !'
            return

        # check if group exists
        if (cmo.groupExists(groupName)==0):
            print 'Group '+groupName+' does not exist - CANNOT add '+
                   userName+' to group '+groupName+' !'
            return

        # check if already member
          if (cmo.isMember(grouName,userName,true)):
            print 'User '+userName+' is already member of group '+groupName+' !'
            return

        # finally :-) add user to group
        cmo.addMemberToGroup(groupName, userName)

    except:
```

To change a user's password, invoke the "changeUserPassword" method of the "UserPasswordEditorMBean", which is extended by the security realm's "AuthenticationProvider MBean". The following WLST online script invokes "changeUserPassword" on the default Authentication Provider.

```
def changeUserpassword(realmName, userName, oldPassword, newPassword):
    try:

cd('/SecurityConfiguration/'+domainName+'/Realms/'+realmName+'/AuthenticationProviders/DefaultAuthent
icator')

        # check if user exists
        if (userExists(userName)==0):
            print 'User '+userName+' does not exist - CANNOT change password !'
            return

        # change the password
        cmo.changeUserPassword(userName, oldPassword, newPassword)
          print "Changed password of user '+userName+' successfully"
    except:
```

Putting it all together

The following example will create a new realm, add the partition admin and some users to the realm, then create a new partition and select the new realm as security realm for the new partition.

Example WLST script:

```
edit()
startEdit()


##########################################################
# create virtual targets

cd('/')
cmo.createVirtualTarget('VirtualTarget-X')

cd('/VirtualTargets/VirtualTarget-X')
cmo.setUriPrefix('/test_x')
set('Targets',jarray.array([ObjectName('com.bea:Name=AdminServer,Type=Server')], ObjectName))

cd('/')
cmo.createVirtualTarget('VirtualTarget-Y')

cd('/VirtualTargets/VirtualTarget-Y')
cmo.setUriPrefix('/test_y')
set('Targets',jarray.array([ObjectName('com.bea:Name=AdminServer,Type=Server')], ObjectName))


##########################################################
# create X realm

cd('/SecurityConfiguration/martin_1221')
cmo.createRealm('MyPartitionXRealm')

cd('/SecurityConfiguration/martin_1221/Realms/MyPartitionXRealm')
cmo.setDeployCredentialMappingIgnored(false)
cmo.createAuthenticationProvider('DefaultAuthenticator',
                                'weblogic.security.providers.authentication.DefaultAuthenticator')
cmo.createAuthenticationProvider('DefaultIdentityAsserter',
                               'weblogic.security.providers.authentication.DefaultIdentityAsserter')
cmo.createAuthorizer('XACMLAuthorizer',
                     'weblogic.security.providers.xacml.authorization.XACMLAuthorizer')
cmo.createRoleMapper('XACMLRoleMapper',
                     'weblogic.security.providers.xacml.authorization.XACMLRoleMapper')
cmo.createAdjudicator('DefaultAdjudicator',
                      'weblogic.security.providers.authorization.DefaultAdjudicator')
cmo.createCredentialMapper('DefaultCredentialMapper',
                           'weblogic.security.providers.credentials.DefaultCredentialMapper')
cmo.createCertPathProvider('WebLogicCertPathProvider',
                           'weblogic.security.providers.pk.WebLogicCertPathProvider')
cmo.setCertPathBuilder(getMBean('/SecurityConfiguration/martin_1221/Realms/MyPartitionXRealm/CertPath
Providers/WebLogicCertPathProvider'))

cmo.createPasswordValidator('SystemPasswordValidator',
'com.bea.security.providers.authentication.passwordvalidator.SystemPasswordValidator')

cd('/SecurityConfiguration/martin_1221/Realms/MyPartitionXRealm/PasswordValidators/SystemPasswordVali
dator')
cmo.setMinPasswordLength(8)
cmo.setMinNumericOrSpecialCharacters(1)

# set Identity Domain idd_x
```

```
cd('/SecurityConfiguration/martin_1221/Realms/MyPartitionXRealm/AuthenticationProviders/DefaultAuthen
ticator')
cmo.setIdentityDomain('idd_x')


##########################################################
# create Y realm

cd('/SecurityConfiguration/martin_1221')
cmo.createRealm('MyPartitionYRealm')

cd('/SecurityConfiguration/martin_1221/Realms/MyPartitionYRealm')
cmo.setDeployCredentialMappingIgnored(false)
cmo.createAuthenticationProvider('DefaultAuthenticator',
                                 'weblogic.security.providers.authentication.DefaultAuthenticator')
cmo.createAuthenticationProvider('DefaultIdentityAsserter',
                                'weblogic.security.providers.authentication.DefaultIdentityAsserter')
cmo.createAuthorizer('XACMLAuthorizer',
                     'weblogic.security.providers.xacml.authorization.XACMLAuthorizer')
cmo.createRoleMapper('XACMLRoleMapper',
                     'weblogic.security.providers.xacml.authorization.XACMLRoleMapper')
cmo.createAdjudicator('DefaultAdjudicator',
                      'weblogic.security.providers.authorization.DefaultAdjudicator')
cmo.createCredentialMapper('DefaultCredentialMapper',
                           'weblogic.security.providers.credentials.DefaultCredentialMapper')
cmo.createCertPathProvider('WebLogicCertPathProvider',
                           'weblogic.security.providers.pk.WebLogicCertPathProvider')
cmo.setCertPathBuilder(getMBean('/SecurityConfiguration/martin_1221/Realms/MyPartitionYRealm/CertPath
Providers/WebLogicCertPathProvider'))

cmo.createPasswordValidator('SystemPasswordValidator',
'com.bea.security.providers.authentication.passwordvalidator.SystemPasswordValidator')

cd('/SecurityConfiguration/martin_1221/Realms/MyPartitionYRealm/PasswordValidators/SystemPasswordVali
dator')
cmo.setMinPasswordLength(8)
cmo.setMinNumericOrSpecialCharacters(1)

# set Identity Domain idd_y
cd('/SecurityConfiguration/martin_1221/Realms/MyPartitionYRealm/AuthenticationProviders/DefaultAuthen
ticator')
cmo.setIdentityDomain('idd_y')

############################################################
# Create partitions

cd('/')
cmo.createPartition('Partition-X')

cd('/Partitions/Partition-X/SystemFileSystem/Partition-X')
cmo.setRoot('/opt/development/wls/wls1221/user_domains/martin_1221/partitions/Partition-X/system')
cmo.setCreateOnDemand(true)
cmo.setPreserved(true)

cd('/Partitions/Partition-X')
cmo.setRealm(getMBean('/SecurityConfiguration/martin_1221/Realms/MyPartitionXRealm'))
cmo.createResourceGroup('default')
set('AvailableTargets',jarray.array([], ObjectName))
cmo.setDefaultTargets(None)
cmo.setRealm(getMBean('/SecurityConfiguration/martin_1221/Realms/MyPartitionXRealm'))
cmo.setPrimaryIdentityDomain('idd_x')

cd('/Partitions/Partition-X')
set('AvailableTargets',jarray.array([ObjectName('com.bea:Name=VirtualTarget-X,Type=VirtualTarget')],
ObjectName))

cd('/Partitions/Partition-X')
set('DefaultTargets',jarray.array([ObjectName('com.bea:Name=VirtualTarget-X,Type=VirtualTarget')],
ObjectName))
cmo.setRealm(getMBean('/SecurityConfiguration/martin_1221/Realms/MyPartitionXRealm'))
cmo.setDataSourceForJobScheduler(None)
cmo.setJobSchedulerTableName('WEBLOGIC_TIMERS')

cd('/')
cmo.createPartition('Partition-Y')

cd('/Partitions/Partition-Y/SystemFileSystem/Partition-Y')
cmo.setRoot('/opt/development/wls/wls1221/user_domains/martin_1221/partitions/Partition-Y/system')
```

```
cmo.setCreateOnDemand(true)
cmo.setPreserved(true)

cd('/Partitions/Partition-Y')
cmo.setRealm(getMBean('/SecurityConfiguration/martin_1221/Realms/MyPartitionYRealm'))
cmo.createResourceGroup('default')
set('AvailableTargets',jarray.array([], ObjectName))
cmo.setDefaultTargets(None)
cmo.setRealm(getMBean('/SecurityConfiguration/martin_1221/Realms/MyPartitionYRealm'))
cmo.setPrimaryIdentityDomain('idd_y')

cd('/Partitions/Partition-Y')
set('AvailableTargets',jarray.array([ObjectName('com.bea:Name=VirtualTarget-Y,Type=VirtualTarget')],
ObjectName))

cd('/Partitions/Partition-Y')
set('DefaultTargets',jarray.array([ObjectName('com.bea:Name=VirtualTarget-Y,Type=VirtualTarget')],
ObjectName))
cmo.setRealm(getMBean('/SecurityConfiguration/martin_1221/Realms/MyPartitionYRealm'))
cmo.setDataSourceForJobScheduler(None)
cmo.setJobSchedulerTableName('WEBLOGIC_TIMERS')
```

Example WLST script for adding users:

```
cd('/SecurityConfiguration/'+domainName+'/Realms/MyPartitionXRealm/AuthenticationProviders/DefaultAut
henticator')
cmo.createUser('admin_x', 'test_1234', 'Partition X Admin')
cmo.addMemberToGroup('Administrators', 'admin_x')
print 'User admin_x has been created !'
cmo.createUser('monitor_x', 'test_1234', 'Partition X Monitor')
cmo.addMemberToGroup('Monitors', 'monitor_x')
print 'User monitor_x has been created !'

cd('/SecurityConfiguration/'+domainName+'/Realms/MyPartitionYRealm/AuthenticationProviders/DefaultAut
henticator')
cmo.createUser('admin_y', 'test_1234', 'Partition Y Admin')
cmo.addMemberToGroup('Administrators', 'admin_y')
print 'User admin_x has been created !'
cmo.createUser('monitor_y', 'test_1234', 'Partition Y Monitor')
cmo.addMemberToGroup('Monitors', 'monitor_y')
```

The reason for having two different scripts is that the domain needs to be restarted after the realms have been created in order to add users.

Different ways to access WebLogic

In the traditional WebLogic security model, an administrative user was always authenticated in the one and only one global security realm. Now with the advent of partition scoped security realms the following question arises: Given a partition administrator, who can only be authenticated in a partition realm. This partition administrator has no login to the domain realm. How can this administrator use WLST and connect to the WebLogic domain?

Oracle has actually implemented an interesting answer to that problem. If – and only if – t3 or t3s is used as the communication protocol, then an extended (new) connection string can be provided which will authenticate the given user directly in the partition security realm. After connected to the WebLogic domain the user will be – in case of the WLST offline mode – placed directly into the partition subtree.

The following table describes the different permissions granted to users depending to which security realm they have logged into.

Role	Logged in to Domain	Logged in to Partition via WLST
Administrator	Full control over domain resources, including partition configuration and management	Write access to partition owned MBeans. Read-only access to own PartitionMBean.Realm and PartitionMBean.PrimaryIdentityDomain attributes. Read-only access to own RealmMBean and its children.
Deployer	Configure resources within the domain and partitions, deploy/redeploy/undeploy/start/stop applications within the domain and partitions.	Configure resources within the partition, deploy/redeploy/undeploy/start/stop applications within the partition.
Operator	Start/stop servers, partitions, resource groups.	Start/stop partition and resource group.
Monitor	Read-only access to domain and partition resources.	Read-only access to partition resources.

© Oracle: https://docs.oracle.com/middleware/1221/wls/WLSMT/config_security.htm

In traditional WLST scripts the "connect" function is used to connect to a WebLogic server (admin or managed-server).

The default syntax is:

This default syntax has now been extended with two new ways to specify the connection URL. It is now possible to specify an URL which points directly to a partition. The side effect here is that the admin needs to know the exact name of the partition. In order to be even more flexible WebLogic has added another new syntax that allows the user to specify an URL which points to a virtual target

Using the "partition-style" connection URL:

```
connect('user','password',"t3://host:port/partitions/partition-name")
```

Using the "virtual-target-style" connection URL:

Summary

WebLogic has finally extended its security model and added limited support for multiple active realms. For its new multitenancy support WebLogic provides two new concepts. It is now possible to have an own active security realm per partition in addition to the default global security realm. Note that on global level and also on partition level WebLogic still enforces the "*only-one-active-security-realm*" model. Secondly, WebLogic has added the optional concept of identity domains which are distinguisher elements and allow to distinguish in which partition a specific user has been authenticated.

A very interesting aspect is that a security domain can be embedded into a partition that also means that this realm will get exported and imported together with the partition.

Beside these new added elements, security realms scoped to partitions are pretty much the same as the globally scoped security realm.

Services for Resource Groups and Partitions

CHAPTER

Introduction

As already discussed in chapter 10, services which are required by the application can be defined as scoped to a partition. Using the new terminology of WebLogic this means that services can be defined as part of a partition resource group and targeted to one of the partition virtual targets. This chapter looks at the different application exposed services (this means services used by applications directly) and how those services can be scoped to a partition (figure 17-1).

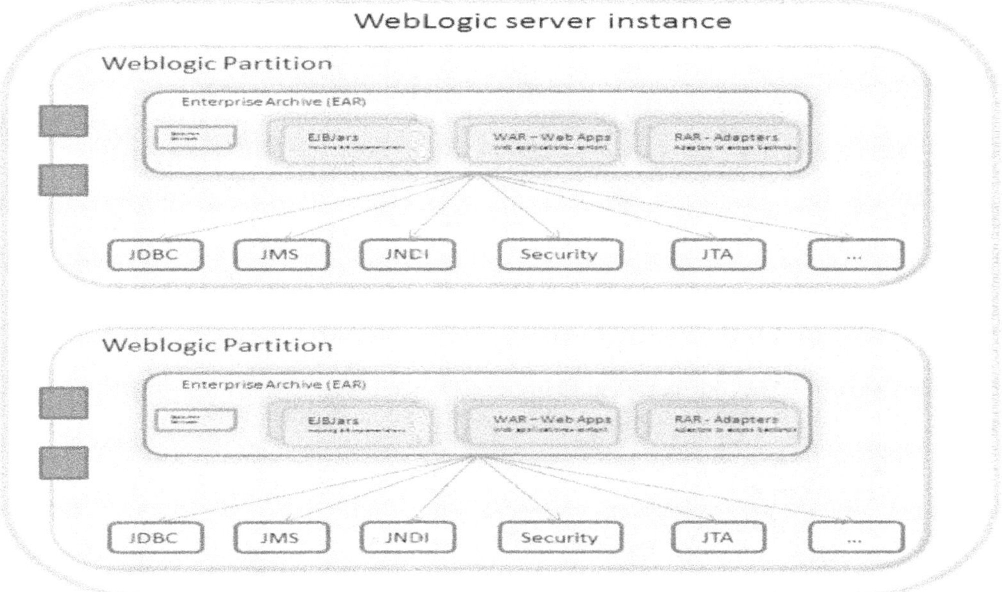

Figure 17-1: WebLogic server with two partitions and only dedicated services

WebLogic offers different ways to define services. They can be defined as part of a resource group template that forms a blueprint for partitions. They can also be defined as part or global or partition scoped resource groups. There are multiple ways to setup systems. In addition, these services can be defined on WebLogic level or on global resource groups. In the subsequent sections of this chapter for the sake of understanding only resource group templates or partition resource groups are discussed.

For all examples in this chapter, the following setup will be used as base setup. This includes two partitions called "X" and "Y". "X" is based on a resource group template whereas "Y" has an own embedded resource group. Scripts and code examples will be kept to a minimum - please see my WLST book for much more detail – as the focus will clearly be on how to scope these services. It is not possible for this book to discuss all details of the different services (figure 17-2).

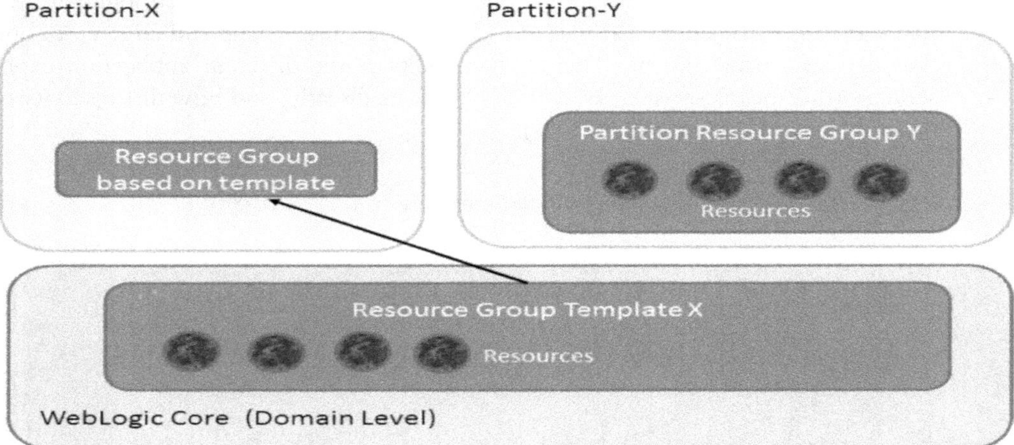

Figure 17-2: Example setup

In the config.xml this is reflected in the following way:

```
...
  <partition>
    <name>Partition-Y</name>
    <resource-group>
      <name>PartitionResourceGroup-Y</name>
      <target></target>
      <use-default-target>true</use-default-target>
    </resource-group>
    <default-target>VirtualTarget-Y</default-target>
    <available-target>VirtualTarget-Y</available-target>
    <realm>MyPartitionYRealm</realm>
    <partition-id>58eec675-0950-4760-a5f4-1d732c67b1c4</partition-id>
    <primary-identity-domain>idd_y</primary-identity-domain>
    <system-file-system>
      <root>/opt/development/wls/wls1221/user_domains/martin_1221/partitions/Partition-
Y/system</root>
      <create-on-demand>true</create-on-demand>
      <preserved>true</preserved>
    </system-file-system>
    <partition-work-manager-ref>PartitionWorkManager-test2</partition-work-manager-ref>
```

```
  </partition>
  <partition>
    <name>Partition-X</name>
    <resource-group>
      <name>ResourceTemplate-X_group</name>
      <resource-group-template>ResourceTemplate-X</resource-group-template>
    </resource-group>
    <default-target>VirtualTarget-X</default-target>
    <available-target>VirtualTarget-X</available-target>
    <realm>MyPartitionXRealm</realm>
    <partition-id>4b882b3b-f416-4369-8862-6779aeefa9ff</partition-id>
    <primary-identity-domain>idd_x</primary-identity-domain>
    <system-file-system>
      <root>/opt/development/wls/wls1221/user_domains/martin_1221/partitions/Partition-
X/system</root>
      <create-on-demand>true</create-on-demand>
      <preserved>true</preserved>
    </system-file-system>
  </partition>
  <resource-group-template>
    <name>ResourceTemplate-X</name>
  </resource-group-template>
```

Namespaces and NameServices

JNDI is a special service as the partition automatically has its own JNDI service. The administrator has no choice as it is not possible to share the JNDI service between partitions. In chapter 22 we discuss how to use the JNDI InitalContext to access partitions.

Integrating into external JNDI Services

Another problem is the integration of foreign JNDI services. In order to hide infrastructure details, WebLogic provides the well-known foreign JNDI service which allows to map foreign JNDI trees.

Foreign JNDI provider in WebLogic enables the administrator to connect different JNDI trees together. JNDI can be roughly compared to a UNIX file system. You have a root directory and underneath a structure of subfolders. Finally in the different folders (on all levels) you have concrete files. Additionally to you create links (comparable to symbolic links in UNIX) and you mount other file system - JNDI (sub)trees.

Referencing other JNDI trees can be compared to mounting file systems.

First you need to define where this file system is and how to connect (host, user, password, file system type).

Secondly, you need to define which folder you want to mount and where this remote folder should appear in your local file system. This is exactly what foreign JNDI providers are good for (figure 17-3).

Foreign JNDI resources

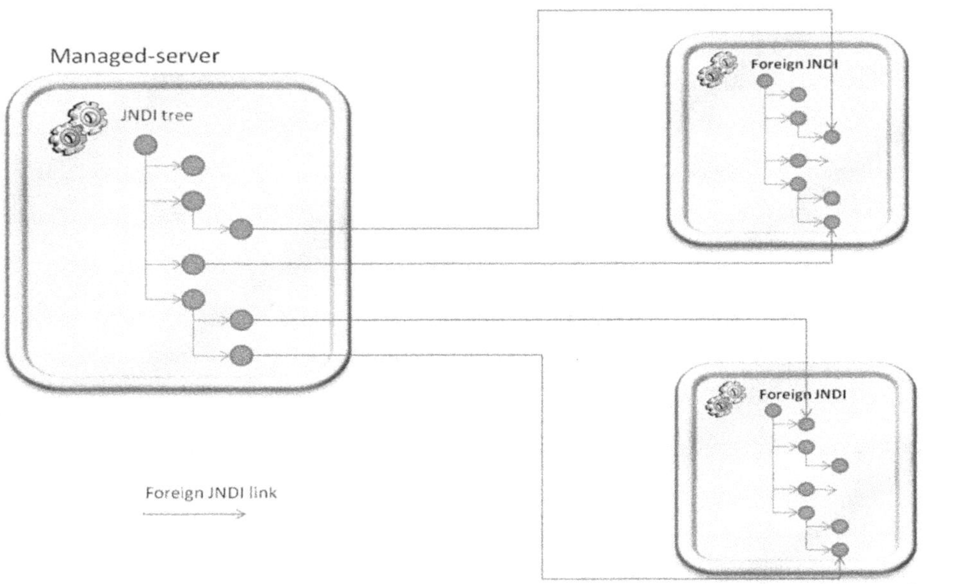

Figure 17-3: Foreign JNDI concept

In the following example, we will create a foreign JNDI provider for our resource group template and another for our partition internal resource group (figure 17-4).

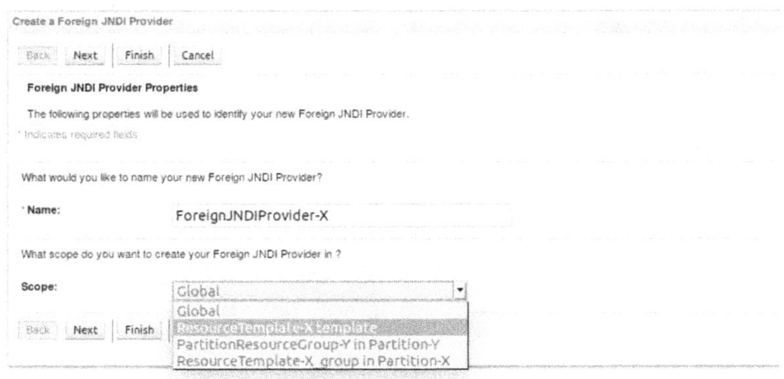

Figure 17-4: Create a foreign provider for a template

Note the scoping in the above screenshot! The new provider will be part of our resource group template and all instances – like our Partition_X – will automatically inherit this provider (figure 17-5).

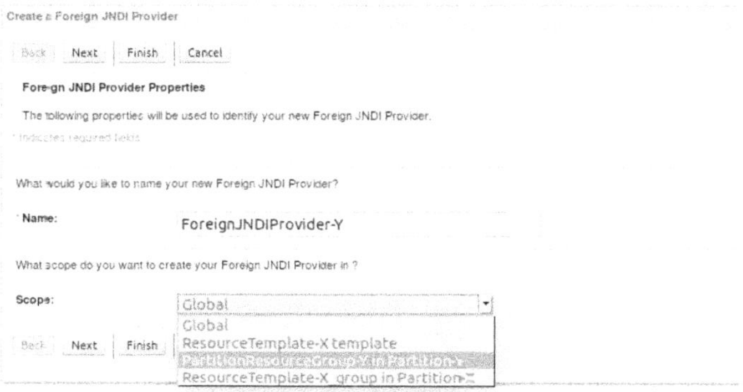

Figure 17-5: Create a provider for a partition internal group

Again, note the specific scoping. This is key for making that provider visible in the right places.

The same providers can also be created using WLST. Note that the following two WLST scripts are basically identical. The only, but important difference is the initial location in the MBean tree which defines the scoping.

Creating the provider for our resource group template

```
cmo.createForeignJNDIProvider('ForeignJNDIProvider-X')

# change to new provider and configure it
cd('ForeignJNDIProviders/ForeignJNDIProvider-X')
cmo.setUser('martin')
cmo.setProviderURL('t3://testhost:7101')
cmo.setInitialContextFactory('weblogic.jndi.WLInitialContextFactory')

# now configuring foreign links
cmo.createForeignJNDILink('MyTestLink')
cd ('ForeignJNDILinks/MyTestLink')
cmo.setLocalJNDIName('jndi/local/testserver/TestServerConnectionFactory')
```

Creating the provider for our partition internal resource group of "Partition_Y"

```
cmo.createForeignJNDIProvider('ForeignJNDIProvider-Y')

# change to new provider and configure it
cd('/Partitions/Partition-Y/ResourceGroups/PartitionResourceGroup-
Y/ForeignJNDIProviders/ForeignJNDIProvider-Y')
cmo.setUser('heinzl')
cmo.setProviderURL('t3://testhost2:9999')
cmo.setInitialContextFactory('weblogic.jndi.WLInitialContextFactory')

# now configuring foreign links
```

```
cmo.createForeignJNDILink('MyTestLink_xyz')
cd ('ForeignJNDILinks/MyTestLink_xyz')
cmo.setLocalJNDIName('jndi/local/xyz')
```

Database access via Datasources

By moving the JDBC pool into the partition it will not only become a part of this partition, but it is now also dedicated with all its resources to this partition. Datasource configurations like user, password, URL, timeouts, ONS or others can be set differently for each partition while for example the JNDI lookup and datasource name can stay the same, if the applications in the different partitions requires that (figure 17-6).

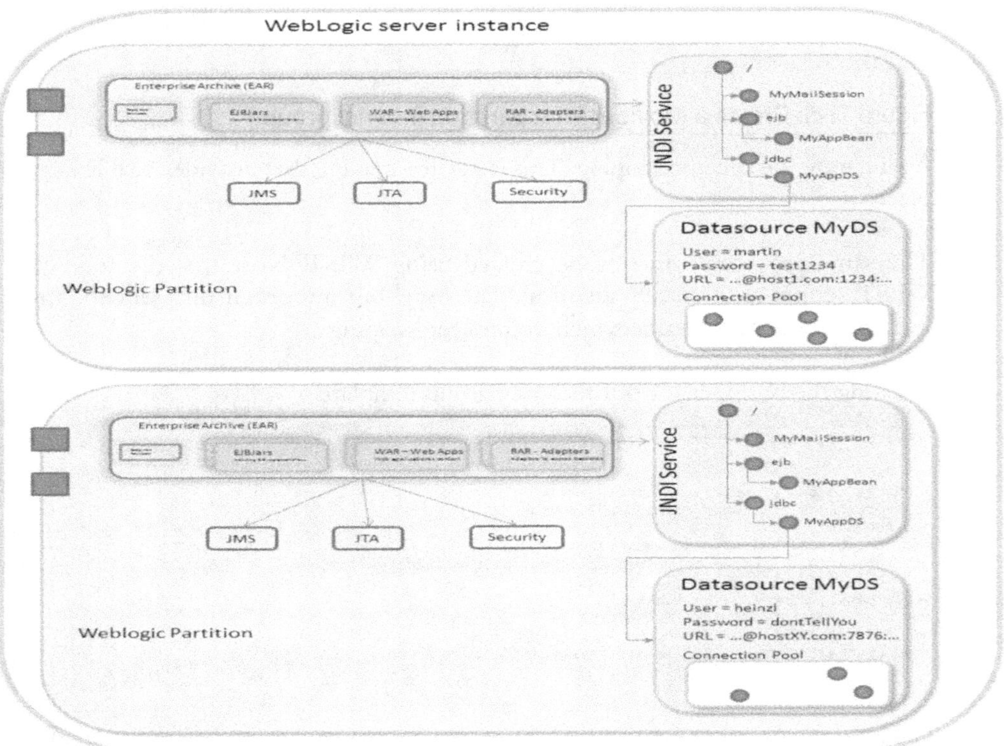

Figure 17-6: Isolated JDBC service

As you can see in the example above, both applications are using an identical JNDI tree, but do not conflict with each other as both are isolated in different partitions.

Example

The following example will create a JDBC datasource for the global resource group template and another datasource for the partition "Y" internal resource group. JDBC data sources can be created using the WebLogic console, WLST, JMX or even REST. The important part is that during datasource creation the correct scoping must be selected. This is either a selection in a drop-down menu, if the Web-UI is used or by selecting the correct base MBean (WLS, JMX) (figure 17-7).

Create a New JDBC Data Source

Back | Next | Finish | Cancel

JDBC Data Source Properties

The following properties will be used to identify your new JDBC data source.

* Indicates required fields

What would you like to name your new JDBC data source?

* Name: JDBC Data Source-groupX

What scope do you want to create your data source in ?

Scope: Global

Global

ResourceTemplate-X template

PartitionResourceGroup-Y in Partition-Y

ResourceTemplate-X_group in Partition-X

What JNDI name would you like to assign to your new

JNDI Name:

/jdbc/myAppDS

Figure 17-7: Select the correct scoping

It is important to note that the drop-down list contains not only the resource group template and the resource group in partition "Y". It is interesting that it also contains the automatically created resource group in partition "X". This depicts that even though a partition is based on a resource group template, it is possible to add services to the group without adding them to the template. Resources which are scoped to these groups are only available in that group but in no other group based on the same template.

After the datasource has been created, it can be seen as part of the resource group template (figure 17-8).

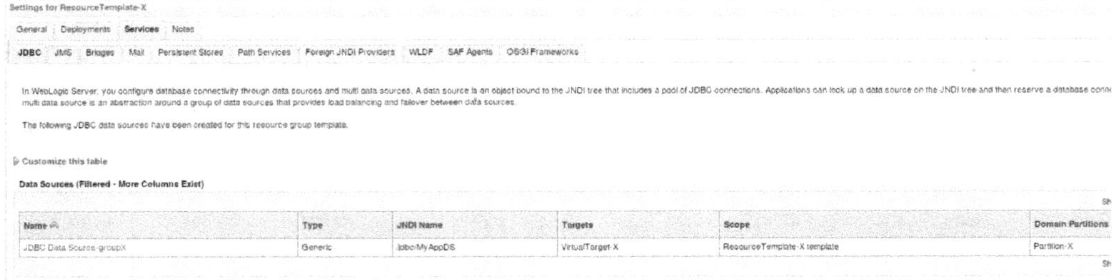

Figure 17-8: JDBC service as part of the resource group template

As the partition "X" is based on the resource group template, it is automatically possible to see the new datasource also on partition level. Note the scope! Any datasourcs can clearly undefined where it is coming from by its individual scope (figure 17-9).

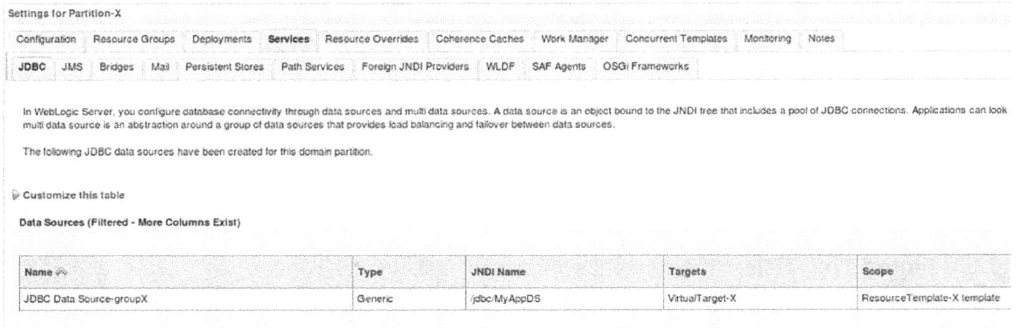

Figure 17-9: Datasource view on partition level

For partition "Y" the datasource must be created in a similar way but scoped to the resource group (not template!) of the partition. See the different scope of the datasource! (figure 17-10).

Figure 17-10: Datasource scoped to a partition resource group

Using the WebLogic console, it is possible to see all defined datasources in the well-known "Services/Data Sources" view. For WebLogic 12.2.x this view has been extended to also show the scope and partition if applicable (figure 17-11).

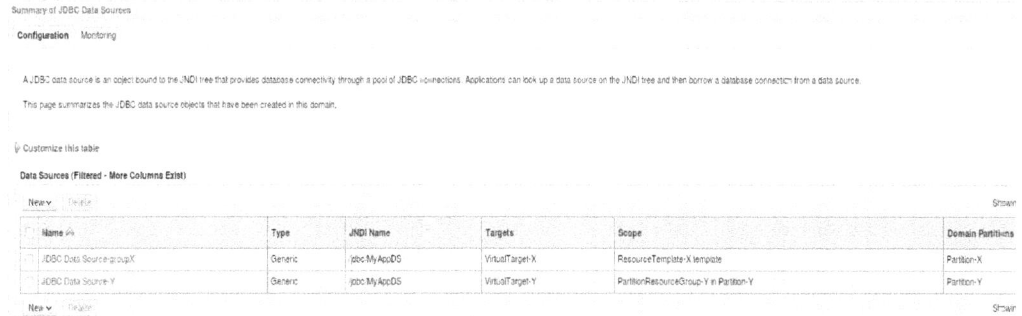

Figure 17-11: Datasource overview in WebLogic

The same datasource can also be created using WLST:

Create the first datasource as part of the resource group template

```
cmo.createJDBCSystemResource('JDBC Data Source-groupX')

cd('/ResourceGroupTemplates/ResourceTemplate-X/JDBCSystemResources/JDBC Data Source-
groupX/JDBCResource/JDBC Data Source-groupX')
cmo.setName('JDBC Data Source-groupX')

cd('/ResourceGroupTemplates/ResourceTemplate-X/JDBCSystemResources/JDBC Data Source-
groupX/JDBCResource/JDBC Data Source-groupX/JDBCDataSourceParams/JDBC Data Source-groupX')
set('JNDINames',jarray.array([String('/jdbc/MyAppDS')], String))
```

```
cd('/ResourceGroupTemplates/ResourceTemplate-X/JDBCSystemResources/JDBC Data Source-groupX/JDBCResource/JDBC Data Source-groupX')
cmo.setDatasourceType('GENERIC')

cd('/ResourceGroupTemplates/ResourceTemplate-X/JDBCSystemResources/JDBC Data Source-groupX/JDBCResource/JDBC Data Source-groupX/JDBCDriverParams/JDBC Data Source-groupX')
cmo.setUrl('jdbc:oracle:thin:@//someDBhost:1521/MyAppDS')
cmo.setDriverName('oracle.jdbc.OracleDriver')

cd('/ResourceGroupTemplates/ResourceTemplate-X/JDBCSystemResources/JDBC Data Source-groupX/JDBCResource/JDBC Data Source-groupX/JDBCDriverParams/JDBC Data Source-groupX/Properties/JDBC Data Source-groupX')
cmo.createProperty('user')

cd('/ResourceGroupTemplates/ResourceTemplate-X/JDBCSystemResources/JDBC Data Source-groupX/JDBCResource/JDBC Data Source-groupX/JDBCDriverParams/JDBC Data Source-groupX/Properties/JDBC Data Source-groupX/Properties/user')
cmo.setValue('myself')

cd('/ResourceGroupTemplates/ResourceTemplate-X/JDBCSystemResources/JDBC Data Source-groupX/JDBCResource/JDBC Data Source-groupX/JDBCDataSourceParams/JDBC Data Source-groupX')
```

Create the second datasource as part of the partition resource group

```
cmo.createJDBCSystemResource('JDBC Data Source-Y')

cd('/Partitions/Partition-Y/ResourceGroups/PartitionResourceGroup-Y/JDBCSystemResources/JDBC Data Source-Y/JDBCResource/JDBC Data Source-Y')
cmo.setName('JDBC Data Source-Y')

cd('/Partitions/Partition-Y/ResourceGroups/PartitionResourceGroup-Y/JDBCSystemResources/JDBC Data Source-Y/JDBCResource/JDBC Data Source-Y/JDBCDataSourceParams/JDBC Data Source-Y')
set('JNDINames',jarray.array([String('/jdbc/MyAppDS')], String))

cd('/Partitions/Partition-Y/ResourceGroups/PartitionResourceGroup-Y/JDBCSystemResources/JDBC Data Source-Y/JDBCResource/JDBC Data Source-Y')
cmo.setDatasourceType('GENERIC')

cd('/Partitions/Partition-Y/ResourceGroups/PartitionResourceGroup-Y/JDBCSystemResources/JDBC Data Source-Y/JDBCResource/JDBC Data Source-Y/JDBCDriverParams/JDBC Data Source-Y')
cmo.setUrl('jdbc:oracle:thin:@//someDBhost:1521/MyAppDS')
cmo.setDriverName('oracle.jdbc.OracleDriver')

cd('/Partitions/Partition-Y/ResourceGroups/PartitionResourceGroup-Y/JDBCSystemResources/JDBC Data Source-Y/JDBCResource/JDBC Data Source-Y/JDBCDriverParams/JDBC Data Source-Y/Properties/JDBC Data Source-Y')
cmo.createProperty('user')

cd('/Partitions/Partition-Y/ResourceGroups/PartitionResourceGroup-Y/JDBCSystemResources/JDBC Data Source-Y/JDBCResource/JDBC Data Source-Y/JDBCDriverParams/JDBC Data Source-Y/Properties/JDBC Data Source-Y/Properties/user')
cmo.setValue('nobodyIsPerfect')

cd('/Partitions/Partition-Y/ResourceGroups/PartitionResourceGroup-Y/JDBCSystemResources/JDBC Data Source-Y/JDBCResource/JDBC Data Source-Y/JDBCDataSourceParams/JDBC Data Source-Y')
```

The interesting fact about the two WLST scripts above is that they are almost identical. Datasource are created always in the same way. Scoping is achieved by selecting the appropriate root MBean (domain root, resource group, resource group template)

Persistent Stores as Resources

Before talking about messaging resources we need to make sure that the base resource for messaging – the persistent store – can be scoped to a resource group or resource group template. A persistent store is a pre-requisite resource which is needed for JMS message persistence. Such a store is required for a JMS server, SAF agent or path service. (figure 17-12).

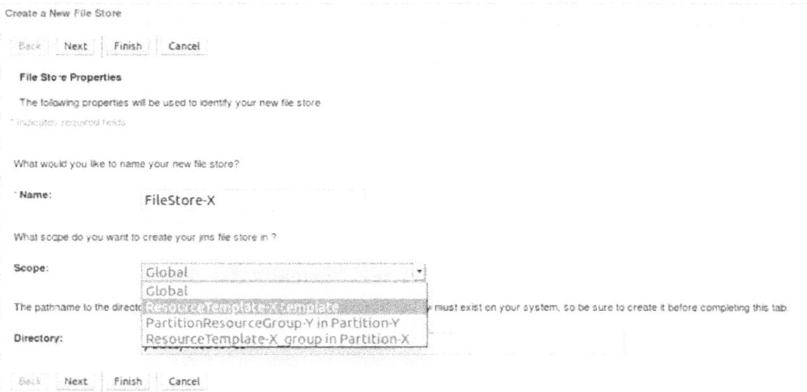

Figure 17-12: Create and scope a filestore

The persistent filestore can also be created using the following WLST script:

```
cd('/ResourceGroupTemplates/ResourceTemplate-X')
cmo.createFileStore('FileStore-X')

cd('/ResourceGroupTemplates/ResourceTemplate-X/FileStores/FileStore-X')
cmo.setSynchronousWritePolicy('Direct-Write')
cmo.setDirectory('/data/x_filestore')
```

The process to create a JDBC persistent store is very similar. The main difference is that a JDBC based persistent store needs an equally scoped datasource.

There are a number of rules for the usage of persistence stores:

- All services like JMS services or SAF agent must reference a persistent store with the same scope (e.g. defined as part of the same template or the same resource group). A null reference is not allowed.
- If a service, which needs a persistent store, is defined as part of a resource group template then the referenced store must also be part of the template. A store which is only scoped to a child instance of this template – a concrete resource group – cannot be referenced.
- Global services can only use global (domain level) persistent stores.

- A JDBC persistent store must reference a datasource with the same scope (e.g. defined as part of the same template or the same resource group). A null reference is not allowed.
- If a JDBC store is defined as part of a resource group template then the referenced datasource must also be part of this particular template. A datasource which is only scoped to a child instance of this template – a concrete resource group – cannot be referenced.

JMS based Messaging

WebLogic provides a complex JMS subsystem, which consists of many different MBeans. The main MBean is the JMSServer which is basically the container for all other JMS resources. Every WebLogic server can host multiple JMS server which consists of JMS system module resources. These artifacts are stored in the domain's config.xml file

All the configuration changes for the JMS will be stored to the config.xml repository and its sub-deployment module descriptor file. Every JMS system module can be defined via a name, its target to servers or cluster, and its related sub-deployments such as a queue or publisher/subscriber topics.

The JMS module is the base module that includes a connection factory as well as queue or topic. Based on your system's requirements, the connection factory needs to be made available for all servers in the domain. The queue, on the other hand, can be targeted to only a single JMS server.

We need to configure a subdeployment per JMS Module. Reasons for subdeployments in the JMS area include avoiding network traffic between JMS components, group connection factories, queues and topics and simplifies the migration.

A subdeployment is a mechanism by which JMS module like queues, topics, and connection factories) are grouped and targeted to a server resource such as JMS servers, server instances, SAF agents, or a cluster. So there would be two different subdeployments 'Default' is for a connection factory and the other is for resources within the JMS module can be the best practice.

It is outside of the scope of this book to look at all JMS artifacts in detail. Please refer to the WLST book for more details. In the same way like datasources and other resources, the definition of JMS components is very similar for domain level services and resource group or resource group template scoped services. Scoping for JMS is also done by selecting the appropriate root MBean for creation.

The following JMS resource can be scoped to resource groups:

- JMS servers
- Store-and-Forward (SAF) agents
- Path services
- Messaging bridges
- JMS system modules and JMS application modules
- JMS connection pools

Due to the complexity of the JMS subsystem, please refer to the Oracle documentation for details and current shortcuts and workarounds. The current list of shortcuts is expected to shrink with every new WebLogic version.

Example

In the first example we will create a JMS server and target it to a resource group template.

Similar to other resources, it is vital to select the correct scoping while creating the JMS server. In this example it will be targeted to our resource group template (figure 17-13).

Figure 17-13: Create and target a JMS server

In a second step the administrator has to configure the persistent store. Note that the Web-UI is smart enough to only offer the persistent stores with the correct scoping (figure 17-14).

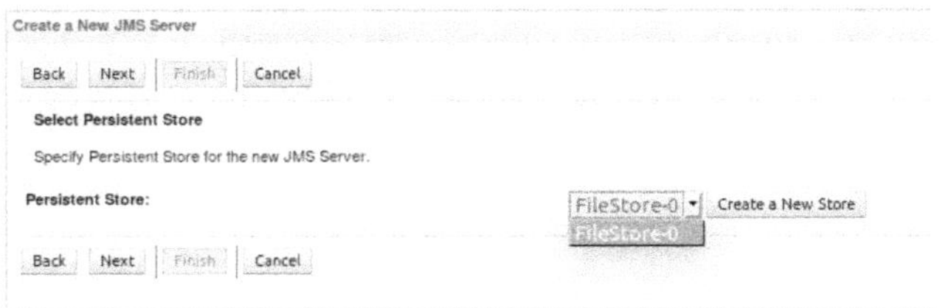

Figure 17-14: Select s persistent store with the correct scoping

Please note that WebLogic 12.2.x support a minimalistic approach and assumes default values wherever possible.

Doing the same using WLST:

```
cmo.createJMSServer('JMSServer-X')

cd('/ResourceGroupTemplates/ResourceTemplate-X/JMSServers/JMSServer-X')
```

Second example

For the second example, we will create a JMS module with a subdeployment and a queue. It will be targeted to our resource group template or to be precise to the JMS server in our resource group template defined in example one (figure 17-15).

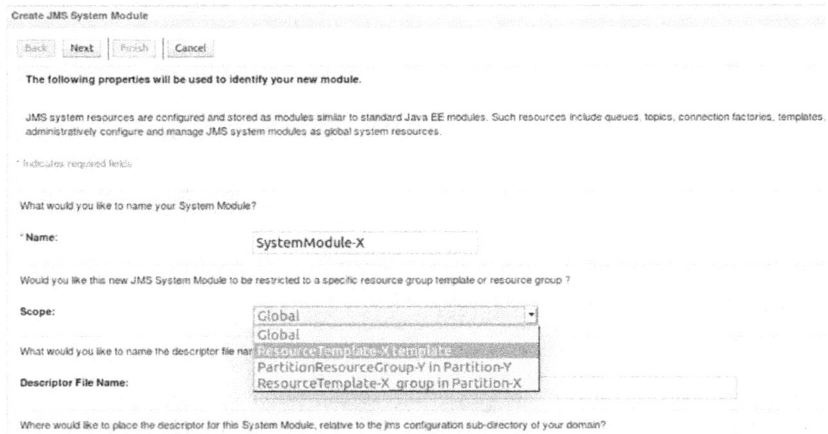

Figure 17-15: Create and target a new JMS module

The other steps are very similar to the "old-fashion" domain level definition of JMS resources. Target will be the JMS server and the queue will be targeted to a subdeployment which is part of the module.

Create the module and queue using WLST:

```
cmo.createJMSSystemResource('SystemModule-X')

cd('/ResourceGroupTemplates/ResourceTemplate-X/JMSSystemResources/SystemModule-X')
cmo.createSubDeployment('SubDepl_X')

cd('/ResourceGroupTemplates/ResourceTemplate-X/JMSSystemResources/SystemModule-
X/SubDeployments/SubDepl_X')
set('Targets',jarray.array([ObjectName('com.bea:ResourceGroupTemplate=ResourceTemplate-
X,Name=JMSServer-X,Type=JMSServer')], ObjectName))

cd('/ResourceGroupTemplates/ResourceTemplate-X/JMSSystemResources/SystemModule-
X/JMSResource/SystemModule-X')
cmo.createUniformDistributedQueue('DistributedQueue-X1')

cd('/ResourceGroupTemplates/ResourceTemplate-X/JMSSystemResources/SystemModule-
X/JMSResource/SystemModule-X/UniformDistributedQueues/DistributedQueue-X1')
cmo.setJNDIName('/jms/queue_x1')
cmo.setDefaultTargetingEnabled(true)
cmo.unSet('Template')
cmo.setUnitOfOrderRouting('Hash')
cmo.setIncompleteWorkExpirationTime(-1)
cmo.setInsertionPausedAtStartup(false)
cmo.setForwardDelay(-1)
cmo.setUnitOfWorkHandlingPolicy('PassThrough')
cmo.setMessagingPerformancePreference(25)
cmo.setSAFExportPolicy('All')
cmo.setProductionPausedAtStartup(false)
cmo.setResetDeliveryCountOnForward(true)
cmo.setDefaultUnitOfOrder(false)
cmo.setConsumptionPausedAtStartup(false)
cmo.setLoadBalancingPolicy('Round-Robin')
cmo.setAttachSender('supports')
```

There are many more JMS components like SAF agents, path services, JMS foreign servers for integration foreign JMS like IBM-MQ, JMS quota, many other JMS components like queues, connection factories, topics and many more; including bridge services.

For all of these components the scoping to resource group templates or (partition) resource groups is very similar to the examples shown above. For more details please consult the WLST book or the Oracle documentation.

Working with Emails

WebLogic Server includes the JavaMail API reference implementation of Sun Microsystems. This API enables applications to use the Internet Message Access Protocol (IMAP) and Simple Mail Transfer Protocol (SMTP)-capable mail servers on the internal or external network, depending on firewall and access permissions.

In WebLogic, you use WLST or JMX (or the Administration Console) to create a mail session instead of doing it in your own code, which configures a javax.mail.Session object and registers it in the WebLogic JNDI tree. Applications can then access the mail session from the JNDI provider.

Likewise, datasources or JMS components, the important aspect is the correct selection of the scope. When a new mail-session is created, the administrator can select the scope (figure 17-16).

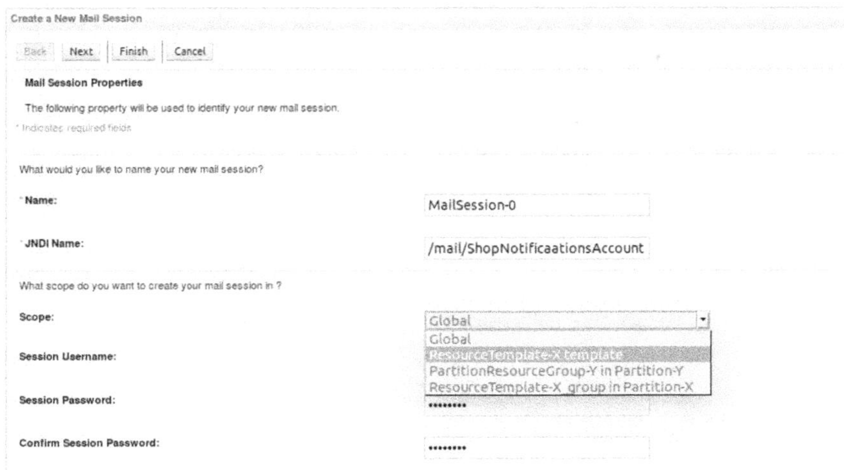

Figure 17-16: Creating a new mail session

After the mail session has been created and as for this example scoped to the resource group template, the mail session is automatically visible as part of the resource group and in our example also directly visible as service for partition "Partition_X" (figure 17-17).

Figure 17-17: Visibility of the new mail session

The mail session can of course also be created using WLST:

```
startEdit();

cd('/ResourceGroupTemplates/ResourceTemplate-X')
cmo.createMailSession('TestNotificationMailSession')

cd('/ResourceGroupTemplates/ResourceTemplate-X/MailSessions/TestNotificationMailSession')
cmo.setSessionUsername('martin')
cmo.setJNDIName('/mail/ShopNotificationsAccount')

properties = java.util.Properties();
properties.put('mail.to','test@multitenancybook.com');
properties.put('mail.from','author@multitenancybook.com');

properties.put('mail.transport.protocol','smtp');
properties.put('mail.smtp.host','mail.multitenancybook.com');
properties.put('mail.smtp.port','25');
properties.put('mail.smtp.user','username');
properties.put('mail.smtp.password','password');
cmo.setProperties(properties);

save();
```

Scoping mail sessions directly to resource groups or partition resource groups only requires to choose another root MBean, similar as discussed already for datasources.

Summary

Services are considered key resources and the most important services can already be scoped to a resource group or even a resource group template. More services will follow in future WebLogic versions.

The main idea of "WebLogic applications" consist in scoping the services to resource groups and embed these resource groups into partitions. This chapter provides an overview over the most important services. WebLogic in the version 12.2.1 already provides a few more like OSGI frameworks or WLDF diagnostics. We will look at WLDF diagnostics later in this book.

WebLogic has implemented an interesting and easy to understand way of creating and scoping resources. The main idea is that resources like datasource, mail-sessions, JMS artifacts and others are always created in the same way, regardless of their intended scope. The scope really depends on the root MBean where the resources are created. Note that the well-known configuration files for the services (like <domain>/config/jdbc/* or <domain>/config/jms/* are stored in different locations if these services are scoped to resource group templates or resource groups.

For the example above the filesystem for our resource group template looks like (figure 17-18).

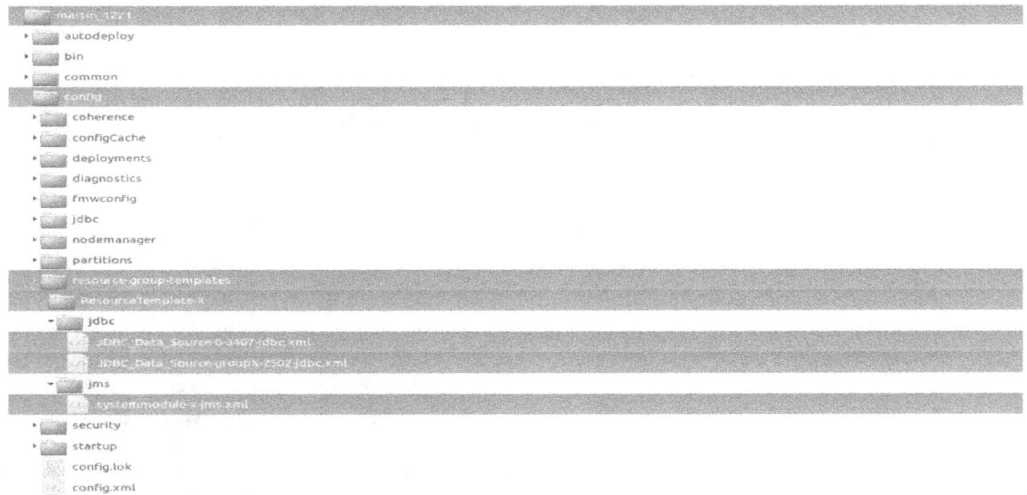

Figure 17-18: File system example for the resource group template

Please note that the jdbc and jms files are located under domain/config/resource-group-templates/name/* directories.

Adapting Resources to Partition Instances

CHAPTER 18

Problem Description

In the last chapter, we looked at the different resources that can be scoped to resource groups and resource group templates. The last chapter discussed the way scope these services. Concrete partition resource groups are nice and easy to configure, especially because the resources only have one instance. The resource group templates though have a problem that needs to be solved. Scoping to a resource group template has great advantages as the resource will be inherited automatically to all resource groups that are referencing this template. But this also reveals the shortcut that all tenants have exactly the same resource setup (figure 18-1).

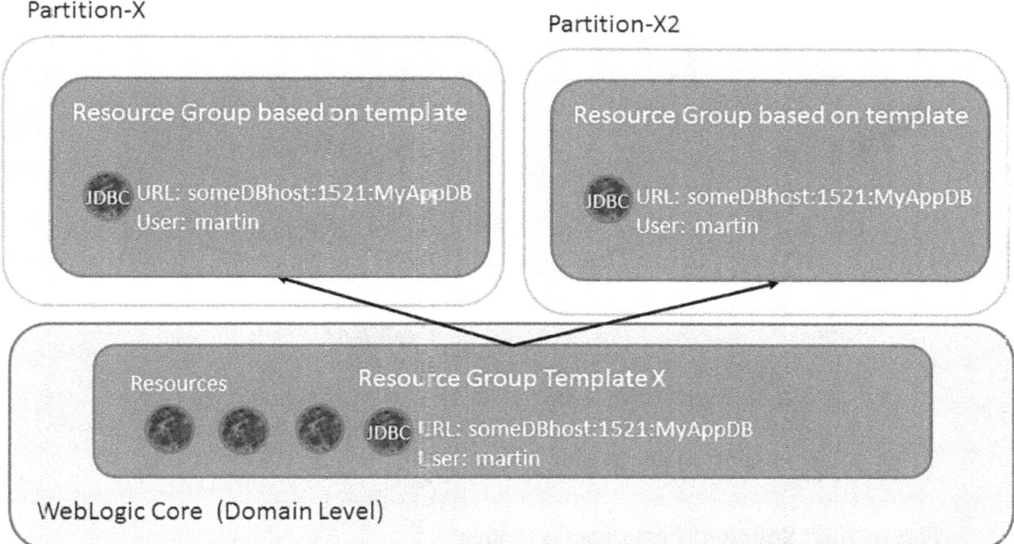

Figure 18-1: Problematic: Both partitions will use the same database URL and login

Consider the following scenario: One resource group template is defined at domain level and two partitions are based on this template. This means that both partitions inherit the same resources. This is what you want for a multitenant setup. The only difference is that both tenants will have their data stored in different databases or at least in different database schemas. So if the resource definition is just inherited, then both tenants will use the same setup and login.

It is vital for multi-tenant setup that all tenants have their individual data access. In many configurations the deployments and resources might be the same but the data content will be different. An example might be a pet food vs. shop for flowers. WebLogic solves this problem with resource overrides. There are two different ways of configuring resource overrides. This chapter will take a closer look at the definitions of MBean overrides. The second option – resource deployment plans – will be discussed in a later chapter.

Resource overrides are defined at partition level and can override inherited resource configurations from the resource group templates. In the example below the resource overrides change the database URL of the configured datasources (figure 18-2):

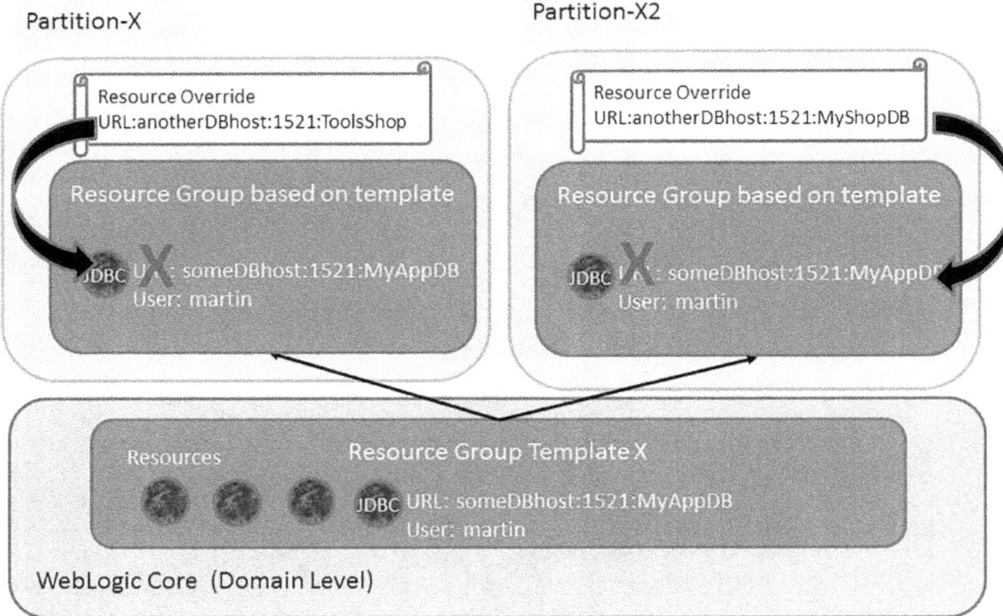

Figure 18-2: Solution: Resource Overrides

WebLogic offers a number of possibilities to override resource settings which have different priorities.

- Some of the resource attributes can be changed using partition level MBean override configurations.
- Resource deployment plans are a new concept of WLS 12.2.x which allow administrators to describe attributes in a XML file. This file can be loaded during partition startup and changes the resource attributes inherited from the resource group templates.
- Partition-specific application deployment plans.

Which override definition will be used in case of conflicting definitions?

If nothing else is provided, then the configuration from the config.xml and its outsourced files will be used. In case a resource deployment plan exists, these configuration have a higher priority and will be applied. If the same attribute is also configured as a MBean override, the MBean override has the highest priority.

MBean Overrides

WebLogic 12.2.1 offers a limited number of override MBeans, albeit it is very likely that this list will increase with 12.2.2 and beyond.

The following override MBeans are available:

- JDBCSystemResourceOverrideMBean
- JMSSystemResourceOverrideMBean
- ForeignServerOverrideMBean
- ForeignConnectionFactoryOverrideMBean
- ForeignDestinationOverrideMBean
- MailSessionOverrideMBean

Examples

The following example describes JDBC resource overrides. Note that the same principles (MBean location, MBean creation and more) also apply to the other override types (figure 18-3):

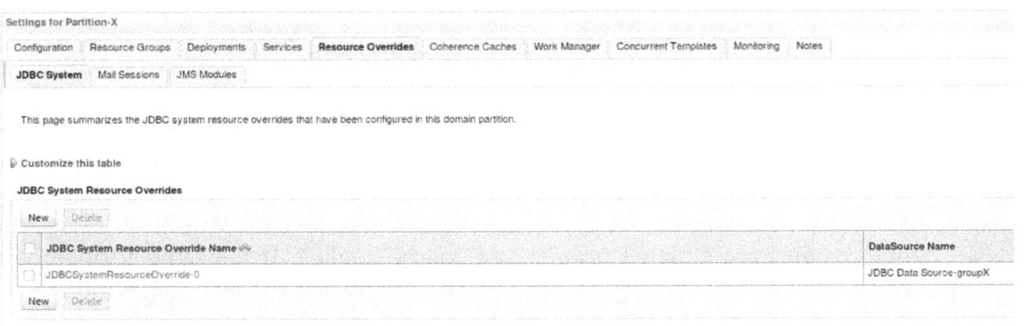

Figure 18-3: Partition level resource overrides

WLST example for creating a resource override

```
startEdit()
cd ('/Partitions/Partition-X')
cmo.createJDBCSystemResourceOverride('JDBCSystemResourceOverride-X')
cd ('JDBCSystemResourceOverrides/JDBCSystemResourceOverride-X')
cmo.setUser('myShopUser')
save()
```

Note that you need to change to the partition root MBean in order to create resource override MBeans.

By looking at the config.xml you can see that the override entries are created on partition level. Unfortunately WebLogic did not design a subtree like <overrides> for all resource overrides. Instead you will find a separate MBean on partition level for each override.

```
    <name>Partition-X</name>
    <resource-group>
      <name>ResourceTemplate-X_group</name>
      <resource-group-template>ResourceTemplate-X</resource-group-template>
    </resource-group>

    <jdbc-system-resource-override>
      <name>JDBCSystemResourceOverride-0</name>
      <data-source-name>JDBC Data Source-groupX</data-source-name>
      <url></url>
      <user>partition_x_user</user>
    </jdbc-system-resource-override>

    <mail-session-override>
      <name>MartinTenantMailOverride</name>
      <session-username>testShop</session-username>
```

```
</mail-session-override>

<default-target>VirtualTarget-X</default-target>
<available-target>VirtualTarget-X</available-target>
<realm>MyPartitionXRealm</realm>
<partition-id>4b882b3b-f416-4369-8862-6779aeefa9ff</partition-id>
<system-file-system>
  <root>/user_domains/martin_1221/partitions/Partition-X/system</root>
  <create-on-demand>true</create-on-demand>
  <preserved>true</preserved>
</system-file-system>

<jms-system-resource-override>
  <name>JMSOverride</name>
</jms-system-resource-override>
```

Multiple overrides of the same type will be created on the same level.

```
<name>Partition-X</name>
<resource-group>
  <name>ResourceTemplate-X_group</name>
  <resource-group-template>ResourceTemplate-X</resource-group-template>
</resource-group>
<jdbc-system-resource-override>
  <name>JDBCSystemResourceOverride-0</name>
  <data-source-name>JDBC Data Source-groupX</data-source-name>
  <url></url>
  <user>partition_x_user</user>
</jdbc-system-resource-override>
<jdbc-system-resource-override>
  <name>JDBCSystemResourceOverride-X</name>
  <data-source-name>JDBC Data Source-0</data-source-name>
  <url></url>
  <user>myShopUser</user>
</jdbc-system-resource-override>
...
```

Summary

Override resources solve a critical problem with resource group templates. In case that the resources are defined in the resource group template, they must be tailored and customized for each partition, based on this template

Resource overrides can be done using different technologies. This chapter looked at the MBean overrides which can be defined using WLST or using the WebLogic console. This way of configuring overrides is also the only way which does not need an external XML file like resource deployment plans or partition deployment plans.

Partitions and System Resources

CHAPTER

Resources are Key

Partitions are the new WebLogic isolation concept that host applications and services. So the major part of all resources used by WebLogic will be used by different partitions and they will compete against each other for those resources. It is therefore key for any administration concept to define how the different partitions share the available resources and how partitions get limited to not hijack all resources they can get ahold of.

There are two major categories of resources that have to be controlled. I prefer to call them WebLogic internal and WebLogic external resources, albeit this is not an official Oracle terminology.

WebLogic external resources

With external resources, I am referring to all resources which WebLogic does not control by itself. This group contains for example java heap space, JVM thread limits, CPU cycles, file descriptors and more. Most of these resources have already been discussed as they can be controlled by the new WebLogic concept *"Resource Manager"*.

WebLogic internal resources

Internal resources are all resources WebLogic controls by itself. The main concept WebLogic offers since a long time are the so called "*WorkManagers*" in WebLogic which control thread pools.

This chapter discusses these two resource categories and what WebLogic offers on partition level to control these resources.

Partition Resource Manager

The technology behind the resource isolation feature is called *Resource Manager*. Even though the configuration is part of the WebLogic configuration, this is all done within the JVM. The resources which can be controlled are mainly file descriptors, CPU and memory.

During the creation of a resource manager it is a very important decision which scope and visibility this resource manager should have. It is possible to scope it globally or locally to a partition. "Global" scope does not mean that it applies to the complete WebLogic server. This means that these resource managers are defined on domain level and can be shared/used by multiple partitions. Each partition will be able to reference such a global resource manager (figure 19-1).

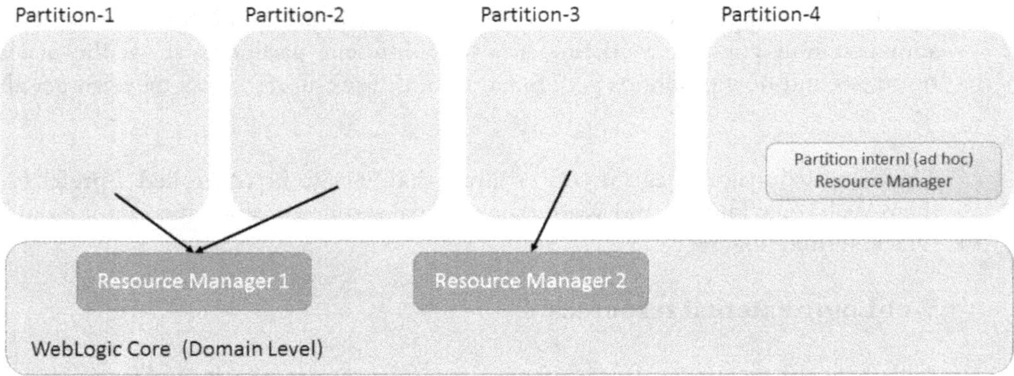

Figure 19-1: Scoping of resource managers

Now we will look at different uses cases for the two different types of resource managers. WebLogic platform admins who are managing a WebLogic multitenancy domain know about the general capacity of the clusters in that domain. For this domain they would create a set of reusable resource managers. When they need to create a new partition, they would choose a resource manager already available in the domain. They may have high, medium, and low resource managers to reflect typical resource usage patterns. Each of these resource managers would be in the domain – also called "global to a domain"

Another pattern is to define the resource manager attributes inside a single partition. This would be useful for a more ad-hoc pattern of creating partitions. The admin would ask what the partition needs, and then define the resource manager attributes for the partition. This should be part of the partition configuration itself, and not something separate. Another difference is that this resource manager will also be exported/imported with the partition, whereas the "global" ones will not.

Please also refer to chapter 9 where resource manager and JVM isolation were already discussed in detail. This chapter will only add and summarize partition scoped resource manager details and will not consider the global resource managers.

Embedded resource managers which will not be shared between partitions. The resource manager defined in the following WLST script is scoped to a partition and therefore in the config.xml also configured as part of the partition.

Using WLST this resource manager can be configured like this:

```
cd('/Partitions/TestPartition')
cmo.createResourceManager('MartinTestPartitionResourceManager')
```

Now examine the config.xml of your domain. You will not find it as part of the global resource-management. You will find it defined as part of the partition!

```
    <name>TestPartition</name>
    <resource-group>
      <name>default</name>
    </resource-group>
    <available-target>VirtualTarget-0</available-target>
    <partition-id>8389f682-1961-4c0e-875c-ddd2b44957f4</partition-id>
     <resource-manager>
       <name>MartinTestPartitionResourceManager</name>
     </resource-manager>
    <system-file-system>

<root>/opt/development/wls_beta/12_2_1/user_projects/domains/test_mt/partitions/TestPartition/system<
/root>
      <create-on-demand>true</create-on-demand>
      <preserved>true</preserved>
    </system-file-system>
```

In opposite to the embedded resource manager, the domain defined resource managers are pretty much useless without partitions referencing them. The partition configuration section offers a way for a partition to reference a domain level resource manager

Using WLST to create a resource manager reference

```
cd('/Partitions/Partition-0')
cmo.setResourceManagerRef(getMBean('/ResourceManagement/test_mt/ResourceManagers/MartinTestResourceMa
nager'))
```

After the reference has been created, this is also reflected in the config.xml through an additional XML tag called <resource-manager-ref>

```
    <name>MyTestPartitionWithGlobalResourceManager</name>
    <resource-group>
      <name>ResourceTemplate-0_group</name>
      <resource-group-template>ResourceTemplate-0</resource-group-template>
    </resource-group>
    <available-target></available-target>
    <partition-id>afe830fd-fa98-4756-beba-d995602657ac</partition-id>
    <resource-manager-ref>MartinTestResourceManager</resource-manager-ref>
    <system-file-system>
      <root>/opt/development/wls_beta/12_2_1/user_projects/domains/test_mt/partitions/Partition-
0/system</root>
      <create-on-demand>true</create-on-demand>
      <preserved>true</preserved>
    </system-file-system>
```

Unfortunately, WebLogic 12.2.1 does not support both types of resource managers for the same partition. If a partition has a partition scoped resource manager and the administrator adds a reference to a domain wide resource manager, the partition scoped resource manager has to be destroyed first.

Example in WLST:

```
cd('/Partitions/TestPartition')
cmo.destroyResourceManager(getMBean('/Partitions/TestPartition/ResourceManagers/MartinTestPartitionRe
sourceManager'))
cmo.setResourceManagerRef(getMBean('/ResourceManagement/test_mt/ResourceManagers/MartinTestResourceMa
nager'))
```

For more details about resource management please refer to chapter 9.

Partition WorkManager

WebLogic internally organizes its main resource – threads – in work managers. Each work manager owns on individual pool of threads. WebLogic already has a large number of different work manager which were either globally scoped (normal case) or application scoped (defined in the EAR components deployment descriptor). Now a new category has been added to WebLogic, a partition scoped work manager.

A work manager consist of different configuration items. In order to restrict, organize, control or manage work you need to define the components of a work manager. WebLogic offers the following components for work managers:

Constraints

- Minimum threads constraint
- Maximum threads constraint
- Capacity constraint

Request components:

- Fair share request class
- Response time request class
- Context request class

A constraint defines the minimum or maximum numbers of threads or the total number of requests. The max threads constraint defines the maximum number of concurrent requests allowed. The minimum threads constraint ensures that the server has always allocated at least this number of threads. The capacity constraint causes the server to reject requests when it has reached its capacity.

Request classes define the way WebLogic allocates threads to requests. WebLogic offers a number of different request classes out of the box. The "fair share request class" defines the average time a thread has been used. The "response time request class" defines the requested response time in milliseconds. This value is not applied to each request but to an average. WebLogic also offers a context request class which allows the administrator to specify context based restrictions dependent e.g. on the current user or group (figure 19-2).

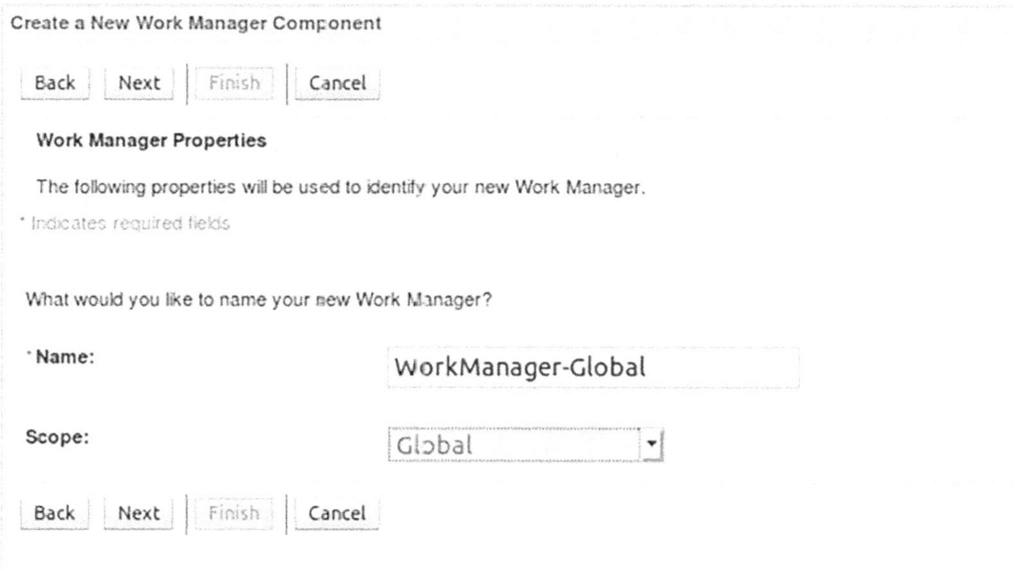

Figure 19-2: Creating a global workmanager

Especially note that you need to select the scope "Global" !

The following WLST script can be used for that:

```
startEdit()

# create work manager domain global
cd('/SelfTuning/martin_1221')
cmo.createWorkManager('WorkManager-Global')

# set target
cd('/SelfTuning/martin_1221/WorkManagers/WorkManager-Global')
set('Targets',jarray.array([ObjectName('com.bea:Name=AdminServer,Type=Server')], ObjectName))
```

On WLST level it is NOT needed to select the scope "Global". This is done automatically as you create the work manager on the domain configuration root level.

Example script to create a new global work manager with max threads and capacity element:

```
# Create a GLOBAL WorkManager
#****************************
def createWorkManager(maxthreads, capacitycount):
    try:
        edit()
        startEdit()

        # change to the domain selftuning instance
        cd('/SelfTuning/'+domainName)

        # create a maxthreads contraint instance
        cmo.createMaxThreadsConstraint('testMaxThreads')
        cd('/SelfTuning/'+domainName+'/MaxThreadsConstraints/testMaxThreads')
        # set count
        cmo.setCount(maxthreads)
        set('Targets',jarray.array([ObjectName('com.bea:Name=MartinTest_Cluster,Type=Cluster')],
            ObjectName))

        # change to the domain selftuning instance
        cd('/SelfTuning/'+domainName)

        # create capacity instance
        cmo.createCapacity('testCapacity')
        cd('Capacities/testCapacity')
        set('Count',capacitycount)
        set('Notes','Defining a capacity instance')
        set('Targets',jarray.array([ObjectName('com.bea:Name=MartinTest_Cluster,Type=Cluster')],
            ObjectName))

        # now create a WorkManager
        cd('/SelfTuning/'+domainName)
        myWorkManager = cmo.createWorkManager('myTestWorkManager')
        cd('/SelfTuning/'+domainName+'/WorkManagers/myTestWorkManager')
        set('Targets',jarray.array([ObjectName('com.bea:Name=MartinTest_Cluster,Type=Cluster')],
            ObjectName))

        # set the maxthreads attribute to the created instance
        cmo.setMaxThreadsConstraint(getMBean('/SelfTuning/'+domainName+
                                    '/MaxThreadsConstraints/testMaxThreads'))
        # set the capacity attribute to the created instance
        cmo.setCapacity(getMBean('/SelfTuning/'+domainName+'/Capacities/testCapacity'))

        save()
        activate()
    except Exception, e:
        print 'Error in script:', e
```

Global WorkManager and applications

An application uses a globally defined work manager as a template. Each application creates its own instance to handle and separate the work associated with this application from the work of other applications. This separation is used to handle traffic directed to two applications that are using the same dispatch policy. Handling each application's work separately, allows an application to be shut down without affecting the thread management of another application. Although each application implements its own work manager instance, the underlying components are shared.

The misleading and confusing aspect on this is, if you are creating a global work manager, WebLogic creates a different (different ObjectName !) MBean for each application and you can see all those MBeans in the runtime MBean tree.

NOTE if the new work manager is not named "default", then this WorkManager will not be used at all unless it is configured in the deployment descriptor (policy overwrite) that this WorkManager is to be used. If you create multiple global work manager, then you will find multiple work manager MBeans underneath each application runtime MBean. This will make a qualified monitoring difficult and confusing.

Partition scoped WorkManager

WebLogic has added support for partition scoped work managers. Every work manager can be created and scoped to a partition (figure 19-3).

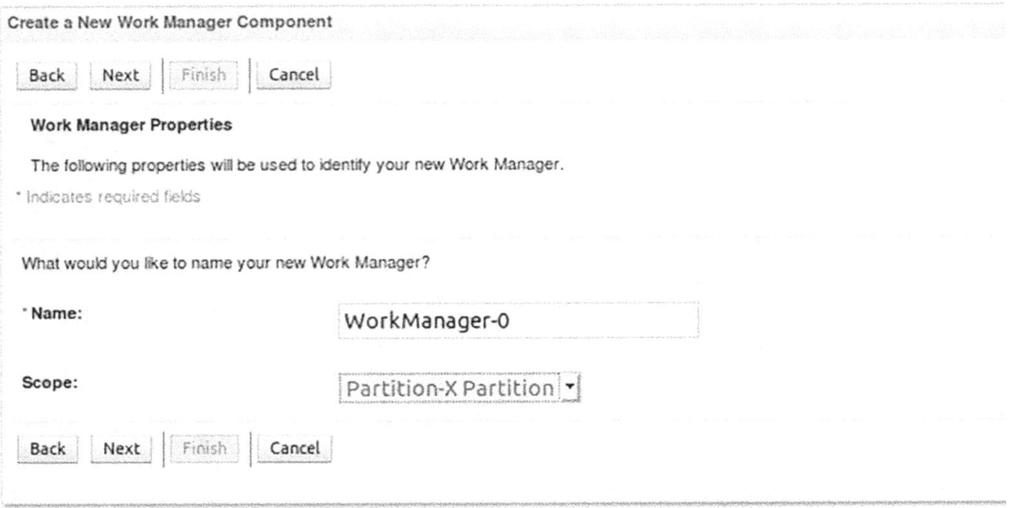

Figure 19-3: Create a partition scoped work manager.

Note that you need to select the partition as scope and only one partition can be selected. A partition scoped work manager cannot be shared by multiple partitions.

Also note that you cannot target this work manager. This work manager will automatically inherit the partition targeting (figure 19-4).

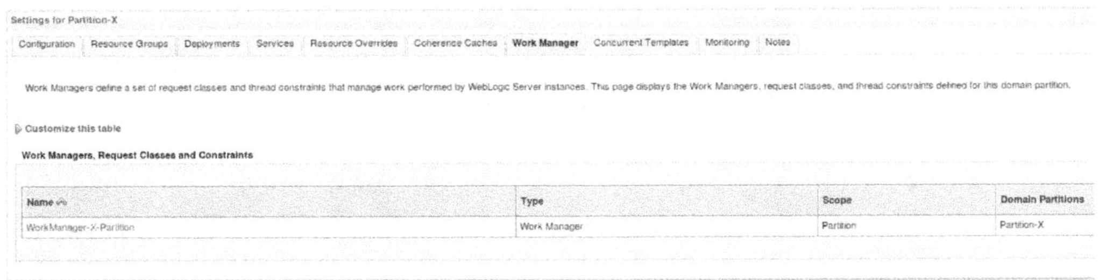

Figure 19-4: Visibility on partition level

After creation this new work manager will be visible at partition level by selecting the "Work Manager" tab. It is possible to create multiple work managers and constraints for a partition (figure 19-5).

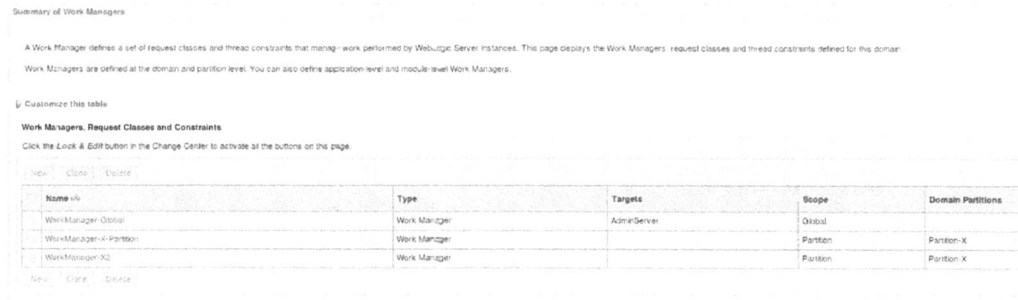

Figure 19-5: Global work manager list

In the list of work managers you can see all available work manager and their scope.

The same can be done using WLST:

```
cd('/Partitions/Partition-X/SelfTuning/Partition-X')
cmo.createWorkManager('WorkManager-X-Partition')
cmo.createWorkManager('WorkManager-X2')
```

The very important point is, that the workmanager will created on partition level and not – like the global work manager – on domain configuration level. This automatically defines the scoping.

The config.xml of WebLogic also reflects the two different resource manager types clearly:

```
  <name>martin_1221</name>
  <domain-version>12.2.1.0.0</domain-version>
...
  <self-tuning>
     <work-manager>
       <name>WorkManager-Global</name>
       <target>AdminServer</target>
     </work-manager>
  </self-tuning>
...
  <partition>
    <name>Partition-X</name>
    <resource-group>
      <name>default</name>
    </resource-group>
    <default-target>VirtualTarget-X</default-target>
    <available-target>VirtualTarget-X</available-target>
    <self-tuning>
       <work-manager>
         <name>WorkManager-X-Partition</name>
       </work-manager>
       <work-manager>
         <name>WorkManager-X2</name>
       </work-manager>
    </self-tuning>
```

```
    <realm>MyPartitionXRealm</realm>
    <partition-id>2ae403ba-9917-44cf-a862-d4c9cd61c6cc</partition-id>
    <primary-identity-domain>idd_x</primary-identity-domain>
    <data-source-for-job-scheduler xsi:nil="true"></data-source-for-job-scheduler>
    <job-scheduler-table-name>WEBLOGIC_TIMERS</job-scheduler-table-name>
    <system-file-system>
      <root>/opt/development/wls/wls1221/user_domains/martin_1221/partitions/Partition-
X/system</root>
      <create-on-demand>true</create-on-demand>
      <preserved>true</preserved>
    </system-file-system>
  </partition>
  ...
```

As you can see from the above domain layout, the work manager is embedded into the partition and can therefore be used only by this partition.

Shared Partition WorkManager

WebLogic has also added support for shared, partition scoped work manager. These work manager can be created and shared between multiple partitions, but cannot be used by applications running outside of a partition.

The concept is basically a mixture of both. These work managers will be created on domain level, but marked as a work manager that can only be used by partitions. On partition level a partition can be assigned to this work manager.

Other than the embedded partition work manager, each partition can have none or one shared partition manager. It is not possible to assign a partition to multiple shared partition work managers (figure 19-6).

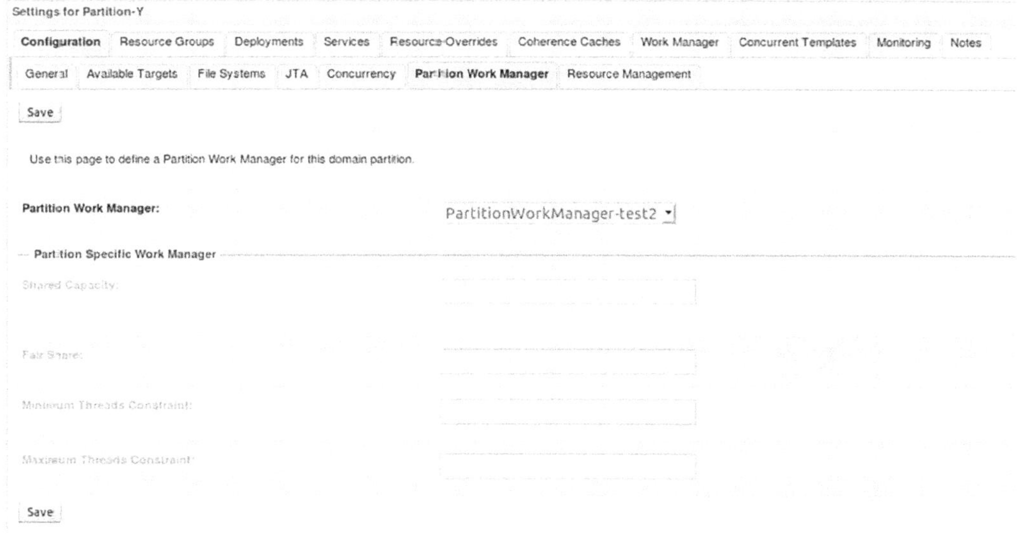

Figure 19-6: Assigning a partition t a shared partition workmanager

In the WebLogic console these shared partition work managers have their own section, where all these work managers and their associated partitions can be seen (figure 19-7).

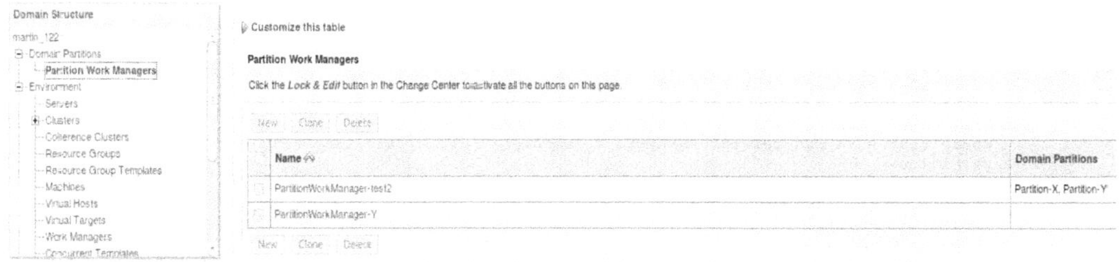

Figure 19-7: Shared Partition WorkManager section

The following WLST script can be used to create a shared partition work manager and assign two partitions to it:

```
startEdit()

# create partition work manager
cmo.createPartitionWorkManager('PartitionWorkManager-test2')

# assign first partition
cd('/Partitions/Partition-X')
cmo.destroyPartitionWorkManager(None)
cmo.setPartitionWorkManagerRef(getMBean('/PartitionWorkManagers/PartitionWorkManager-test2'))
```

```
# assign second partition
cd('/Partitions/Partition-Y')
cmo.destroyPartitionWorkManager(None)
cmo.setPartitionWorkManagerRef(getMBean('/PartitionWorkManagers/PartitionWorkManager-test2'))
```

In the following domain layout (config.xml) you can see the differences between a global work manager, a partition embedded and a shared partition work manager:

```
...
  <self-tuning>
    <work-manager>
      <name>WorkManager-Global</name>
      <target>AdminServer</target>
    </work-manager>
  </self-tuning>
...
  <partition>
    <name>Partition-X</name>
    <resource-group>
      <name>default</name>
    </resource-group>
    <default-target>VirtualTarget-X</default-target>
    <available-target>VirtualTarget-X</available-target>
    <self-tuning>
      <work-manager>
        <name>WorkManager-X-Partition</name>
      </work-manager>
      <work-manager>
        <name>WorkManager-X2</name>
      </work-manager>
    </self-tuning>
    <realm>MyPartitionXRealm</realm>
    <partition-id>2ae403ba-9917-44cf-a862-d4c9cd61c6cc</partition-id>
    <primary-identity-domain>idd_x</primary-identity-domain>
    <data-source-for-job-scheduler xsi:nil="true"></data-source-for-job-scheduler>
    <job-scheduler-table-name>WEBLOGIC_TIMERS</job-scheduler-table-name>
    <system-file-system>
      <root>/opt/development/wls/wls1221/user_domains/martin_1221/partitions/Partition-
X/system</root>
      <create-on-demand>true</create-on-demand>
      <preserved>true</preserved>
    </system-file-system>
    <partition-work-manager-ref>PartitionWorkManager-test2</partition-work-manager-ref>
  </partition>
  <partition>
    <name>Partition-Y</name>
    <resource-group>
      <name>default</name>
    </resource-group>
    <default-target>VirtualTarget-Y</default-target>
    <available-target>VirtualTarget-Y</available-target>
    <realm>MyPartitionYRealm</realm>
    <partition-id>58eec675-0950-4760-a5f4-1d732c67b1c4</partition-id>
    <primary-identity-domain>idd_y</primary-identity-domain>
    <data-source-for-job-scheduler xsi:nil="true"></data-source-for-job-scheduler>
    <job-scheduler-table-name>WEBLOGIC_TIMERS</job-scheduler-table-name>
    <system-file-system>
      <root>/opt/development/wls/wls1221/user_domains/martin_1221/partitions/Partition-
Y/system</root>
      <create-on-demand>true</create-on-demand>
      <preserved>true</preserved>
    </system-file-system>
    <partition-work-manager-ref>PartitionWorkManager-test2</partition-work-manager-ref>
  </partition>
...
  <partition-work-manager>
    <name>PartitionWorkManager-Y</name>
  </partition-work-manager>
  <partition-work-manager>
    <name>PartitionWorkManager-test2</name>
  </partition-work-manager>
```

The sections marked in bold in this domain layout are the last discussed shared partition work managers and the reference to them from the partition (<partition-work-manager-ref>)

Shared Partition vs. Embedded WorkManager

Administrators need to think carefully which of the work manager model they want to use. Both have their disadvantages and advantages.

Embedded partition work managers are only usable within one partition. These partition managers in return will be included in the partition import and export. This means that work manager is always available and will always have the same values. So this model shall be used if the partition has a static resource model in all environments and if this partition does not need to share a work manager with other partitions.

Shared partition work manager have a different nature. Note though that shared does not mean that they MUST be shared by different partitions. It is of course also possible to define one shared partition work manager for EACH partition. As the partition only references this work manager, this also implies that this work manager definition must pre-exist in all domains for importing such a partition. On the other had this provides the administrator with a great flexibility to define different resource requirements for this partition in different environments (domains) by providing the same shared partition work manager (same name !) in all domains. But with a potentially different configuration.

Different WorkManagers

WebLogic now supports many different types of work managers:

- Global workmanager
- Default global workmanager
- Application scoped work manager
- Embedded partition work manager
- Shared partition work manager

WorkManager vs. ResourceManager

Resource Managers are similar to WebLogic work managers, but configured and operated far below on the level of the Java virtual machine (JVM).

Work managers have been around for a long time in WebLogic and are heavily used to provide many different pools of threads for different purposes. Each work manager can be configured with different policies like maximum and minimum amount of threads and more. But work manager expect that whenever they need they can get more threads from the Java virtual machine.

The last assumption – to get more threads from the JVM when needed – is the assumption that endangers multi-tenant environments. The new resource manager fills this gap and controls physically on JVM level how many threads a partition can allocate.

On domain and also on partition level many work managers can be defined. Applications can have their own work manager or share a platform or default workmanager. Only by using work managers it is possible to limit the maximum amount of threads used. This can easily be changed, e.g. by deploying an application with its own work manager.

So by only using work managers a hard thread limit cannot be guaranteed. ResourceManager can now jump in and define a hard limit for a partition on JVM level. Regardless how many work mangers will be defined within a partition, together they cannot utilize more threads than the ResourceManager will allow them to allocate.

Summary

Partitions are using resources on different levels. All resources can be controlled by different managers. On the JVM level, the new resource manager controls the physical resources that can be allocated. The available physical resources can then be used by the partition. Threads are a special resource as threads control the amount of parallel activities in the partition. WebLogic has a sophisticated thread management on WebLogic level called "work manager". Both managers work together to control resources on all levels.

Deploying Applications to Partitions

CHAPTER

Overview

The last chapters discussed resources that can be scoped to domain or partition level. For partitions resource overrides are supported to adapt resources from resource group templates to a specific partition instances. Resources are required to run applications. After resources have been configured the administrators can deploy applications to a partition. Application deployment in WebLogic is a rather complicated process with many different options, starting from staging options up to application deployment plans.

This chapter focus on application deployments to partitions and assumes that the reader has already a solid understanding of WebLogic application deployment. We will discuss standard application deployment to partition and customized deployments using a deployment plan on application level. A special deployment case are resource adapters, because WebLogic supports standalone deployments of resource adaptors also with partition scope.

Application deployment was always a rather complicated task and WebLogic supports a number of different technologies like "side-to-side" deployment, application deployment plans and more. For more details please consult the Oracle documentation.

General deployment aspects

Application deployment always was the process of deploying applications (EARs, WARs, EJBJars) or components like libraries or RARs to a WebLogic domain. It was possible to select the target of these deployments. Targets could be managed-servers or clusters of managed-servers. All deployments were always scoped to domain level, as it was the only available option.

With the new multitenancy technologies, application deployment gets more options. So it is up to the administrator choose the appropriate scope for the deployment of an application.

Using the WLS console, deployment works like any other deployment, except that you need to select the scope (figure 20-1):

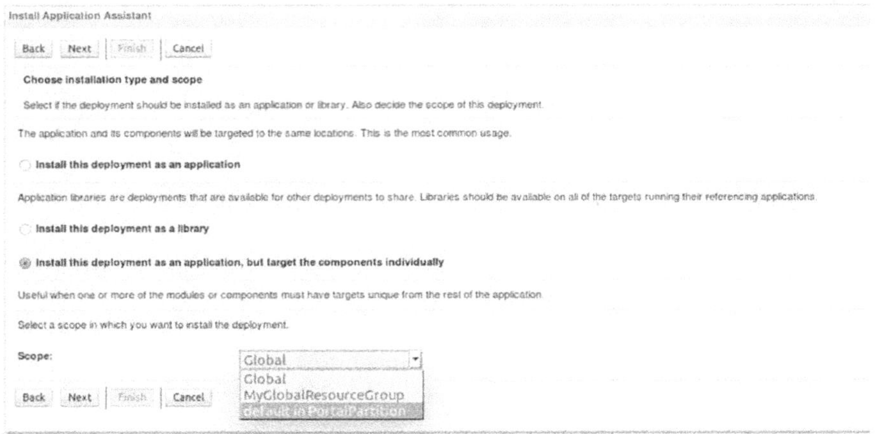

Figure 20-1: Deployment using the WLS console

Possible deployment scopes in WebLogic 12.21 and above

Scope	Description
Global or domain level	Same as deployment to WLS 12.1.3 or earlier versions. This is a standard deployment without using any special multi-tenancy features
Resource group on domain level	Similar to domain level deployment. The difference is that due to its scope to a global resource group it is possible that this resource group can be referenced by multiple partitions
Resource group template level	Also a deployment on domain level but with a significant difference! As resource group templates do not have a target and also no concrete instances, there will never be a real instance of this deployment at domain level. Partitions based on this template will also inherit these deployments.
Resource group within a partition	This deployment is the only deployment which is limited to exactly one partition. It is the only deployment done directly at partition and not at domain level. There will also be one and only one instance of this application.

Deployments in WebLogic can have a number of options. The following sections assume that readers are familiar with application deployment plans. The focus of this chapter is on the scoping of applications. Other deployment options like deployment order or others are not used in order to keep the examples simple.

The rest of the chapter will only use the WLST scripting language in order to perform deployments. This is the best and recommended way. I do not recommend to use the WLS console unless it is really for a one-time and then throw-away test only. The main reason is that deployments using scripts can be repeated and can be kept in a version control system. It is also possible for a development group to develop deployment scripts and hand them over to operations.

Deploying applications to resource group templates

Deploying applications to resource group template is actually the most powerful way in order to work with applications and multitenancy. It is the only deployment method which will actually create multiple instances of these applications. One instance in each partition which is based on this resource group template will be created. Albeit the resource group template – and therefore also the deployment – is scoped to domain level, there will never be a real instance of this deployment at domain level.

Benefits of this deployment type:

- One time deployment but update of all partitions based on this template.
- Easy way in order to keep application versions in different partition in sync.

Disadvantages of this deployment type:

- Different partitions cannot run different versions of the application.
- Application will be deployed one time. If the application needs to be adapted to the different partitions, then an own application deployment plan PER partition is required.

In order to deploy an application to a resource group template you need to specify a number of attributes to the "deploy" function in WLST. You need to specify the resource group template name, the application name, the path to the application's binary and – if needed – the path to a deployment plan. Very important for deployments to a resource group template is, that you must not specify targets.

In order to give the reader an idea about the different options that can be used for a deployment, the following help information is provided. This can always be retrieved by using "help('deploy')" in WLST:

```
Description:
Deploys an application to a WebLogic Server instance. The deploy command returns a WLSTProgress
object that you can access to check the status of the command. Note that if there is an edit session
in progress, the deploy command does not block user interaction until the deployment is complete.

Syntax:

deploy(appName, path, [targets], [stageMode], [planPath], [resourceGroup], [resourceGroupTemplate],
[partition], [options])
- appName = Name of the application or standalone J2EE module to be  deployed.

- path = Name of the application directory, archive file, or root of  the exploded archive directory
to be deployed.

- targets = Optional. Comma-separated list of the targets. Each target  may be qualified with a J2EE
module name (for example, module1@server1) enabling you to deploy different modules of the
application archive on different servers. This argument defaults to the server to which WLST is
currently connected.

- stageMode = Optional. Staging mode for the application you are deploying. Valid values are stage,
nostage, and external_stage. This argument defaults to null.

- planPath = Optional. Name of the deployment plan file. The filename can be absolute or relative to
the application directory. This argument defaults to the plan/plan.xml file in the application
directory, if one exists.

- resourceGroup = Optional. Name of the resource group this deployment is scoped to. Specify a
resource group when deploying to a partition resource group or domain resource group. The specified
resource group needs to be pre-existed before executing the deployment command.

- resourceGroupTemplate = Optional. Name of the resource group template this deployment is scoped to.
The specified resource group template needs to exist before executing the deployment command.

- partition = Optional. Name of the partition this deployment is scoped to. The partition name will
be derived from the current invocation context if not specified. The specified partition need to be
pre-existed before executing the deployment command.

- options = Optional. Comma-separated list of deployment options, specified as name-value pairs.
Valid options include:
o altDD = Location of the alternate application deployment descriptor on the admin server.

 o altWlsDD = Location of the alternate WebLogic application deployment descriptor on the admin
server.

 o archiveVersion = Archive version number.

 o block = (true|false) Boolean value specifying whether WLST should block user interaction until the
command completes.

 o clusterDeploymentTimeout = Time, in milliseconds, granted for a cluster deployment task on this
application.

 o createPlan = (true|false) Boolean value indicating that user would like to create a default plan.
This option defaults to false.

 o defaultSubmoduleTargets = (true|false) Boolean value indicating that targeting for any JMS
submodules should be derived by the system.

 o deploymentPrincipalName = String value specifying the principal for deploying the file or archive
during server starts (static deployment; it does not effect the current deployment task). Make sure
the user exists. This option adds deployment-principal-name to the app-deployment element in the
config.xml file.

 o forceUndeployTimeout = Time (in seconds) to wait for in-flight work to complete before undeploying
the application.
```

```
 o gracefulIgnoreSessions = (true|false) Boolean value specifying whether the graceful production to
Admin mode operation should ignore pending HTTP sessions. This option defaults to false and only
applies if gracefulProductionToAdmin is set to true.

 o gracefulProductionToAdmin = (true|false) Boolean value specifying whether the production to Admin
mode operation should be graceful. This option defaults to false.

 o libImplVersion = Implementation version of the library, if it is not present in the manifest.

 o libraryModule = (true|false) Boolean value specifying whether the module is a library module. This
option defaults to false.

 o libSpecVersion = Specification version of the library, if it  is not present in the manifest.

 o planVersion = Plan version number.

 o retireGracefully = (true|false) Retirement policy to gracefully retire an application only after
it has completed all in-flight work. This policy is only meaningful for stop and redeploy operations
and is mutually exclusive to the retire timeout policy.

 o retireTimeout = Time (in seconds) WLST waits before retiring an application that has been replaced
with a newer version. This option default to -1, which specifies graceful timeout.

 o rmiGracePeriod = Time (in seconds) WLST waits for RMI requests before retiring an application that
has been replaced with a newer version.

 o securityModel = Security model. Valid values include: DDOnly, CustomRoles, CustomRolesAndPolicy,
and Advanced.

 o securityValidationEnabled = (true|false) Boolean value specifying whether security validation is
enabled.

 o subModuleTargets = Submodule level targets for JMS modules. For example,
 submod@mod-jms.xml@target | submoduleName@target.

 o adminMode = (true|false) Boolean value specifying whether to start the Web application with
restricted access. This option defaults to false.

 o timeout = Time (in milliseconds) that WLST waits for the deployment process to complete before
canceling the operation. A value of 0 indicates that the operation will not time out. This argument
defaults to 300,000 ms (or 5 minutes).

 o upload = (true|false) Boolean value specifying whether the application files are uploaded to the
WebLogic Server Administration Server's upload directory prior to deployment. Use this option when
you are on a different machine from the Administration Server and you cannot copy the deployment
files by other means. This option defaults to false.

 o remote = (true|false) Boolean value specifying whether the operation will be remote from the file
system that contains the source. Use this option when you are on a different machine from the
dministration Server and the deployment files are already at the specified location where the
Administration Server is located. This option defaults to false.

 o deploymentOrder = deployment order in Integer. Specify the deployment order of the application.
The application with the lowest deployment order value is deployed first.

 o versionIdentifier = Version identifier.

 o planStageMode = Staging mode for the deployment plan. Valid values are stage, nostage, and
```

There are a number of related WLST functions like "redeploy" or "undeploy" that have a very similar set of arguments and options.

The second important WLST function is used in order to distribute the application to the referencing partitions. This is done by using the function "distributeApplication"

```
Description:
```

```
Copies the deployment bundle to the specified targets. The deployment bundle includes module,
configuration data, and any additional generated code. The distributeApplication command does not
start deployment.

Syntax:


distributeApplication(appPath, [planPath], [targets], [resourceGroup], [resourceGroupTemplate],
[partition], [options])
- appPath = Name of the archive file or root of the exploded archive directory to be deployed.

- planPath = Optional. Name of the deployment plan file. The filename can be absolute or relative to
the application directory. This argument defaults to the plan/plan.xml file in the application
directory, if one exists.

- targets = Optional. Comma-separated list of the targets. Each target may be qualified with a J2EE
module name (for example, module1@server1) enabling you to deploy different modules of the
application archive on different servers. This argument defaults to the server to which WLST is
currently connected.

- resourceGroup = Optional. Name of the resource group this deployment is scoped to. Specify a
resource group when deploying to a partition resource group or domain resource group. The specified
resource group needs to be pre-existed before executing the deployment command.

- resourceGroupTemplate = Optional. Name of the resource group template this deployment is scoped to.
The specified resource group template needs to be pre-existed before executing the deployment
command.

- partition = Optional. Name of the partition this deployment is scoped to. The partition name will
be derived from the current invocation context if not specified. The specified partition need to be
pre-existed before executing the deployment command.

- options = Optional. Comma-separated list of deployment options, specified as name-value pairs.
Valid options include:
 o altDD = Location of the alternate application deployment descriptor on the admin server.

 o altWlsDD = An alternate WebLogic application deployment descriptor on the admin server.

 o archiveVersion = Archive version number.

 o block = (true|false) Boolean value specifying whether WLST should block user interaction until the
command completes. This option defaults to true. If set to false, WLST returns control to the user
after issuing the command

 o clusterDeploymentTimeout = Time (in ms) granted for a cluster deployment task on this application.

 o createPlan = (true|false) Boolean value indicating that user would like to create a default plan.
This option defaults to false.

 o defaultSubmoduleTargets = (true|false) Boolean value indicating that targeting for any JMS
submodules should be derived by the system.

 o forceUndeployTimeout = Force undeployment timeout value.

 o gracefulIgnoreSessions = (true|false) Boolean value specifying whether the graceful production to
Admin mode operation should ignore pending HTTP sessions. This option defaults to false and only
applies if gracefulProductionToAdmin is set to true.

 o gracefulProductionToAdmin = (true|false) Boolean value specifying whether the production to Admin
mode operation should be graceful. This option defaults to false.

 o libImplVersion = Implementation version of the library, if it is not present in the manifest.

 o libraryModule = (true|false) Boolean value specifying whether the module is a library module. This
option defaults to false.

 o libSpecVersion = Specification version of the library, if it is not present in the manifest.

 o planVersion = Plan version number.

 o retireGracefully = (true|false) Retirement policy to gracefully retire an application only after
it has completed all in-flight work. This policy is only meaningful for stop and redeploy operations
and is mutually exclusive to the retire timeout policy.

 o retireTimeout = Time (in seconds) WLST waits before retiring an application that has been replaced
with a newer version. This option default to -1, which specifies graceful timeout.
```

```
o rmiGracePeriod = Time (in seconds) WLST waits for RMI requests before retiring an application that
has been replaced with a newer version. RMI requests arriving within a grace period of prior request
scheduled within the grace period will be accepted, and otherwise rejected. This option default to -
1, which specifies no grace period.

o securityModel = Security model. Valid values include: DDOnly, CustomRoles, CustomRolesAndPolicy,
and Advanced.

o securityValidationEnabled = (true|false) Boolean value specifying whether security validation is
enabled.

o subModuleTargets = Submodule level targets for JMS modules. For example, submod@mod-jms.xml@target
| submoduleName@target.

o adminMode = (true|false) Boolean value specifying whether to start the Web application with
restricted access. This option defaults to false.

o timeout = Time (in milliseconds) that WLST waits for the deployment process to complete before
canceling the operation. A value of 0 indicates that the operation will not time out.

o upload = (true|false) Boolean value specifying whether the application files are uploaded to the
WebLogic Server Administration Server's upload directory prior to deployment. Use this option when
you are on a different machine from the Administration Server and you cannot copy the deployment
files by other means. This option defaults to false.

o remote = (true|false) Boolean value specifying whether the operation will be remote from the file
system that contains the source. Use this option when you are on a different machine from the
Administration Server and the deployment files are already at the specified location where the
Administration Server is located. This option defaults to false.
```

WLST Examples

From the option list above note that there are two different optional attributes. One is an option called "resourceGroupTemplate" and the other is an option called "resourceGroup".

For the following examples let us assume that we have an application called "MyShop" with an EAR file located in /opt/applications/binaries/MyShop.ear

Deployment of the application to a resource group template with minimal arguments

```
connect(...)

# switch to edit mode and start session
edit()
startEdit()

# deploy the application
deploy(appName='MyShop', path='/opt/applications/binaries/MyShop.ear',
resourceGroupTemplate='GeneralShopResourceGroupTemplate')

# activate the changes
```

The most important aspect here is to specify the optional attribute "resourceGroupTemplate". Otherwise, the application would be deployed to the domain level. In case you want to use a deployment plan, you can also add the attribute "planPath" to the deploy function.

There are two additional functions defined in WLST. One is used in order to redeploy an already deployed application and the other can be used to update a deployed application. Both have similar command-lines than the "deploy" function, except that it is not necessary to specify the location of the EAR file.

Redeploy (planPath can be added if required):

Update an application (planPath can be added if required. Most likely this only makes sense if an application deployment plan has changed):

```
updateApplication(appName='MyShop', resourceGroupTemplate='GeneralShopResourceGroupTemplate',
```

After the application is deployed, it is required to distribute it.

```
connect(…)

# switch to edit mode and start session
edit()
startEdit()

# deploy the application
distributeApplication(appPath='/opt/applications/binaries/MyShop.ear',
resourceGroupTemplate='GeneralShopResourceGroupTemplate')

# activate the changes
```

Application deployment plans

Personally, I do not like application deployment plans, as they make things more complicated. Many – if not all – problems which an application deployment plan solves could be solved in a different way by e.g. using proper resource setups and resource overrides or by storing configuration options that are environment specific in a dedicated table of a database.

But there are many applications which require a plan in order to adapt certain settings to the runtime environment. Using the resource group template method reveals a weak point: One deployment is done to the template, but the deployment plan may differ for each referencing partition. WebLogic has solved this by allowing partitions to overwrite the plan location.

You need to perform the following steps in order to use partition specific deployment plans even if you deploy your application to a resource group template.

1) Deploy your application to the resource group template
2) Redeploy to a specific partition and changing the deployment plan

Example:

```
connect(...)

# switch to edit mode and start session
edit()
startEdit()

# deploy the application
deploy(appName='MyShop', path='/opt/applications/binaries/MyShop.ear',
resourceGroupTemplate='GeneralShopResourceGroupTemplate',
planPath='/opt/applications/plans/MyShop/GeneralShopResourceGroupTemplatePlan.xml')

# now redeploy to different partitions using a partition specific plan
redeploy(appName='MyShop', partition='ToysShopPartition',
planPath='/opt/applications/plans/MyShop/ToysShopPlan.xml')

redeploy(appName='MyShop', partition='FurnitureShopPartition',
planPath='/opt/applications/plans/MyShop/'FurnitureShopPlan.xml')

# activate the changes
```

Interesting is that you do not need to specify the partition resource group or the resource group template because WebLogic can identify it from the combination of application name and partition name.

Deploying applications to Resource Groups

Deploying applications to resource groups instead of resource group templates, is a very similar task. But there are a number of important differences. The most important difference is that a resource group is a real instance with real targets. There are two different flavors of resource groups: Domain scoped groups and partition scoped groups. Please note that – similar to resources – applications can also be deployed to partition resource groups directly even if these groups are based on a resource group template.

Benefits of this deployment type:

- One time deployment but concrete deployment. No change of a plan for each partition is required.
- Easy way in order to use different application versions in different partitions.

Disadvantages of this deployment type:

- More difficult to run the same version of the application in different partitions as one deployment per partition is needed.

In order to deploy an application to a resource group, you need to specify a number of attributes to the "deploy" function in WLST. You need to specify the resource group name, the application name, the path to the application binary and – if needed – the path to a deployment plan. In case you deploy it to a partition scoped resource group, then you also need to specify the partition name.

Another difference to resource group template deployment is that for resource groups WebLogic supports lifecycle operations like "start" and "stop". Lifecycle operations are supported for resource groups because resource groups have concrete targets.

WLST Examples

From the "deploy" option list shown in the last section we need the option called "resourceGroup".

For the following examples let us assume that we have an application called "MyShop" with an EAR file located in /opt/applications/binaries/MyShop.ear.

Deployment of the application to a domain level resource group template with minimal arguments

```
connect(…)

# switch to edit mode and start session
edit()
startEdit()

# deploy the application
deploy(appName='MyShop', path='/opt/applications/binaries/MyShop.ear',
resourceGroup='DomainPetShopResourceGroup')

# activate the changes
```

For deployment to a partition scoped group you need to add the partition name:

```
connect(…)

# switch to edit mode and start session
edit()
startEdit()

# deploy the application
deploy(appName='MyShop', path='/opt/applications/binaries/MyShop.ear',
resourceGroup='PetShopPartitionResourceGroup', partition='PetShopPartition')

# activate the changes
```

In case you want to use a deployment plan, you can also add the attribute "planPath" to the deploy function.

After the application is deployed, it is required to distribute it.

```
connect(...)

# switch to edit mode and start session
edit()
startEdit()

# deploy the application
distributeApplication(appPath='/opt/applications/binaries/MyShop.ear',
resourceGroup='PetShopPartitionResourceGroup', partition='PetShopPartition')

# activate the changes
```

In case of domain scoped resource groups:

```
connect(...)

# switch to edit mode and start session
edit()
startEdit()

# deploy the application
distributeApplication(appPath='/opt/applications/binaries/MyShop.ear',
resourceGroup='PetShopDomainResourceGroup')

# activate the changes
```

As resource group are real instances, applications can be started and stopped. WLST does support lifecycle operations on resource groups. These are supported for domain level and partition scoped resource groups.

Starting an application requires only the application name and the partition name. It is not required to specify the name of the resource group as application names must be unique within a partition. WebLogic can determine the resource group name from the configuration of the partition.

Please note that there are a number of additional options that you could specify for application start.

```
Description:
Starts an application, making it available to users. The application must be fully configured and
available in the domain.

Syntax:
startApplication(appName, [partition], [options])
- appName = Name of the application to start, as specified in the plan.xml file.

- partition = Optional. Name of the partition this deployment is scoped to. The partition name will
be derived from the current invocation context if not specified. The specified partition need to be
pre-existed before executing the deployment command.

- options = Optional. Comma-separated list of deployment options, specified as name-value pairs.
Valid options include:
 o altDD = An alternate application deployment descriptor on the admin server.

 o altWlsDD = Location of the alternate WebLogic application deployment descriptor on the admin
server.

 o archiveVersion = Archive version number.
```

```
 o block = (true|false) Boolean value specifying whether WLST should block user interaction until the
command completes. This option defaults to true. If set to false, WLST returns control to the user
after issuing the command

 o clusterDeploymentTimeout = Time (ms), granted for a cluster deployment task on this application.

 o createPlan = (true|false) Boolean value indicating that user would like to create a default plan.
This option defaults to false.

 o defaultSubmoduleTargets = (true|false) Boolean value indicating that targeting for any JMS
submodules should be derived by the system.

 o forceUndeployTimeout = Force undeployment timeout value.

 o gracefulIgnoreSessions = (true|false) Boolean value specifying whether the graceful production to
Admin mode operation should ignore pending HTTP sessions.

 o gracefulProductionToAdmin = (true|false) Boolean value specifying whether the production to Admin
mode operation should be graceful. This option defaults to false.

 o libImplVersion = Implementation version of the library, if it is not present in the manifest.

 o libraryModule = (true|false) Boolean value specifying whether the module is a library module. This
option defaults to false.

 o libSpecVersion = Specification version of the library, if it is not present in the manifest.

 o planVersion = Plan version number.

 o retireGracefully = (true|false) Retirement policy to gracefully retire an application only after
it has completed all in-flight work.

 o retireTimeout = Time (in seconds) WLST waits before retiring an application that has been replaced
with a newer version. This option default to -1, which specifies graceful timeout.

 o rmiGracePeriod = Time (in seconds) WLST waits for RMI requests before retiring an application that
has been replaced with a newer version. RMI requests arriving within a grace period of prior request
scheduled within the grace period will be accepted, and otherwise rejected. This option default to -
1, which specifies no grace period.

 o securityModel = Security model. Valid values include: DDOnly, CustomRoles, CustomRolesAndPolicy,
and Advanced.

 o securityValidationEnabled = (true|false) Boolean value specifying whether security validation is
enabled.

 o subModuleTargets = Submodule level targets for JMS modules.

 o targets = Comma-separated list of targets on which you would like this application to be started.

 o adminMode = (true|false) Boolean value specifying whether to start the Web application with
restricted access. This option defaults to false.
```

Here is an example that starts an application deployed to a partition resource group

```
connect(...)

# switch to edit mode and start session
edit()
startEdit()

# start the application
startApplication(appName='MyShop', partition='PetShopPartition')

# activate the changes
```

Starting an application in a domain level scoped resource group:

Stopping applications which are deployed to a resource group is very similar. It is only required to name the application and – in case of a partition scoped group – the partition name.

Example which stops an application deployed to a partition resource group

```
connect(…)

# switch to edit mode and start session
edit()
startEdit()

# stop the application
stopApplication(appName='MyShop', partition='PetShopPartition')

# activate the changes
```

Stopping an application in a domain level scoped resource group:

Resource group considerations

With resource groups there are a number of points I would recommend readers to notice and take into consideration:

1) Even if a partition is based on a resource group template, it is still possible to deploy applications directly into the partition resource group. This has the huge benefit that all partitions are based on the same resource setup, but can run different software versions. This is very helpful for testing different versions or patch-level of the same application.
2) As it is a concrete deployment, there is no need for overwriting an application deployment plan on partition level.
3) Regardless how many resource groups you may have defined in your partition, the application names must be unique within the whole partition.
4) In case of partition scoped resource groups: This deployment scope is the only scope which allows partition admins to also deploy applications. All other deployment variations require domain admin access.

Parallel deployment

WebLogic recently has added the feature of parallel deployment. In case of multiple deployments, this increases the performance and improves the startup time of managed servers. WebLogic domains starting with version 12.2.1, have this feature enabled by default. The attributes which need to be set on domain level in order to activate this feature are called "ParallelDeployApplications" and "ParallelDeployApplicationModules".

For partitions this is not activated by default, but it can be activated by setting the corresponding attributes on partition level. WebLogic also supports at partition level both kinds of parallel deployment.

In order to allow partitions to deploy their applications in parallel, it is only necessary to configure the ParallelDeployApplications attribute of the PartitionMBean. Please note that the partition level setting has a higher priority than the domain wide configuration setting and therefore overrides settings at domain level.

Either on partition level or even at application level it is possible to allow WebLogic to deploy the different application modules in parallel.

For a partition wide permission you need to configure the "ParallelDeployApplicationModules" attribute of the PartitionMBean. In case you only want to define this for certain applications, it is necessary to configure the "ParallelDeployModules" attribute of the "AppDeploymentMBean". Whenever this is set on application level, it has the highest priority. Settings on application level overrides partition or domain settings.

Summary

Deployment of applications is a complex task with many possible configurations and variations. With the multitenancy support, WebLogic has increased the different scopes for deployments which now include domain level, resource group template and resource group level.

Most of the deployment arguments are also available for the new deployment scopes. Similar to the resource scoping discussed in previous chapters, the most important change for application deployment is also to decide the appropriate scope level.

WebLogic offers a wide range of deployment processes which enables customers to implement different use cases.

Partition Lifestyle

CHAPTER

Overview

Partitions are the core unit of the new multitenancy support. The last chapters discussed in detail how you can setup partitions. WebLogic has a number of different ways and technologies how to do this. It can be done either by domain scoped resource group templates. It is also possible to use partition scoped resource group or by referencing and sharing global resource groups. Applications can also be deployed in different ways in order to meet the requirements of the different use cases.

Partitions can be viewed as the new service level of WebLogic by providing "WebLogic applications" to a WebLogic platform that I earlier called WaaS (WebLogic as a Service). This also requires that partitions as a whole have common lifecycle operations. This chapter looks at the operations that can be done on partition level. The most important operations are start, stop, export and import. Just these operations make the partition based platform as powerful as it really is.

Lifecycle Operations

Each partition can be looked at as associated unit. This includes the partition scoped resource groups as well as resource managers, work-manager and of course also applications. This unit also has lifecycle operations which act on a complete partition.

All lifecycle operations are available through the "PartitionLifeCycleRuntime MBean" of the partition. Some of them are also available using the WLS Console.

Use WLST to navigate to the PartitionLifeCycleRuntime of the partition. Note that each partition has its own PartitionLifeCycleRuntime MBean.

```
connect('weblogic','...','t3://localhost:12001')

# switch to domain runtime
domainRuntime()
```

```
# change to the lifecycle mbean of the partition - in this case Partition_X
cd ('/DomainPartitionRuntimes/Partition_X/PartitionLifeCycleRuntime/Partition_X')

# inspect the available methods
ls()
dr--   ResourceGroupLifeCycleRuntimes
dr--   Tasks

-r--   Name                  Partition_X
-r--   State                 SHUTDOWN
-r--   Type                  PartitionLifeCycleRuntime

-r-x   forceShutdown         WebLogicMBean :
-r-x   forceShutdown         WebLogicMBean : Integer(timeout)
-r-x   forceShutdown         WebLogicMBean : WebLogicMBean[](targets)
-r-x   forceSuspend          WebLogicMBean :
-r-x   forceSuspend          WebLogicMBean : WebLogicMBean[](targets)
-r-x   getState              String : WebLogicMBean(serverMBean)
-r-x   purgeTasks            Void :
-r-x   resume                WebLogicMBean :
-r-x   resume                WebLogicMBean : WebLogicMBean[](targets)
-r-x   shutdown              WebLogicMBean :
-r-x   shutdown              WebLogicMBean : Integer(timeout),Boolean(ignoreSessions)
-r-x   shutdown              WebLogicMBean : Integer(timeout),Boolean(ignoreSessions),
                                             Boolean(waitForAllSessions)
-r-x   shutdown              WebLogicMBean : Integer(timeout),Boolean(ignoreSessions),
                                             Boolean(waitForAllSessions),WebLogicMBean[](targets)
-r-x   shutdown              WebLogicMBean : Integer(timeout),Boolean(ignoreSessions),
                                             WebLogicMBean[](targets)
-r-x   shutdown              WebLogicMBean : WebLogicMBean[](targets)
-r-x   start                 WebLogicMBean :
-r-x   start                 WebLogicMBean : String(initialState),Integer(timeOut)
-r-x   start                 WebLogicMBean : WebLogicMBean[](targets)
-r-x   startInAdmin          WebLogicMBean :
-r-x   startInAdmin          WebLogicMBean : WebLogicMBean[](targets)
```

The WLS console also provides access to these methods via the "control" tab of the partition list (figure 21-1).

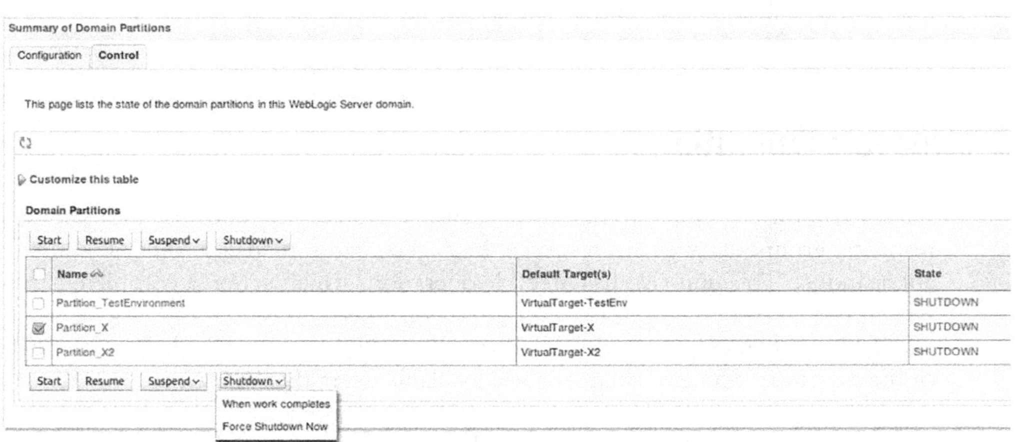

Figure 21-1: Select partition and perform operation

WebLogic supports a number of different lifecycle operations which can be invoked from this PartitionLifeCycleRuntime MBean. Some of these operations have different methods accepting a different list of arguments.

Operation	Description
start	Start the partition, if the partition is in the stopped or failed state
startInAdmin	Start the partition in admin mode
resume	Resume a partition which is in admin mode
suspend	Suspend a running partition into admin mode
forceSuspen	Force a partition into admin mode
shutdown	Shutdown a partition nicely
forceShutdown	Force shutdown and shutdown immediately

Starting Partitions

One possible operation is "start". This means that the complete partition and all its resources, resource managers and applications will be started and then can be used by consumers.

Start a partition without any further options:

```
connect('weblogic','...','t3://localhost:12001')

# switch to domain runtime
domainRuntime()

# change to the lifecycle mbean of the partition - in this case Partition_X
cd ('/DomainPartitionRuntimes/Partition_X/PartitionLifeCycleRuntime/Partition_X')

# start the partition
```

As you can see from the listing above, WebLogic offers a number of different start commands. It is also possible to specify a list of targets and a startup timeout.

Stopping Partitions

The opposite action is to stop or shutdown a partition. The difference between stop and suspend is that "stop" will shut down the partition completely and "suspend" will bring the partition into admin mode, so that the administrator and especially the partition administrator can still access the partition using the administration interface in order to do analysis.

Shutdown a partition without any further options:

```
connect('weblogic','...','t3://localhost:12001')

# switch to domain runtime
domainRuntime()

# change to the lifecycle mbean of the partition - in this case Partition_X
cd ('/DomainPartitionRuntimes/Partition_X/PartitionLifeCycleRuntime/Partition_X')

# start the partition
```

Resource deployment plans

Before we discuss exporting and importing partitions in more detail, we need to solve an open issue with partition.

Environment specific overrides

Exporting a partition means to create an archive of the filesystem with the partition content. Importing partitions back into the same domain is no problem. This is usually done as part of a backup concept or if you need to re-activate an archived or older version. Section five of this book (use-cases) will discuss a number of these use-cases.

But before we can import partitions into another domain we need to find a way to customize the partition resources to the new domain environment. Given e.g. that you want to migrate a partition from UAT to production. In this case it is absolutely necessary to adjust the resource to the new infrastructure. Very common examples are JDBC settings like URL, user and password. Please note that this CANNOT be done by using the MBean resource overrides which was discussed in chapter 18. These overrides are used to customize an instance of a resource group template to a partition instance.

WebLogic supports another concept for resource adaption in case a partition gets migrated to another domain. This concept is called "Resource Deployment plan". The idea is very similar to the well-known application deployment plans, with the only, but important difference, that it is only used for customizing resources. A resource deployment plan is an XML file which defines attributes the administrator wants to change, add or delete. Every partition can have at most one of these resource deployment plans.

Resource MBean Overrides vs. Resource Deployment Plan

Earlier we discussed MBean overrides which can be used in order to customize instances of resource group templates for a given partition. Together with the config.xml settings the administrator has three different techniques to set resource attributes. These three possibilities can be used by administrators together to provide resource overrides. WebLogic will first look at the config.xml. In case an attribute is defined in a resource deployment plan, then this attribute overrides the setting in the config.xml. The highest priority though have attributes defined as MBean overrides.

Resource Deployment Plan Content

Resource deployment plans have a unique and new syntax. Unfortunately, Oracle did not use a generic way by allowing to override any attribute. Oracle has invented a new syntax where new keywords and types must match predefined constants. Therefore, resource deployment plans can override many items, but not all. An important aspect is that you need to create a two-level process: First you need to create variables and then the place(s) where this variable is used to override or add information.

A resource deployment plan consists of three main sections:

1) **Definition of variables**
   A list of variables specified by a name and a value. The name can be anything as it is used only within this plan.
2) **External-resource-overrides**
   Override places which are not defined in the core config.xml file, but in outsourced descriptor files. Datasource properties like URL or credentials are a very common use-case.
3) **Config-resource-overrides**
   All other overrides which changes the content of the core config.xml file.

General syntax of a resource deployment plan:

```
description
version
variable-definition
  variable*
    name
    value
external-resource-override*
  resource-name
  resource-type
  root-element
  variable-assigment*
    name
    xpath
config-resource-override*
  resource-name
  resource-type
  variable-assigment*
    name
    xpath
```

© Oracle documentation

WebLogic supports a number of different resources that can be overridden. This includes resource properties in external files as well as properties within the config.xml. Currently WebLogic supports CoherenceClusterSystemResource, FileStore, ForeignJNDIProvider, JDBCStore, JDBCSystemResource, JMSBridgeDestination, JMSServer, JMSSystemResource, MailSession, ManagedExecutorService, ManagedScheduledExecutorService, ManagedThreadFactory, MessagingBridge, PathService, SAFAgent and WLDFSystemResource.

Example resource deployment plan

Deployment plans are XML files. The content of these files follows the syntax described above.

Example resource deployment plan

```
  xmlns="http://xmlns.oracle.com/weblogic/resource-deployment-plan"
  xmlns:xsi="http://www.w3.org/2001/XMLSchema"
  xsi:schemaLocation="http://xmlns.oracle.com/weblogic/resource-deployment-plan
http://xmlns.oracle.com/weblogic/resource-deployment-plan/1.0/resource-deployment-plan.xsd"
>
  <description>Martin Example Resource Deployment Plan</description>

  <variable-definition>
    <variable>
      <name>myNewJNDIName</name>
      <value>/jndi/prod/PortalDS</value>
    </variable>
    <variable>
      <name>fileStoreLocation</name>
      <value>/prod/stores/portal.store</value>
    </variable>
  </variable-definition>

  <external-resource-override>
    <resource-name>PortalDS</resource-name>
    <resource-type>jdbc-system-resource</resource-type>
    <root-element>jdbc-data-source</root-element>
    <variable-assignment>
      <name>myNewJNDIName</name>
      <xpath>/jdbc-data-source/jdbc-data-source-params/jndi-name </xpath>
    </variable-assignment>
  </external-resource-override>

  <config-resource-override>
    <resource-name>PortalFileStore</resource-name>
    <resource-type>file-store</resource-type>
    <variable-assignment>
      <name>fileStoreLocation</name>
      <xpath>/file-store/directory</xpath>
    </variable-assignment>
  </config-resource-override>
```

Constructing a resource deployment plan

At first glance, the deployment plan looks rather difficult. External-resource-overrides and config-resource-overrides have both an important detail in common. Resources are uniquely identified with a combination of name (<resource-name>) and type (<resource-type>).

Oracle did not include the different type names in its documentation, but a quick look at the partition definition in the config.xml reveals the secret. The type names are identical to the xml tags used in the partition or resource group template configuration.

Example partition

```
    <name>PortalPartition</name>
    <resource-group>
      <name>default</name>
      <app-deployment>...</app-deployment>
      <jms-server>
        <name>PortalJMSServer</name>
        <persistent-store>PortalFileStore</persistent-store>
      </jms-server>
      <file-store>
        <name>PortalFileStore</name>
        <directory>/tmp</directory>
      </file-store>
      <jms-system-resource>
        <name>PortalSystemModule</name>
        <descriptor-file-name>partitions/PortalPartition/jms/portalsystemmodule-jms.xml</descriptor-
file-name>
      </jms-system-resource>
      <jdbc-system-resource>
        <name>PortalDS</name>
        <descriptor-file-name>partitions/PortalPartition/jdbc/PortalDS-4171-jdbc.xml</descriptor-
file-name>
      </jdbc-system-resource>
    </resource-group>
    ...
```

For the config-resource-override of a file store, the type name in the resource deployment plan is <***file-store***>. For the external resource override of a datasource the type name in the resource deployment plan is <***jdbc-system-resource***>.

For external overrides the root element is also not difficult to find. Open the referenced file. E.g. for a datasource:

```
<jdbc-data-source>
  <name>PortalDS</name>
  <datasource-type>GENERIC</datasource-type>
  <jdbc-driver-params>
    <url>jdbc:oracle:thin:@//localhost:1521/ORCL</url>
    <driver-name>oracle.jdbc.OracleDriver</driver-name>
    <properties>
      <property>
        <name>user</name>
        <value>test</value>
      </property>
    </properties>
  </jdbc-driver-params>
  <jdbc-connection-pool-params>
    <test-table-name>SQL ISVALID</test-table-name>
  </jdbc-connection-pool-params>
```

```
<jdbc-data-source-params>
  <jndi-name>/jdbc/portalDS</jndi-name>
  <global-transactions-protocol>OnePhaseCommit</global-transactions-protocol>
</jdbc-data-source-params>
```

The root element is the XML root of this file. For a datasource this is ***<jdbc-data-source>***. As a last information the XPath needed to specify the location is the absolute path based on the resource root.

Example for a datasource:

```
<resource-name>PortalDS</resource-name>
<resource-type>jdbc-system-resource</resource-type>
<root-element>jdbc-data-source</root-element>
<variable-assignment>
  <name>myNewJNDIName</name>
  <xpath>/jdbc-data-source/jdbc-data-source-params/jndi-name </xpath>
</variable-assignment>
```

This example will override the "jndiName" configured in datasource "PortalDS".

Using a resource deployment plan

Resource deployment plans are designed to be added to a partition. WLST can be used in order to attach a plan to the partition. During the next start of the partition all non-dynamic changes will be applied.

```
connect(…)

# switch to the edit mode
edit()

# start editing
startEdit()

# get hold of the already created (or imported !) partition
partition=cmo.lookupPartition('PortalPartition')

# attach the resource deployment plan to this partition
partition.setResourceDeploymentPlanPath('data/partition/plans/portalPartition/uatPlan.xml')

# save changes and activate
save()
```

For existing partitions this is an acceptable process. Unfortunately, Oracle did not add a feature to specify a resource deployment plan as an argument to the "importPartition" function. This means that you need to import the partition first and then attach the plan.

Alternative approach

The resource partition plan is definitely the cleanest approach as you separate the exported partition and the plan. The plan can also be attached to an already deployed partition.

In real life this has also drawbacks. Possible drawbacks include

- Partitions and plans are separate entities which might lead to backup and version issues
- Resource deployment plans do not support all possible changes. For example they do not support work-manager or resource-manager.

For all of you who do not like these drawbacks or for whom the resource deployment plan is not sufficient, there is an easy workaround.

Just create a copy of the exported partition archive. Open the archive and edit the file partition-config.xml or one of the outsourced xml files directly. This actually provides the greatest flexibility and allow you to change everything. And it is also an easy way back to the former configuration, as you now have a backup!

Drawback of this workaround is that you get multiple – different (!) – copies of the exported partition. This could end of in a mess of partition versions. But nobody said, that you cannot have these copies versioned in a software version control system like SVN. Just tag it and you can reproduce it in case you need it. And it also provide some advantages in regard to be a bit more audit-save.

Exporting and Importing Partitions

One of the most interesting features of partitions is the fact that they can be exported as a whole. The complete "WebLogic application" can be exported into an archived format. This archive – especially the JSON file and the deployment plans – can be adjusted by the deployment team and afterwards imported into another WebLogic domain if required.

Exporting Partitions

The complete "WebLogic application" can be exported into an archived format. This also includes the secret key for encryption and decryption of sensible data like passwords and all resources and resource overrides.

Exporting partitions is the required technology for many use-cases like partition migrations, partition backups and more.

Partitions are exported as an archive file. The following artifacts will be included in the export:

- The configuration of the partition.
- All resource groups are scoped to this partition. In case these groups are instances of resource group templates, then these templates will also be included.
- All artifacts stored in the partition's file system.
- All applications deployed to this partition. This is optionally and can be deselected in case the administrator only wants to export the partition with resources, but not the application deployments.

The following table provides an overview of the different possible files which can be included in the exported partition.

Files and Directories	Description
partition-config.xml	Contains the partition configuration and resource group templates configuration from config.xml.
MANIFEST.MF	Includes a time stamp and domain information for the archive.
<PartitionName>-attributes.json	Contains the MBean attributes and properties which can be changed by the administrator while importing the partition. In addition to being contained in the archive, a copy of this file is also located with the archive in the file system to make it easier to update.
expPartSecret	Contains the encrypted secret key used for encrypting and decrypting encrypted attributes.
domain/config/resource-group-templates/<resource_template_name>/*	If there is a resource group template associated with this partition, then the files

	related to the resource group template are copied to this location.
domain/config/partitions/<partition-name>/*	All the configuration files are located at domain/config/partitions/<partition-name>/config/*.
pfs/config/*	Contains the <partition-file-system>/config directory content. This would also include system resources (JMS, JDBC, and such) descriptor files.
domain/upload/resource-group-templates/<resource_template_name>/<application_name>/	Contains resource group template-level binaries.
pfs/upload/<application_name>/	Contains resource group level application binaries.

(© Oracle: https://docs.oracle.com/middleware/1221/wls/WLSMT/export_import.htm#WLSMT1397)

The following example will export a small partition which only has a JDBC datasource defined in a resource group and no application deployed into it.

In the WLS console you need to go to the list of partitions and select the partition you want to export. After that you can start the export by pressing the "Export" button (figure 21-2).

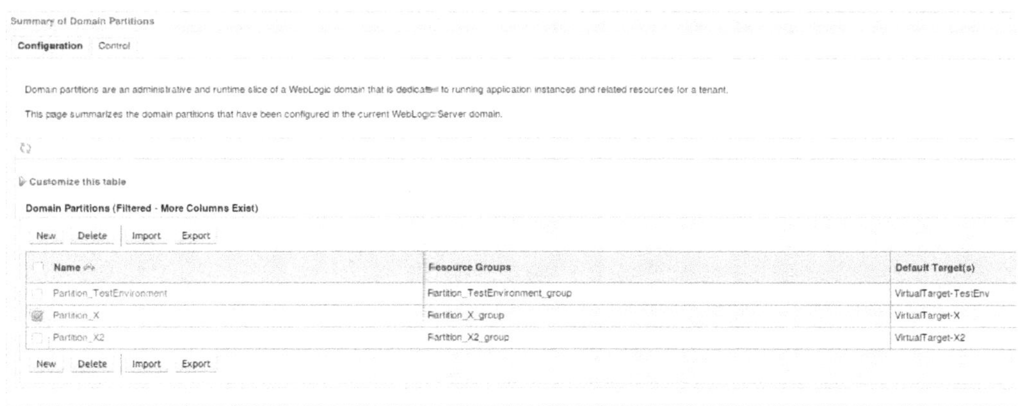

Figure 21-2: Select partitions in order to perform export

As a second step it is possible to specify a number of options, including path names (figure 21-3).

Export a Domain Partition

OK | Cancel

Export a Domain Partition

Select or enter the directory where the domain partition archive should be placed. Each domain partition should be located in its own directory. The domain partition archive will be overwritten if it already exists

Domain Partition Name: Partition_X

Do you want to include the installed applications in the exported ZIP file?

Include Application Bits

What is the full path to the key file you want to use to encrypt attributes in the partition archive?

Full path to the Key File:

Where do you want the domain partition archive to be placed ?

Path: /opt/development/archived_partitions

Recently Used Paths: (none)

Current Location: localhost / opt / development / wls / wls1221 / user_domains / usecase_1

autodeploy
bin
common
config
console-ext
generated_classes
init-info
lib
original
pending
resources
security
servers
sysman
tmp

OK | Cancel

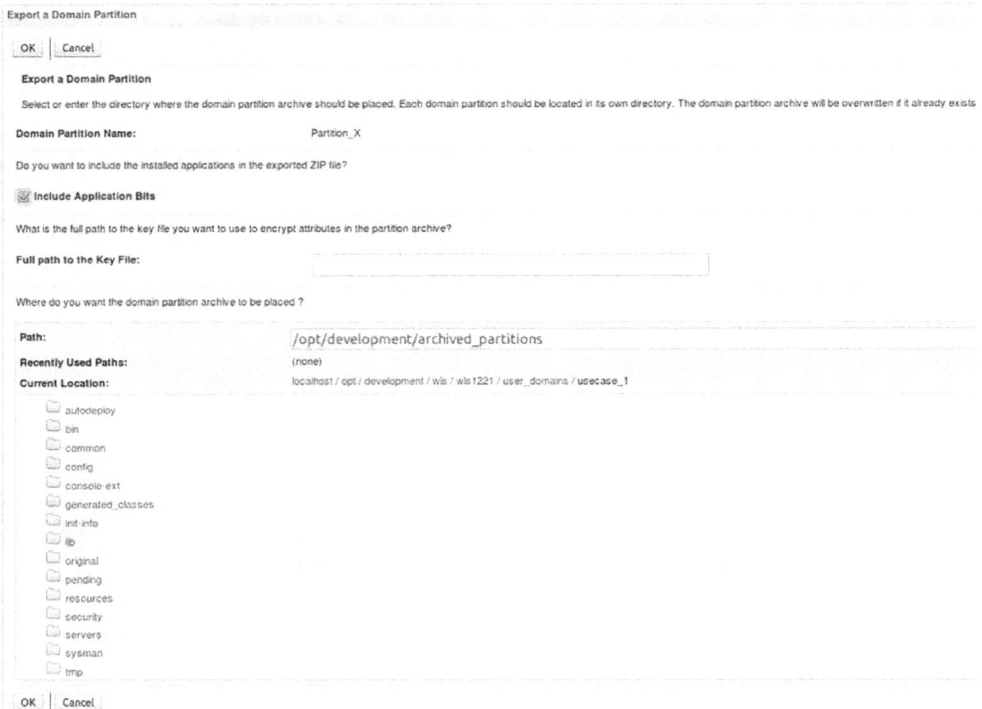

Figure 21-3: Specify details for export

The same export (recommended!) can also be done using WLST. WLST offers a special function called "exportPartition" which is not part of an MBean. The main reason for doing so is that a partition can be exported in online and offline mode.

```
Description:
Exports a partition into a partition archive that can be used later with the importPartition command.
Copies a partition's configuration into the archive file as well as (optionally) the partition's
applications and libraries. Also creates an attributes.json file that can be used to modify the
partitions configuration on import.

Syntax:

exportPartition(partitionName, expArchPath, [includeAppsNLibs], [keyFile])
- partitionName = The name of the partition to export
- expArchPath = Full path to a directory to save the partition archive to.  The path must be
reachable by the admin server. The archive file will be  named PartitionName.zip.
- includeAppsNLibs = Optional. True to include application and library binaries in the partition
archive. False to not include them. Defaults to true.
- keyFile = Optional. Full path to a file containing a string to use as the encryption key to encrypt
attributes in the partition archive. The path must be reachable by the admin server. Defaults to
```

For our example, the command looks like this:

After this export has been done, the following two files were generated in the target folder:

```
total 16
drwxrwxr-x  2 martin martin 4096 Jan 31 14:41 ./
drwxr-xr-x 19 martin martin 4096 Jan 31 14:39 ../
-rw-r-----  1 martin martin  872 Jan 31 14:41 Partition X-attributes.json
```

One of the files is the partition as a zip file and the other is the JSON description file. The content of this partition (in this case with only a datasource and no deployments) is:

```
 Date       Time  Name
---------- ----- ----
2016-01-31 14:41 Partition_X-attributes.json
2016-01-31 14:41 resource-group-templates/ResourceGroupTemplate_X/jdbc/TestDataSource-2617-jdbc.xml
2016-01-31 14:41 partition-config.xml
```

For this small example the json file looks like:


```
    "partition": {
        "name": "Partition_X",
        "primary-identity-domain": "idd_Partition_X",
        "default-target": [{"virtual-target": {"name": "VirtualTarget-X"}}],
        "jdbc-system-resource-override": {
            "name": "JDBCSystemResourceOverride-TestDataSource",
            "data-source-name": "TestDataSource",
            "url": "jdbc:oracle:thin:@\/\/mydb.com:1521\/ORCL",
            "user": "martin"
        },
        "available-target": [{"virtual-target": {"name": "VirtualTarget-X"}}]
    },
    "resource-group": {"name": "Partition_X_group"},
    "resource-group-template": {
        "name": "ResourceGroupTemplate_X",
        "jdbc-system-resource": {
            "name": "TestDataSource",
            "descriptor-file-name": "resource-group-
templates\/ResourceGroupTemplate_X\/jdbc\/TestDataSource-2617-jdbc.xml"
        }
    }
```


The other important file is the file called "partition-config.xml". For this example this looks like:


```
<domain>
  <name>${DOMAIN_NAME}</name>
  <domain-version>${DOMAIN_VERSION}</domain-version>
  <security-configuration>
    <default-realm xsi:nil="true"></default-realm>
  </security-configuration>
  <partition>
    <name>Partition_X</name>
    <resource-group>
      <name>Partition_X_group</name>
      <resource-group-template>ResourceGroupTemplate_X</resource-group-template>
    </resource-group>
    <jdbc-system-resource-override>
      <name>JDBCSystemResourceOverride-TestDataSource</name>
```

```
      <data-source-name>TestDataSource</data-source-name>
      <url>jdbc:oracle:thin:@//mydb.com:1521/ORCL</url>
      <user>martin</user>
    </jdbc-system-resource-override>
  </partition>
  <resource-group-template>
    <name>ResourceGroupTemplate_X</name>
    <notes>My ResourceTemplate called ResourceGroupTemplate_X</notes>
    <jdbc-system-resource>
      <name>TestDataSource</name>
      <descriptor-file-name>resource-group-templates/ResourceGroupTemplate_X/jdbc/TestDataSource-
2617-jdbc.xml</descriptor-file-name>
    </jdbc-system-resource>
  </resource-group-template>
```

Importing Partitions

The contrary operation to the partition export is the import of a partition into an existing domain. Before a new partition can get imported into a domain, a few pre-requisites must be available. It might be necessary to configure those before the important operation can be done. Among those pre-requisites are any dependency of the partition to existing configuration artifacts which are not part of the exported archive like

- virtual targets
- security realms
- resource group templates
- external/shared resource groups which are referenced

Note that the resource group templates are part of the export and that WebLogic has an option to avoid name clashed. In case the existing resource group template does not fit the needs of the resource group template which was used to create the partition resource group then the administrator might need to update it first.

In addition to the changes an administrator might need to do before importing a partition, the administrator has an additional option to override settings as part of the import.

WebLogic supports different deployment plans for partitions which can be used to customize partition content.

1) A Resource deployment plan can be created in order to adapt resource setups like JDBC URLs, user names, passwords or other settings
2) Partition deployment plans can be used to customize applications deployed to a partition. These are partition scoped application deployment plans.

Importing partitions can be done using WLST or the WebLogic console (figure 21-4).

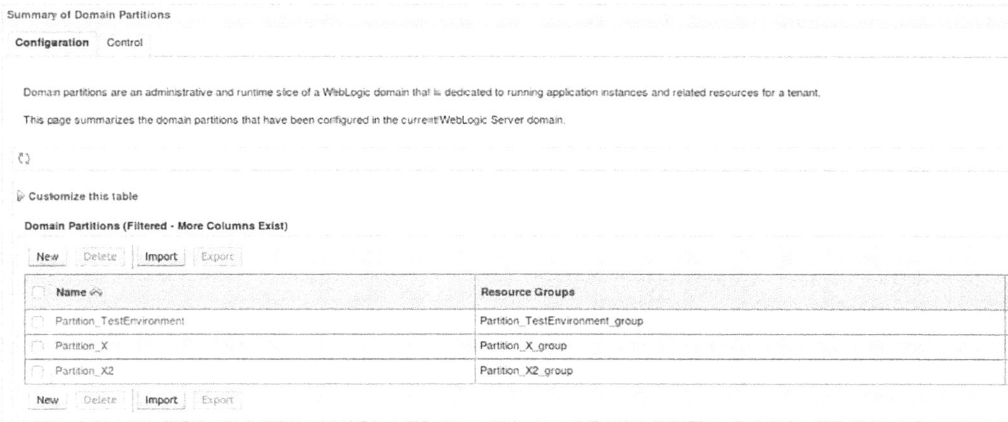

Figure 21-4: Select "import" in order to import a partition

In a second step, the administrator or deployer can specify a number of options, like paths (figure 21-5).

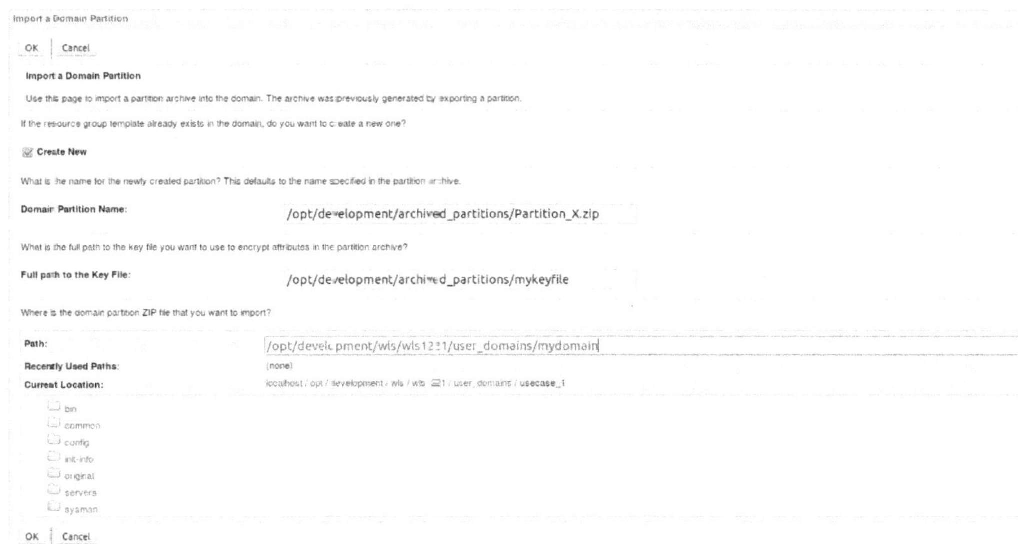

Figure 21-5: Specify import options

Note that the "Create New" option can be used to specify the behavior in case that a resource group template already exist in the destination domain. If this option is checked then the system will NOT use the existing one, but create a new resource group template based on the information in the exported partition.

Using WLST

The same import (recommended!) can also be done using WLST. WLST offers a special function called "importPartition" which is not part of an MBean. The main reason for doing so is that a partition can be exported in online and offline mode.

```
Description:

Imports a partition archive (generated by the exportPartition command)into a domain. Supports an
attributes.json file that can be used to modify the partitions configuration on import.

Syntax:

importPartition(archiveFileName, [partitionName], [createNew], [keyFile])
- archiveFileName = full path to the partition archive to import. Path must be reachable by the admin
server. importPartition will also look for a file, PartitionName-attributes.json, in the same
directory as the partition archive. If it is found then the values in that file will override those
in the partition archive.
- partitionName = Optional. Name to use for partition when created in the new domain. Defaults to the
original name of the partition.
- createNew = Optional. Controls how resource group template conflicts are handled. All resource
group templates used by the partition are contained in the partition archive and are imported along
with the partition into the domain. If the resource group template already exists in the domain and
this flag is false, then the existing resource group template is used. If this flag is true, then a
new resource group template is created using a new name. If this flag is not specified, then the
import will fail if the resource group template already exists in the  domain.
- keyFile = Optional. Full path to a file containing a string to use as the encryption key to decrypt
attributes in the partition archive. The path must be reachable by the admin server. Defaults to
```

For our example the command looks like:

What about encrypted values?

WebLogic encrypts sensitive data like JDBC passwords and others with a domain specific key. The problem now arises when a partition gets imported into a different domain. The destination domain has another secret key. This results in the fact that none of the encrypted values can be decrypted anymore.

The solution implemented by WebLogic is easy and logical. As part of the export operation, a new – partition specific – secret key will be generated. All sensitive data will be re-encrypted using this new key. The key-file itself will be stored in the exported partition ZIP file. If you prefer to use your own key instead of a generated key for this partition, then you can override the key using the keyFile option.

During import the secret key or the overridden user specific key is read. All values in the partition configuration will be decrypted and then re-encrypted using the secret key of the destination domain.

Backup and other Partition Operations

In almost all organizations sooner or later the administrator group has to think about a way to backup application and domain setups. Most of them would most likely just archive the complete domain folder. This has a number of disadvantages like the fact that you need to archive all domain folders on all hosts where servers are running. This archive is also bound to the filesystem layout so that it cannot be recovered to any new domain folder.

Other may use the "domainToScript" like features offered in WebLogic. This an interesting approach but not 100% reliable as that this generator will not catch all possible settings. Furthermore, binary files like deployments are not considered. In addition, security settings, especially users, groups, policies and all other LDAP content is not included.

Using the partition export functionality discussed above can really help here, as the export of a partition does a nice job of exporting everything needed to recover this partition, including application deployments. The exported partition files can easily be archived to a backup drive or tape. They can also be recovered into another domain if needed so that most of the restrictions mentioned above do not apply to this backup method.

Migrating to Partitions

Most companies already do have a number of WebLogic domains up and running. After the decision has been made that the new partition technology should be used most customers need to think about a transition plan of how to migrate existing applications and domains to the new partition technology.

There are two different approaches to that:

1) Create a new WebLogic 12.2.1 domain, with resource groups, partitions and all other new technology components. Then deploy your applications to these new partitions.

This is probably the cleanest approach as everything will be setup from scratch without any legacy settings.

2) In case the first approach is too time consuming Oracle has created a new utility which help with the process of converting existing WebLogic domains into partitions.

This new tool is called Domain to Partition Conversion Tool (DPCT). This utility implements a migration process that can convert an existing WebLogic domain (10.3.6, 12.1.2, 12.1.3 or 12.2.1) into a WebLogic partition. It consists of two tools: an export tool, which is used on the source domain; and an import tool, which is used on the target WebLogic Server 12.2.1 installation. You can use D-PCT to create and configure partitions, resource groups, and resource group templates. By default, D-PCT moves all applications, libraries, and resources to the new partition. Optionally, it also provides a mechanism for selecting individual applications, libraries, and resources.

In the first release this tool is provided by Oracle apart from the WebLogic 12.2.1.0 installation as separate download. Staring with 12.2.1.1 this tool will be provided as part of the WebLogic 12.2.x installation.

Summary

Operations on partitions as a whole are very important in order to really operate on partitions or – as defined earlier – on WebLogic applications. The available operations can be grouped into two categories: Lifecycle operations and Migration operations (export/import).

Lifecycle operations enable administrators work with partitions available to the given domain and start or stop them.

Migration operations enable administrators to export partitions for backup or migration and in order to import partitions either for recovery or for migrating them to a different domain.

Working with Partitions

CHAPTER

Introduction

After discussing partitions, resourcing, scoping, isolation, security and many other partition services in detail, question may arise like: "How on earth do I operate this new world ?".

As partitions are a new service layer above the WebLogic core that focus on density, multi-tenancy, application isolation and more, the following questions will trouble administrators:

- How do I know which partition has written which log entries?
- How can I access and analyze a specific partition?

Partition specific logging

A single WLS server may host (and most likely will host) a number of different partitions. All of these partitions will write log files, notification and error messages. It is vital for the administrator to identify clearly which partition has protocolled which error message or warning. For troubleshooting debug logs are also very important and the administrator must be able to identify which partition has written the log entries.

WebLogic supports partitions specific log files for a number of log messages. For this reason WebLogic maintains by default partition log files in the directory:

```
partitions/<partition>/system/servers/<server-name>
```

This applies to the following log files.

Log File	Contents
ServerLog	Log records for Weblogic Server events generated when doing work within the scope of a partition. The server log is not available within the partition file system — it is available only

Log File	Contents
	through the WLDF data accessor. (For more details see my WLDF book)
DomainLog	Log records domain-scope events generated on behalf of a partition. The domain log is not available within the partition file system — it is available only through the WLDF data accessor.
HTTPAccessLog (partition scope virtual target access log)	The `access.log` file for each virtual target's web server is maintained in separately for each partition and can be accessed by the partition user.
HarvestedDataArchive	MBean metrics applicable to a partition are collected by the WLDF Harvester component. This file is available only through the WLDF data accessor.
EventsDataArchive	Events generated by the WLDF Instrumentation component. This file is available only through the WLDF data accessor.
JMSMessageLog (partition scope)	Log records for partition scope JMS resources. An individual log file is maintained for each partition and may be accessed by the partition user.
JMSSAFMessageLog (partition scope)	Log records for partition scope SAF agent resources. An individual log file is maintained for each partition and may be accessed by the partition user.
DataSourceLog	Data source profile records generated when doing work within the scope of a partition.
WebAppLog (partition scope)	Servlet context logs from partition scope applications. An individual log file is maintained for each partition and may be accessed by the partition user.
ConnectorLog (partition scope)	Java Connector Architecture resource adapter logs from partition scope resource adapters. An individual log file is maintained for each partition and may be accessed by the partition user.

© Oracle: http://docs.oracle.com/middleware/1221/wls/WLSMT/monitoring.htm

Logging from applications deployed to a partition

In WebLogic, it is possible to configure application specific log levels for partition scoped deployments. The only requirement is that the application must use java.util.logging.Loggers. The settings ONLY apply to the partition. Other partitions – even if their applications are using the same logger name – are not affected.

To activate this feature the WebLogic servers must be started with an additional JVM argument:

Example script in order to set these logging levels:

```
connect(...)

# switch to edit mode
edit()
```

```
startEdit()

# lookup the partition
cd('/')
myPartition = cmo.lookupPartition('PortalPartition')

# get the Partition Logging MBean
myPartitionLogs = myPartition.getPartitionLog()

# set your apps debug properties
myAppDebugProps = java.util.Properties()
props.put('portal.access.logging','WARNING')
props.put('portal.database.logging','WARNING')
props.put('portal.common.logging','INFO')

# set loggin arguments for the partition
myPartitionLogs.setPlatformLoggerLevels(props)

# save changes and activate
save()
```

Debugging Partitions

WebLogic offers a large number of debug options to be activated for each WebLogic server. Albeit these options are very useful, a multitenancy setup may require to enable these options for troubleshooting only for certain partitions.

WebLogic also supports these debug flags for individual partitions only. For this case each partition offers a special PartitionLogMBean. Partition scoped debug flags must be set using this MBean.

Example to set DebugJDBCSQL for a specific partition

```
connect(...)

# switch to edit mode
edit()
startEdit()

# lookup the partition
cd('/Partitions/PortalPartition/PartitionLog/PortalPartition')

# set debug flags only for partition, e.g.: DebugJDBCSQL
cmo.addEnabledServerDebugAttribute("DebugJDBCSQL")

# save changes and activate
save()
```

Before this script is executed, the MBean had an empty list of debug flags in its EnabledServerDebugAttributes attribute

```
-r--   DynamicallyCreated                         false
-rw-   EnabledServerDebugAttributes               null
-r--   Id                                         0
-rw-   Name                                       PortalPartition
-rw-   Notes                                      null
```

```
-rw-   PlatformLoggerLevels                    null
-rw-   Tags                                    null
-r--   Type                                    PartitionLog

-r-x   addEnabledServerDebugAttribute          Boolean : String(name)
-r-x   addTag                                  Boolean : String(tag)
-r-x   freezeCurrentValue                      Void : String(attributeName)
-r-x   getInheritedProperties                  String[] : String[](propertyNames)
-r-x   isInherited                             Boolean : String(propertyName)
-r-x   isSet                                   Boolean : String(propertyName)
-r-x   removeEnabledServerDebugAttribute       Boolean : String(name)
-r-x   removeTag                               Boolean : String(tag)
-r-x   restoreDefaultValue                     Void : String(attributeName)
```

After the script has been run, the debug flag has been added to the attribute:

```
-r--   DynamicallyCreated                      false
-rw-   EnabledServerDebugAttributes            java.lang.String[DebugJDBCSQL]
-r--   Id                                      0
-rw-   Name                                    PortalPartition
-rw-   Notes                                   null
-rw-   PlatformLoggerLevels                    null
-rw-   Tags                                    null
-r--   Type                                    PartitionLog
```

An interesting fact is that the debug flag on the server level is still marked as disabled:

```
dr--   DebugScopes
dr--   Server

...
-rw-   DebugJDBCONS                            false
-rw-   DebugJDBCRAC                            false
-rw-   DebugJDBCRMI                            false
-rw-   DebugJDBCReplay                         false
-rw-   DebugJDBCSQL                            false
-rw-   DebugJDBCUCP                            false
-rw-   DebugJMSAME                             false
-rw-   DebugJMSBackEnd                         false
```

The reason is simple. If the debug flag would have been also enabled on the server level, then the domain itself would also generate debug output. IN this case the administrator only wants to get the debug output from the partition.

WLST Domain connect vs. Partition connect

In traditional WLST scripts the "connect" function is used to connect to a WebLogic server (admin or managed-server).

The default syntax is:

This default syntax has now been extended with two new ways to specify the connection URL. It is now possible to specify an URL which points directly to a partition. The side effect here is that the admin needs to know the exact name of the partition. In order to be more flexible, WebLogic has even added another new syntax, to allow the user to specify an URL which points to a virtual target.

Using the "partition-style" connection URL:

```
connect('user','password',"t3://host:port/partitions/partition-name")
```

Using this method WLST will start in the root MBean folder of this partition. Depending on the user being used for authentication it is still possible to switch to the domain main root MBean.

```
Initializing WebLogic Scripting Tool (WLST) ...

Welcome to WebLogic Server Administration Scripting Shell

Type help() for help on available commands

wls:/offline> connect('weblogic','welcome1','t3://localhost:12001/partitions/PortalPartition')
Connecting to t3://localhost:12001/partitions/PortalPartition with userid weblogic ...
Successfully connected to partition "PortalPartition".
```

This may be accomplished by using the "virtual-target-style" connection URL:

Surprisingly WLST in this case will switch to the domain root MBean. It would have been better to also switch to the partition root MBean.

```
Initializing WebLogic Scripting Tool (WLST) ...

Welcome to WebLogic Server Administration Scripting Shell

Type help() for help on available commands

wls:/offline> connect('weblogic','welcome1','t3://localhost:12001/VirtualTarget-Portal')
Connecting to t3://localhost:12001/VirtualTarget-Portal with userid weblogic ...
Successfully connected to Admin Server "AdminServer" that belongs to domain " martinDomain ".
```

JMX Domain connect via. Partition connect

A JMX connect is different from a WLST or JNDI connect. This is because WebLogic is not running an own runtime MBeanServer for each partition. Therefore the JMX connect must be done using the standard domain port or the port used in the VirtualTarget.

If a user is allowed to access a specific MBean depends on the user authentication and the user rights.

JNDI access from external clients

External clients do not care if an application is hosted on domain level or inside a partition. For external clients this MUST be completely transparent. Using http requests, this is relatively easy as a virtual target either has a unique set of host and port or a unique URL prefix.

But there are cases – e.g. direct access to an EJB (RMI call) to access to a partition scoped JMX service – where clients need to access partition services from outside of WebLogic. In fact the same information is required if a partition wants to talk to another partition.

This section discusses the way an external client can be used to access the partition specific JNDI tree. Consider the following source code with the different PROVIDER_URLs. The following code uses a standard JNDI InitialContext connection and print all the visible root elements and after that all elements available under "/jdbc".

```
import java.util.*;

public class PartitionJNDIAccessTest {

  public static void main(String[] args) throws Exception
  {
     Context ctx = null;
     Hashtable ht = new Hashtable();
     ht.put(Context.INITIAL_CONTEXT_FACTORY,"weblogic.jndi.WLInitialContextFactory");

     ht.put(Context.PROVIDER_URL,"t3://localhost:12001");
     //ht.put(Context.PROVIDER_URL,"t3://localhost:12001/partitions/PortalPartition");
     //ht.put(Context.PROVIDER_URL,"t3://localhost:12001/VirtualTarget-Portal");

     ctx = new InitialContext(ht);
```

```
        NamingEnumeration<NameClassPair> list = ctx.list("/");
        while (list.hasMore()) {
            System.out.println(list.next().getName());
        }

        System.out.println("\n JDBC subcontext :");

        list = ctx.list("jdbc");
        while (list.hasMore()) {
            System.out.println(list.next().getName());
        }

        ctx.close();
    }
```

First, we will use the standard domain provider URL: "t3://localhost:12001". This will produce the following output:

```
jmx
javax
weblogic
__WL_GlobalJavaApp
_WL_internal_Cou0FU0pRttDzFN9yiosYYtjJ3hhzTRn4iqT95S80aqyoyHbWJX2h2ojn0Z3s9hE
ejb
java:global
tangcsol
eis
```

You can see all root level objects of the standard WebLogic JNDI context.

As a second example, we will use the partition provider URL: "t3://localhost:12001/partitions/PortalPartition ". This will produce the following output:

```
mtTestdyeTest_jarTestDelegateBean_Home
weblogic
jdbc
Test1#de
java:global
eis
TestDelegateBean#de
jmx
javax
__WL_GlobalJavaApp
mtTestdyeTest_jarTest1Bean_Home
_WL_internal_Cou0FU0pRttDzFN9yiosYYtjJ3hhzTRn4iqT95S80aqyoyHbWJX2h2ojn0Z3s9hE
mtTestdyeTest_jarTest1Bean_Test1BeanRemote

JDBC subcontext :
```

This lists the partition JNDI root context. As the partition has one datasource defined with the JNDI name "/jdbc/portalDS", this time the listing of "/jdbc" does find this datasource.

Similar to the WLST connect, the VirtualTarget syntax of the connect (PROVIDER_URL=t3://localhost:12001/VirtualTarget-Portal) points to the domain JNDI root:

```
jmx
javax
weblogic
__WL_GlobalJavaApp
_WL_internal_Cou0FU0pRttDzFN9yiosYYtjJ3hhzTRn4iqT95S80aqyoyHbWJX2h2ojn0Z3s9hE
ejb
java:global
tangosol
```

Summary

The new concept of partitions which offers a WebLogic service platform similar to PaaS offering has many advantages that we will discuss in the next chapters. The previous chapter provided the technology components needed to build such a platform.

Due to this new WebLogic infrastructure layer, a complete new set of challenges and tasks are needed. Due to security isolation features but also due to direct access requirements to a single partition, a number of tasks needs to be examined.

This chapter discussed a number of the most common connectivity and administrative challenges that came along with the new partition concept.

Part V

Real world use cases demonstrating multitenancy value

Introduction to real world examples

CHAPTER

Importance of real word scenarios

This part about use-cases is the heart of the book. Whatever technology is invented, it is useless unless it offers real business values. Without proper business or technically value added for a user new technology is a nice toy but will not be used. Therefore it is important to discuss use cases where this new multitenancy technology offers real value to the users of WebLogic.

There are many use cases which offer added value. I have chosen 11 of them as I think their benefits are pretty obvious, easy to achieve and last, but not least, show the power of the new features.

Note that there is sometimes a bit of overlapping between the different use cases but this can be avoided as some use cases automatically have others as prerequisite or just work nicely hand in hand with others Nevertheless each use case has its main focus on a specific advantage of multitenancy. This is also the reason use cases are wrapped into own chapters.

Please note that this section of the book is designed to be useful for everybody. Business decision makers as well as administrators, (infrastructure) architects and all others will find useful information in the different use case chapters.

Structure of the use cases

Each use-case will start with a business case consideration. Whatever we do in our world is business driven. Oracle would not have implemented this complex new WebLogic multitenancy model, if this model would not benefit the business. For (business) decision makers each use case will look at the business case first so that readers who are not so much interested in technology details can get the benefit behind the use-case. I have tried to select a number of use-cases with a broad range of scenarios so that not every use-case will be applicable for every reader. It is also expected that in many cases combinations of use-cases might make sense. Experience with different other technology areas has proven that most likely many readers may benefit from some use-cases even though they did not expect that they had these areas of potential improvements.

After a brief discussion, the business case whereas the non-multitenancy setup will be compared with a possible multitenancy setup. The second part of each use-case chapter will dig into details of how this could be implemented. These descriptions expect that the reader is familiar with the technology building bricks which were explained in the previous part (part IV) of the book.

Whenever possible and useful, example setup scripts will be provided. In case these scripts are too big, only relevant parts are printed but all of these scripts are available for download. Note that scripts might be similar for different use cases but they are provided to get a better understanding of each use case without referring to scripts or script parts of other use cases. All example scripts and codes are provided as WLST scripts as it is widely used and easier to understand than JMX or REST.

Base WebLogic domain for the use cases

All use cases assume that a base domain will be created. The following script is used in order to create the base domain(s). Only exception is that some use-cases might need multiple clusters. In this case more managed-server and more clusters will be created.

```
import sys
from java.util import Properties
from java.io import FileInputStream
from java.io import File
from java.util import ArrayList
from java.util import HashMap


# -------- global parameters ---------------------------------------

domainLocationRoot = '/opt/development/wls/wls1221/user_domains/';
domainName     ="usecase_1"
adminUserName = 'weblogic'
adminPassword = 'welcome1'
jvmLocation='/opt/development/jdk1.8.0_60'



######################################################################
# Get instance properties
######################################################################
def createDirIfNotExists(dirname):
   try:
      os.makedirs(dirname)
   except OSError:
      if os.path.exists(dirname):
         # We are nearly safe
         pass
      else:
         # There was an error on creation, so make sure we know about it
         raise
```

```
###################################################################
# Create the boot.properties file
###################################################################
def createBootProperties(serverName):
    try:
        # domain root folder
        domainLocation = domainLocationRoot + '/' + domainName
        createDirIfNotExists(domainLocation + "/servers/" + serverName + "/security")
        filename=domainLocation + "/servers/" + serverName + "/security/boot.properties"

        print '    Create boot property file ' + filename
        f=open(filename, 'w')
        # better encrypt !!  line='username=  + encrypt(adminUserName, domainLocation + "/" +
domainName) + '\n'
        line='username=' + adminUserName + '\n'
        f.write(line)
        # better encrypt !!  line='password='  + encrypt(adminPassword, domainLocation + "/" +
domainName) + '\n'
        line='password=' + adminPassword + '\n'
        f.write(line)
        f.flush()
        f.close()
    except OSError:
        print 'Exception while creating boot.properties for server '+serverName+'. You need to
control/create this file manually !';
        dumpStack()

###################################################################
# Create and configure all managed servers
###################################################################
def createManagedServer(actual_managedserver_name, plain_port, ssl_port, cluster_name):
    try:
        print 'Creating managedserver: '+str(actual_managedserver_name)

        cd('/');
        create(actual_managedserver_name, 'Server')

        # create server
        cd('/Servers/'+actual_managedserver_name)
        print 'Configure managedserver - '+str(actual_managedserver_name)
        set('ListenAddress','localhost')
        set('ListenPort',int(plain_port))
        set('ListenPortEnabled',true)
        set('JavaCompiler','javac')
        set('ClientCertProxyEnabled',false)

        # Add to machine
        #print '    Adding server to machine ;
        #assign('Server', actual_managedserver_name,'Machine', actual_managedserver_machine);

        # Cluster y/n ?
        if ('None' != cluster_name):
           print 'Adding server to cluster  +str(cluster_name)
           assign('Server',actual_managedserver_name,'Cluster',cluster_name)

        # SSL
        print 'Configure SSL';
        create(actual_managedserver_name,'SSL')
        cd('/Servers/'+actual_managedserver_name+'/SSL/'+actual_managedserver_name)
        set('Enabled', 'true')
        set('ListenPort', int(ssl_port))
    except:
        dumpStack();
        print 'Exception while configuring managed servers !'
        exit()



if __name__== "main":
    print '###################################################################';
    print '#                  MT Domain Creation                             #';
    print '###################################################################';

    try:
```

```
# test arguments
if len(sys.argv) != 2 :
        print 'Usage:   createDomain.sh <domainname>';
        exit();

domainName = sys.argv[1];
domainLocation = domainLocationRoot + domainName

print 'Creating the domain : ' + domainName

print 'Selecting templates for multitenancy domain : ' + domainName

selectTemplate("Basic WebLogic Server Domain", "12.2.1")
selectTemplate("Oracle Enterprise Manager-Restricted JRF", "12.2.1")

print 'Loading the templates or multitenancy domain : ' + domainName
loadTemplates()

# Setting the username/password
cd('/Security/base_domain/User/weblogic');
cmo.setName(adminUserName);
cmo.setPassword(adminPassword);

print 'Setting StartUp Options...'
setOption('ServerStartMode', 'prod');
setOption('JavaHome', jvmLocation);
setOption('OverwriteDomain', 'false');

cd('/')
cd('NMProperties')
setOption('NodeManagerType','ManualNodeManagerSetup')

# configureAdminServer
# ------------------------------------------
# Setting listen address/port
print 'Configure Admin Server...'
cd('/Server/AdminServer')
set('ListenAddress','localhost')
set('ListenPort',12001)

# SSL Settings
create('AdminServer','SSL')
cd('SSL/AdminServer')
set('Enabled', 'true')
set('ListenPort', 12002)

# disable hostname verification
cd('/Servers/AdminServer/SSL/AdminServer')
cmo.setHostnameVerificationIgnored(true)
cmo.setHostnameVerifier(None)

print 'Admin Server Configuration Completed.'


# create machines and nodemnager
# to do

# createCluster (only one for now)
# ----------------------------------------------------------------
print 'Creating the cluster Cluster1 ...'
cd('/')
create('Cluster1', 'Cluster')
cd('Cluster/Cluster1')
set('ClusterMessagingMode', 'unicast')
set('FrontendHTTPSPort', 0)
set('FrontendHTTPPort', 0)
set('WeblogicPluginEnabled', 'false')

# create managed servers
print 'Start creating the managed servers ...'
createManagedServer('MS1', '12101', '12102', 'Cluster1')
createManagedServer('MS2', '12201', '12202', 'Cluster1')

# update domain to disk
# -----------------------------
print 'Writing Domain: '+ domainLocation
try:
    writeDomain(domainLocation)
```

```
        except:
            dumpStack()

        print 'Finished writing Domain: '+ domainLocation

        closeTemplate();
        print 'Resources closed: Domain written to disk: '+ domainLocation

        # boot properties
        print '\nCreate boot.properties for all servers\n'
        createBootProperties('AdminServer')
        createBootProperties('MS1')
        createBootProperties('MS2')


        print '\nChange memory for server startup to 1G \n'

        # change memory arguments for admin start
        scriptLocation = domainLocation + '/bin/'

        os.system('sed \'s/\\-Xms256m\\ \\-Xmx512m/\\-Xms1024m\\ \\-Xmx1024m/\'
'+scriptLocation+'setDomainEnv.sh > '+scriptLocation+'tmp1.sh')
        os.system('sed \'s/\\-Xms512m\\ \\-Xmx512m/\\-Xms1024m\\ \\-Xmx1024m/\'
'+scriptLocation+'tmp1.sh > '+ scriptLocation+'tmp2.sh')
        os.system('sed \'s/\\-XX:PermSize=128m/\\-XX:PermSize=196m/\' '+scriptLocation+'tmp2.sh > '
+scriptLocation+'tmp3.sh')
        os.system('sed \'s/\\-XX:PermSize=48m/\\-XX:PermSize=196m/\' '+scriptLocation+'tmp3.sh >
'+scriptLocation+'tmp4.sh')
        os.system('sed \'s/\\-XX:MaxPermSize=128m/\\-XX:PermSize=256m/\' '+scriptLocation+'tmp4.sh >
' +scriptLocation+'tmp5.sh')
        os.system('sed \'s/JAVA_OPTIONS=\\"\\${JAVA_OPTIONS}\\
\\${JAVA_PROPERTIES}\\"/JAVA_OPTIONS=\\"\\${JAVA_OPTIONS}\\ \\-XX\\:\\+UnlockCommercialFeatures\\ \\-
XX\\:\\+ResourceManagement\\ \\-XX\\:\\+UseG1GC\\ \\${JAVA_PROPERTIES}\\"/\'
'+scriptLocation+'tmp5.sh > ' +scriptLocation+'tmp6.sh')

        os.system('cp '+scriptLocation+'tmp6.sh '+scriptLocation+'setDomainEnv.sh')
        os.system('chmod +x '+scriptLocation+'setDomainEnv.sh')
        os.system('rm '+scriptLocation+'tmp*.sh')

        print '\n\n\nDOMAIN creation and configuration finished !\n'

    except:
        print 'Exception while creating domain !'
        dumpStack();
```

Summary

After discussing the technical foundations, it is – especially for decision makers and architects – very useful to think about use cases where this new technology can be used. But the most important aspect is not where it can be used but where it can be used and will bring valuable business benefit.

Part III of this book discussed the main level of isolation which are a prerequisite for multitenancy. In part IV this book discussed the necessary technology bits. The different use cases will bring those together and discuss situations where this technology can be used and can bring different improvements for your business.

Please note that there is no priority or ordering for the difference use-case chapters. All use cases are treated individually. Only if one use case references another then the references will be discussed in a previous chapter to make reading easier.

Introduction to real world examples

CHAPTER

Importance of real word scenarios

This part about use-cases is the heart of the book. Whatever technology is invented, it is useless unless it offers real business values. Without proper business or technically value added for a user new technology is a nice toy but will not be used. Therefore it is important to discuss use cases where this new multitenancy technology offers real value to the users of WebLogic.

There are many use cases which offer added value. I have chosen 11 of them as I think their benefits are pretty obvious, easy to achieve and last, but not least, show the power of the new features.

Note that there is sometimes a bit of overlapping between the different use cases but this can be avoided as some use cases automatically have others as prerequisite or just work nicely hand in hand with others. Nevertheless each use case has its main focus on a specific advantage of multitenancy. This is also the reason use cases are wrapped into own chapters.

Please note that this section of the book is designed to be useful for everybody. Business decision makers as well as administrators, (infrastructure) architects and all others will find useful information in the different use case chapters.

Structure of the use cases

Each use-case will start with a business case consideration. Whatever we do in our world is business driven. Oracle would not have implemented this complex new WebLogic multitenancy model, if this model would not benefit the business. For (business) decision makers each use case will look at the business case first so that readers who are not so much interested in technology details can get the benefit behind the use-case. I have tried to select a number of use-cases with a broad range of scenarios so that not every use-case will be applicable for every reader. It is also expected that in many cases combinations of use-cases might make sense. Experience with different other technology areas has proven that most likely many readers may benefit from some use-cases even though they did not expect that they had these areas of potential improvements.

After a brief discussion, the business case whereas the non-multitenancy setup will be compared with a possible multitenancy setup. The second part of each use-case chapter will dig into details of how this could be implemented. These descriptions expect that the reader is familiar with the technology building bricks which were explained in the previous part (part IV) of the book.

Whenever possible and useful, example setup scripts will be provided. In case these scripts are too big, only relevant parts are printed but all of these scripts are available for download. Note that scripts might be similar for different use cases but they are provided to get a better understanding of each use case without referring to scripts or script parts of other use cases. All example scripts and codes are provided as WLST scripts as it is widely used and easier to understand than JMX or REST.

Base WebLogic domain for the use cases

All use cases assume that a base domain will be created. The following script is used in order to create the base domain(s). Only exception is that some use-cases might need multiple clusters. In this case more managed-server and more clusters will be created.

```
import sys
from java.util import Properties
from java.io import FileInputStream
from java.io import File
from java.util import ArrayList
from java.util import HashMap

# -------- global parameters ---------------------------------------

domainLocationRoot = '/opt/development/wls/wls1221/user_domains/';
domainName     ="usecase_1"
adminUserName = 'weblogic'
adminPassword = 'welcome1'
jvmLocation='/opt/development/jdk1.8.0_60'



####################################################################
# Get instance properties
####################################################################
def createDirIfNotExists(dirname):
   try:
      os.makedirs(dirname)
   except OSError:
      if os.path.exists(dirname):
         # We are nearly safe
         pass
      else:
         # There was an error on creation, so make sure we know about it
         raise
```

```
###################################################################
# Create the boot.properties file
###################################################################
def createBootProperties(serverName):
    try:
        # domain root folder
        domainLocation = domainLocationRoot + '/' + domainName
        createDirIfNotExists(domainLocation + "/servers/" + serverName + "/security")
        filename=domainLocation + "/servers/" + serverName + "/security/boot.properties"

        print '     Create boot property file ' + filename
        f=open(filename, 'w')
        # better encrypt !!  line='username=' + encrypt(adminUserName, domainLocation + "/" +
domainName) + '\n'
        line='username=' + adminUserName + '\n'
        f.write(line)
        # better encrypt !!  line='password=' + encrypt(adminPassword, domainLocation + "/" +
domainName) + '\n'
        line='password=' + adminPassword + '\n'
        f.write(line)
        f.flush()
        f.close()
    except OSError:
        print 'Exception while creating boot.properties for server '+serverName+'. You need to
control/create this file manually !';
        dumpStack()

###################################################################
# Create and configure all managed servers
###################################################################
def createManagedServer(actual_managedserver_name, plain_port, ssl_port, cluster_name):
    try:
        print 'Creating managedserver: '+str(actual_managedserver_name)

        cd('/');
        create(actual_managedserver_name, 'Server')

        # create server
        cd('/Servers/'+actual_managedserver_name)
        print 'Configure managedserver - '+str(actual_managedserver_name)
        set('ListenAddress','localhost')
        set('ListenPort',int(plain_port))
        set('ListenPortEnabled',true)
        set('JavaCompiler','javac')
        set('ClientCertProxyEnabled',false)

        # Add to machine
        #print '     Adding server to machine ';
        #assign('Server', actual_managedserver_name,'Machine', actual_managedserver_machine);

        # Cluster y/n ?
        if ('None' != cluster_name):
           print 'Adding server to cluster '+str(cluster_name)
           assign('Server',actual_managedserver_name,'Cluster',cluster_name)

        # SSL
        print 'Configure SSL';
        create(actual_managedserver_name,'SSL')
        cd('/Servers/'+actual_managedserver_name+'/SSL/'+actual_managedserver_name)
        set('Enabled', 'true')
        set('ListenPort', int(ssl_port))
    except:
        dumpStack();
        print 'Exception while configuring managed servers !'
        exit()



if __name__== "main":
    print '###################################################################';
    print '#                      MT Domain Creation                        #';
    print '###################################################################';

    try:
```

```
# test arguments
if len(sys.argv) != 2 :
        print 'Usage:   createDomain.sh <domainname>';
        exit();

domainName = sys.argv[1];
domainLocation = domainLocationRoot + domainName

print 'Creating the domain : ' + domainName

print 'Selecting templates for multitenancy domain : ' + domainName

selectTemplate("Basic WebLogic Server Domain", "12.2.1")
selectTemplate("Oracle Enterprise Manager-Restricted JRF", "12.2.1")

print 'Loading the templates or multitenancy domain : ' + domainName
loadTemplates()

# Setting the username/password
cd('/Security/base_domain/User/weblogic');
cmo.setName(adminUserName);
cmo.setPassword(adminPassword);

print 'Setting StartUp Options...'
setOption('ServerStartMode', 'prod');
setOption('JavaHome', jvmLocation);
setOption('OverwriteDomain', 'false');

cd('/')
cd('NMProperties')
setOption('NodeManagerType','ManualNodeManagerSetup')

# configureAdminServer
# ----------------------------------------
# Setting listen address/port
print 'Configure Admin Server...'
cd('/Server/AdminServer')
set('ListenAddress','localhost')
set('ListenPort',12001)

# SSL Settings
create('AdminServer','SSL')
cd('SSL/AdminServer')
set('Enabled', 'true')
set('ListenPort', 12002)

# disable hostname verification
cd('/Servers/AdminServer/SSL/AdminServer')
cmo.setHostnameVerificationIgnored(true)
cmo.setHostnameVerifier(None)

print 'Admin Server Configuration Completed.'


# create machines and nodemnager
# to do

# createCluster (only one for now)
# --------------------------------------------------------------
print 'Creating the cluster Cluster1 ...'
cd('/')
create('Cluster1', 'Cluster')
cd('Cluster/Cluster1')
set('ClusterMessagingMode', 'unicast')
set('FrontendHTTPSPort', 0)
set('FrontendHTTPPort', 0)
set('WeblogicPluginEnabled', 'false')

# create managed servers
print 'Start creating the managed servers ...'
createManagedServer('MS1', '12101', '12102', 'Cluster1')
createManagedServer('MS2', '12201', '12202', 'Cluster1')

# update domain to disk
# ----------------------------
print 'Writing Domain: '+ domainLocation
try:
    writeDomain(domainLocation)
```

```
        except:
            dumpStack()

        print 'Finished writing Domain: '+ domainLocation

        closeTemplate();
        print 'Resources closed: Domain written to disk: '+ domainLocation

        # boot properties
        print '\nCreate boot.properties for all servers\n'
        createBootProperties('AdminServer')
        createBootProperties('MS1')
        createBootProperties('MS2')

        print '\nChange memory for server startup to 1G \n'

        # change memory arguments for admin start
        scriptLocation = domainLocation + '/bin/'

        os.system('sed \'s/\\-Xms256m\\ \\-Xmx512m/\\-Xms1024m\\ \\-Xmx1024m/\'
'+scriptLocation+'setDomainEnv.sh > '+scriptLocation+'tmp1.sh')
        os.system('sed \'s/\\-Xms512m\\ \\-Xmx512m/\\-Xms1024m\\ \\-Xmx1024m/\'
'+scriptLocation+'tmp1.sh > '+ scriptLocation+'tmp2.sh')
        os.system('sed \'s/\\-XX:PermSize=128m/\\-XX:PermSize=196m/\' '+scriptLocation+'tmp2.sh > '
+scriptLocation+'tmp3.sh')
        os.system('sed \'s/\\-XX:PermSize=48m/\\-XX:PermSize=196m/\' '+scriptLocation+'tmp3.sh >
'+scriptLocation+'tmp4.sh')
        os.system('sed \'s/\\-XX:MaxPermSize=128m/\\-XX:PermSize=256m/\' '+scriptLocation+'tmp4.sh >
' +scriptLocation+'tmp5.sh')
        os.system('sed \'s/JAVA_OPTIONS=\\"\\${JAVA_OPTIONS}\\
\\${JAVA_PROPERTIES}\\"/JAVA_OPTIONS=\\"\\${JAVA_OPTIONS}\\ \\-XX\\:\\+UnlockCommercialFeatures\\ \\-
XX\\:\\+ResourceManagement\\ \\-XX\\:\\+UseG1GC\\ \\${JAVA_PROPERTIES}\\"/\'
'+scriptLocation+'tmp5.sh > ' +scriptLocation+'tmp6.sh')

        os.system('cp '+scriptLocation+'tmp6.sh '+scriptLocation+'setDomainEnv.sh')
        os.system('chmod +x '+scriptLocation+'setDomainEnv.sh')
        os.system('rm '+scriptLocation+'tmp*.sh')

        print '\n\n\nDOMAIN creation and configuration finished !\n'

    except:
        print 'Exception while creating domain !'
        dumpStack();
```

Summary

After discussing the technical foundations, it is – especially for decision makers and architects – very useful to think about use cases where this new technology can be used. But the most important aspect is not where it can be used but where it can be used and will bring valuable business benefit.

Part III of this book discussed the main level of isolation which are a prerequisite for multitenancy. In part IV this book discussed the necessary technology bits. The different use cases will bring those together and discuss situations where this technology can be used and can bring different improvements for your business.

Please note that there is no priority or ordering for the difference use-case chapters. All use cases are treated individually. Only if one use case references another then the references will be discussed in a previous chapter to make reading easier.

Optimized usage of memory by co-locating different environments

CHAPTER

Overview

One of the major technical advantages is a much higher density of resource utilization. A very popular example are test environments. It is often necessary for a project to have multiple test environments for different development teams or for different versions of a product. In the traditional approach all of them would be installed, use their space on the file system and as they are usually up and running using memory and so on. With multitenancy this could become a one installation environment with the different test environments being different tenants.

Real world example

Imagine a development company for an online shop. The company has as a core product a sophisticated shop. This shop can be extended with different plugins, can be localized with different languages and is used by customers worldwide in different countries. Of course this company has a support and test department in order to confirm customer support cases and to test patches in case of defects.

In order to serve all customers, the company must have test environments for all possible systems and for all possible scenarios (figure 24-1).

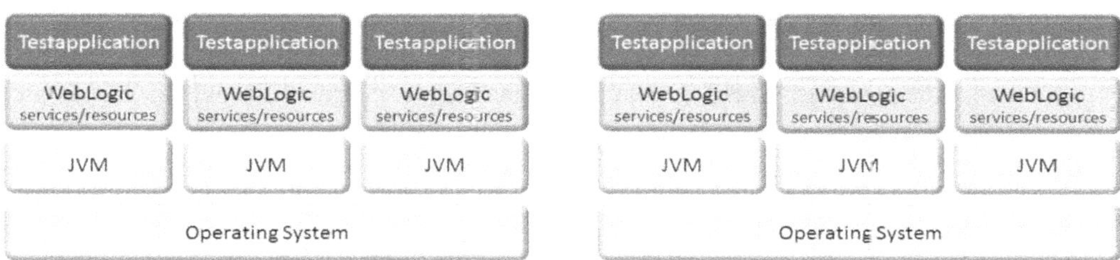

Figure 24-1: Common setup

A common setup is that a configured environment for each version has to be created and maintained. It really depends on the nature of the applications if multiple environments can be setup on the same machine, but this is a quite common approach.

In case these machines and setups are all maintained individually, it is only necessary to have enough file system space in order to setup all the WebLogic domains. Please note that a real world setup is even more complex than depicted above as it also involves AdminServer, NodeManager, cluster setup and possible much more.

In case of a hosting and automated platform like an internal cloud or even an external cloud, the automated mechanism will also reserve all necessary resources for all environments like heap. The customer will be billed for all environments even though almost always only a very small number of environments will be running at the same time.

With the multitenancy approach test environments and their services can be bundled and setup as own partitions. This will save a lot of operating costs (less machines, less machine based licenses, less physical memory and more) and also less administrative costs due to less hardware and resources (figure 24-2).

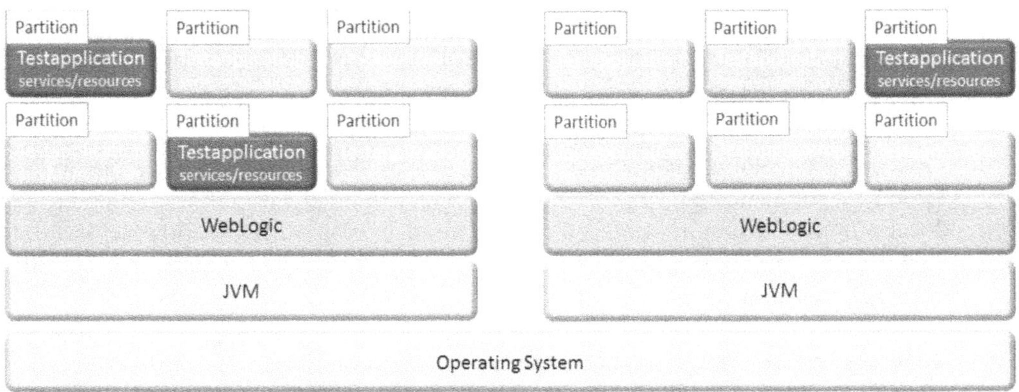

Figure 24-2: Example multitenancy setup

Due to the setup as "WebLogic applications" services are no longer on WebLogic but on partition level.

Drawback using the traditional WLS setup

The traditional (non-multitenancy) setup has a number of disadvantages. Depending on the mode of operation in your company not all of them may apply to you.

Much more resources are needed. As each environment requires an own WebLogic domain or at least on own WebLogic cluster, each environment requires its own heap space, its own process, its own filesystem.

In case of a full domain setup for each environment there is also a need for a lot admin server processes.

Due to the higher amount of resources, most likely more hardware (more machines) will be needed. This is quite a big factor as many licenses are machine/CPU based.

More machines means more work for the administrators. More work for patching, network and security. In case of real hardware (virtual machines are much more common) this also requires more physical space in a datacenter.

It is also not that easy to just deploy another environment on an existing WebLogic as the services (especially database access) is configured on WebLogic level. Therefore a test setup is a combination of the deployments and of the WebLogic domain (or at least cluster) configuration.

Advantages gained using Multitenancy

The multitenancy approach eliminates many of these disadvantages:

- Higher density of test environments.
- Less amount of hardware, which in turn also means less work for unis and network teams
- Cost savings for hardware and licenses

Now partitions combine application code and resource setup, so resources are no longer defined on domain level. It is very easy to host multiple test environments (= partitions) in the same domain, even on the same cluster of managed servers as these environments are sufficient isolated against each other.

Even if multiple test environments may be needed at the same time, the new resource management features can ensure that the WebLogic servers will not run out of memory or utilize too many threads.

Partitions (I like to call them WebLogic applications) can also easily be exported from one domain and kept archived (e.g. older versions!) on the file system. Just in case one may need them at a later point in time (e.g. an audit), they can be brought back very fast and reliable.

Test environment partitions can also easily be exported and migrated to different domains in case one domain is too busy or overloaded.

Especially in automated hosting environments there are massive cost savings as the hosting costs are usually related to resources (machines, memory, etc.) ordered. In the multitenancy case only a minimum of resources are reserved from the platform as all partitions use the same heap (but not necessarily at the same time). Other than the non-multitenancy environment there is no need to reserve heap and hosting (cloud) resources for all environments

Technical steps and details

As in our example we are setting up a farm of test environments, it is very likely that all partitions have a similar setup. In this case we can even use resource group templates to setup all resources which are needed for all partitions. All partitions will be configured with appropriate resource overrides in order to adapt the resources which are inherited from the template to the specific partition instance.

The suggestion would be to use virtual targets with port overrides so that URLs will always be the same. This makes testing easier, especially as in almost all cases automated test suites will be used. One suggestion from the author would be to start the different WebLogic instances always on ports like 10000 or 20000. This makes for a maximum of 6 domains per machine. Every partition defines a port offset so that regardless on which domain the partition runs, it always has the same port offset or – if we only consider the last 4 digest – can be seen to always have the same port.

As it is expected that almost always only one or at least only a few partitions are active, this use case benefits from a global resource manager which is shared by all partitions. This allows the administrators to adjust the available resources based on physical machine boundaries, but also ensure that all partitions together will not break the WebLogic JVM process.

Export and import automations are highly needed in order to move test environments around. To make testing easier, it is recommended to define a well-known port schema and setup every machine with all required virtual targets so that migrating partitions can be done with minimal downtime as the required targets are already defined in all WLS domains.

It is not expected that partitions will share resources so that all resources are scoped on partition level by either add them to the resource group template (which is the foundation for all partitions) or directly add them to the automatically created partition resource group. This also simplifies export and import of partitions.

Automation Example

The following example creates three different partitions. Two of these partitions can be considered to be different environments for the same software. Because of that both are based on the same resource group templates. The resource group template contains a datasource. The third partition is based on a different resource group template.

Script in order to create the resource group template (in case it does not exist), the virtual target and finally the partition.

```
from java.util import Properties
from java.io import FileInputStream
from java.io import File

setupProps = Properties();
input = FileInputStream(sys.argv[1])
setupProps.load(input)
input.close()

# connect to admin
connect(setupProps.getProperty('option_connect_user'),
setupProps.getProperty('option_connect_password'), setupProps.getProperty('option_connect_url'));

# start edit
edit()
startEdit()


# create resource group template
# --------------------------------------------------
cd('/')

if
cmo.lookupResourceGroupTemplate(setupProps.getProperty('option_resourcegrouptemplate_name'))==None:
    print 'Create resource group template ' -
setupProps.getProperty('option_resourcegrouptemplate_name')
    cmo.createResourceGroupTemplate(setupProps.getProperty('option_resourcegrouptemplate_name'))

    cd('/ResourceGroupTemplates/'+setupProps getProperty('option_resourcegrouptemplate_name'))
    cmo.setNotes('My ResourceTemplate called
'+setupProps.getProperty('option_resourcegrouptemplate_name'))


    # create datasource in resource group template
    # --------------------------------------------------
```

```
    cd('/ResourceGroupTemplates/'+setupProps.getProperty('option_resourcegrouptemplate_name'))
    cmo.createJDBCSystemResource(setupProps.getProperty('option_datasource_name'))


cd('/ResourceGroupTemplates/'+setupProps.getProperty('option_resourcegrouptemplate_name')+'/JDBCSyste
mResources/'+setupProps.getProperty('option_datasource_name')+'/JDBCResource/'+setupProps.getProperty
('option_datasource_name'))
    cmo.setDatasourceType('GENERIC')
    cmo.setName(setupProps.getProperty('option_datasource_name'))


cd('/ResourceGroupTemplates/'+setupProps.getProperty('option_resourcegrouptemplate_name')+'/JDBCSyste
mResources/'+setupProps.getProperty('option_datasource_name')+'/JDBCResource/'+setupProps.getProperty
('option_datasource_name')+'/JDBCDataSourceParams/'+setupProps.getProperty('option_datasource_name'))
    cmo.setJNDINames(jarray.array([String(setupProps.getProperty('option_datasource_jndiname'))],
String))
    cmo.setGlobalTransactionsProtocol('OnePhaseCommit')


cd('/ResourceGroupTemplates/'+setupProps.getProperty('option_resourcegrouptemplate_name')+'/JDBCSyste
mResources/'+setupProps.getProperty('option_datasource_name')+'/JDBCResource/'+setupProps.getProperty
('option_datasource_name')+'/JDBCDriverParams/'+setupProps.getProperty('option_datasource_name'))
    cmo.setUrl(setupProps.getProperty('option_datasource_url'))
    cmo.setDriverName('oracle.jdbc.OracleDriver')

    cd('/ResourceGroupTemplates/'+setupProps.getProperty('option_resourcegrouptemplate_name')+
    '/JDBCSystemResources/'+setupProps.getProperty('option_datasource_name')+'/JDBCResource/'+
    setupProps.getProperty('option_datasource_name')+'/JDBCDriverParams/'+
    setupProps.getProperty('option_datasource_name')+'/Properties/'+
    setupProps.getProperty('option_datasource_name'))

    cmo.createProperty('user')


cd('/ResourceGroupTemplates/'+setupProps.getProperty('option_resourcegrouptemplate_name')+'/JDBCSyste
mResources/'+setupProps.getProperty('option_datasource_name')+'/JDBCResource/'+setupProps.getProperty
('option_datasource_name')+'/JDBCDriverParams/'+setupProps.getProperty('option_datasource_name')+'/Pr
operties/'+setupProps.getProperty('option_datasource_name')+'/Properties/user')
    cmo.setValue(setupProps.getProperty('option_datasource_user'))


cd('/ResourceGroupTemplates/'+setupProps.getProperty('option_resourcegrouptemplate_name')+'/JDBCSyste
mResources/'+setupProps.getProperty('option_datasource_name')+'/JDBCResource/'+setupProps.getProperty
('option_datasource_name')+'/JDBCConnectionPoolParams/'+setupProps.getProperty('option_datasource_nam
e'))
    cmo.setTestTableName('SQL ISVALID')
else:
    print 'Resource group template ' + setupProps.getProperty('option_resourcegrouptemplate_name')+'
already exists - skip create'



# create virtual target
# -----------------------------------
cd('/')

if cmo.lookupVirtualTarget(setupProps.getProperty('option_virtualtarget_name'))==None:
    print 'Create virtual target ' + setupProps.getProperty('option_virtualtarget_name')

    cmo.createVirtualTarget(setupProps.getProperty('option_virtualtarget_name'))

    cd('/VirtualTargets/'+setupProps.getProperty('option_virtualtarget_name'))
    cmo.setUriPrefix(setupProps.getProperty('option_virtualtarget_prefix'))

set('Targets',jarray.array([ObjectName('com.bea:Name='+setupProps.getProperty('option_virtualtarget_t
arget')+',Type='+setupProps.getProperty('option_virtualtarget_targettype'))], ObjectName))
else:
    print 'Virtual target ' + setupProps.getProperty('option_virtualtarget_name')+' already exists -
skip create'


# create partition with override
# -----------------------------------------------------------
cd('/')
cmo.createPartition(setupProps.getProperty('option_partition_name'))

cd('/Partitions/'+setupProps.getProperty('option_partition_name')+'/SystemFileSystem/'+setupProps.get
Property('option_partition_name'))
```

```
cmo.setRoot('/opt/development/wls/wls1221/user_domains/martin_1221/partitions/'+setupProps.getPropert
y('option_partition_name')+'/system')
cmo.setCreateOnDemand(true)
cmo.setPreserved(true)

cd('/Partitions/'+setupProps.getProperty('option_partition_name'))
cmo.createResourceGroup(setupProps.getProperty('option_partition_name')+'_group')

cd('/Partitions/'+setupProps.getProperty('option_partition_name')+'/ResourceGroups/'+setupProps.getPr
operty('option_partition_name')+'_group')
cmo.setResourceGroupTemplate(getMBean('/ResourceGroupTemplates/'+setupProps.getProperty('option_resou
rcegrouptemplate_name')))

cd('/Partitions/'+setupProps.getProperty('option_partition_name'))
set('AvailableTargets',jarray.array([ObjectName('com.bea:Name='+setupProps.getProperty('option_virtua
ltarget_name')+',Type=VirtualTarget')], ObjectName))
set('DefaultTargets',jarray.array([ObjectName('com.bea:Name='+setupProps.getProperty('option_virtualt
arget_name')+',Type=VirtualTarget')], ObjectName))

cd('/Partitions/'+setupProps.getProperty('option_partition_name')+'/ResourceGroups/'+setupProps.getPr
operty('option_partition_name')+'_group')


# create overrides
# --------------------
cd ('/Partitions/'+setupProps.getProperty('option_partition_name'))
cmo.createJDBCSystemResourceOverride('JDBCSystemResourceOverride-
'+setupProps.getProperty('option_datasource_name'))
cd ('JDBCSystemResourceOverrides/JDBCSystemResourceOverride-
'+setupProps.getProperty('option_datasource_name'))
cmo.setDataSourceName(setupProps.getProperty('option_datasource_name'))
cmo.setURL(setupProps.getProperty('option_datasource_url'))
cmo.setUser(setupProps.getProperty('option_datasource_user'))


# save and activate
# -----------------------
save()
```

Property files which can be used to setup the discussed three partitions.

Partition "X"

Properties file

```
option_connect_user=weblogic
option_connect_password=welcome1

option_virtualtarget_name=VirtualTarget-X
option_virtualtarget_prefix=/test_x
option_virtualtarget_target=Cluster1
option_virtualtarget_targettype=Cluster

option_resourcegrouptemplate_name=ResourceGroupTemplate_X
option_datasource_name=TestDataSource
option_datasource_url=jdbc:oracle:thin:@//mydb.com:1521/ORCL
option_datasource_jndiname=/jdbc/testDS
option_datasource_user=martin
```

Script output

```
Initializing WebLogic Scripting Tool (WLST) ...
...

Starting an edit session ...
Started edit session, be sure to save and activate your changes once you are done.
Create resource group template ResourceGroupTemplate_X
Create virtual target VirtualTarget-X
```

```
Saving all your changes ...
Saved all your changes successfully.
Activating all your changes, this may take a while ...
The edit lock associated with this edit session is released once the activation is completed.

The following non-dynamic attribute(s) have been changed on MBeans
that require server re-start:
MBean Changed : com.bea:Name=usecase_1,Type=SecurityConfiguration
Attributes changed : AdministrativeIdentityDomain
```

Partition "X2"

Properties file

```
option_connect_user=weblogic
option_connect_password=welcome1

option_virtualtarget_name=VirtualTarget-X2
option_virtualtarget_prefix=/test_x2
option_virtualtarget_target=Cluster1
option_virtualtarget_targettype=Cluster

option_resourcegrouptemplate_name=ResourceGroupTemplate_X
option_datasource_name=TestDataSource
option_datasource_url=jdbc:oracle:thin:@//mydb.com:1521/O2
option_datasource_jndiname=/jdbc/testDS
option_datasource_user=martin
```

Script output

```
Initializing WebLogic Scripting Tool (WLST) ...
...

Starting an edit session ...
Started edit session, be sure to save and activate your changes once you are done.
Resource group template ResourceGroupTemplate_X already exists - skip create
Create virtual target VirtualTarget-X2
Saving all your changes ...
Saved all your changes successfully.
Activating all your changes, this may take a while ...
The edit lock associated with this edit session is released once the activation is completed.
```

Partition "Test"

Properties file

```
option_connect_user=weblogic
option_connect_password=welcome1

option_virtualtarget_name=VirtualTarget-TestEnv
option_virtualtarget_prefix=/test_env
option_virtualtarget_target=Cluster1
option_virtualtarget_targettype=Cluster

option_resourcegrouptemplate_name=ResourceGroupTemplate_TestEnv
option_datasource_name=TestDataSource
option_datasource_url=jdbc:oracle:thin:@//uat.com:1521/Test
option_datasource_jndiname=/jdbc/testDS
option_datasource_user=martin
```

Script output

```
Initializing WebLogic Scripting Tool (WLST) ...
...
Starting an edit session ...
Started edit session, be sure to save and activate your changes once you are done.
Create resource group template ResourceGroupTemplate_TestEnv
Create virtual target VirtualTarget-TestEnv
Saving all your changes ...
Saved all your changes successfully.
Activating all your changes, this may take a while ...
The edit lock associated with this edit session is released once the activation is completed.
```

The domain set which is stored in the config.xml looks like:

```
<domain>
  <name>usecase_1</name>
  <domain-version>12.2.1.0.0</domain-version>

  <virtual-target>
    <name>VirtualTarget-X</name>
    <target>Cluster1</target>
    <uri-prefix>/test_x</uri-prefix>
    <web-server>
      <web-server-log>
        <number-of-files-limited>false</number-of-files-limited>
      </web-server-log>
    </web-server>
  </virtual-target>
  <virtual-target>
    <name>VirtualTarget-X2</name>
    <target>Cluster1</target>
    <uri-prefix>/test_x2</uri-prefix>
    <web-server>
      <web-server-log>
        <number-of-files-limited>false</number-of-files-limited>
      </web-server-log>
    </web-server>
  </virtual-target>
  <virtual-target>
    <name>VirtualTarget-TestEnv</name>
    <target>Cluster1</target>
    <uri-prefix>/test_env</uri-prefix>
    <web-server>
      <web-server-log>
        <number-of-files-limited>false</number-of-files-limited>
      </web-server-log>
    </web-server>
  </virtual-target>

  <partition>
    <name>Partition_X</name>
    <resource-group>
      <name>Partition_X_group</name>
      <resource-group-template>ResourceGroupTemplate_X</resource-group-template>
    </resource-group>
    <jdbc-system-resource-override>
      <name>JDBCSystemResourceOverride-TestDataSource</name>
      <data-source-name>TestDataSource</data-source-name>
      <url>jdbc:oracle:thin:@//mydb.com:1521/ORCL</url>
      <user>martin</user>
    </jdbc-system-resource-override>
    <default-target>VirtualTarget-X</default-target>
    <available-target>VirtualTarget-X</available-target>
    <partition-id>9ac9087e-8486-4835-83e2-66eca814f2cf</partition-id>
    <system-file-system>
<root>/opt/development/wls/wls1221/user_domains/martin_1221/partitions/Partition_X/system</root>
      <create-on-demand>true</create-on-demand>
      <preserved>true</preserved>
    </system-file-system>
  </partition>
  <partition>
    <name>Partition_X2</name>
    <resource-group>
```

```
      <name>Partition_X2_group</name>
      <resource-group-template>ResourceGroupTemplate_X</resource-group-template>
    </resource-group>
    <jdbc-system-resource-override>
      <name>JDBCSystemResourceOverride-TestDataSource</name>
      <data-source-name>TestDataSource</data-source-name>
      <url>jdbc:oracle:thin:@//mydb.com:1521/O2</url>
      <user>martin</user>
    </jdbc-system-resource-override>
    <default-target>VirtualTarget-X2</default-target>
    <available-target>VirtualTarget-X2</available-target>
    <partition-id>87192735-4ea1-4adb-8cd7-9b8482e20453</partition-id>
    <system-file-system>

<root>/opt/development/wls/wls1221/user_domains/martin_1221/partitions/Partition_X2/system</root>
      <create-on-demand>true</create-on-demand>
      <preserved>true</preserved>
    </system-file-system>
  </partition>
  <partition>
    <name>Partition_TestEnvironment</name>
    <resource-group>
      <name>Partition_TestEnvironment_group</name>
      <resource-group-template>ResourceGroupTemplate_TestEnv</resource-group-template>
    </resource-group>
    <jdbc-system-resource-override>
      <name>JDBCSystemResourceOverride-TestDataSource</name>
      <data-source-name>TestDataSource</data-source-name>
      <url>jdbc:oracle:thin:@//uat.com:1521/Test</url>
      <user>martin</user>
    </jdbc-system-resource-override>
    <default-target>VirtualTarget-TestEnv</default-target>
    <available-target>VirtualTarget-TestEnv</available-target>
    <partition-id>953181db-26d1-43aa-a6af-9b1d8047bd76</partition-id>
    <system-file-system>

<root>/opt/development/wls/wls1221/user_domains/martin_1221/partitions/Partition_TestEnvironment/syst
em</root>
      <create-on-demand>true</create-on-demand>
      <preserved>true</preserved>
    </system-file-system>
  </partition>
  <resource-group-template>
    <name>ResourceGroupTemplate_X</name>
    <notes>My ResourceTemplate called ResourceGroupTemplate_X</notes>
    <jdbc-system-resource>
      <name>TestDataSource</name>
      <descriptor-file-name>resource-group-templates/ResourceGroupTemplate_X/jdbc/TestDataSource-
2617-jdbc.xml</descriptor-file-name>
    </jdbc-system-resource>
  </resource-group-template>
  <resource-group-template>
    <name>ResourceGroupTemplate_TestEnv</name>
    <notes>My ResourceTemplate called ResourceGroupTemplate_TestEnv</notes>
    <jdbc-system-resource>
      <name>TestDataSource</name>
      <descriptor-file-name>resource-group-
templates/ResourceGroupTemplate_TestEnv/jdbc/TestDataSource-2617-jdbc.xml</descriptor-file-name>
    </jdbc-system-resource>
  </resource-group-template>
```

Summary

WebLogic up to now had a number of restrictions which enforces administrators in many cases to deploy different applications or even different application components into separate domains. The main problem was the limited security (one realm model). Also the global availability of all resources was causing conflicts and in some cases serious security risks.

Using the new partition model, it is possible to collocate different environments. This use-case, showed with a common example with different environments where not all of these environments were running all the time. Partitions in this case even allow for a very efficient way to use existing resources and reduce the number of administrative components (adminserver).

Optimized usage of computing resources

CHAPTER

Overview

Applications, hosted as multiple tenants, can share resources. In case of WebLogic, resource sharing is a flexible and configurable process which allow applications to either share resources like JMS or JDBC or use (part of them) exclusively. In addition sharing means that there is no network overhead like t3 calls or http calls involved as all tenants are co-located in the same address space. Multitenancy concepts of course already exist for resource systems like databases or caches (e.g. coherence).

Real world example

Imagine a company which uses a payment system and a customer database. Both need to access data which is stored in the same database. Furthermore both systems need to talk to each other for every transaction. Nevertheless both system also have their own requirements and own deployments as they are different applications. Both applications have to fulfill a requirement for amount of parallel invocations.

See the following diagram. Both applications are co-hosted on the same machine to save network latency. Both WebLogic domains have their own JDBC pool and their own thread pool (figure 25-1).

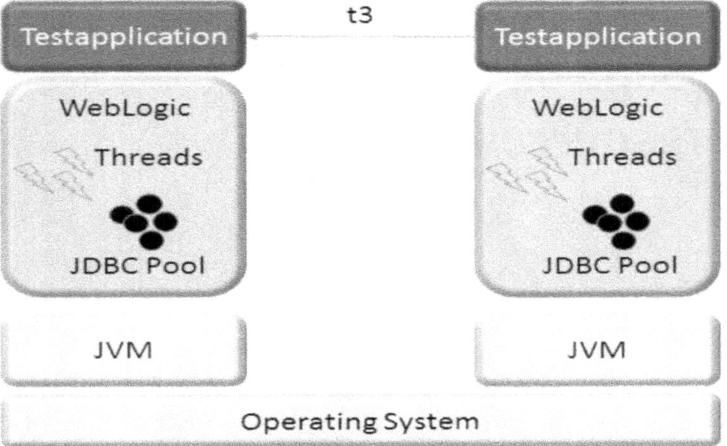

Figure 25-1: Traditional setup

A common setup is that a configured domain for each application has to be created and maintained.

Both domains have their own resource pool defined on WebLogic domain level. Threads are needed to fulfill the parallel requirement as for each parallel invocation an own thread is needed.

As for our example both applications access data from the same database, both WebLogic domains have to be setup with the same datasources and have to maintain the same JDBC pool. Remember that all pools combined must not request more connections as the database can offer. In this case it might be possible that both pools need to be configured with a smaller maximum in order to avoid database overload.

With the multitenancy approach this scenario could be improved. Both applications will be configured as a partition which allow the administrators to configure both partitions with all resources they need. In our example this would be an own thread pool. In order to get the optimal resource usage a shared JDBC pool can be used in order to avoid multiple pools for the same connection setup (figure 25-2).

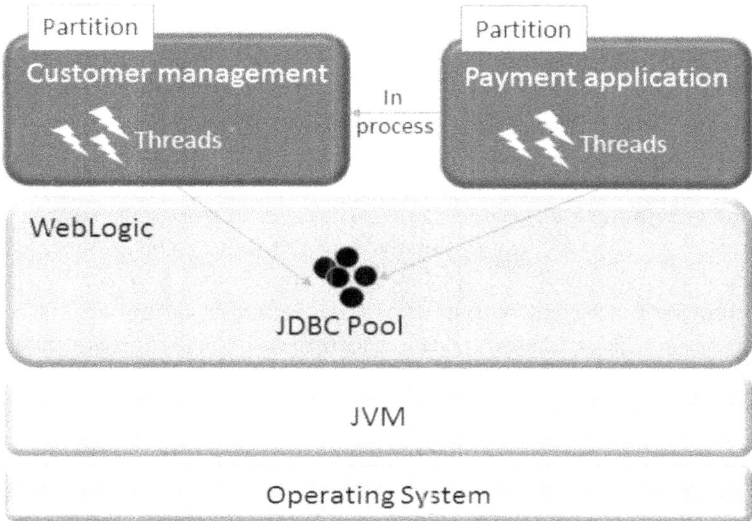

Figure 25-2: Possible Multitenancy setup

A possible multitenancy setup could bundle both applications in different partitions, but deploy and target both partitions to the same WebLogic cluster or managed servers. Every partition get is own – partition scoped – work manager and thread management. In order to optimize the resources (JDBC pool in our example) both partitions access the same JDBC pool which is scoped to a global (domain scoped) resource group.

Drawback using the traditional WLS setup

The non-multitenancy setup has a number of disadvantages. The example discussed above consider a combination of different components which are hosted in different domains, but working together and even using the same database or other common resources. It is quite common that bigger and more complex applications are split into different components or that different applications need to work together.

The main drawback in this example is the fact that this setup duplicates resource usage for certain types of resources. This kind of setup requires that different virtual machines with completely separated memory heaps have to be created. It also requires that resources like JDBC pools need to be duplicated. It is much more efficient, if they will be shared!

It is impossible to use the same heap more efficiently as both components are running in different JVMs.

Duplicated JDBC pools can be quite difficult to handle, as the administrator must ensure that at no point in time all systems together will open more database connections than can be handled by the database.

Communication between these two components – as isolation is required – must in this case use TCP based communication connections, at least in this case. In case of very high traffic or many short calls, this will definitely slow down the response time.

Due to the communication between both domains there are also a number of security issues to take into account like authentication, authorization but also domain trust.

Last but not least it also requires more disk space as two WebLogic domains must be setup.

Advantages gained using Multitenancy

Using a multitenancy setup can avoid many of the drawbacks discussed in the previous section. The main aspect here is that components can be co-located to make better use of resources without abandon their level of isolation.

By using different partitions for the different components, both applications can be deployed (imported) into the same WebLogic cluster. By running both in the same WebLogic the amount of domains – which also means the amount of admin servers – will be reduced to one. This also reduces the filesystem footprint

One aspect of this use-case is that resources which are configured at domain level can be shared by both partitions. This example is using a JDBC connection pool that is configured on domain level. As it is configured outside of the partitions, it can be shared by both partitions.

Given as an example that the database can only open 100 concurrent connection, the administrator does not need to worry about how to distribute these 100 connections between the different domains. As there is only one JDBC pool both applications can use connections from this pool. Administrators only need to take the amount of managed servers of this cluster into account.

This setup also simplifies the security setup of the domain as for example domain trust is no longer required.

Technical steps and details

The multitenancy setup described in this use case can be setup using the new WebLogic feature. It is advisable to consider the following points while doing the setup:

As both components work together it is advisable (albeit not required) to only use the global security realm as this makes security easier. It is also possible to use partition security realms and also identity domains but this makes the setup more complicated, especially because of the cross partition communication.

On domain level a resource manager controls the resource usage of both partitions. In case both partitions have different requirements (like different heap requirements) it might be worthwhile considering an own resource manager for each partition.

Also on domain level the global JDBC datasource can be setup in a global resource group. Note that it cannot be setup using a resource group template as the pool will be instantiated on domain level.

Especially JMS resources and their usage can be setup much better using this approach because the JMS server can be instantiated on the domain level and extra components like SAF or foreign server configurations are not necessary.

All other resources which are not shared between both applications will be setup on partition level in order to keep the isolation and the bundling of resources and applications.

Automation Example

The following example creates a globally (domain) scoped JDBC datasource. In order to show another feature of partitions, this example uses a shared partition workmanager. Each partition also has an own resource manager with a heap trigger. The example creates two partitions. The partition setup includes the setup of the shared workmanager if – and only if – it does not yet exist. Note that both scripts contain the shared workmanager setup in case partitions will get imported and not created.

Script in order to setup the global resources of the domain.

```
import sys
from java.util import Properties
from java.io import FileInputStream
from java.io import File

setupProps = Properties();
input = FileInputStream(sys.argv[1])
setupProps.load(input)
```

```
input.close()

# connect to admin
connect(setupProps.getProperty('option_connect_user'),
setupProps.getProperty('option_connect_password'), setupProps.getProperty('option_connect_url'));

# start edit
edit()
startEdit()


# create shared partition workmanager - IF NOT EXIST
# -------------------------------------------------------
cd('/')

if cmo.lookupPartitionWorkManager('MySharedPartitionWorkManager')==None:
    print 'Create shared partition workmanager:MySharedPartitionWorkManager'
    cmo.createPartitionWorkManager('MySharedPartitionWorkManager')

    cd('/PartitionWorkManagers/MySharedPartitionWorkManager')
    cmo.setSharedCapacityPercent(100)
    cmo.setFairShare(50)
    cmo.setMinThreadsConstraintCap(0)
    cmo.setMaxThreadsConstraint(200)
else:
    print 'Shared partition workmanager:MySharedPartitionWorkManager already exists - skip create'


# Setup domain level global datasource  ( and other shared resources)
# -------------------------------------------------------------------
cd('/')
cmo.createJDBCSystemResource('MyGDS')

cd('/JDBCSystemResources/MyGDS/JDBCResource/MyGDS')
cmo.setName('MyGDS')

cd('/JDBCSystemResources/MyGDS/JDBCResource/MyGDS/JDBCDataSourceParams/MyGDS')
set('JNDINames',jarray.array([String('/global/jdbc/gds')], String))

cd('/JDBCSystemResources/MyGDS/JDBCResource/MyGDS')
cmo.setDatasourceType('GENERIC')

cd('/JDBCSystemResources/MyGDS/JDBCResource/MyGDS/JDBCDriverParams/MyGDS')
cmo.setUrl('jdbc:oracle:thin:@//localhost:1521/ORCL')
cmo.setDriverName('oracle.jdbc.OracleDriver')

cd('/JDBCSystemResources/MyGDS/JDBCResource/MyGDS/JDBCConnectionPoolParams/MyGDS')
cmo.setTestTableName('SQL ISVALID\r\n')

cd('/JDBCSystemResources/MyGDS/JDBCResource/MyGDS/JDBCDriverParams/MyGDS/Properties/MyGDS')
cmo.createProperty('user')

cd('/JDBCSystemResources/MyGDS/JDBCResource/MyGDS/JDBCDriverParams/MyGDS/Properties/MyGDS/Properties/
user')
cmo.setValue('ttttt')

cd('/JDBCSystemResources/MyGDS/JDBCResource/MyGDS/JDBCDataSourceParams/MyGDS')
cmo.setGlobalTransactionsProtocol('OnePhaseCommit')

cd('/JDBCSystemResources/MyGDS')
set('Targets',jarray.array([ObjectName('com.bea:Name=Cluster1,Type=Cluster')], ObjectName))

# save and activate
# ----------------------
save()
```

Script in order to setup a partition, which includes the virtual target, the partition resource manager and if needed the shared workmanager.

```
import sys
from java.util import Properties
from java.io import FileInputStream
from java.io import File
```

```
setupProps = Properties();
input = FileInputStream(sys.argv[1])
setupProps.load(input)
input.close()

# connect to admin
connect(setupProps.getProperty('option_connect_user'),
setupProps.getProperty('option_connect_password'), setupProps.getProperty('option_connect_url'));

# start edit
edit()
startEdit()


# create shared partition workmanager - IF NOT EXIST
# --------------------------------------------------------
cd('/')

if cmo.lookupPartitionWorkManager('MySharedPartitionWorkManager')==None:
    print 'Create shared partition workmanager:MySharedPartitionWorkManager'
    cmo.createPartitionWorkManager('MySharedPartitionWorkManager')

    cd('/PartitionWorkManagers/MySharedPartitionWorkManager')
    cmo.setSharedCapacityPercent(100)
    cmo.setFairShare(50)
    cmo.setMinThreadsConstraintCap(0)
    cmo.setMaxThreadsConstraint(200)
else:
    print 'Shared partition workmanager:MySharedPartitionWorkManager already exists - skip create'


# create virtual target
# -------------------------------------
cd('/')

if cmo.lookupVirtualTarget(setupProps.getProperty('option_virtualtarget_name'))==None:
    print 'Create virtual target ' + setupProps.getProperty('option_virtualtarget_name')

    cmo.createVirtualTarget(setupProps.getProperty('option_virtualtarget_name'))

    cd('/VirtualTargets/'+setupProps.getProperty('option_virtualtarget_name'))
    cmo.setUriPrefix(setupProps.getProperty('option_virtualtarget_prefix'))

set('Targets',jarray.array([ObjectName('com.bea:Name='+setupProps.getProperty('option_virtualtarget_t
arget')+',Type='+setupProps.getProperty('option_virtualtarget_targettype'))], ObjectName))
else:
    print 'Virtual target ' + setupProps.getProperty('option_virtualtarget_name')+' already exists -
skip create'


# create partition
# ----------------------------------------------------------
cd('/')
cmo.createPartition(setupProps.getProperty('option_partition_name'))

cd('/Partitions/'+setupProps.getProperty('option_partition_name')+'/SystemFileSystem/'+setupProps.get
Property('option_partition_name'))
cmo.setRoot('/opt/development/wls/wls1221/user_domains/martin_1221/partitions/'+setupProps.getPropert
y('option_partition_name')+'/system')
cmo.setCreateOnDemand(true)
cmo.setPreserved(true)

# shared work manager reference
cd('/Partitions/'+setupProps.getProperty('option_partition_name'))
cmo.setPartitionWorkManagerRef(getMBean('/PartitionWorkManagers/MySharedPartitionWorkManager'))


# set partition resource manager with heap trigger
cd('/Partitions/'+setupProps.getProperty('option_partition_name'))
cmo.createResourceManager('ResourceManager-'+setupProps.getProperty('option_partition_name'))

cd('/Partitions/'+setupProps.getProperty('option_partition_name')+'/ResourceManager/ResourceManager-
'+setupProps.getProperty('option_partition_name'))
cmo.createHeapRetained('HeapRetainedResource')
```

```
cd('/Partitions/'+setupProps.getProperty('option_partition_name')+'/ResourceManager/ResourceManager-
'+setupProps.getProperty('option_partition_name')+'/HeapRetained/HeapRetainedResource')
cmo.createTrigger('Trigger-2GB-Heap', 2048, 'slow')

# target
cd('/Partitions/'+setupProps.getProperty('option_partition_name'))
set('AvailableTargets',jarray.array([ObjectName('com.bea:Name='+setupProps.getProperty('option_virtua
ltarget_name')+',Type=VirtualTarget')], ObjectName))
set('DefaultTargets',jarray.array([ObjectName('com.bea:Name='+setupProps.getProperty('option_virtualt
arget_name')+',Type=VirtualTarget')], ObjectName))


# save and activate
# -----------------------
save()
```

Setup the first partition

Property file to setup the first partition

```
option_connect_user=weblogic
option_connect_password=welcome1

option_virtualtarget_name=VirtualTarget-PaymentManagement
option_virtualtarget_prefix=/payment
option_virtualtarget_target=Cluster1
option_virtualtarget_targettype=Cluster
```

Output while running the script

```
Initializing WebLogic Scripting Tool (WLST) ...

Connecting to t3://localhost:12001 with userid weblogic ...

Location changed to edit tree.

Starting an edit session ...
Started edit session, be sure to save and activate your changes once you are done.
Create shared partition workmanager:MySharedPartitionWorkManager
Create virtual target VirtualTarget-PaymentManagement
Saving all your changes ...
Saved all your changes successfully.
Activating all your changes, this may take a while ...
The edit lock associated with this edit session is released once the activation is completed.

The following non-dynamic attribute(s) have been changed on MBeans
that require server re-start:
MBean Changed : com.bea:Name=usercase_2,Type=SecurityConfiguration
Attributes changed : AdministrativeIdentityDomain
```

Setup the second partition

Property file to setup the first partition

```
option_connect_user=weblogic
option_connect_password=welcome1

option_virtualtarget_name=VirtualTarget-CustomerManagement
option_virtualtarget_prefix=/customerMgmt
```

```
option_virtualtarget_target=Cluster1
option_virtualtarget_targettype=Cluster
```

Output while running the script

```
Connecting to t3://localhost:12001 with userid weblogic ...

Location changed to edit tree.
This is a writable tree with DomainMBean as the root.

Starting an edit session ...
Started edit session, be sure to save and activate your changes once you are done.
Shared partition workmanager:MySharedPartitionWorkManager already exists - skip create
Create virtual target VirtualTarget-CustomerManagement
Saving all your changes ...
Saved all your changes successfully.
Activating all your changes, this may take a while ...
The edit lock associated with this edit session is released once the activation is completed.
```

After all scripts did run, the domain has the following configuration

```
  <name>usercase_2</name>

  <virtual-target>
    <name>VirtualTarget-PaymentManagement</name>
    <target>Cluster1</target>
    <uri-prefix>/payment</uri-prefix>
    <web-server>
      <web-server-log>
        <number-of-files-limited>false</number-of-files-limited>
      </web-server-log>
    </web-server>
  </virtual-target>

  <virtual-target>
    <name>VirtualTarget-CustomerManagement</name>
    <target>Cluster1</target>
    <uri-prefix>/customerMgmt</uri-prefix>
    <web-server>
      <web-server-log>
        <number-of-files-limited>false</number-of-files-limited>
      </web-server-log>
    </web-server>
  </virtual-target>

  <jdbc-system-resource>
    <name>MyGDS</name>
    <target>Cluster1</target>
    <descriptor-file-name>jdbc/MyGDS-6250-jdbc.xml</descriptor-file-name>
  </jdbc-system-resource>

  <partition>
    <name>Partition_PaymentManagement</name>
    <default-target>VirtualTarget-PaymentManagement</default-target>
    <available-target>VirtualTarget-PaymentManagement</available-target>
    <partition-id>ef92fb84-faec-4053-a18b-824a988d2407</partition-id>
    <resource-manager>
      <name>ResourceManager-Partition_PaymentManagement</name>
      <heap-retained>
        <name>HeapRetainedResource</name>
        <trigger>
          <name>Trigger-2GB-Heap</name>
          <value>2048</value>
          <action>slow</action>
        </trigger>
      </heap-retained>
    </resource-manager>
    <system-file-system>
```

```
      <root>/opt/development/wls/partitions/Partition_PaymentManagement/system</root>
      <create-on-demand>true</create-on-demand>
      <preserved>true</preserved>
    </system-file-system>
    <partition-work-manager-ref>MySharedPartitionWorkManager</partition-work-manager-ref>
  </partition>

  <partition>
    <name>Partition_CustomerManagement</name>
    <default-target>VirtualTarget-CustomerManagement</default-target>
    <available-target>VirtualTarget-CustomerManagement</available-target>
    <partition-id>a1edd8fb-c82b-4e66-ad10-d99e83ca700e</partition-id>
    <resource-manager>
      <name>ResourceManager-Partition_CustomerManagement</name>
      <heap-retained>
        <name>HeapRetainedResource</name>
        <trigger>
          <name>Trigger-2GB-Heap</name>
          <value>2048</value>
          <action>slow</action>
        </trigger>
      </heap-retained>
    </resource-manager>
    <system-file-system>
      <root>/opt/development/wls/partitions/Partition_CustomerManagement/system</root>
      <create-on-demand>true</create-on-demand>
      <preserved>true</preserved>
    </system-file-system>
    <partition-work-manager-ref>MySharedPartitionWorkManager</partition-work-manager-ref>
  </partition>

  <partition-work-manager>
    <name>MySharedPartitionWorkManager</name>
    <shared-capacity-percent>100</shared-capacity-percent>
    <fair-share>50</fair-share>
    <min-threads-constraint-cap>0</min-threads-constraint-cap>
    <max-threads-constraint>200</max-threads-constraint>
  </partition-work-manager>
```

Summary

In our world of permanently growing system landscapes and additionally shrinking IT budgets, it is a high priority for all administrators to use the available resources as efficiently as possible.

Hosting multiple applications in different partitions helps to save resources by providing a better memory (heap) usage, less network traffic and it also decreases the administration overhead. All of these benefits can be measured in a reduction of costs.

A new way of looking at applications by including their resources

CHAPTER

Overview

The biggest packaging format defined in the J2EE standard is the EAR file. An EAR file contains all deployments for the different application server container. It can contain standard archives (like EJBs, WARs and RARs) but also vendor specific ones. All these components together form a deployable application. But it does not contain the resources and resource definitions needed by this application like JDBC pools, JMS destinations, JNDI trees or network endpoint to name a few. WebLogic multitenancy changes this by defining a new application container (called "partition") which combines all these.

Real world example

All companies have the problem of handing over developed programs to operation and production. Many attempts have been made to improve these processes – see e.g. DevOps. Regardless of the process there is always the problem that application code (e.g. packaged as EAR) has to be deployed into environments which then uses resources of these environments. The handover process of course also needs to define and describe the resources needed but anyway these two components are almost always treated separately.

None of the common environments really define a way to combine resources and applications into a single unit. J2EE for example define resource references in order to decouple application code from real resources, but it does not contain the description of the resources – and this was designed on purpose.

Looking at a common scenario: An EAR file will be provided for the application logic. In addition the administrator gets a number of queue and topic names which reside on a remote (or local) JMS system. Now the administrator has to setup all the queues and topics first, makes sure the JMS environment is ready and works (should be automated of course) and afterwards he can deploy the application EAR. He cannot do this together (figure 26-1).

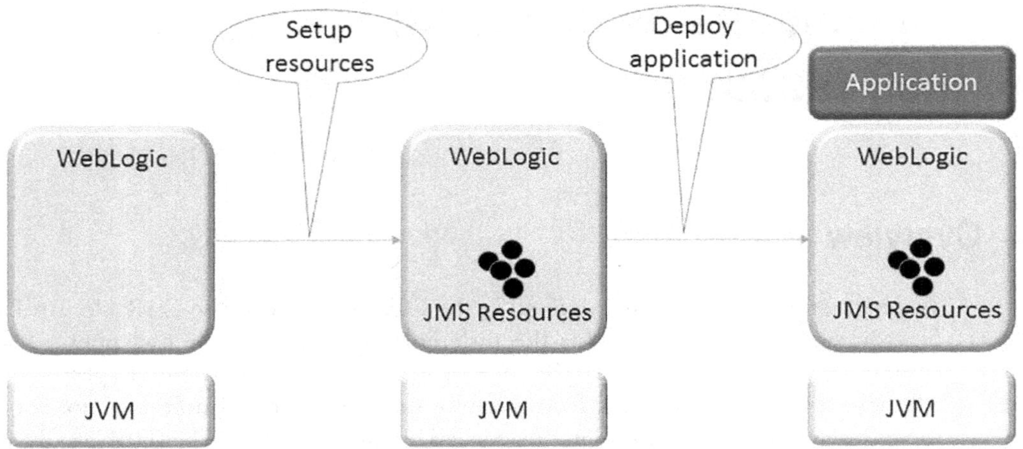

Figure 26-1: Standard way to setup and deploy to WebLogic

WebLogic now – albeit it is not a standard, but a proprietary way – offers the ability to define what I earlier introduced as "WebLogic applications" where resources and applications can be bundled together, so they can be deployed (imported) together into a destination environment (figure 16-2).

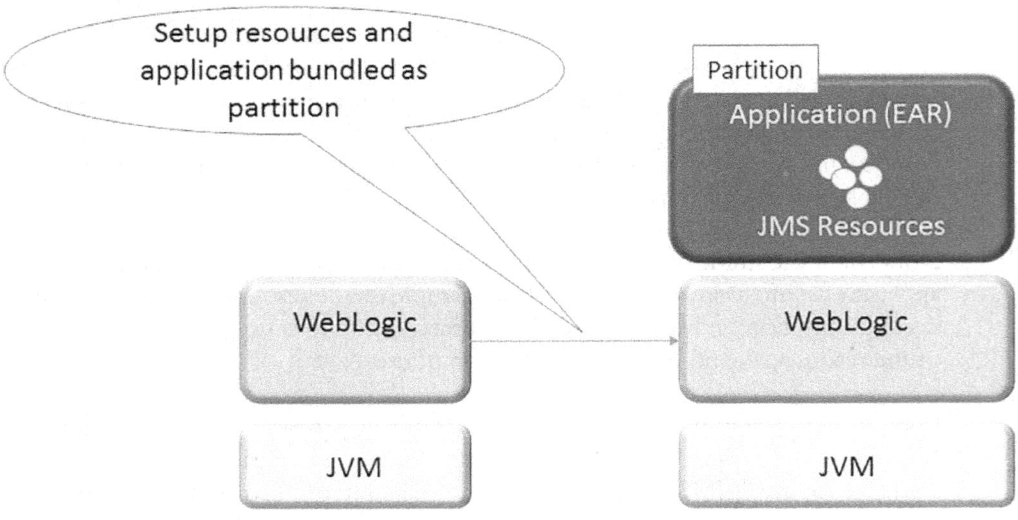

Figure 26-2: Import partitions

Drawback using the traditional WLS setup

This use-case looks at the core idea of partitions. Using the traditional setup reveals an issue all WebLogic admins in our world know. The main issue is that applications require resources. Without those resources being setup before the application gets deployed, the deployment most likely will fail (depends on the resource).

Problems with this setup are that the development team must handover a description of the required resources to the administrators. The only professional way of doing this is to handover a script which can be configured with external parameters and which the admin can run to setup the resources before the administrator will deploy the applications.

As all environments are different, especially with regards to machine names, network setup, amount of managed servers and more. So the deployment description – in many companies called deployment runbook – must describe all the resources and their environment specific configurations.

Usually WLST scripts are the best way of configuring WebLogic domains. In many companies it is required that scripts and in general deployment artifacts must be handed over to a staging environment. Then the admin will setup integration environments, after that UAT (user acceptance test) or NFT (non-functional test) environments and finally production. All environment migrations need to follow the same process as that the administrator needs to setup resources first and afterwards deploy the application. It not only avoids a lot of errors, but it also makes a setup reproducible. This may be a requirement or a prescription by law. Aside from that, it works much faster than doing it by hand.

Advantages gained using Multitenancy

A multitenancy setup changes this process fundamentally as resources and applications are no longer treated separately. Partitions provide the technical implementation to bundle resources and applications into a single deployable unit. In earlier chapters I called this "WebLogic application".

It is now possible for the development team to setup a partition with all the necessary resources. A resource deployment plan will be provided so that administrators can override infrastructure differences like JDBC URLs.

Consider especially JMS components. It is not unusual that a JMS setup consists of dozens or even hundreds of queues and topics. These could be either local or even remote queues. It is very cumbersome to analyze error situations in production only to find out that some resources in the production environment are accidentally pointing to the UAT environment.

Bundling resources and applications not only provide better isolation between components but also combine them together by configuration into a single unit.

Technical steps and details

The technical implementation is done using WebLogic partitions. Partitions support the new concept of WebLogic applications which provide a way of creating a new deployment unit.

Partitions can contain resources like JDBC, JMS, threads or email configurations and applications. All of this can be exported and imported together as a single deployment unit.

As of the example above all resources which are targeted to a partition can be easily bundled. Global resource groups which are targeted to the domain or even traditional resource setups should be avoided if possible as this breaks the partition and isolation concept.

There is no longer a need for administrators to setup resources apart from applications. This makes the deployment and configuration process for administrators much easier, reduce the error rate and speed up deployments. Especially the higher grade of automation will increase the efficiency and reliability of all environments.

Automation Example

The following example creates a virtual target and a partition where all is defined within the partition. This includes resources, workmanager, resource manager and more. As an example this partition has a datasource, a JMS server and a JMS module with a queue.

Script to setup the domain

```
import sys
from java.util import Properties
from java.io import FileInputStream
from java.io import File
```

```
setupProps = Properties();
input = FileInputStream(sys.argv[1])
setupProps.load(input)
input.close()

# connect to admin
connect(setupProps.getProperty('option_connect_user'),
setupProps.getProperty('option_connect_password'), setupProps.getProperty('option_connect_url'));

# start edit
edit()
startEdit()


# create virtual target
# ------------------------------------
cd('/')
cmo.createVirtualTarget('VirtualTarget-Portal')

cd('/VirtualTargets/VirtualTarget-Portal')
cmo.setUriPrefix('/portal')
set('Targets',jarray.array([ObjectName('com.bea:Name=Cluster1,Type=Cluster')], ObjectName))


# create partition
# ------------------------------------
cd('/')
cmo.createPartition('PortalPartition')

cd('/Partitions/PortalPartition/SystemFileSystem/PortalPartition')
cmo.setRoot('/opt/development/wls/wls1221/user_domains/usercase_2/partitions/PortalPartition/system')
cmo.setCreateOnDemand(true)
cmo.setPreserved(true)


# define realm
# ------------------------------
cd('/Partitions/PortalPartition')
cmo.setRealm(getMBean('/SecurityConfiguration/usercase_2/Realms/myrealm'))

# create resource group
# ------------------------------
cmo.createResourceGroup('default')
set('AvailableTargets',jarray.array([ObjectName('com.bea:Name=VirtualTarget-
Portal,Type=VirtualTarget')], ObjectName))
set('DefaultTargets',jarray.array([ObjectName('com.bea:Name=VirtualTarget-
Portal,Type=VirtualTarget')], ObjectName))


# Add JDBC datasource to partition resource group
# ------------------------------
cd('/Partitions/PortalPartition/ResourceGroups/default')
cmo.createJDBCSystemResource('PortalDS')

cd('/Partitions/PortalPartition/ResourceGroups/default/JDBCSystemResources/PortalDS/JDBCResource/Port
alDS')
cmo.setName('PortalDS')

cd('/Partitions/PortalPartition/ResourceGroups/default/JDBCSystemResources/PortalDS/JDBCResource/Port
alDS/JDBCDataSourceParams/PortalDS')
set('JNDINames',jarray.array([String('/jdbc/portalDS')], String))

cd('/Partitions/PortalPartition/ResourceGroups/default/JDBCSystemResources/PortalDS/JDBCResource/Port
alDS')
cmo.setDatasourceType('GENERIC')

cd('/Partitions/PortalPartition/ResourceGroups/default/JDBCSystemResources/PortalDS/JDBCResource/Port
alDS/JDBCDriverParams/PortalDS')
cmo.setUrl('jdbc:oracle:thin:@//localhost:1521/ORCL')
cmo.setDriverName('oracle.jdbc.OracleDriver')

cd('/Partitions/PortalPartition/ResourceGroups/default/JDBCSystemResources/PortalDS/JDBCResource/Port
alDS/JDBCConnectionPoolParams/PortalDS')
cmo.setTestTableName('SQL ISVALID\r\n')

cd('/Partitions/PortalPartition/ResourceGroups/default/JDBCSystemResources/PortalDS/JDBCResource/Port
alDS/JDBCDriverParams/PortalDS/Properties/PortalDS')
```

```
cmo.createProperty('user')

cd('/Partitions/PortalPartition/ResourceGroups/default/JDBCSystemResources/PortalDS/JDBCResource/Port
alDS/JDBCDriverParams/PortalDS/Properties/PortalDS/Properties/user')
cmo.setValue('test')

cd('/Partitions/PortalPartition/ResourceGroups/default/JDBCSystemResources/PortalDS/JDBCResource/Port
alDS/JDBCDataSourceParams/PortalDS')
cmo.setGlobalTransactionsProtocol('OnePhaseCommit')


# Create a JMS filestore and scope it to the partition resource group
# ----------------------------------------------------------------------
cd('/Partitions/PortalPartition/ResourceGroups/default')
cmo.createFileStore('PortalFileStore')

cd('/Partitions/PortalPartition/ResourceGroups/default/FileStores/PortalFileStore')
cmo.setDirectory('/tmp')


# Create a JMS Server and scope it to the partition resource group
# ----------------------------------------------------------------------
cd('/Partitions/PortalPartition/ResourceGroups/default')
cmo.createJMSServer('PortalJMSServer')

cd('/Partitions/PortalPartition/ResourceGroups/default/JMSServers/PortalJMSServer')
cmo.setPersistentStore(getMBean('/Partitions/PortalPartition/ResourceGroups/default/FileStores/Portal
FileStore'))


# Create a JMS Module with a queue and scope it to the partition resource group
# ----------------------------------------------------------------------
cd('/Partitions/PortalPartition/ResourceGroups/default')
cmo.createJMSSystemResource('PortalSystemModule')

cd('/Partitions/PortalPartition/ResourceGroups/default/JMSSystemResources/PortalSystemModule/JMSResou
rce/PortalSystemModule')
cmo.createQueue('PortalQueue')

cd('/Partitions/PortalPartition/ResourceGroups/default/JMSSystemResources/PortalSystemModule/JMSResou
rce/PortalSystemModule/Queues/PortalQueue')
cmo.setJNDIName('/jms/PortalQueue')
cmo.setDefaultTargetingEnabled(true)



# Create a partition internal resource manager
# ---------------------------------------------
cd('/Partitions/PortalPartition')
cmo.createResourceManager('PortalResourceManager')

cd('/Partitions/PortalPartition/ResourceManager/PortalResourceManager')
cmo.createHeapRetained('HeapRetainedResource')

cd('/Partitions/PortalPartition/ResourceManager/PortalResourceManager/HeapRetained/HeapRetainedResour
ce')
cmo.createTrigger('Trigger-2GB', 2048, 'notify')
cmo.createTrigger('Trigger-4GB', 4096, 'shutdown')


# Setup the partition internal default work manager
# ------------------------------------------------
cd('/Partitions/PortalPartition')
cmo.createPartitionWorkManager('PortalPartition-PartitionWorkManager')

cd('/Partitions/PortalPartition/PartitionWorkManager/PortalPartition-PartitionWorkManager')
cmo.setMinThreadsConstraintCap(10)
cmo.setMaxThreadsConstraint(200)

cd('/Partitions/PortalPartition/JTAPartition/PortalPartition')
cmo.setTimeoutSeconds(90)


# save and activate
# -----------------------
save()
```

The following snippet shows how the partition setup looks like in the config.xml

```
...

<partition>
  <name>PortalPartition</name>
  <resource-group>
    <name>default</name>
    <jms-server>
      <name>PortalJMSServer</name>
      <persistent-store>PortalFileStore</persistent-store>
    </jms-server>
    <file-store>
      <name>PortalFileStore</name>
      <directory>/tmp</directory>
    </file-store>
    <jms-system-resource>
      <name>PortalSystemModule</name>
      <descriptor-file-name>partitions/PortalPartition/jms/portalsystemmodule-jms.xml</descriptor-
file-name>
    </jms-system-resource>
    <jdbc-system-resource>
      <name>PortalDS</name>
      <descriptor-file-name>partitions/PortalPartition/jdbc/PortalDS-4171-jdbc.xml</descriptor-
file-name>
    </jdbc-system-resource>
  </resource-group>
  <default-target>VirtualTarget-Portal</default-target>
  <available-target>VirtualTarget-Portal</available-target>
  <realm>myrealm</realm>
  <partition-id>8dae4915-f0f6-4c9b-b44b-560Cefb65956</partition-id>
  <jta-partition>
    <timeout-seconds>90</timeout-seconds>
  </jta-partition>
  <resource-manager>
    <name>PortalResourceManager</name>
    <heap-retained>
      <name>HeapRetainedResource</name>
      <trigger>
        <name>Trigger-2GB</name>
        <value>2048</value>
        <action>notify</action>
      </trigger>
      <trigger>
        <name>Trigger-4GB</name>
        <value>4096</value>
        <action>shutdown</action>
      </trigger>
    </heap-retained>
  </resource-manager>
  <system-file-system>

<root>/opt/development/wls/wls1221/user_domains/usercase_2/partitions/PortalPartition/system</root>
    <create-on-demand>true</create-on-demand>
    <preserved>true</preserved>
  </system-file-system>
  <partition-work-manager>
    <name>PortalPartition-PartitionWorkManager</name>
    <min-threads-constraint-cap>10</min-threads-constraint-cap>
    <max-threads-constraint>200</max-threads-constraint>
  </partition-work-manager>
</partition>

...
```

Especially note that this partition does not have references to global or shared resources. All of them are defined on partition level!

Summary

All application servers so far treated applications and resources as different entities. It was actually one of the major drivers behind the J2EE specification to separate application and infrastructure so that this is no surprise.

Partitions do NOT revert this J2EE achievement back! Features and resources partitions offer to administrators and users are part of a bigger packaging and isolation concept which extends the concepts of the J2EE specification. J2EE focuses mainly on development and that the code must be infrastructure neutral.

With the partition this has not changed. Partitions just enlarge the scope and define a packaging concept which take the J2EE packages (like EARs) together with the infrastructure resources just by this application and create an overall application package.

Application Update/Versioning

CHAPTER

Overview

How do updates usually work? Well, usually a second server environment is build, configured and tested. Then during a downtime the connectivity and real traffic is redirected to this new environment. Or in a downtime like a bet and pray approach all configuration will be done on the live system. The first option is resource consuming and the second option is just gambling.

With multitenancy a new tenant can be setup on the production system and when finished, the traffic can be redirected. Afterwards the old tenant is archived. This is much more efficient and less error prone and provides a fall-back solution, just in case there are some unexpected issues and one has to bring up the former version again.

Real world example

How do you do versioning and backup? WebLogic is a complex environment which consists of domain setup and resource (JDBC, JMS and more) configurations. In case of JMS there could be potentially hundreds of queues or topics. It is vital to keep the setup scripts in the same version as the application otherwise you will be never able to setup an older version correctly. Neither are you able to reproduce any former setup. This may become a serious issue, if one has to prove traceability.

So application versioning usually means to keep a number of related artifacts like application binaries, WLST scripts or even domain setup scripts or more. Another alternative is to archive the whole domain folder including all configurations and binaries but this has the disadvantage that many items in a domain configuration have absolute paths in it. Regardless which backup process you choose it is very important to carefully organize it and it always consists of different parts.

The following diagram shows two different options (of course there are others as well) for backup and versioning of applications (figure 27-1).

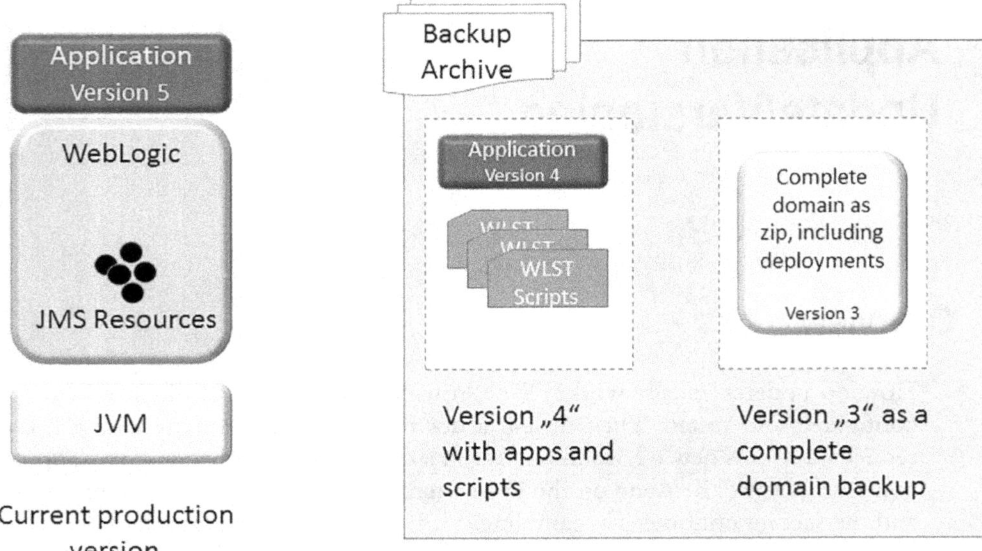

Figure 27-1: Possible traditional backup methods

Using multitenancy and the new WebLogic partitions, this can be done much easier with exported partitions which also contains all the resource setups (like e.g. queues and topics or datasource) See figure 27-2:

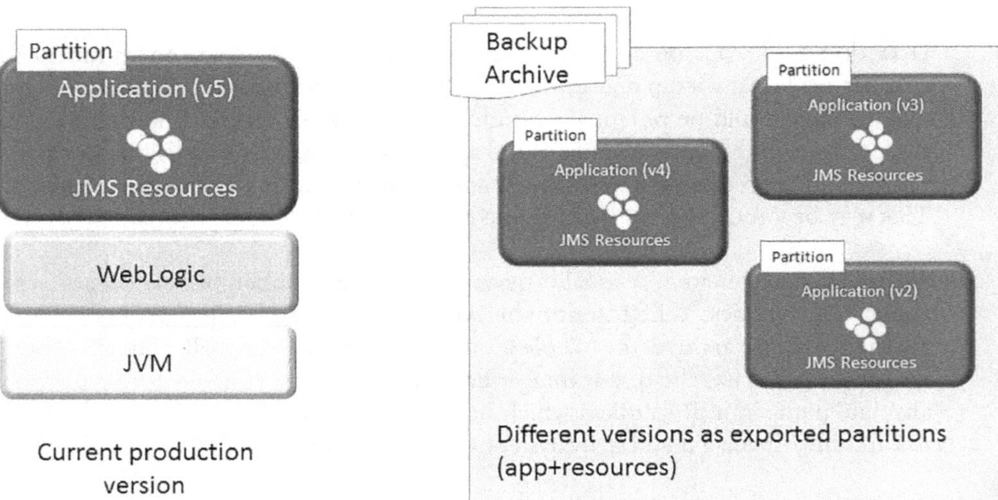

Figure 27-2: Versioning using partitions

Especially if partition setups change over time without reflecting this in the original scripts, this backup has a number of important benefits.

Drawback using the traditional WLS setup

Everybody has the problem of versioning and archiving. Software is always a living and evolving animal and after a while multiple versions of this software do exist. The question here is how to backup software? Just archiving the EAR somewhere is not enough. In case this version must be reactivated, it must also be possible to setup all required resources again.

Typical backup strategies:

- Backup only the EAR file(s). This backup process is incomplete and very dangerous as it usually does not allow to setup this software again, unless no special resources are needed which I have never seen in all that years.
- Backup the EAR file(s) and a description which resources are needed. Description might be as document or spreadsheet. This backup requires administrators to manually re-do all the setup in case this version needs to be installed again.
- Backup the EAR file(s) and all WLST scripts used to setup the resources. This is the most flexible backup as it allows to recover the resources easily and it also allows to re-setup the software in other domains.
- Backup the complete domain with all configurations and deployments. This is an easy backup. It contains everything but it has a number of restrictions like absolute paths and more.

All of the above setup methods have to implement a backup process where deployments and resource setup processes (description, WLST or something else) must be conserved together as both are needed to recover this version again.

Another unfortunately not uncommon issue is that often there are no setup scripts anymore. Maybe because the software has been setup a long time ago and the scripts were lost or it was setup manually. It is also possible that due to change requests the current setup differs from the original scripts. Actually administrators in this case – unless they backup the full domain – would be required to update old scripts or create some setup scripts. WebLogic offers help with a “domainToScript” feature but this is only a starting point.

Advantages gained using Multitenancy

Using multitenancy features of WebLogic both processes – updating and archiving – can be improved.

Updating an application means that the old partition will be stopped, exported and archived and a new partition can then be imported. Why do I say export first? As it is expected that the users after the update will continue to work as they were used to, the new partition will use the same virtual target. It is not possible that multiple partitions share a virtual target, therefore it is not enough to just stop the old partition. It must also be archived.

As the exported partition also contains all the resources – regardless if setup using WLST or done manually using the console – the WebLogic domain is immediately free to host a new version. There is no need to delete old resources and setup new resources. Resources targeted to resource groups will be imported together with their partitions.

This means that there is only a minimal downtime during export of the old and then import of the new partition. Long downtimes due to setup activities are not needed and the risk of roll-backs becomes much smaller.

Also for archiving applications the partition approach has a number of benefits. All resources which are targeted to the partition – or to be precise to the resource group of the partition – will be archived together with the partition. There is no need to also archive WLST scripts or setup documents, albeit you of course should always archive whatever is available. It is in some aspects similar to the backup of the full domain. But there are some important differences. The main difference is that an exported partition has no domain dependency or absolute filesystem path settings. Together with a deployment plan this partition can be re-used in basically any other domain. But this exported partition has the latest and most up-to-date setup of all the resource.

By archiving exported partitions together with their deployment plans, backup and versioning is made much simpler. And if you would like to be really sure, your backup is valid, you could try to restore the partition on another machine, run some automated regression tests and see if they show the expected results. So now a backup, can be considered a really backup.

Technical steps and details

The main technology used is the core functionality of WebLogic partitions. All resources are targeted to the partition resource group or alternatively to a resource group template which acts as a blueprint for this partition.

The greatest benefits in this use case are achieved if ALL resources are scoped to the partition and none of the partition is using any domain level scoped resource.

As for the update process the new software version also needs to be targeted to the same virtual target, it is not possible to have both versions loaded at the same time into the same WebLogic domain. This use case does not support parallel deployment and long-term migration (this is covered in another use-case).

WLST has been extended to support partition lifecycle operations. This also includes exporting and importing of partitions. This means this use-case utilizes the new features of WLST not only for the creation of the initial partition but also for imports and exports.

Even though resources are scoped to partitions, each environment has its own requirements like different JDBC URLs. Partitions support different means of resource overrides (see part 4 of this book). Together with partitions a deployment plan is used to adapt a partition to a given environment. This is useful but not required if the partition only lives in one special WebLogic domain.

Automation Example

This example will use the same partition setup as discussed in the previous use-case. Please refer to previous chapters about the scripts for creating and setting up the domain and partition. The only extension is that this partition will get a deployment.

Partition configuration:

```
<name>PortalPartition</name>
<resource-group>
  <name>default</name>
  <app-deployment>
    <name>mtTest</name>
    <module-type>ear</module-type>
    <source-path>/opt/development/mtTest.ear</source-path>
    <security-dd-model>DDOnly</security-dd-model>
    <staging-mode>stage</staging-mode>
    <plan-staging-mode xsi:nil="true"></plan-staging-mode>
    <cache-in-app-directory>false</cache-in-app-directory>
  </app-deployment>
  <jms-server>
    <name>PortalJMSServer</name>
    <persistent-store>PortalFileStore</persistent-store>
  </jms-server>
```

```
      <file-store>
        <name>PortalFileStore</name>
        <directory>/tmp</directory>
      </file-store>
      <jms-system-resource>
        <name>PortalSystemModule</name>
        <descriptor-file-name>partitions/PortalPartition/jms/portalsystemmodule-jms.xml</descriptor-
file-name>
      </jms-system-resource>
      <jdbc-system-resource>
        <name>PortalDS</name>
        <descriptor-file-name>partitions/PortalPartition/jdbc/PortalDS-4171-jdbc.xml</descriptor-
file-name>
      </jdbc-system-resource>
    </resource-group>
    <default-target>VirtualTarget-Portal</default-target>
    <available-target>VirtualTarget-Portal</available-target>
    <realm>myrealm</realm>
    <partition-id>8dae4915-f0f6-4c9b-b44b-56d0efb65956</partition-id>
    <jta-partition>
      <timeout-seconds>90</timeout-seconds>
    </jta-partition>
    <resource-manager>
      <name>PortalResourceManager</name>
      <heap-retained>
        <name>HeapRetainedResource</name>
        <trigger>
          <name>Trigger-2GB</name>
          <value>2048</value>
          <action>notify</action>
        </trigger>
        <trigger>
          <name>Trigger-4GB</name>
          <value>4096</value>
          <action>shutdown</action>
        </trigger>
      </heap-retained>
    </resource-manager>
    <system-file-system>
      <root>/opt/development/wls/partitions/PortalPartition/system</root>
      <create-on-demand>true</create-on-demand>
      <preserved>true</preserved>
    </system-file-system>
    <partition-work-manager>
      <name>PortalPartition-PartitionWorkManager</name>
      <min-threads-constraint-cap>10</min-threads-constraint-cap>
      <max-threads-constraint>200</max-threads-constraint>
    </partition-work-manager>
```

The idea of this use-case is to use the export functionality for partitions in order to create backup archives. The following script demonstrates the export of a partition. Note that export is a NON blocking call so that we need to get the instance of the "ImportExportPartitionTaskMBean" and query the process status.

```
# -------------------------------------------------------------------

from weblogic.management.mbeanservers.edit.internal import ImportExportPartitionTaskMBean

# define a function which converts the state into a readable name
# -------------------------------------------------------------------
def stateName(currentState):
   if (currentState==ImportExportPartitionTaskMBean.STATE_NOT_STARTED):
      return "NOT_STARTED"
   elif (currentState==ImportExportPartitionTaskMBean.STATE_STARTED):
      return "STARTED"
   elif (currentState==ImportExportPartitionTaskMBean.STATE_FINISHED):
      return "FINISHED"
   elif (currentState==ImportExportPartitionTaskMBean.STATE_FAILED):
      return "FAILED"
   else:
      return "UNKNOWN"
```

```
# -------------------------------------------------------------
connect('weblogic','welcome1','t3://localhost:12001')

# get the task MBean
ppTask = exportPartition("PortalPartition", "/opt/development/archived_partitions")

# while not finished print state
while ppTask.getState()==ImportExportPartitionTaskMBean.STATE_NOT_STARTED or
      ppTask.getState()==ImportExportPartitionTaskMBean.STATE_STARTED:
     print 'Current State of export activity: ' + stateName(ppTask.getState())

# After task finished print result - failed or sucess
if (ppTask.getState()==ImportExportPartitionTaskMBean.STATE_FAILED):
   print 'Export task failed with error: ' + str(ppTask.getError())
elif (ppTask.getState()==ImportExportPartitionTaskMBean.STATE_FINISHED):
   print 'Export task finished successfully'
else:
```

After the export has finished, a ZIP file contains the exported partition (figure 27-3):

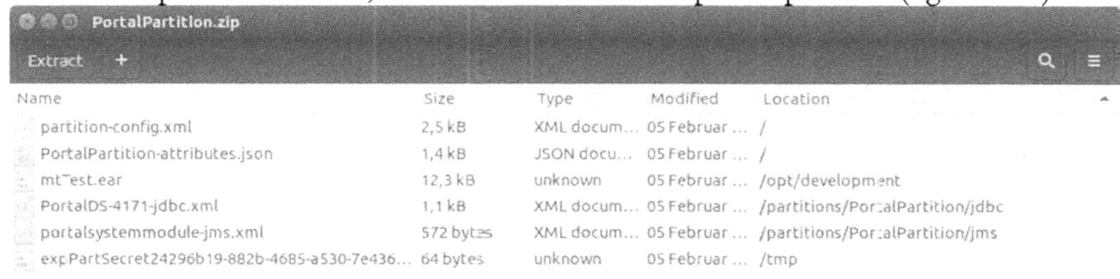

Name	Size	Type	Modified	Location
partition-config.xml	2,5 kB	XML docum...	05 Februar ...	/
PortalPartition-attributes.json	1,4 kB	JSON docu...	05 Februar ...	/
mtTest.ear	12,3 kB	unknown	05 Februar ...	/opt/development
PortalDS-4171-jdbc.xml	1,1 kB	XML docum...	05 Februar ...	/partitions/PortalPartition/jdbc
portalsystemmodule-jms.xml	572 bytes	XML docum...	05 Februar ...	/partitions/PortalPartition/jms
expPartSecret24296b19-882b-4685-a530-7e436...	64 bytes	unknown	05 Februar ...	/tmp

Figure 27-3: Partition ZIP content

As you can see, the exported partition archive contains all deployments, the partition setup and all resource configurations.

Also note that – compared to the previous example – the WLST setup script did not do the deployment. In this case we used the script to setup WLS and then used another script or the console to deploy. The exported archive does contain all.

The PortalPartition-attributes.json file has the following content:

```
    "partition": {
        "name": "PortalPartition",
        "primary-identity-domain": "idd_PortalPartition",
        "default-target": [{"virtual-target": {"name": "VirtualTarget-Portal"}}],
        "realm": {"name": "myrealm"},
        "available-target": [{"virtual-target": {"name": "VirtualTarget-Portal"}}]
    },
    "resource-group": {
        "name": "default",
        "app-deployment": {
            "name": "mtTest",
            "module-type": "ear",
            "source-path": "\/opt\/development\/mtTest.ear",
            "security-dd-model": "DDOnly",
            "staging-mode": "stage",
            "plan-staging-mode": {
                "@xmlns:xsi": "http:\/\/www.w3.org\/2001\/XMLSchema-instance",
```

```
                "@xsi:nil": "true"
            },
            "cache-in-app-directory": false
        },
        "jms-server": {
            "name": "PortalJMSServer",
            "persistent-store": "PortalFileStore"
        },
        "file-store": {
            "name": "PortalFileStore",
            "directory": "\/tmp"
        },
        "jdbc-system-resource": {
            "name": "PortalDS",
            "descriptor-file-name": "partitions\/PortalPartition\/jdbc\/PortalDS-4171-jdbc.xml"
        },
        "jms-system-resource": {
            "name": "PortalSystemModule",
            "descriptor-file-name": "partitions\/PortalPartition\/jms\/portalsystemmodule-jms.xml"
        }
    }
```

Summary

Archiving and updating of software is a daily job of all (WebLogic) administrators worldwide. Many more or less useful ways have been invented to make this process easier, more automated, more reliable and safer. All of those processes in the end have to deal with the drawbacks discussed earlier in this chapter.

The partition concept together with partition export and import lifecycle operations can make this process much easier, safer and more reliable. And even this would make it a very valuable feature, as it will reduce unplanned downtimes, errors and a high effort for trouble shooting. This only would already make a nice business case.

Optimized usage of CPU power by co-locating apps with different resource footprint

CHAPTER

Overview

It is a day to day business nightmare for many companies running global applications. An application which serves e.g. Europe has high CPU requirements during European day time. Another application which serves the US has CPU requirements during US time and applications for Asia need system resources for the Asian day time. But as all applications are installed and reserve their resources they usually are installed on different hardware. This also means that the hardware is basically idle for 66% of the time. By hosting them as different tenants on the same infrastructure companies can reduce their hardware installation and have a much better CPU utilization

Real world example

Consider an office application which a company is using worldwide in 3 different regions – e.g. EMEA, APAC and US. For our example this is be branch office application of a reseller (but could be anything else of course). This application is used in 3 different regions only during office times. In addition this application has region specific setups like language support, currencies or similar differences.

Initially the company hosted this application on 3 different machine clusters. This results in a cluster of machines per region. An analysis revealed that the machines are only 33% of the day loaded and 66% more or less idle, except for some smaller activities.

The following diagram explain the findings (whereas only one machine per region is shown but of course for the sake of load balancing and failover a cluster per region is used) as per figure 28-1.

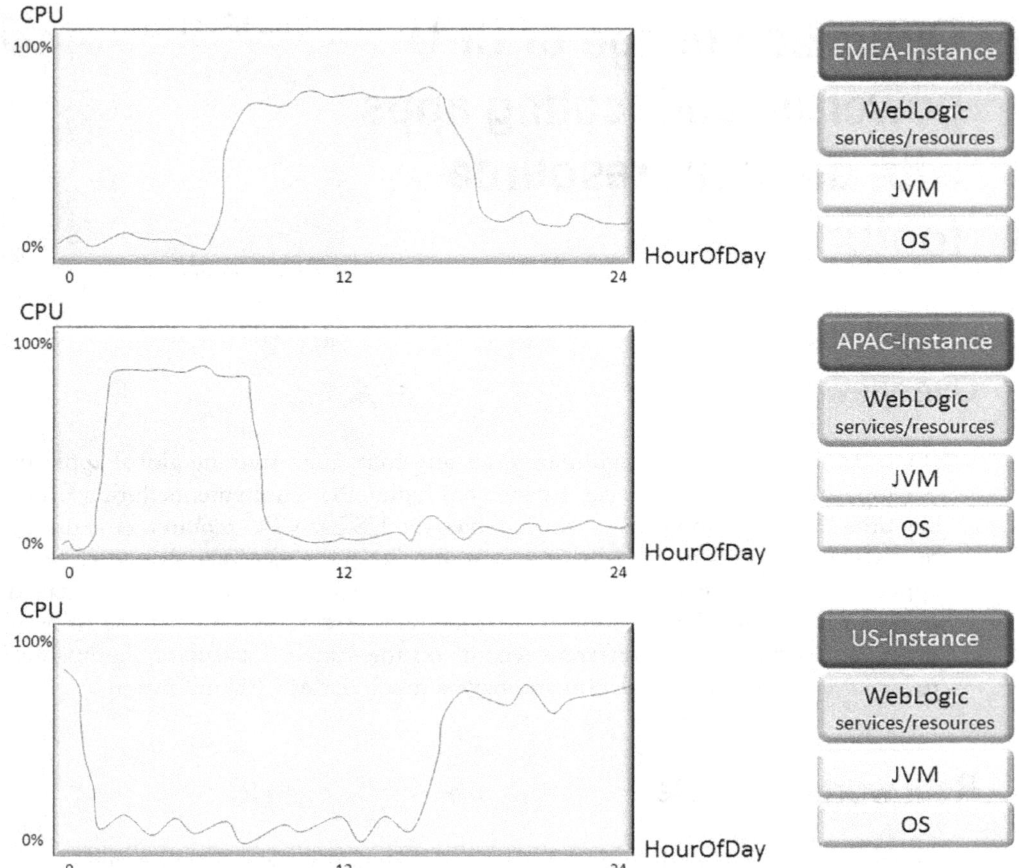

Figure 28-1: One separate application cluster per region

After verifying that the latency is insignificant, the company decided to cohost these three applications. Due to the different machine utilization all three application instances could be hosted on a single cluster. This reduced the cost for hardware, maintenance and licenses up to 66%.

As this application also has the same codebase and only uses different region specific setup, using the partition model together with resource blueprints (templates) even reduced footprint and maintenance (figure 28-2).

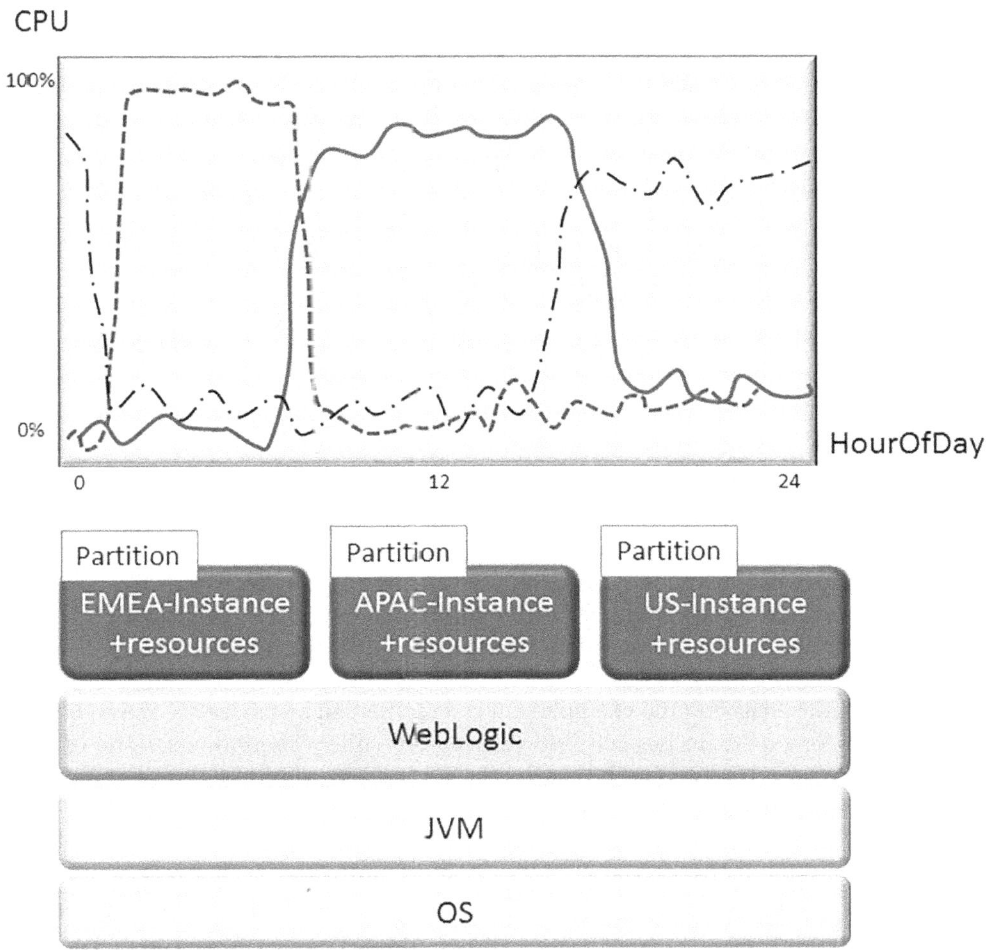

Figure 28-2: Possible multitenancy setup

After migration to multitenancy, a setup and utilization similar to the example above was possible.

Drawback using the traditional WLS setup

The usual setup is that all of these applications will be configured in separate WebLogic domains. In the above example these domains were initially located on different hosts.

The main point we are looking at with this use case is that all domains were using resources only during certain times and that the same resources were allocated to these instances but more or less unused. Resources in this case can machines, CPU, filesystem space and also machine memory (JVM heap space).

The example above shows a common case which has a lot of resources being unused most of the time.

Advantages gained using Multitenancy

For this use case someone can argue that it is not necessary to use the new partition features in order to co-locate the different instances onto a single machine cluster. This is correct but there is more to this example then only the machine itself.

By carefully analyzing the example you can see that all instances are active all the time, but only one of them has full load (the region with working hours). The others have some activities. This could be anything starting from employees working later or early up to automated batch jobs.

This also means that all instances must be up and running all the time and this also means that all instances do allocate their resources all the time. This is especially true for memory (heap).

Co-locating the instances on one machine cluster is independent from any multitenancy features but the new partition features will grant you more benefits. It is possible to construct one partition for each application and to deploy all of them to the same WebLogic cluster. As discussed in the chapters about isolation, WebLogic offers the new resource management features. Using fair-share policies for example will even allow administrators to save physical memory by allowing partitions with high load to reuse memory from the partitions which are idler.

So even without violating the isolation between the different applications it is possible to reuse resources like memory from other instances during the time those instances do not need them.

Technical steps and details

Co-locating on the same machine can simply be done by hosting the different applications in different domains on the same machine cluster. This can always be done and has nothing to do with multitenancy.

The implementation of this use case assumes a different, more advanced setup where the different applications will be using the new partition concept. The partition concept will allow them to keep their level of isolation which they are used to. In addition they use partition scoped resource groups to isolate their resources against each other.

The second benefit of colocation is that administrators can configure an advanced memory model by using shared resource manager configuration and appropriate policies like fair share.

Example calculation: Given as an example that every application under full load needs 4GB of RAM and therefore each domain 5GB (extra RAM for WLS and the JVM). This means without multitenancy all three applications together use 15 GB on each machine of the cluster. It has been proven that partitions during the low load period only need a maximum of around 500MB. This means that for the multitenancy setup it is enough to use 1GB for WLS + 4GB for the full load partition + 2x 500MB for the two other partition with low load. This sums up to 6GB of RAM.

As the calculation shows it is possible to save up to 9GB of RAM on each machine of the cluster using the partition and colocation features together with the new resource manager. This frees a lot of space for other applications, e.g. a webshop.

Summary

In our world of permanently growing need for infrastructure it is very important to save resources wherever possible. This is especially true for hosting providers or cloud based providers, regardless if company internal or external. Especially applications with different resource requirements are suitable for colocation. The given example is a very common use case for applications which are rolled out to different regions and whereas all the different instances are used during different hours during the day with close to no overlapping.

Improved long-term migration between application versions

CHAPTER

Overview

This scenarios is also a well-known nightmare. Given that an application "A" has to be replaced by "A_v2" but users have a grace period (days or even weeks) to migrate from "A" to "A_v2". This means that the company has to run both in parallel for the same time. The user load will stay all the time the same, but will be shifted from "A" to "A_v2". Hosting them on the same hardware/middleware as multiple tenants has a significant benefit that no additional hardware/middleware is needed. Additionally the migration period can easily extended, if needed.

Real world example

This is actually a very common scenario. Imagine for example a system to deal with customer cases (like a support system). Customer cases usually take some time to complete, including creating, delivering and testing fixes or solutions. Now imagine a company has such a system in production and in use by 10,000 employees. After some time the company decided to move to a newer version with new features. Due to the new features only new cases can be handled in the new system and the old system must be up and running until all old cases are closed.

As both systems need to run in parallel, the company is required to double the resources as the old system at the beginning requires 100% resources and the new close to 0% but this is steadily changing over time until the new system uses 100% and the old system close to 0%. After the last old case has been closed the old system can be shut down.

The complete system use always the same resources but the distribution of usage is shifting over time from old to new. Nevertheless the company has to provide 2x the complete resources during the migration process. Even worse if a hosting provider like a cloud infrastructure is used as this also means double provisioning, double costs and so on (figure 29-1).

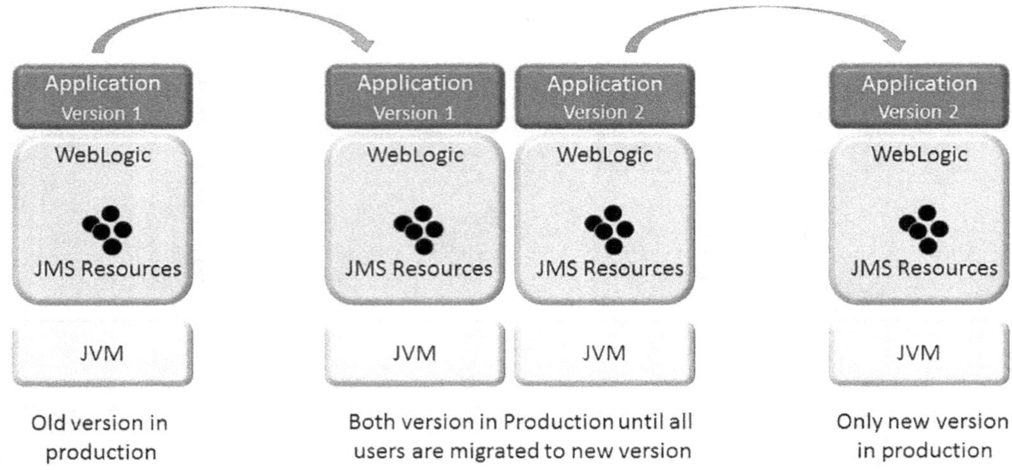

Figure 29-1: Traditional long term migration

The main issue here is that even though the resource usage will not increase the company has to provide twice the resource during migration.

Using the multitenancy approach, this is not needed, as both versions can be hosted in different partitions sharing the same heap so that it is no needed to duplicate resources (figure 29-2).

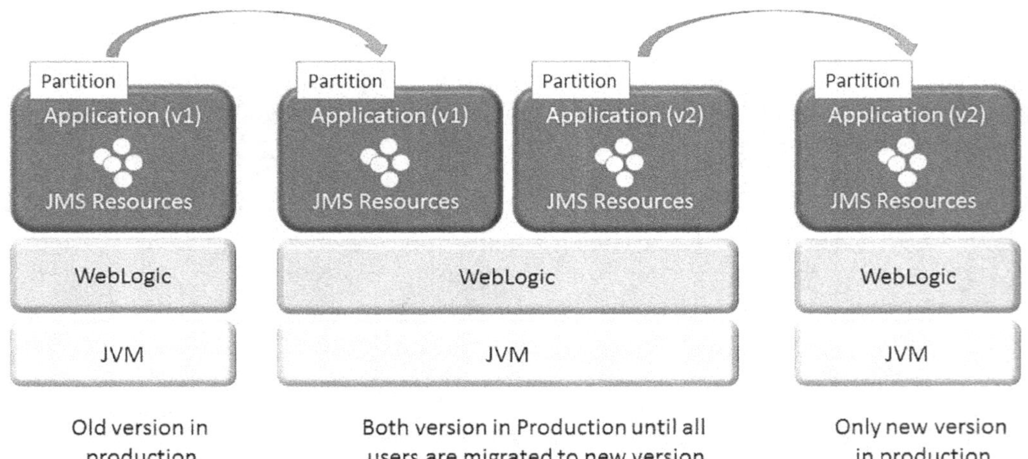

Figure 29-2: Possible multitenancy setup

An even bigger benefit can be gained if core resources – controlled by a resource manager are shared between partitions (figure 29-3).

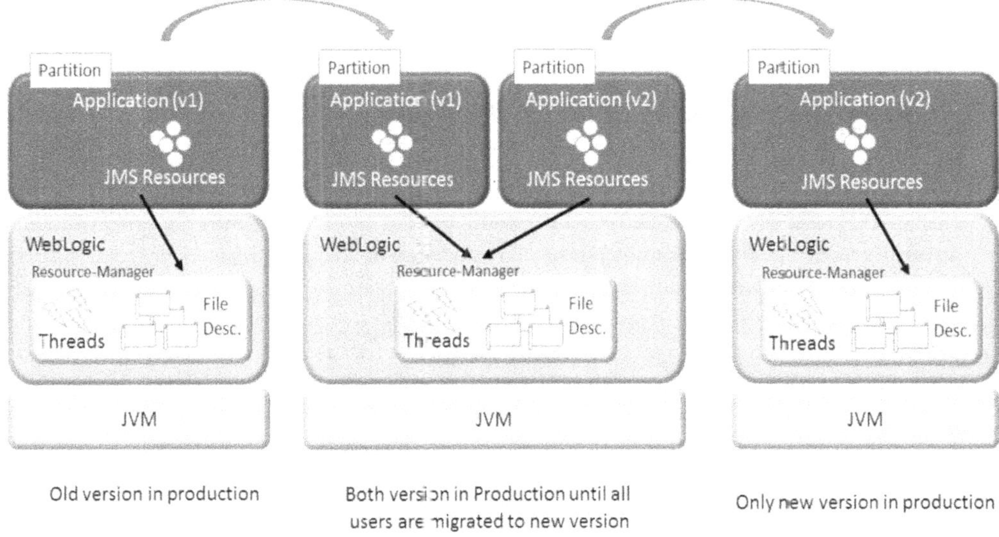

Figure 29-3: Possible multitenancy setup with shared core resources

Drawback using the traditional WLS setup

This is a use case with significant drawbacks for the traditional setup. As both applications will be live for a certain amount of time. Until the last case have been completed in the old system, the administrator is requested to allocate the same amount of resources for the old production and the new production. This is necessary but in fact oversized as the amount of users or the load has not changed or at least in most cases not significantly.

In this case the administrator has to operate two different domains. One with the current production and a new domain for the new production. Both domains will be up and running until all users have been migrated to the new system. In a classical support system this usually means until all old cases have been closed as users need to finish old cases in the new system but create new cases already in the new system.

Two domains means two times memory (heap). In this case both domains need the full amount of memory because at the beginning the old system has the full load and the new system close to nothing. This changes over time and at the end the new system has the full load but the old system close to nothing. It also means two domains, two admin servers, two times the filesystem footprint and more.

Advantages gained using Multitenancy

Using the partition approach really helps to save resources. Similar to the previous use-case the memory (heap) will be first used by the old system and the amount needed shifts gracefully to the new system. By running both partitions isolated in the same WLS cluster they do not interfere with each other, but many resources like heap or file descriptors or threads can be shifted from the old to the new application. This means that the amount of resources needed in this setup is only slightly higher than the maximum need of each partition. In the traditional setup it was double the amount needed by one application.

And there is another very valuable aspect with directly reflects in costs. If this system is hosted on a hosting platform each hosting unit (usually memory and/or CPU) costs money. In the traditional setup the costs during migration would double (double hosting size). Using the multitenancy setup the costs will stay the same or increase only a little bit.

Technical steps and details

Technology wise the proposed multitenancy setup will make use of the partition feature. Resources are targeted to the partition in order to keep isolation.

Note that if resources can be shared the effect in cost saving is even bigger. It is advisable in this case to use a shared work manager so that the thread pool can be shared. At any given time the amount of used threads during migration is not (significantly) higher than before as users get shifted between applications. So resources like threads or file descriptors and especially heap should be shared resources.

Partition themselves are isolated but if a resource manager is used to control the heap and also resources like file descriptors then it is possible to use appropriate policies to distribute resources according to the changing needs during migration.

Resource deployment plans can be used to customize the partitions. This enables administrators to modify partition resources. It also allows to import a second partition alongside with other partitions.

OTD (Oracle Traffic Director) can be used to maintain load-balancing and routing for the different partitions.

Summary

For all system which implement work processes – like support cases – this use case is relevant if the current tasks cannot be continued in the new version. Long-term migrations are seen frequently in our industry. Usually administrators have to allocate double resources during that period, which reflects in double costs.

Multitenancy can greatly improve that by co-hosting both application versions in different isolated partitions but with shared resource manager which are allowed to shift resources from one partition to the other alongside with the migration process.

Shared app server/domain - Reduced administrative costs

CHAPTER

Overview

Have you ever administered environments with hundreds or even thousands of domains? Well this is really no fun without proper automation. A reduction of domains by combining applications as multiple tenants into fewer domains reduces the administrative overhead a lot. As well as discussed earlier may lead to less hardware running and causing costs.

Real world example

Usually each application will be deployed in WebLogic into its own domain. This result in many WebLogic domains, each with an own AdminServer. All domains need to be setup, needs to be patched, needs to be configured and maintained. Especially the limitations in WebLogic with regards to security (only one security realm per domain) usually prohibits administrators to use one domain for multiple applications.

Beside the security restriction, resources are defined on domain level. Yes it is of course possible to configure resources for different applications into one domain by using different names, but there is always a risk of mixing applications and resources as resources and applications are not tightly coupled.

Albeit it is possible, for many - especially security – reasons, in most cases one WebLogic domain will only be used for one application.

The following diagram shows a very typical setup throughout our industry (figure 30-1).

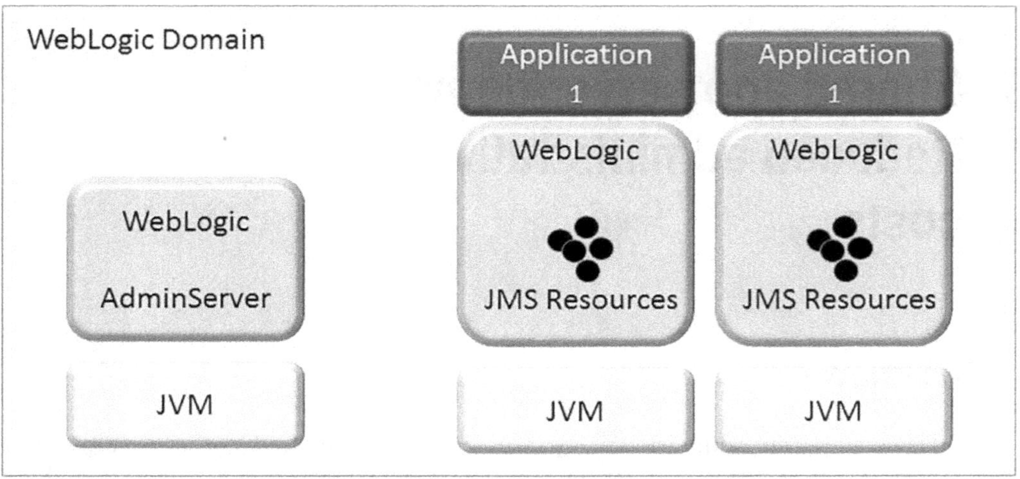

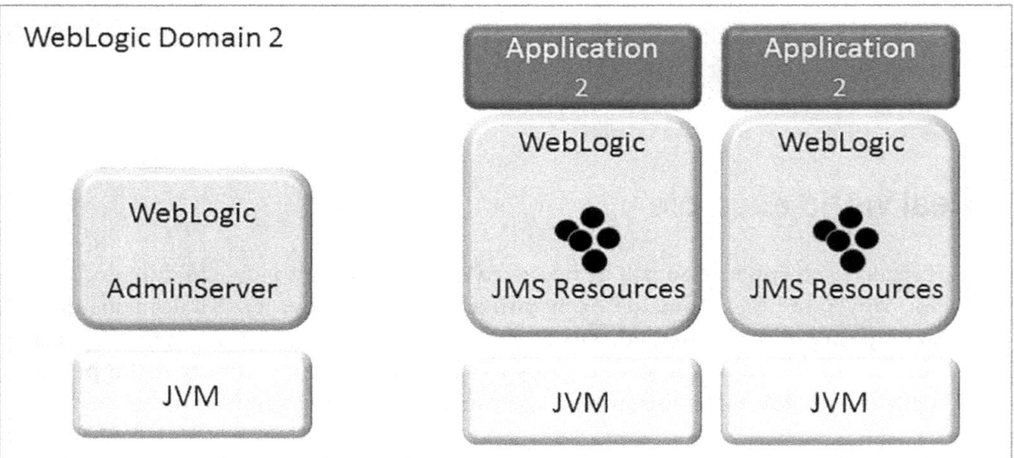

Figure 30-1: Typical domain setup in industry and hosting environments

With the new multitenancy technology, it is now possible to reduce the amount of domains, which also reduces the amount of admin servers and therefore the number of web UIs to log into.

Two new technology features allow this new model without losing features administrators were used to in the traditional setup (see above). The new model is possible with the new security model as it allows an own security realm per partition and the tight coupling of resources and application into a partition (figure 30-2).

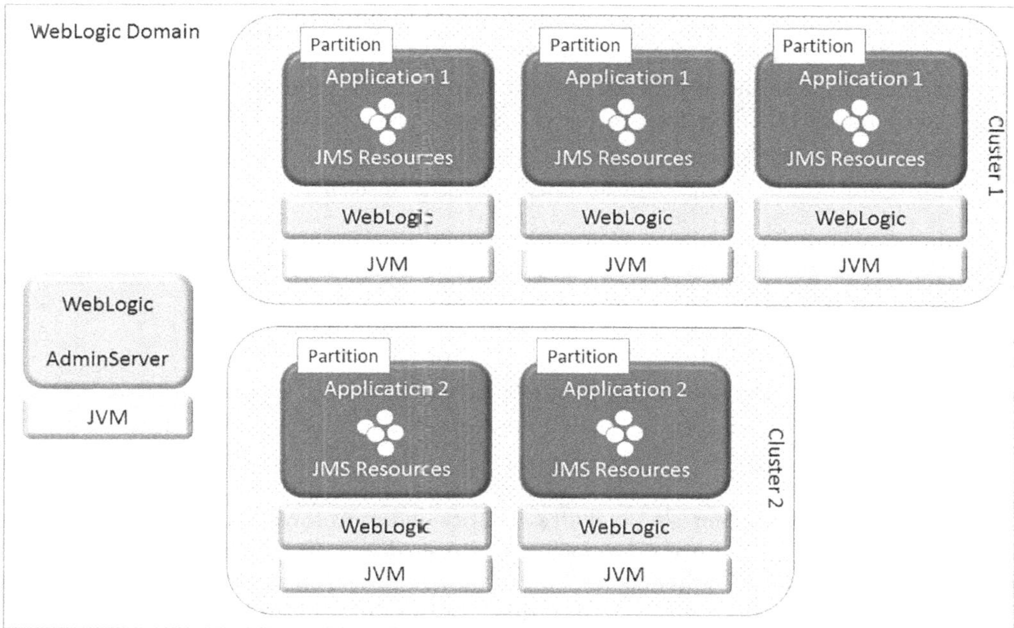

Figure 30-2: Possible multitenancy setup

Drawback using the traditional WLS setup

Have you ever talked to administrators who are cursing every day because they need to repeat certain actions like monitoring or even setup activities hundreds or even thousands of times?

The traditional capabilities of WebLogic often require administrators to setup small domains and deploy only one application per domain. This leads to an administrative nightmare of having many domains and therefore also many admin servers. For security reasons, especially in hosting environments this also means that administrative passwords and access will be different for all domains.

Questions may be asked by readers like: WebLogic supports multi-cluster domains since ages, so that this is already possible? This is right, but the traditional WebLogic setup has a number of disadvantages which in many cases prohibit the usage of multi-cluster domains. First and most important is the restriction of having only a single security realm. All applications in the same domain – even if deployed to different clusters – must share the same security realm which may result in security and audit issues. Secondly all resources like datasources or JMS setup must be done globally at domain level. It is of course possible (and necessary) to target these resources to the same cluster as the application, but in case multiple applications need resources with the same JNDI setup then this is not possible. Also misuse of resources by the other applications is possible.

Advantages gained using Multitenancy

The aforementioned disadvantages do not apply to the new partition concept. Partitions are isolated environments whereas resources can be targeted to partition internal resource groups so that conflicts or even misuse between applications is very unlikely.

The isolation concept also includes security and therefore each partition can have its own full security realm. Users get authenticated in their partition and each partition have its own set of authentication and authorization mechanism. Together with identity domains it is also possible to distinguish the same user being authenticated to different partitions given that each partition has its own identity domain.

Technical steps and details

Beside the partition concept as such the main foundation for this use case is the fact that partitions can also have their sown security setup. From an implementation perspective each application is setup into an own partition with an own security realm. Users get authenticated in the partition security realm and therefore the security layer is no longer a global domain security layer, but a private isolated security layer in the partition. The additional, albeit optional feature called identity domain can add a partition specific identity tag. The default authentication and authorization provider in WebLogic 12.2.1 and above support identity domains.

In addition resources scoped to partitions using partition internal resource groups provide isolation of resources between the different applications as each partition has its own JNDI service. JNDI conflicts are therefore impossible between applications hosted in different partitions.

Summary

Also in many traditional setups administrators tried to deploy applications to different clusters instead of different domains in order to reduce the administrative overhead. Due to WebLogic restrictions w.r.t. security or the lack of resource isolation this was in many cases not possible.

The new partition concept also offers solutions in this area, especially with the partition internal security realm and partition scoped resource groups.

Technical benefits by using the new isolation stack (one partition model)

CHAPTER

Overview

Another technical benefit of using the new multitenancy (partition) model in WebLogic is the fact that Oracle has improved the lower level stack - the Java VM in this case - to support resource isolation. Even with only a single tenant which is equal to the traditional hosting the new lower level stack features can be used.

Real world example

In many cases one WebLogic domain hosts exactly one application. Given as an example, a company needs more than that and also uses different operating system users. Also they want have additional requirements of isolation, which they do not want do miss in the future.

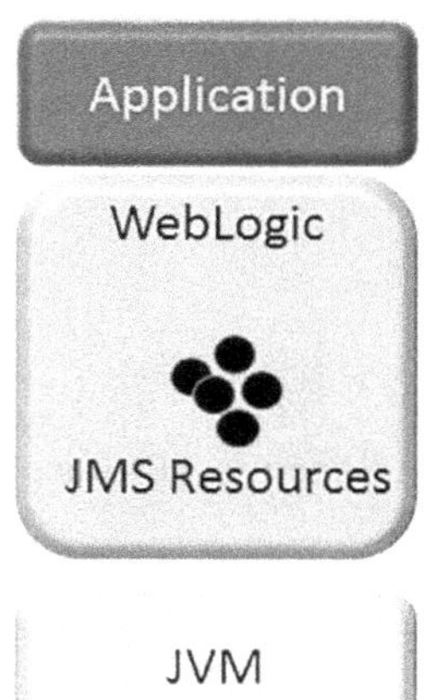

Their question here might be, how can a one partition model only help them or improve their infrastructure. Even if it is not planned to host multiple partitions the partition model can be beneficial for companies.

In the traditional setup resources are configured on domain level and are therefore only loosely coupled to applications. Furthermore, traditional setup cannot make use of the new resource manager which can control threads, file descriptors, CPU and threads on JVM level.

Figure 31-1: Traditional setup

Oracle recommends to migrate existing domains to multitenancy domains based on the partition model in order to take advantage from the new components like resource and application bundling into a partition and also to take advantage of the resource management. This resource management is only available for partitions. Applications deployed on domain level cannot benefit from this resource management feature of WebLogic.

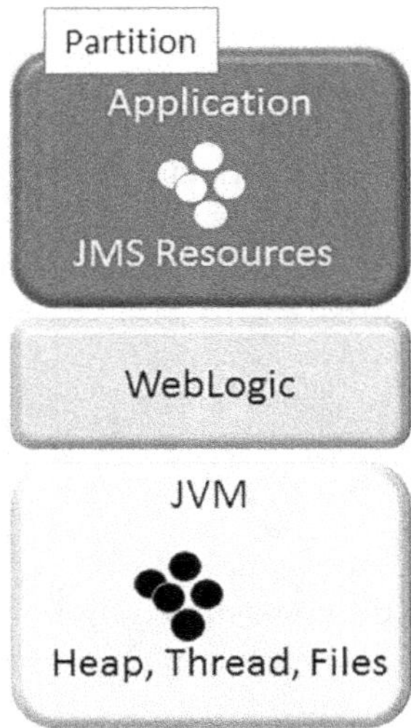

Figure 31-2: Possible Multitenancy setup

Drawback using the traditional WLS setup

The traditional setup has some disadvantages (as already mentioned in all other use cases) that resources and application are not bundled together.

There is another area in WebLogic where traditional WebLogic setup have shortcuts. WebLogic has the concept of workmanager which controls the usage of threads. Control of other resources is out of scope of a traditional setup. WebLogic was always vulnerable to errors like Out-Of-Memory which affects the complete WLS instance.

Another typical and difficult to detect and debug area are file descriptors. An often observed scenario is that a certain number of users can work, but additional user have issues getting a connection to the server. In almost all cases this has its root cause in either the server running out of threads OR the WebLogic instance running out of file descriptors.

Advantages gained using Multitenancy

Somebody may argue that a one partition setup is the same as a traditional setup. This is partly true as from an isolation perspective there is only a small difference of targeting resources to the domain or to the only available partition.

The advantages in this case are the lifecycle functionality added for partitions. Exporting partitions together with their resources helps a lot for application migration, testing and versioning.

Another major advantage is the new resource manager feature which can be used to control file descriptors, JVM heap and threads. Resource managers can only be used together with partitions and not on domain level. Defining resource manager policies for file descriptors or heap can avoid that the entire WLS instance is running out of resources. Out-of-Memory exceptions which affects the WebLogic instance in total, are then very unlikely. If the partition gets too hungry for resources it can be slowed down or even stopped depending on the requirements or intention of the business.

Technical steps and details

The concept of this use case is based on the WebLogic partition feature. In addition the new resource manager control mechanism will be used to avoid that the hosting WebLogic server runs out of resources. The implementation uses resource manager policies to slowdown and even stop partitions in case the resource requests are getting too high.

Export and import functionalities of the partition enable administrators to easily do configurations, deployments and archiving. Partitions can be exported together with their resource setup.

Summary

The new partition model has its greatest advantages in co-hosting of applications in different isolated partitions. This use case also demonstrates that the new partition model in WebLogic also has a number of benefits even if only one partition is deployed to a WebLogic domain. Especially the new resource manager features can only be used in combination with a partition.

Reducing platform footprint

CHAPTER

Overview

Installation of application servers need a significant amount of disk space. Even if done right and the binaries are separated from the WebLogic domain so that these are not duplicated, still domain structures and all sorts of standard files need space. In a multitenancy environment this can be reduces to a small number of real application server installations which reduces the amount of disc space (and also backup, tape space and so on) necessary.

Real world example

Given for example a company who has deployed three different applications into three different domains. Due to better machine utilization all application share the same hardware cluster (figure 32-1).

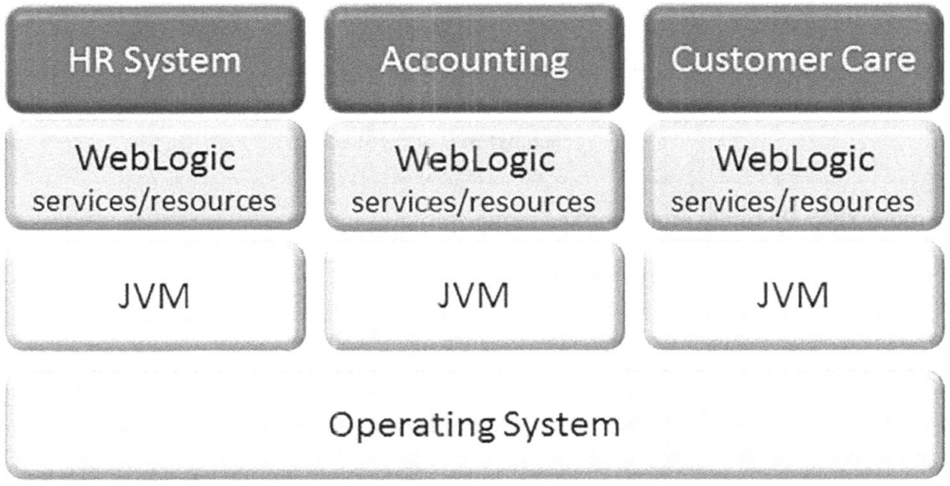

Figure 32-1: Traditional setup

Even though if I assume that there is only one WebLogic binary installation there is still the need to setup three different domains with all their resources, files, LDAP databases and more. In addition three different admin servers are needed.

Using the multitenancy approach, all three different applications will be moved from own domains into partitions. This reduces the filesystem footprint from three domains down to one, which makes also backup, recovery and file system setup easier.

In addition it reduces the platform footprint by reducing the amount of the WebLogic admin server from three down to one and also the amount of WebLogic clusters could be reduced. If the partitions will be hosted in the same WebLogic cluster then even the memory footprint can be reduced due to the fact that a resource manager can be used to do smart memory management (figure 32-2).

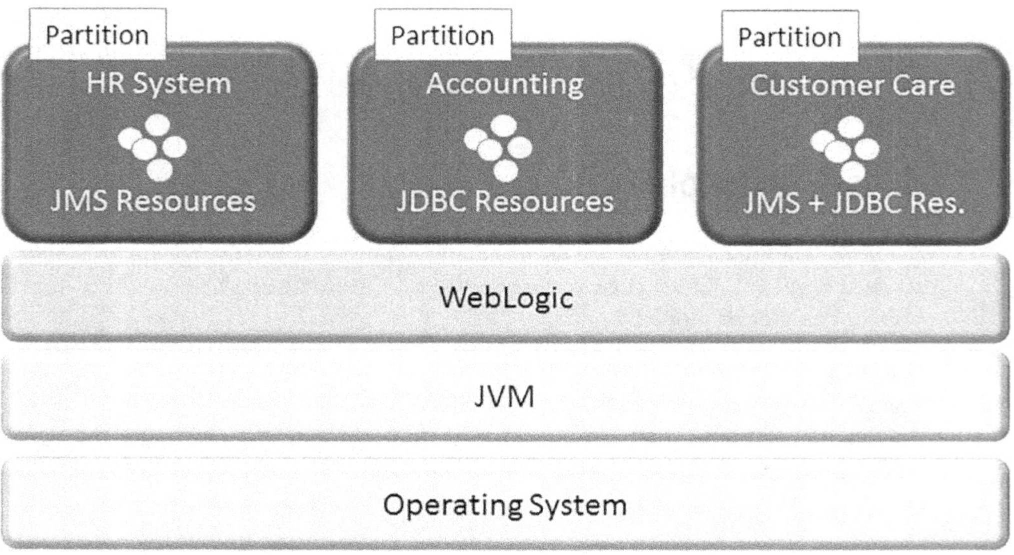

Figure 32-2: Possible multitenancy setup

Drawback using the traditional WLS setup

One complain heard often is that WebLogic has a heavy footprint on the platform with regards to filesystem usage. Even though most administrators will have to setup the application binaries apart from the domain anyway in order to avoid security holes, each domain uses space on the filesystem.

Also each domain needs automation around it for startup, shutdown, restart in case of system failures and much more. Each WebLogic domain needs an administrative unit called AdminServer which controls the other server in the domain. The more domains an environment has, the more admin server it needs.

All of these points lead in summary to a rather big footprint on the servers and a large number of administrative tasks and artifacts.

Unfortunately in many environments it cannot be avoided to have a large number of domains due to security and isolation reasons.

Advantages gained using Multitenancy

The new partition concept can help to significantly reduce the size of the platform and the administrative footprint.

The isolation concept of partitions where resources get targeted to partition internal resource groups and where partitions do have their own security realms allow administrators to co-host different applications in different partitions into the same WLS domain or at least into different clusters of the same WLS domain. A WebLogic domain changes its level from a former application level down to a platform level of its own.

This results in less domains, less admin servers and less filesystem storage used. It also ease the life of administrators as there are less domains to maintain with less adminservers.

Technical steps and details

The technical foundation is the partition with its resource and security isolation. Together with a resource manager on the platform level, different applications can be isolated cohosted.

The difference of this use case it that it does not even consider to reduce the number of machines. The goal is to reduce the footprint of the overall WebLogic infrastructure. Applications are moved from different domains into different partitions, regardless if these applications are hosted in the same WLS cluster or in different ones.

Even if each application partition will be targeted to a different WebLogic cluster, the amount of domains and the amount of adminservers are reduced. And this also reduces the amount of operating system users and the amount of filesystem storage together with backup storage.

Summary

In our world of cost explosions and increased costs for hosting services, one central goal is to reduce platform footprints as much as possible.

Another major cost factor in our world are we human beings. Administrators costs money and if the workload of the administration group is reduced due to optimized footprint then this also reduces the overall costs for the administration team.

Lightweight application transitioning and migration

CHAPTER

Overview

An application is usually configured and tested in an integration environment. After that this application has to be installed in the "UAT (user acceptance test)" environments in order to test non-functional requirements and very often production like setups, e.g. end-to-end connectivity. The names of these environments and the order in which they are used depends on the company internal processes. This may differ significantly between companies.

By using the new partition model, applications together with their resources can be copied from one environment to the next without the need of updating/re-installing a WebLogic server environment. This makes the transition much faster and easier. Similar benefits exist for the migration between different servers or even for a migration to new a WebLogic version.

Real world example

It is also very easy to imagine this use case is more or less the same in any company. Imagine a company which is running a branch office software on a central server cluster (but of course could be any other software).

The software gets developed and after development is finished, handed over in order to deploy it into an integration environment. This means that on that integration environment the WLS domain needs to be setup, then (hopefully with automated WLST scripts) all necessary resources like JDBC datasources, JMS configurations and other resources must be configured. Finally after the domain has been prepared the application components (e.g. EARs, WARs or RARs) can be deployed.

After all integration tests are done and signed off, the same process needs to be repeated in order to get the software into the UAT environment. Usually this environment is used to perform all non-functional tests. Again all resources need to be setup on the domain and afterwards the application components need to be deployed.

After UAT signoff, handover and deployment to the production environment will follow the same process again. The biggest disadvantage is that there are always different steps involved which belong together and must be performed in a specific order (figure 33-1).

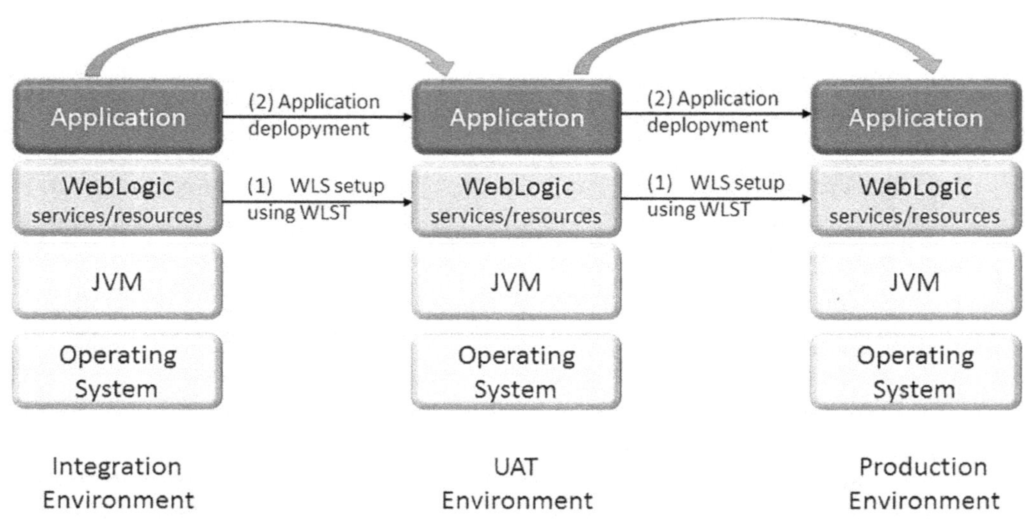

Figure 33-1: Typical deployment and handover process

By using a multitenancy approach the principle process still stays the same: Handover and deployment to the integration environment. After integration signoff handover to the UAT environment.

After all – including UAT – tests are done and UAT signoff has been given, software will be handed over and deployed to production.

Using multitenancy though means that the technical process has a great advantage. Handover and installation into the next level of environments only involves one step and no longer a series of multiple and depending steps. Resource setup and applications are bundles into a partition and this means that it is much more unlikely that a resource will be setup in a wrong way or a setup step will be missed. Beside necessary resource adjustment done via a deployment plan, the only step needed is to handover an exported partition and import this partition into the next environment (figure 33-2).

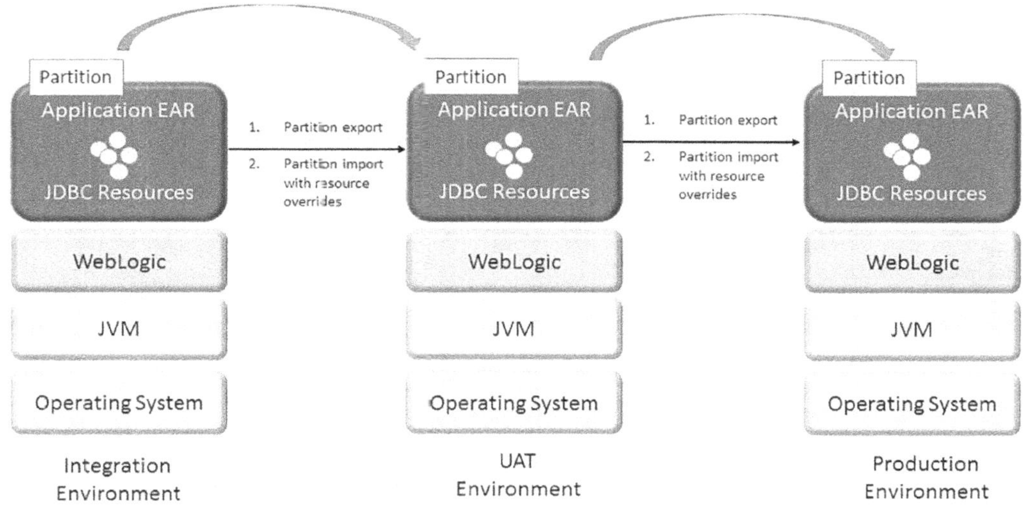

Figure 33-2: Multitenancy approach

Drawback using the traditional WLS setup

For setting up the first environment (e.g. integration) it might be common sense that all resources like JDBC and JMS must be setup in order to deploy and test the application.

The real drawback of this approach appears when the application has passed integration test and shall be moved to higher level environments like UAT or NFT testing. If this move happens for the first time then it is also very obvious that resources must be setup up. But in case a new patch is migrated to higher environments it might easily happen that changes in resources or complete resource setups get lost.

Another very common drawback (by the way I highly discourage ALL users to do that) happens if the resource and domain setup in integration happens via WLS console and not via scripts. How do you migrate this application to UAT? Either you have a description what has to be done and admins do this using the console (very bad idea) or admins need to create a script for that. Who verifies that this script is correct?

Migration between two environments always means that resource setup or resource updates must be in sync with the application version. Resources and application are only loosely coupled which makes this difficult and quite error prone.

Advantages gained using Multitenancy

The bundling of resources and applications into partitions makes this process much easier. Of course I recommend to always setup also the first environment (integration in our example) using a WLST script but if the partition approach is used the way how integration was setup will be less important.

If WLST is used or if the WLS console is used results both in the same result that the resources will targeted to the partition. Migration and transition into higher level environments do not require a script. Administrators will export the complete partition including all resources and import it into the next environment.

Please note that this benefit gets lost if the partition also uses domain level scoped resources.

Technical steps and details

The technical implementation of this use case also requires the new partition concept and isolated resource which are targeted to the partition internal resource group.

Given that the main benefits for this use case are the new lifecycle operations which are built into WLST which allow administrators to export and import whole partitions and their resources and security settings.

This makes the separation into resource setup or update and the application deployment unnecessary.

As partitions get migrated between different environments, a resource deployment plan can be used in order to customize the partition resources to the different environments.

Automation Example

The following example will extract a partition from the source domain. Based on requirements a resource deployment plan will be provided for each destination environment.

Source partition configuration

```
    <name>PortalPartition</name>
    <resource-group>
      <name>default</name>
      <app-deployment>
        <name>mtTest</name>
        <module-type>ear</module-type>
        <source-path>/opt/development/mtTest ear</source-path>
        <security-dd-model>DDOnly</security-dd-model>
        <staging-mode>stage</staging-mode>
        <plan-staging-mode xsi:nil="true"></plan-staging-mode>
        <cache-in-app-directory>false</cache-in-app-directory>
      </app-deployment>
      <jms-server>
        <name>PortalJMSServer</name>
        <persistent-store>PortalFileStore</persistent-store>
      </jms-server>
      <file-store>
        <name>PortalFileStore</name>
        <directory>/tmp</directory>
      </file-store>
      <jms-system-resource>
        <name>PortalSystemModule</name>
        <descriptor-file-name>partitions/PortalPartition/jms/portalsystemmodule-jms.xml</descriptor-
file-name>
      </jms-system-resource>
      <jdbc-system-resource>
        <name>PortalDS</name>
        <descriptor-file-name>partitions/PortalPartition/jdbc/PortalDS-4171-jdbc.xml</descriptor-
file-name>
      </jdbc-system-resource>
    </resource-group>
    <jta-partition>
      <timeout-seconds>90</timeout-seconds>
    </jta-partition>
    <resource-manager>
      <name>PortalResourceManager</name>
      <heap-retained>
        <name>HeapRetainedResource</name>
        <trigger>
          <name>Trigger-2GB</name>
          <value>2048</value>
          <action>notify</action>
        </trigger>
        <trigger>
          <name>Trigger-4GB</name>
          <value>4096</value>
          <action>shutdown</action>
        </trigger>
      </heap-retained>
    </resource-manager>
    <partition-work-manager>
      <name>PortalPartition-PartitionWorkManager</name>
      <min-threads-constraint-cap>10</min-threads-constraint-cap>
      <max-threads-constraint>200</max-threads-constraint>
    </partition-work-manager>
  </partition>
```

Export the partition

```
# ---------------------------------------------------------------
from weblogic.management.mbeanservers.edit.internal import ImportExportPartitionTaskMBean
```

```
# define a function which converts the state into a readable name
# ---------------------------------------------------------------
def stateName(currentState):
   if (currentState==ImportExportPartitionTaskMBean.STATE_NOT_STARTED):
      return "NOT_STARTED"
   elif (currentState==ImportExportPartitionTaskMBean.STATE_STARTED):
      return "STARTED"
   elif (currentState==ImportExportPartitionTaskMBean.STATE_FINISHED):
      return "FINISHED"
   elif (currentState==ImportExportPartitionTaskMBean.STATE_FAILED):
      return "FAILED"
   else:
      return "UNKNOWN"


# ---------------------------------------------------------------
connect('weblogic','welcome1','t3://localhost:12001')

# get the task MBean
ppTask = exportPartition("PortalPartition", "/opt/development/archived_partitions")

# while not finished print state
while ppTask.getState()==ImportExportPartitionTaskMBean.STATE_NOT_STARTED or
ppTask.getState()==ImportExportPartitionTaskMBean.STATE_STARTED:
     print 'Current State of export activity: ' + stateName(ppTask.getState())
     os.time.sleep(20)

# After task finished print result - failed or sucess
if (ppTask.getState()==ImportExportPartitionTaskMBean.STATE_FAILED):
   print 'Export task failed with error: ' + str(ppTask.getError())
elif (ppTask.getState()==ImportExportPartitionTaskMBean.STATE_FINISHED):
   print 'Export task finished successfully'
else:
```

Resource deployment plan for the destination environment

```
   <description>Martin Example Resource Deployment Plan</description>
   <variable-definition>
     <variable>
       <name>myNewJNDIName</name>
       <value>/jndi/prod/PortalDS</value>
     </variable>
     <variable>
       <name>fileStoreLocation</name>
       <value>/prod/stores/portal.store</value>
     </variable>
   </variable-definition>

   <external-resource-override>
     <resource-name>PortalDS</resource-name>
     <resource-type>jdbc-system-resource</resource-type>
     <root-element>jdbc-data-source</root-element>
     <descriptor-file-path>partitions/PortalPartition/jdbc/PortalDS-4171-jdbc.xml</descriptor-file-
path>
     <variable-assignment>
       <name>myNewJNDIName</name>
       <xpath>/jdbc-data-source/jdbc-data-source-params/jndi-name </xpath>
     </variable-assignment>
   </external-resource-override>

   <config-resource-override>
     <resource-name>PortalFileStore</resource-name>
     <resource-type>file-store</resource-type>
     <variable-assignment>
       <name>fileStoreLocation</name>
       <xpath>/file-store/directory</xpath>
     </variable-assignment>
   </config-resource-override>
```

Script to prepare destination domain for import (in this case setup virtual target if it does not exist)

```
import sys
from java.util import Properties
from java.io import FileInputStream
from java.io import File

setupProps = Properties();
input = FileInputStream(sys.argv[1])
setupProps.load(input)
input.close()

# connect to admin
connect(setupProps.getProperty('option_connect_user'),
setupProps.getProperty('option_connect_password'), setupProps.getProperty('option_connect_url'));

# start edit
edit()
startEdit()

# create virtual target
# -----------------------------------
cd('/')
cmo.createVirtualTarget('VirtualTarget-Portal')

cd('/VirtualTargets/VirtualTarget-Portal')
cmo.setUriPrefix('/portal')
set('Targets',jarray.array([ObjectName('com.bea:Name=Cluster1,Type=Cluster')], ObjectName))

# save and activate
# -----------------------
save()
```

Import script, which also attaches the deployment plan to the partition if required

```
# -------------------------------------------------------------

from weblogic.management.mbeanservers.edit.internal import ImportExportPartitionTaskMBean

# define a function which converts the state into a readable name
# -------------------------------------------------------------
def stateName(currentState):
   if (currentState==ImportExportPartitionTaskMBean.STATE_NOT_STARTED):
      return "NOT_STARTED"
   elif (currentState==ImportExportPartitionTaskMBean.STATE_STARTED):
      return "STARTED"
   elif (currentState==ImportExportPartitionTaskMBean.STATE_FINISHED):
      return "FINISHED"
   elif (currentState==ImportExportPartitionTaskMBean.STATE_FAILED):
      return "FAILED"
   else:
      return "UNKNOWN"


# -------------------------------------------------------------
connect('weblogic','welcome1','t3://localhost:12001')

# get the task MBean
ppTask = importPartition("/opt/development/archived_partitions/PortalPartition.zip")

# while not finished print state
while ppTask.getState()==ImportExportPartitionTaskMBean.STATE_NOT_STARTED or
ppTask.getState()==ImportExportPartitionTaskMBean.STATE_STARTED:
     print 'Current State of export activity: ' + stateName(ppTask.getState())
     os.time.sleep(20)

# After task finished print result - failed or sucess
if (ppTask.getState()==ImportExportPartitionTaskMBean.STATE_FAILED):
   print 'Export task failed with error: ' + str(ppTask.getError())
```

```
elif (ppTask.getState()==ImportExportPartitionTaskMBean.STATE_FINISHED):
   print 'Export task finished successfully'
   print 'Attach resource deployment plan'
   edit()
   startEdit()

   # get hold of the already created (or imported !) partition
   partition=cmo.lookupPartition('PortalPartition')

   # attach the resource deployment plan to this partition
   partition.setResourceDeploymentPlanPath('data/partition/plans/portalPartition/uatPlan.xml')

   save()
   try:
       activate()
   except:
       dumpStack()

else:
```

In case you want to de-couple import and resource deployment plan, the following script just sets the deployment plan:

```
connect('weblogic','welcome1','t3://localhost:12001')

# switch to the edit mode
edit()

# start editing
startEdit()

# get hold of the already created (or imported !) partition
partition=cmo.lookupPartition('PortalPartition')

# attach the resource deployment plan to this partition
partition.setResourceDeploymentPlanPath('/archiv/portal_resource_deployment_plan.xml')

# save changes and activate
save()
try:
   activate()
except:
```

Summary

Every company and application has the issue of migrating software versions from different test environments to user acceptance tests up to production. Migration always includes setup of applications and all resources required by this application.

Partition can dramatically simplify this process by using the new exporting and importing features provided by WebLogic through WLST.

Improved/Optimized (production like) testing and troubleshooting

CHAPTER

Overview

Even more important than the previous use case is the problem of re-creating production issues. Typically a reference environment exist which can be used to reproduce production issues. But both need to be setup and maintained.

Using the WebLogic multitenancy model it is possible to take a snapshot of the production model (with WebLogic 12.2.1 onwards only an offline snapshot, but maybe in the future even a hot snapshot with production states) and moves it to the reference system.

This guarantees that application and resources are really identical to the production which had the issue. Furthermore this allows that the reference system can be used to reproduce issues from different production systems and versions which is a bit benefit w.r.t. to time, cost and resources.

Real world example

I believe that all companies are familiar with the following example. An application was tested and went productive. After being live for a while production issues appear, which were never seen in UAT or NFT test environments. It is now necessary to reproduce this error in a production like reference environment.

Question now is: Does the reference environment really has the exact same setup as production? If yes then it is fine, but if not what needs to be done to bring the reference environment to the same configuration as the production. It might even be the case that no reference environment exists at all. In all cases it is needed to get a production like reference environment up and running as fast as possible. After the issue has been solved, it is necessary to verify, that the provided patch really solves the problem. After this has been verified, the partition will be exported and deployed in production. This way one can (most likely) be sure, that the issue will be finally gone.

Setting up the reference environment (in case it is not already setup) requires to setup all resources like datasource, JMS queues and topics and other resources and to deploy the same version of the application as production.

In case the company already has a reference environment then it only must be verified that this environment has the same setup and application version as production (see following diagram) as shown in figure 34-1.

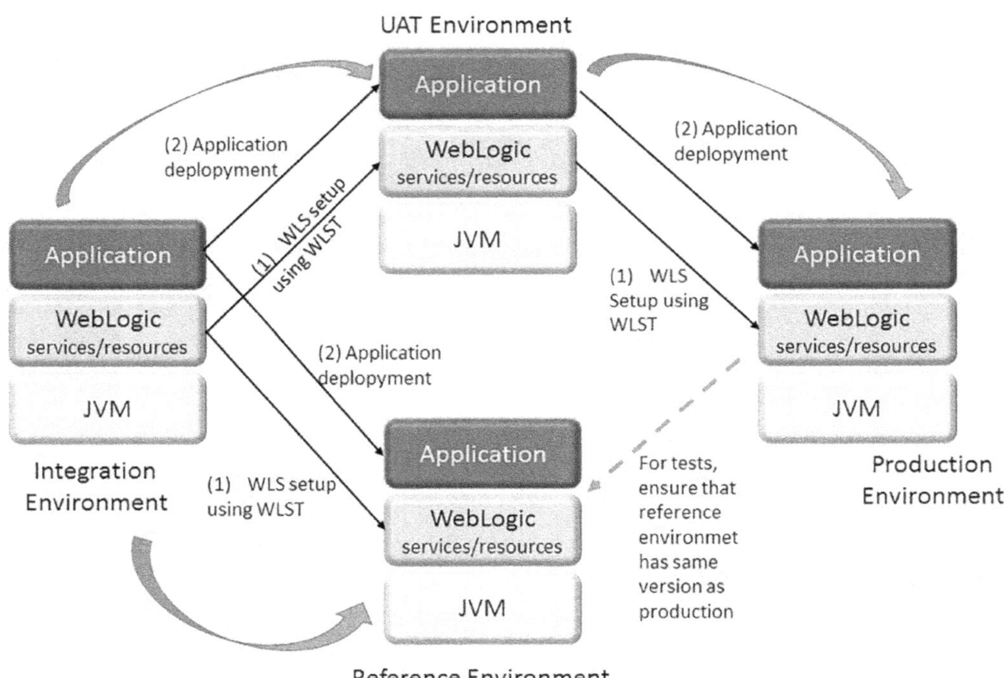

Figure 34-1: Existing reference environment must be verified to have a production like setup

In case the company does not have a reference environment or – also not uncommon – has a reference environment which is shared for all software and versions, it is important to configure the reference environment alike the production.

In this case the next series of questions pop up. Does the company has WLST scripts or other automation tools to do this setup automatically? Best would be to reuse the scripts which have been used to setup the production itself. Also it is important to clarify if the production setup were changed after the initial setup (e.g. though emergency (configuration) changes)? In this case even the automated scripts are not sufficient, as the emergency changes are nor included and must be repeated by hand. One can be lucky, if all of these changes were well documented (figure 34-2).

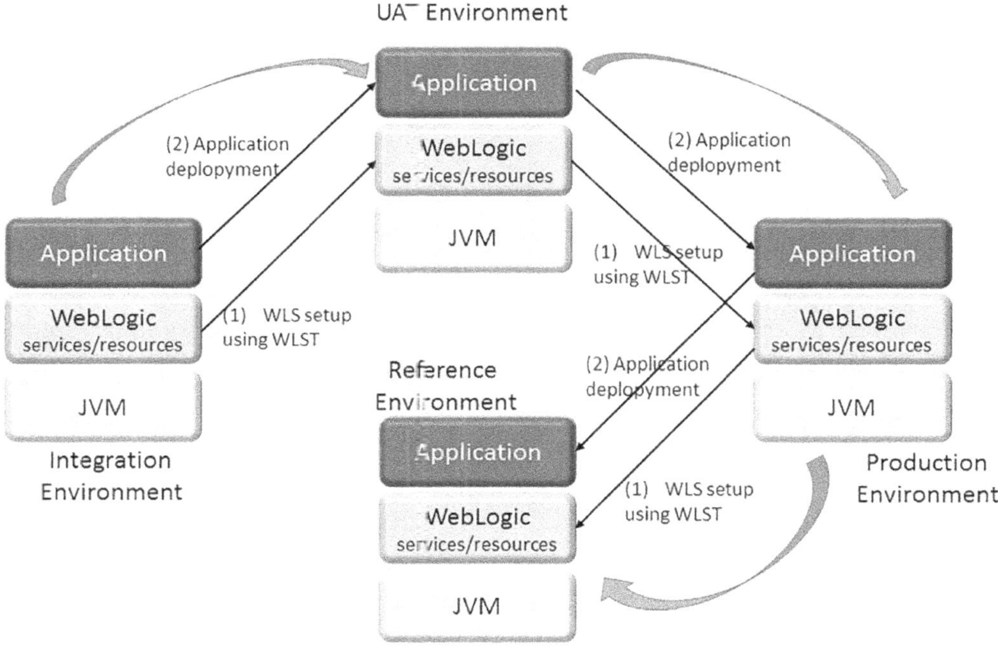

Figure 34-2: Reference environment must be setup like the production environment

Using the new multitenancy features the administrators have a new way of doing it. Note that this is not compulsory. It is a new option. My opinion definitely is that the best option is always to have a reference environment setup whenever a software goes live and all changes in production must immediately copied to the reference environment so that this environment is always production like and always ready to be used for testing.

In case of multitenancy the new option is that the administrators do not have to worry about setting all resources first and to make sure that they have all resources (like all JMS queues or all datasources) and finally deploy the application. The partition concepts allow administrators to export the current production state and import the exact same setup (except environment change defined in a resource deployment plan) into the reference environment. This will setup resources and applications in one deployment step (figure 34-3).

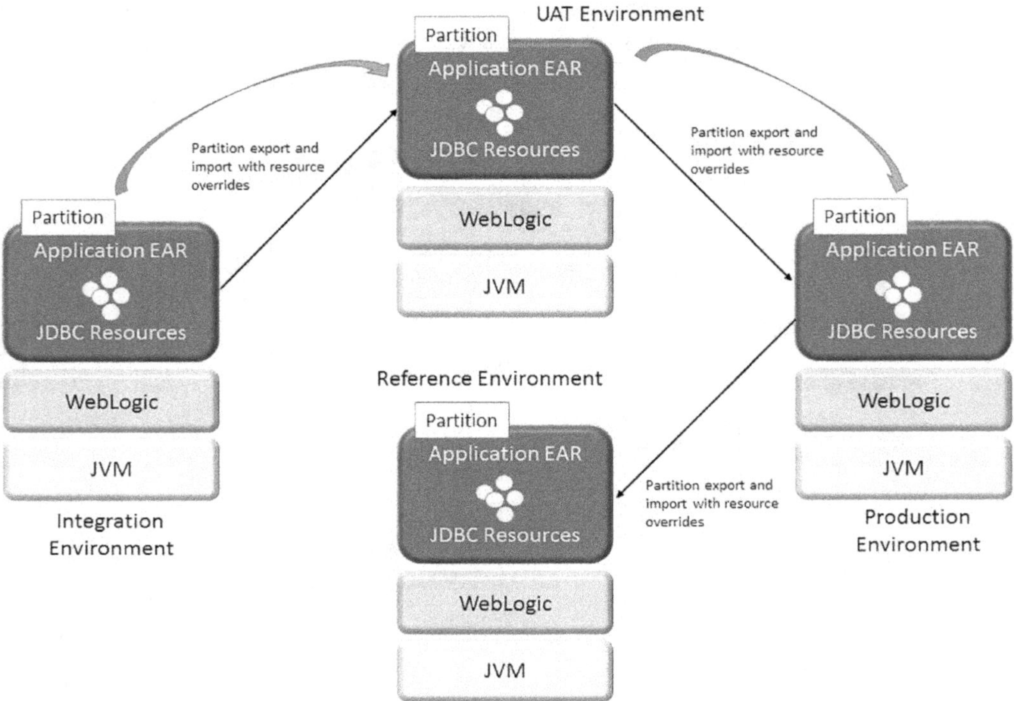

Figure 34-3: Multitenancy approach in case no reference environment exists

Not shown as an own diagram but of course it is definitely always advisable to keep a reference environment. The partition approach can help you to deploy the same application always from UAT to production and reference. This would be the best approach.

Drawback using the traditional WLS setup

The main issue with the traditional setup is that it is quite hard - unless you have a well-defined release and deploy process - to ensure that a reference environment always have a production like setup. Whenever a production issue occurred it is important that this issue can be reproduced in a non-production environment which has the same setup as the production. It is vital that the test environment to reproduce production issues has the same setup of resources, the same version of the application and so on.

As the traditional setup separates resources and applications, both aspects must be checked and verified otherwise test results might be useless. This is especially true in case patches needs to be created and tested and after the tests released to the production environment.

In case the release and deployment process is well defined, then this might not be an issue but many companies do not have it. But nevertheless, there is no better way, than to automate (almost) anything. Otherwise one can never reproduce anything. Also it might become an issue for an audit, because it is not traceable!

This problem especially exists for older systems which are running for a longer time in production and where the production setup even might have been changed over time without reflecting all changes also in the test environments of the environment setup scripts.

Advantages gained using Multitenancy

The process of testing and troubleshooting can be significantly improved using the WebLogic partition concept. With partitions it is possible that in case of a production issue the production partition will be exported and - based on a deployment plan - imported into the test environment. This ensures that all resources are also setup and configured production like.

It also provides a MUCH better usage of resources as the infrastructure is not forced to keep testing environments for all the production versions. The WebLogic domains can be used for other purposes until a troubleshooting session is required. Due to the bundling of resources into partition resource groups, it is very easy to change the WebLogic (resource) setup and host another application.

Technical steps and details

Technically the multitenancy solution uses the partition feature. Rather than working with separated WLST scripts or even manual instructions to setup the testing environment, the resources are targeted to the partition resource group and therefore installed and configured together with the partition.

In addition the new automated partition lifecycle features like import and export are part of this solution in order to automatically create partition archives and to install partitions. For troubleshoot testing it is even possible to write one, rather short script which exports the partition from the production system and import it using an appropriate resource deployment plan to the troubleshoot/test environment.

For this use case it is beneficial if the application and the resources are completely isolated. This means that all resources are targeted to the partition internal resource group so that all resources get exported and imported together with the partition.

From an implementation perspective the scripts needed for this use-case are identical to the previous use-case. This example just has much more resource deployment plans and therefore it is essential that these plans are maintained properly. This includes also putting them into a version control system.

Summary

This use case is a very common one, as many issues are only seen in real production environments and were not covered by test cases. In case the company does not have a reference environment that always has the identical setup than the production environment troubleshooting of production issues are challenging tasks.

Also companies may not have an own reference environment for every application. This means that the reference environment needs to be changed for each troubleshooting case.

The partition technology is particularly helpful in this case. Due to the bundling of application and resources together with a resource deployment plan, the exported production partition can be easily imported into the reference environment.

Microservice Architectures

CHAPTER

Overview

During the last years a new terminology in the area of software architecture became more and more popular. With "Microservice Architecture" many architects describe software development as a special way of breaking down an application into a number of independently deployable services.

"Microservice Architecture" does not have a precise definition, but a number of common characteristics. This includes among others the definition of access points, usage of standards and deployments. Each module supports a specific business goal and uses a simple, well-defined interface to communicate with other modules.

Microservices have a similar characteristics like SOA (Service Oriented Architecture) services but there is a fundamental difference. SOA is an enterprise approach whereas the enterprise as a whole is divided into (re-useable) services. A SOA approach normally affects the complete enterprise or at least a department and looks at the overall service landscape. Microservices usually focus on one particular application and divide this application into services with well-defined interfaces and more.

An interesting overview of common design patterns around Microservices can be found at: http://blog.arungupta.me/microservice-design-patterns. Arun discusses the agility, flexibility and scalability which can be gained by functional decompositions using a number of design patterns. These patterns include:

- Aggregator Microservice Design Pattern
- Proxy Microservice Design Pattern
- Chained Microservice Design Pattern
- Branch Microservice Design Pattern
- Asynchronous Messaging Microservice Design Pattern

WebLogic multitenancy and the partition technology provide a solid foundation that can be used to implement a Microservice architecture. Partitions can be designed to be small, independent services. Due to its small overhead, a WebLogic domain can host many of these services (figure 35-1).

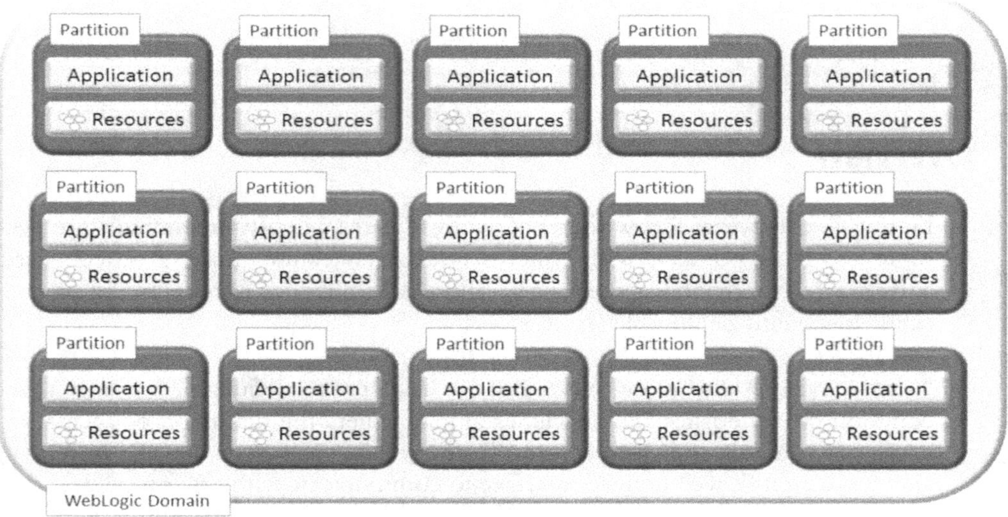

Figure 35-1: Multitenancy WebLogic Domain using a Microservice Architecture

Microservices tend to be small, use limited resources and have a well-defined interface. All these characteristics make them an interesting candidate for partitions. (figure 35-2)

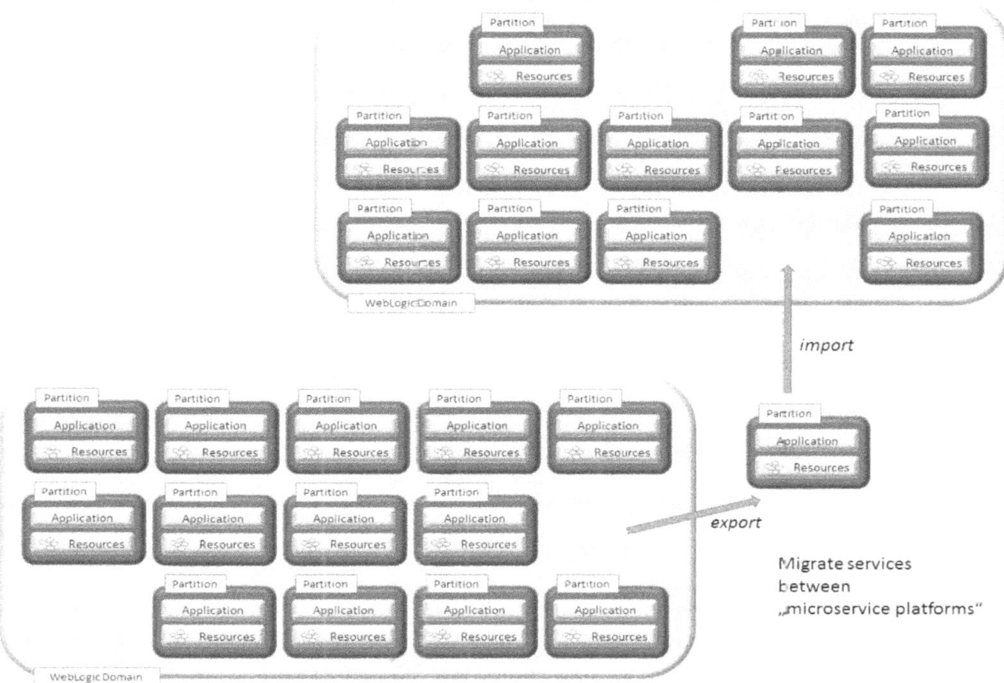

Figure 35-2: Microservice migration

The available technology in WebLogic support services migrations. Exporting/Importing partitions have already been discussed in detail in the technology section of this book.

Real world example

Given as an example an online shop. This online shop consists of a web frontend and an EJB based application which provides a shopping card implementation. In addition this application has components which communicate with other company systems. For this example: A messaging based access to check customer data on a mainframe and a payment component with a JDBC backend.

The complete application has been developed by different teams and finally built and provided to the operations team as a typical J2EE application as one EAR file. The operations team has to deploy the EAR file to a WebLogic cluster. Due to its nature, all components will be running on all managed servers. This implies that the administrators need to configure all required resources for all managed servers (figure 35-3).

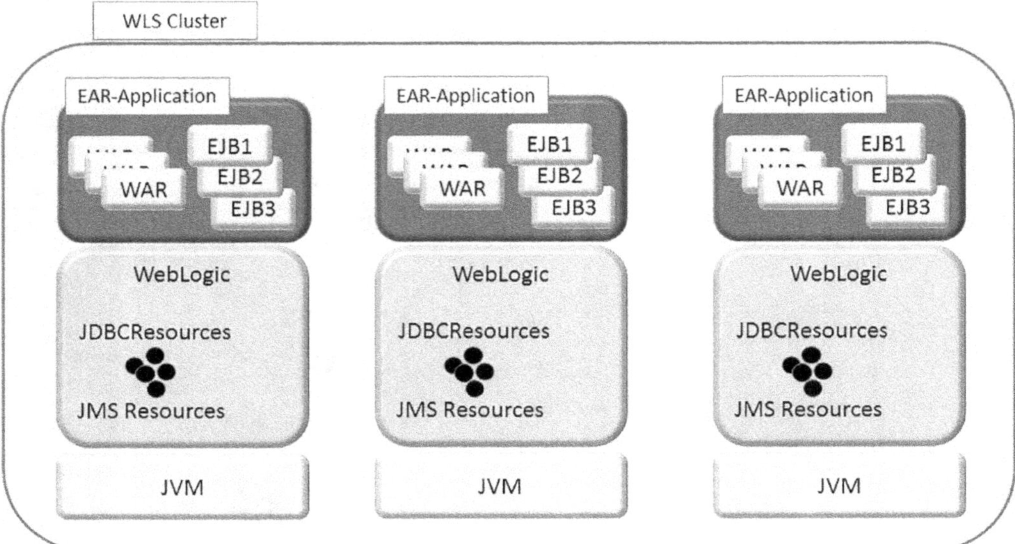

Figure 35-3: All managed-servers have the same EAR file deployed and require all resources

After reading through the other use-cases, it is obvious that combining the application and resources into a partition will provide a number of benefits. This will also ease deployments and migrations.

In this case let us focus on the application itself. Online shops usually have 90% or more of the traffic in the web portal. This is caused by visitors browsing the products, but not shopping anything. Given the approach above this means that the operators need to scale out this application to more hosts due to high traffic. Scaling out also means that the backend components also get scaled out, even though there is only low traffic on them.

Microservices break down this application into its components and make them deployable as individual artifacts. Each of the application component requires only a subset of the services. Combining the breakdown with the partition isolation features and the abilities to bundle component and resources into a "WebLogic application" has a number of benefits (figure 35-4).

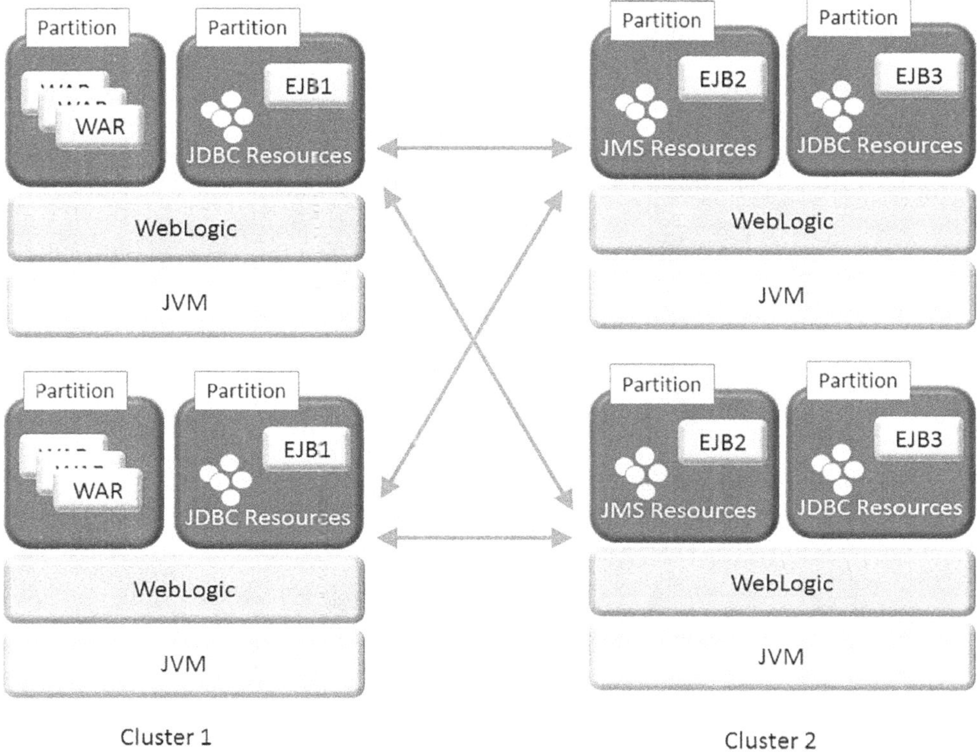

Figure 35-4: Microservice architecture combined with partition isolation

Note that for simplicity the above diagram does not include load-balancer (like OTD) or other infrastructure components.

The above diagram shows one possible way to break down application components into smaller (micro) services and bundle these components with all the resources they need.

Given the above setup allow administrators to scale out the web frontend as needed. The backends do not need to scale together with the web frontend. Using the partition migration features, it is also easy for administrators to change the combination of co-deployments. For example the two backends ("EJB2" and "EJB3") can easily be separated into different partition clusters if needed. As the resources are bundled together with the component into a partition this would not even require a change in the WebLogic setup (beside the virtual target migration).

Drawback using the traditional WLS setup

The main issue with the traditional setup is that the J2EE design pattern recommend to combine all application components into one deployment archive – called EAR. Indeed, this has a number of benefits like classloader isolation, common environmental naming context and more. It also simplifies the deployment.

In the example above this approach suffers from the fact that the load on the different components is very different.

In a non-multitenancy setup it is also possible to deploy the different components alone. E.g.: deploy the WAR files to the web cluster, then EJBs to the EJB cluster. This does not require the partition isolation.

The difficulties arise for the deployment team. They need to perfectly understand which cluster will have which application component and therefore requires which set of resources. Every change in the distribution requires a re-configuration or re-targeting of resources.

It gets even more complicated if the administrators decide that – e.g. for security reasons – the components need to be hosted into different domains.

Advantages gained using Multitenancy

Using the partition technology instead of just deploying the different components alone has a number of advantages. The most visible advantage is clearly the combination of the component and all its required resources into a single deployment unit. By doing this, each component can benefit from the new technologies like resource management, partition deployment and migration.

Practically this approach is breaking down one J2EE application (EAR) into a number of even better isolated "WebLogic applications"

Technical steps and details

Technically the multitenancy solution uses the partition feature. For each component an own resource group template will be created. All resources needed for this component get scoped to this resource group template. For each component the administrator needs to create an own partition that is based on the corresponding resource group template. Each partition can be equipped with an own resource managers to manage threads, IO and more. The application component will be deployed to its partition. For each component the administrator creates an own virtual target. Resource deployment plans for the different environments, (e.g. integration, UAT or production) can be used to customize the environment specific settings.

The benefit is that it is even possible for the development groups to handover exported partitions and the resource deployment plans to the deployment teams. The deployment teams only need to create the virtual targets and the security setup before they can import the provided partitions.

Summary

Microservices focus on breaking down complex applications or deployments into smaller chunks. These chunks need to be well designed and equipped with standard interfaces.

The WebLogic partition technology can help combine these application chunks into isolated deployment units with all the resources this service needs.

By using partitions and not full dedicated managed server clusters, many advantages discussed earlier – like reduced footprint, better density and more – can be utilized for these services.

Part VI

Advanced Multitenancy Aspects

Integrating Partitions and Oracle Traffic Director

CHAPTER

Introduction

The main part of the book focused on the new technology features around partitions in WebLogic. Partitions form the foundation for multitenancy and can be used as a base technology for cloud services.

In chapter 5, the new concepts are introduced. We are now revisiting the key concepts of the multitenancy strategy of Oracle – see the diagram below. Up to now the book discussed multitenancy at the WebLogic level, including all the new technologies and features.

Within this advanced section of the book we will extend our scope and include the missing technologies. First of all, we will discuss the load-balancing capabilities offered by Oracle. In the subsequent chapter we will examine Oracle's multitenancy extension into other products, especially into the distributed "Coherence Caches" (figure 36-1).

Key Concepts

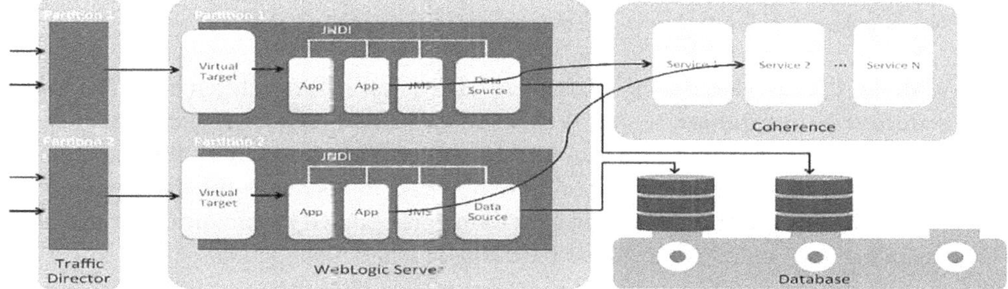

Figure 36-1: Extending Multitenancy into the OTD loadbalancer © Oracle

Load-balancing Technologies for WebLogic

Oracle offers two different technologies for load-balancing web applications. This includes a plugin to the Apache Webserver and the Oracle product OTD (Oracle Traffic Director).

Unfortunately, Oracle did not extend the Apache plugin in order to support multitenancy in a special way. The Apache plugin can of course be used to load-balance traffic to partitions. In case partitions get moved to different servers or more instances of the partition need to be started, a manual change in the Apache plugin is required to update the load-balancer setup. The configuration of the Apache plugin for partitions is therefore identical to a load-balancing to a standard WebLogic domain.

This chapter focus on the "Oracle Traffic Director" (short OTD). Oracle has implemented a direct support for multitenancy into OTD. Due to this support, the OTD configuration will get updated automatically if partitions get moved or additional instances gets started.

Introduction to Oracle Traffic Director

Oracle Traffic Director (OTD) implements a layer-7 software load balancer. Similar to the Apache Webserver, the OTD can be used for reliable HTTP, HTTPS and also (this is different to Apache) TCP communication. OTD acts as a reverse proxy and/or load-balancer to application server clusters sitting in the core network (backend). Oracle Traffic Director provides different load-balancing methods and rules. Like other web-server it also supports caching. OTD also supports a number of additional quality of service features. Instances of Oracle Traffic Director can be grouped together to form active-active or active-passive clusters.

With the 12.2.x. release Oracle has also added support for multitenancy. The interesting feature is an integration to the WebLogic domains hosting the partition cluster. This integration enables the infrastructure to get notified as soon as the partition cluster changes. A change may be that additional partition instances for this cluster had been started. In this case the OTD configuration gets updated automatically so that the load-balancing also includes the added partitions.

Oracle Traffic director adds the missing load-balancing and failover technology in front of a partition cluster (figure 36-2).

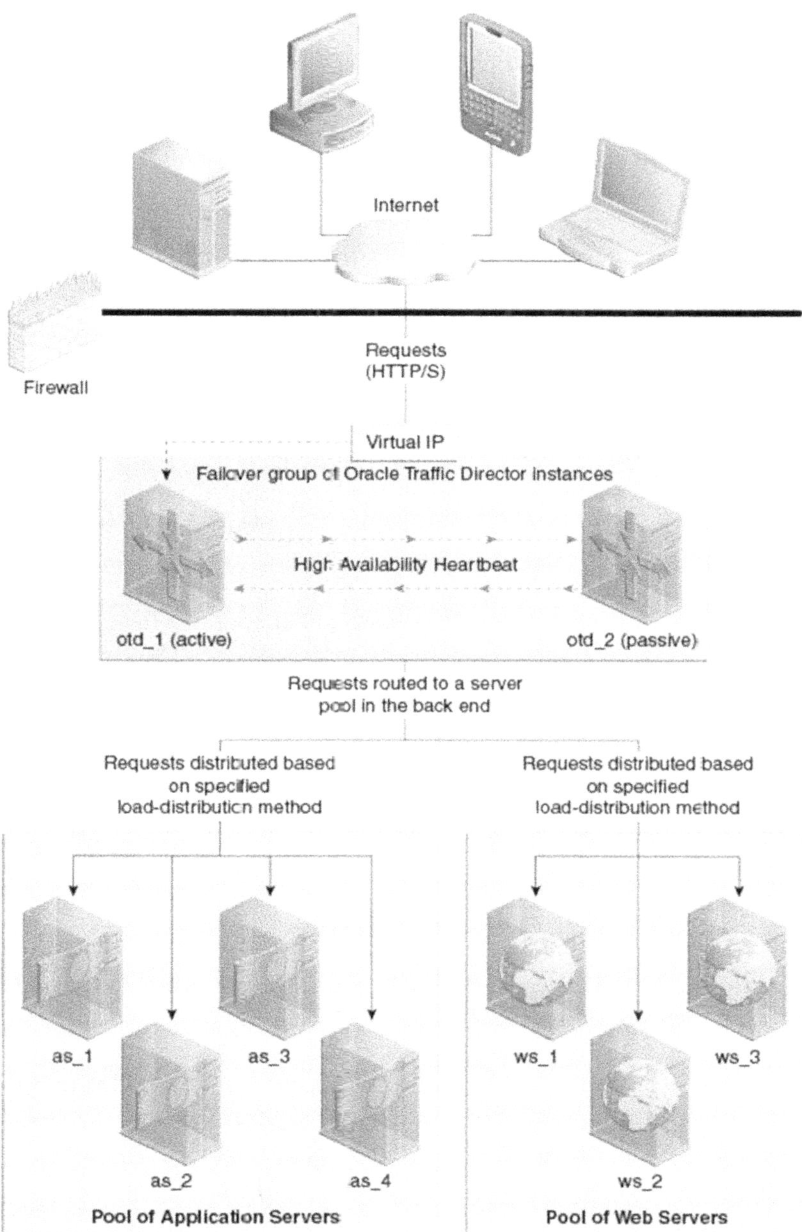

Figure 36-2: Oracle Traffic Director – © Oracle Documentation

Instances of Oracle Traffic Director are in almost all cases hosted in a different domain than the partitions. Usually the Oracle Traffic Director instances are located in a DMZ environment or at least on dedicated server and forward traffic to application server cluster in secure networks. Albeit it is possible to co-locate OTD into the same WebLogic domain as the multitenancy application partitions, I consider this setup as unusual. This section will assume that OTD and application partitions are deployed into different, separated domains.

The integration implemented by Oracle is called "OTD Runtime". Partitions on the WebLogic multitenancy domains can be associated with an OTD Runtime for load-balancing.

Configure Multitenancy Setups in OTD

Please refer to the Oracle documentation for the installation and the configuration of an OTD domain. It is required to install WebLogic and OTD into the same directory as we will manage OTD through WebLogic. This means that on each machine where you want to run OTD, you need to install WebLogic and OTD.

It is required to create an OTD runtime in the OTD domain first. On each WebLogic domain, it is required to activate the Lifecycle Manager. Then you can create links between these two domains.

Create an OTD runtime in the OTD domain

The first step is to create a new OTD domain. As in our case we manage OTD through the WebLogic administration, the OTD domain can be created using the standard WebLogic configuration wizard, or a WLST script.

After setting up the OTD domain, the OTD node-manager and the OTD machines we can start to create OTD runtime configurations.

The following screenshots demonstrate the creation of an OTD runtime using the Enterprise Manger Fusion Middleware Console (figure 36-3).

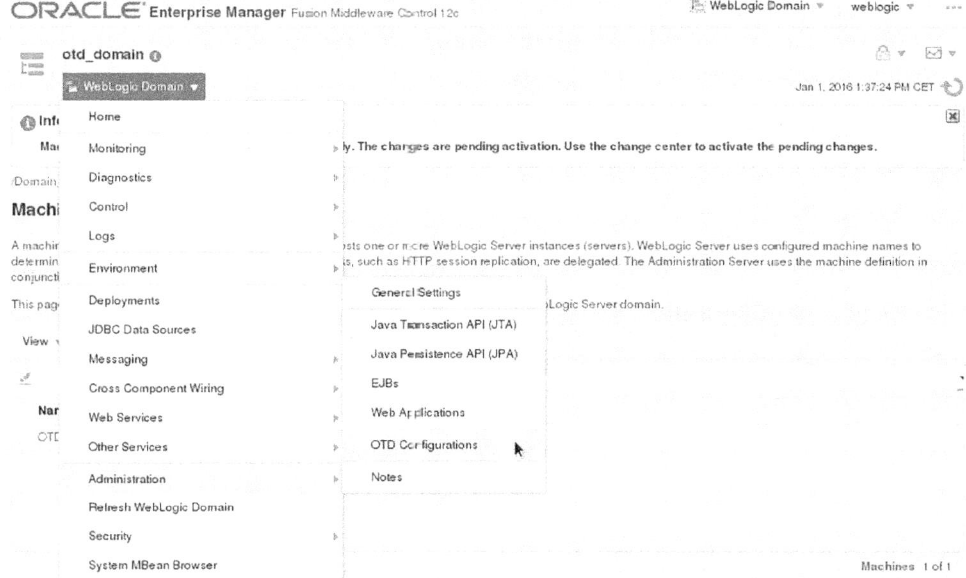

Figure 36-3: Start to configure OTD

As the OTD is managed by WebLogic, the drop-down menus also contain all the resource and security wizards used to setup a standard WebLogic domain. For each load-balancing service we need to configure an a new OTD configuration in the OTD domain. (figure 36-4)

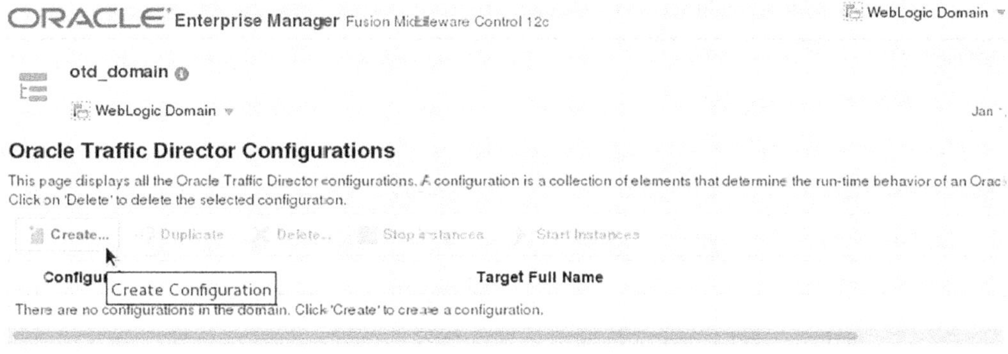

Figure 36-4: Create a configuration

Start the creation of the OTD configuration by clicking on "Create" in the OTD configurations wizard. The wizard will guide you through the different steps, which are required to create a new configuration (figure 36-5).

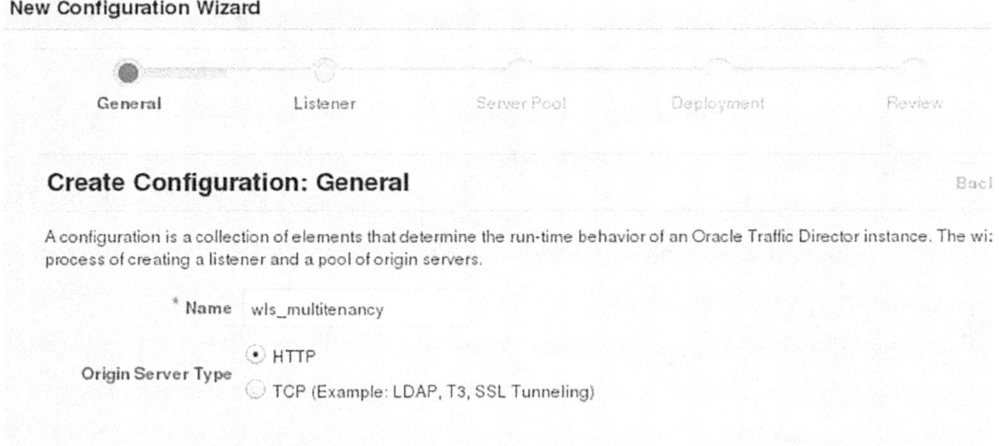

Figure 36-5: Configure the OTD Configuration

First choose a unique name. Later on we link up the WebLogic domain to this configuration. It is recommended to use a meaningful name.

The OTD – other than Apache – does not only offer HTTP load-balancing. It also offers load-balancing for other protocols like t3 or even SSL tunneling. In our example we want to load-balance HTTP requests to our partitions, therefore we choose HTTP (figure 36-6).

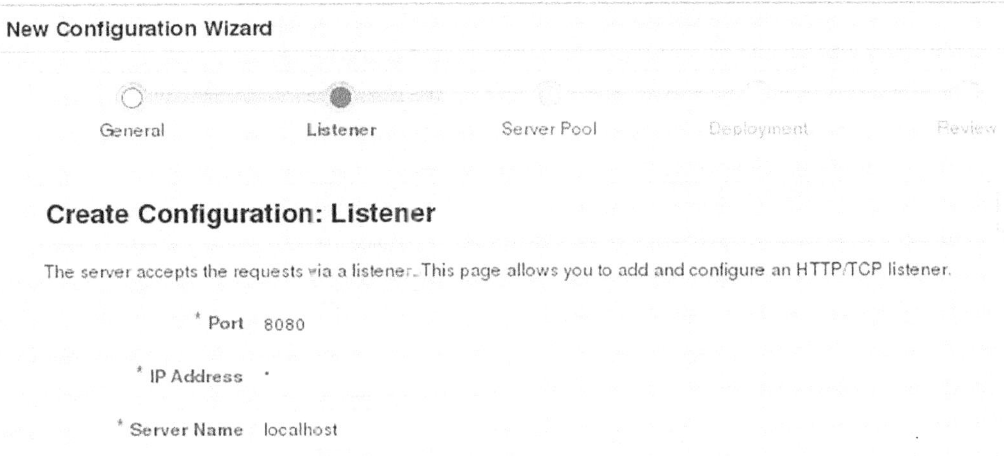

Figure 36-6: Select the OTD listener port

In the second step, you need to configure the listener port of the OTD load-balancer. If you do not want OTD to listen on all network adapter, then it is possible to choose a network adapter and server name which OTD should listen on.

The next step allows the administrator to configure all the remote WebLogic servers to which OTD should load-balance requests to (figure 36-7).

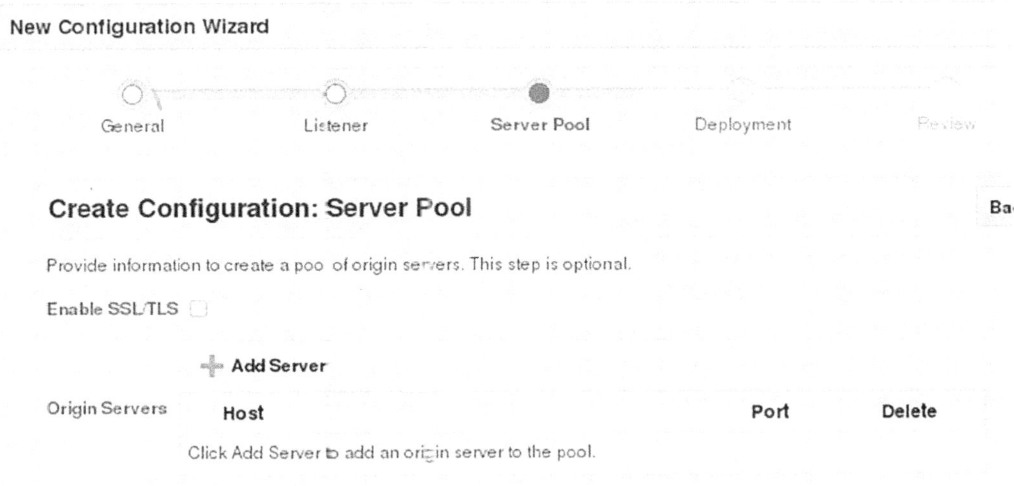

Figure 36-7: Load-balancing setup

In the section we will "link" OTD to a WLS12.2.x domain. WebLogic starting with version 12.2.1 is able to pass its configurations of the partition cluster to OTD. Therefore it is not required to configure these servers for a multitenancy setup (figure 36-8).

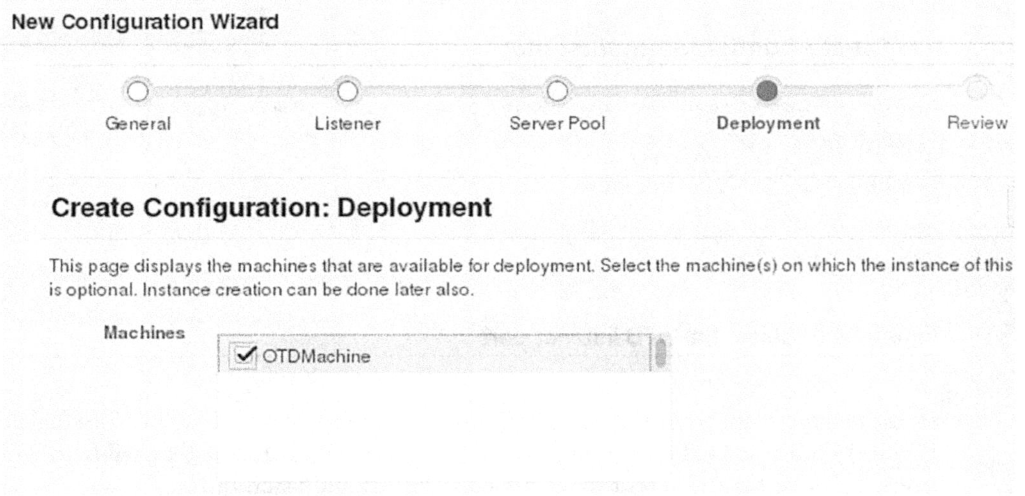
New Configuration Wizard
General
Listener
Server Pool
Deployment
Review
Create Configuration: Deployment
This page displays the machines that are available for deployment. Select the machine(s) on which the instance of this
is optional. Instance creation can be done later also.
Machines
OTDMachine

Figure 36-8: Deployment of your configuration

As a last configuration step we need to deploy (or target) our configuration to one or more OTD servers. In this example we deploy the configuration to a single OTD server called "OTDMachine".

After a chance to review our settings, the configuration is completed (figure 36-9).

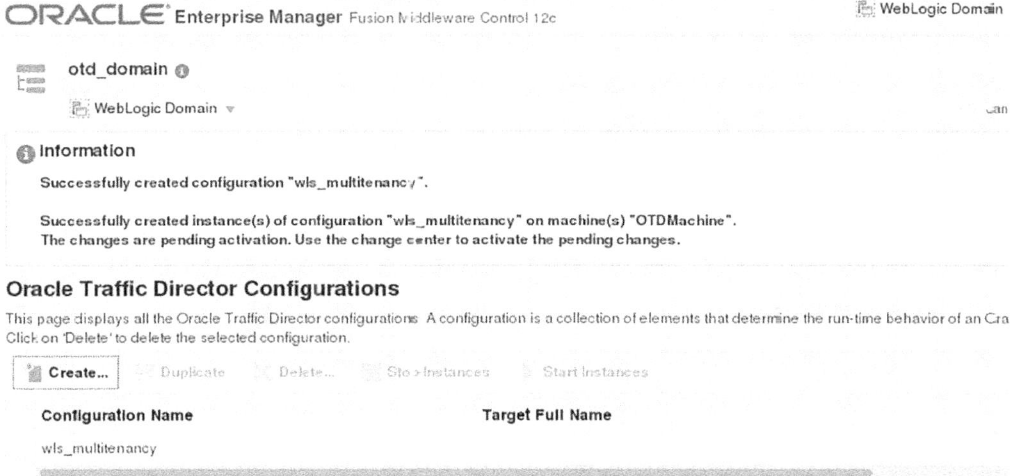

Figure 36-9: Configuration has been created

Similar to changes in standard WebLogic server, we need to activate our changes (figure 36-10).

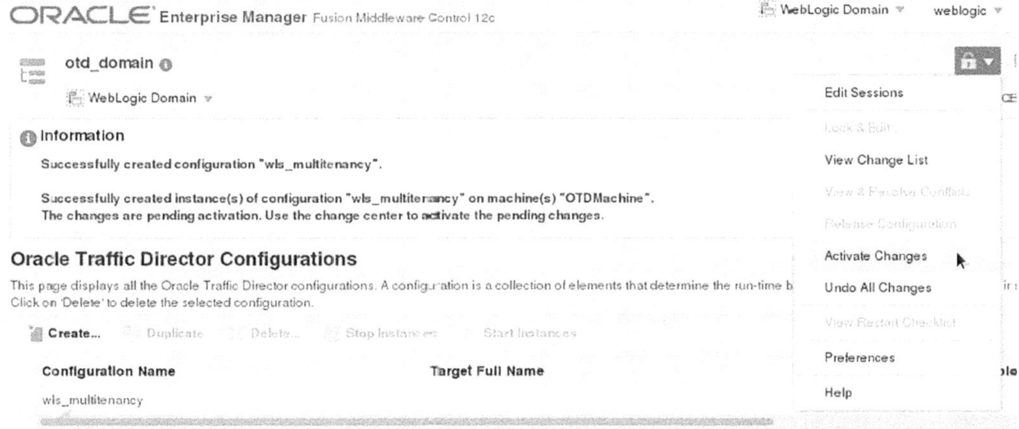

Figure 36-10: Activate the configuration settings

A deployed and activated configuration must be started so that requests can be processed and forwarded to the backend server. Similar to WebLogic managed server or partitions, the OTD offers lifecycle operations for its configurations.

You need to perform a "start" operation in order to start the configuration (figure 36-11).

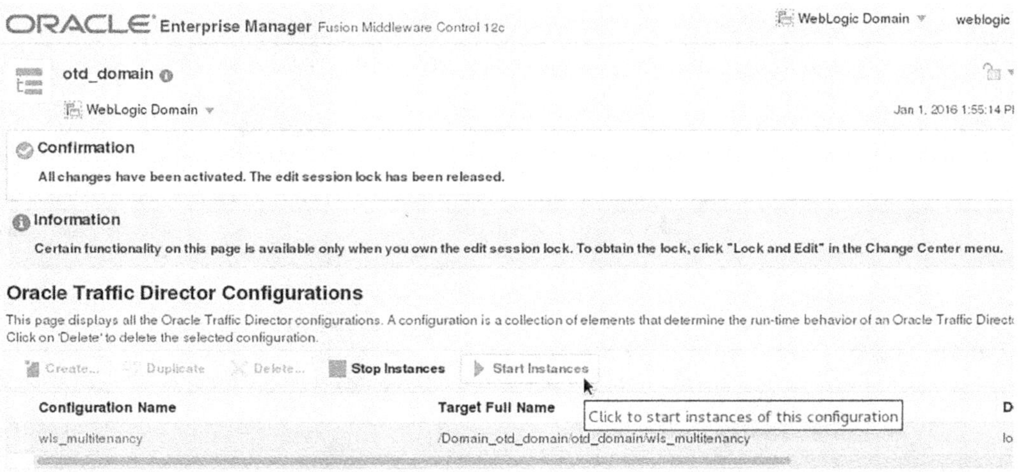

ORACLE Enterprise Manager Fusion Middleware Control 12c
WebLogic Domain
weblogic
otd_domain
WebLogic Domain
Jan 1, 2016 1:55:14 PI
Confirmation
All changes have been activated. The edit session lock has been released.
Information
Certain functionality on this page is available only when you own the edit session lock. To obtain the lock, click "Lock and Edit" in the Change Center menu.
Oracle Traffic Director Configurations
This page displays all the Oracle Traffic Director configurations. A configuration is a collection of elements that determine the run-time behavior of an Oracle Traffic Direct
Click on 'Delete' to delete the selected configuration.
Create...
Duplicate
Delete...
Stop Instances
Start Instances
Configuration Name
Target Full Name
Click to start instances of this configuration
wls_multitenancy
/Domain_otd_domain/otd_domain/wls_multitenancy

Figure 36-11: Start the configuration

OTD also offers monitoring capabilities. Each configuration has changed after its activation into a link. By clicking on the link, OTD will bring up the monitoring page for this configuration (figure 36-12, figure 36-13).

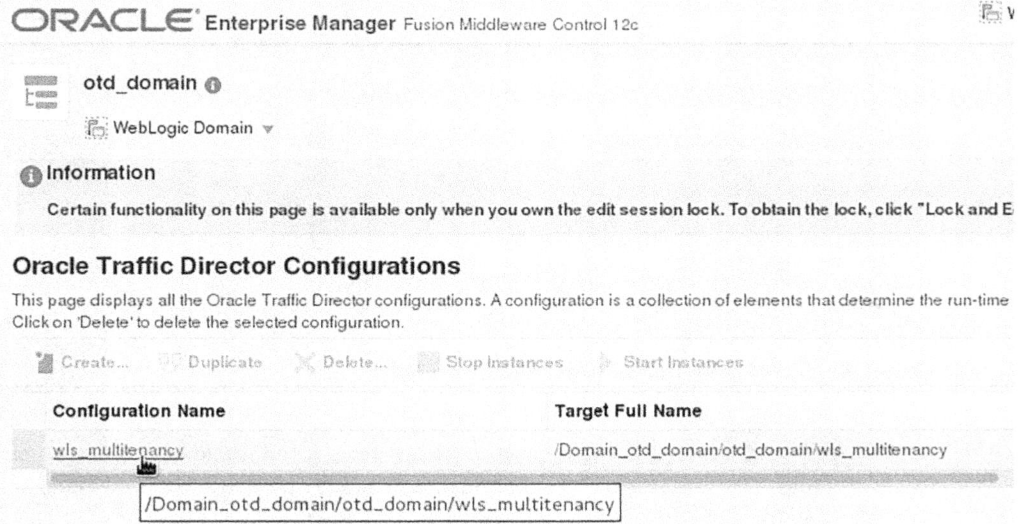

ORACLE Enterprise Manager Fusion Middleware Control 12c
otd_domain
WebLogic Domain
Information
Certain functionality on this page is available only when you own the edit session lock. To obtain the lock, click "Lock and E
Oracle Traffic Director Configurations
This page displays all the Oracle Traffic Director configurations. A configuration is a collection of elements that determine the run-time
Click on 'Delete' to delete the selected configuration.
Create...
Duplicate
Delete...
Stop Instances
Start Instances
Configuration Name
Target Full Name
wls_multitenancy
/Domain_otd_domain/otd_domain/wls_multitenancy
/Domain_otd_domain/otd_domain/wls_multitenancy

Figure 36-12: Selecting link to see the monitoring page

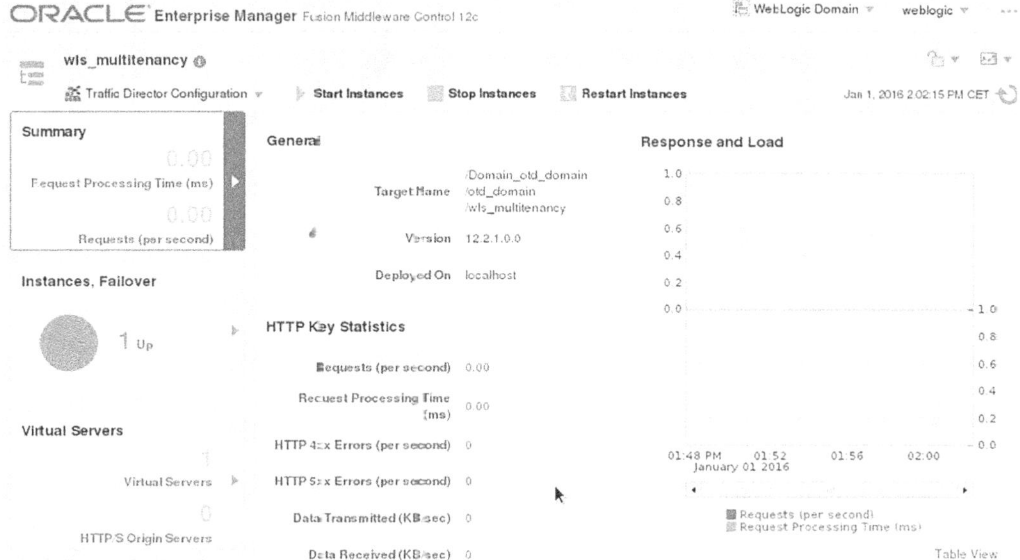

Figure 36-13: Monitoring page for this OTD configuration

Activate the Lifecycle Manager in the WebLogic domain

By default, the "LifecycleManager" is disabled in WebLogic. Note that this section changes the configuration of the WebLogic multitenancy domain and no longer the OTD domain!

You can enable the LifecycleManager using the WebLogic Console or the WebLogic EM Console (figure 36-14).

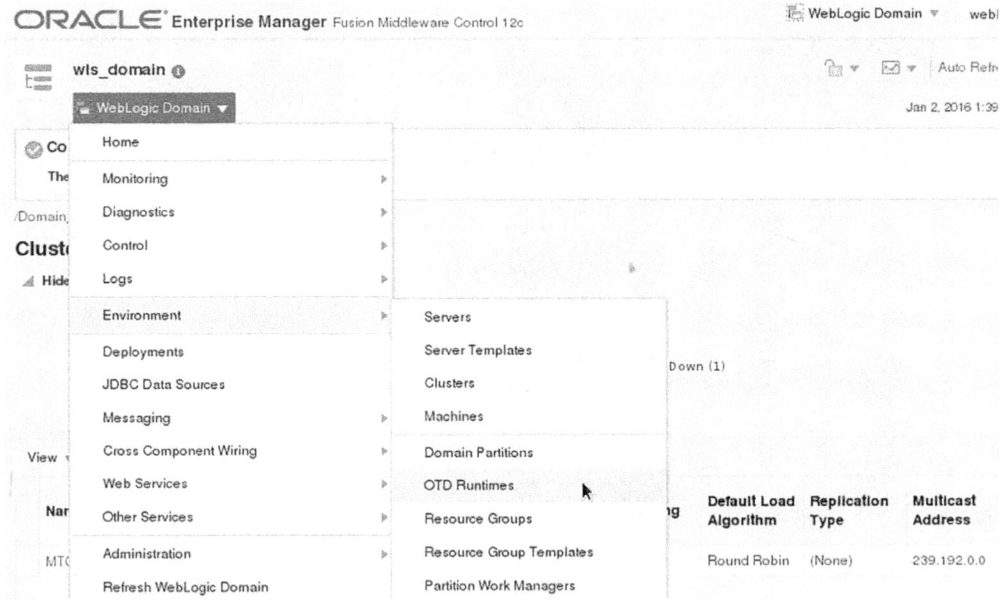

Figure 36-14: Choose OTD Runtimes

In the WebLogic domain – not OTD domain (!) – you need to choose the "OTD Runtimes" configuration section.

By default the LifecycleManager is disabled (figure 36-15).

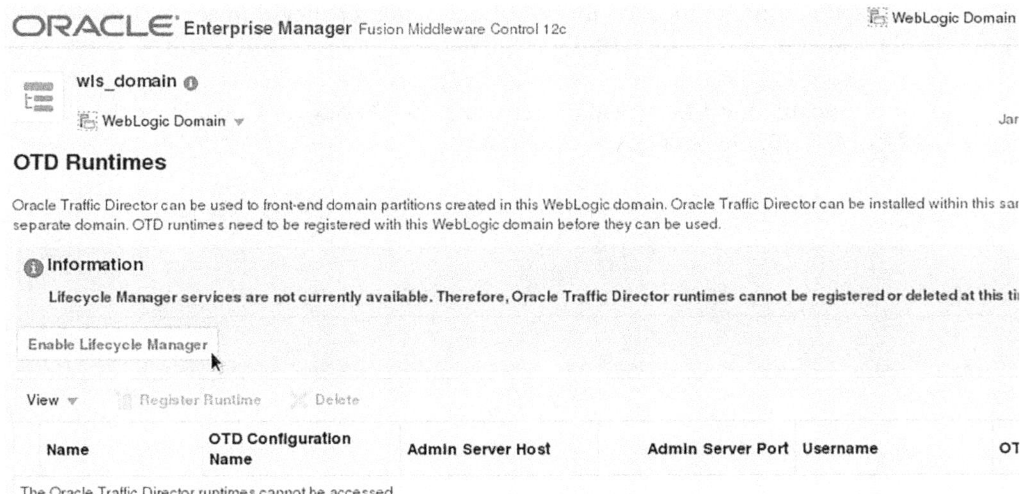

Figure 36-15: Click to enable the Lifecycle Manager

After clicking the above button, the Lifecycle Manager gets enabled and you need to restart the domain as this is a non-dynamic change.

The same activity can also be automated using the following WLST script:

```
connect('weblogic','welcome1','t3://localhost:12001')

# change to the lifecycle manager MBean
cd ('LifecycleManagerConfig/'+domainName)
```

This script will provide the following output, which shows the Lifecycle Manager setup.

```
dr--   ConfiguredEndPoints
dr--   EndPoints
dr--   Target

-rw-   DataSourceName                                null
-rw-   DeploymentType                                none
-r--   DynamicallyCreated                            false
-r--   Enabled                                       false
-r--   Id                                            0
-rw-   Name                                          usecase_10
-rw-   Notes                                         null
-rw-   OutOfBandEnabled                              false
-rw-   PersistenceType                               XML
-rw-   Tags                                          null
-rw-   Target                                        null
-r--   Type                                          LifecycleManagerConfig

-r-x   addTag                                        Boolean : String(tag)
-r-x   freezeCurrentValue                            Void : String(attributeName)
-r-x   getInheritedProperties                        String[] : String[](propertyNames)
-r-x   isInherited                                   Boolean : String(propertyName)
-r-x   isSet                                         Boolean : String(propertyName)
-r-x   removeTag                                     Boolean : String(tag)
-r-x   restoreDefaultValue                           Void : String(attributeName)
```

This lifecycle manager must be enabled. The following WLST script can be used to do that (unless you want to use the WebConsole or EMConsole):

```
connect('weblogic','welcome1','t3://localhost 12001')

# switch to the edit mode
edit()

# change to the lifecycle manager MBean
cd ('LifecycleManagerConfig/'+domainName)

# activate the lifecycle manager and set it to "local admin". The corresponding parameter is "admin"
cmo.setOutOfBandEnabled(true)
cmo.setDeploymentType('admin')

# save and activate changes
save()
```

After this script has been run, you need to restart the domain.

Create the link between both domains

After the Lifecycle Manager has been enabled, the administrator has to configure OTD runtime configurations in the multitenancy (!) domain. These runtime configurations contain a link and login details to the OTD domain and the OTD runtime defined in the OTD domain.

As a second step, the administrator can now define partitions in the multitenancy domain. The partitions can be configured with the information that load-balancing will be done using a specific OTD runtime. This link enabled the WebLogic multitenancy domain to feedback setup information for this OTD runtime from the multitenancy domain to the OTD domain.

Create an OTD runtime link

The OTD link is a configuration on domain level and does not (yet) have anything to do with partitions (figure 36-16).

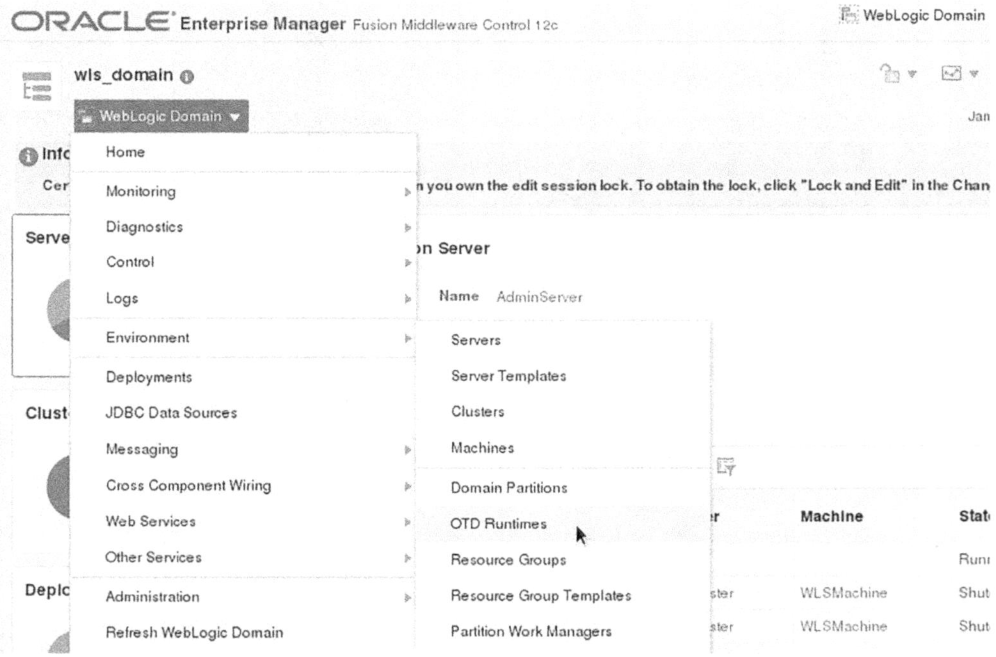

Figure 36-16: Select OTD runtimes in the multitenancy domain

In this configuration wizard you can configure the different OTD runtime links. Click on "Register Runtime" in order to create a new OTD runtime link (figure 36-17).

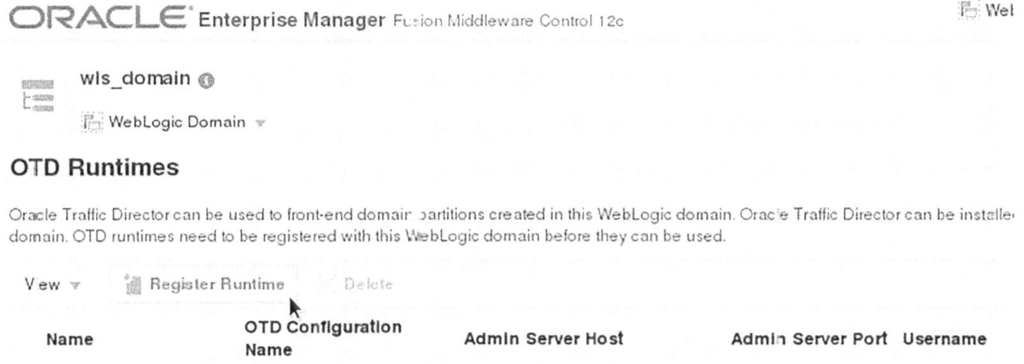

Figure 36-17: Register a runtime to create a new link

You need to provide login details to the OTD domain that hosts the load-balancing runtime. It is also required to provide the runtime name – "wls_multitenancy" - which we used earlier to create the runtime in the OTD domain (figure 36-18).

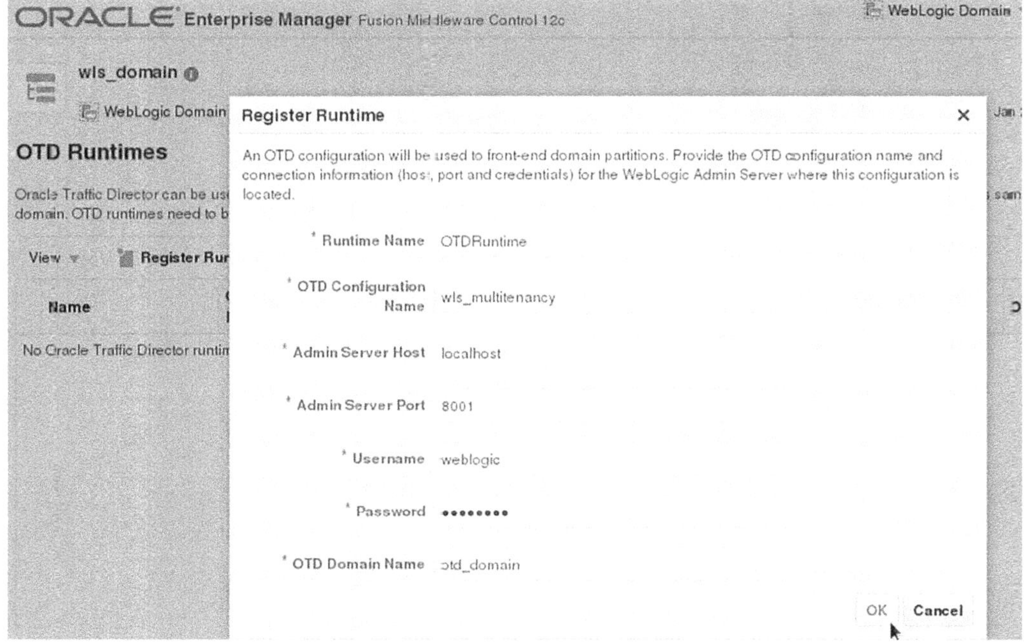

Figure 36-18: Provide remote runtime details

After all changes have been activated, we have successfully created our OTD runtime link to a remote OTD domain runtime configuration (figure 36-19).

Figure 36-19: Runtime link registered

After the runtime link has been created, the administrator can configure partitions with reference to the OTD runtime link (figure 36-20).

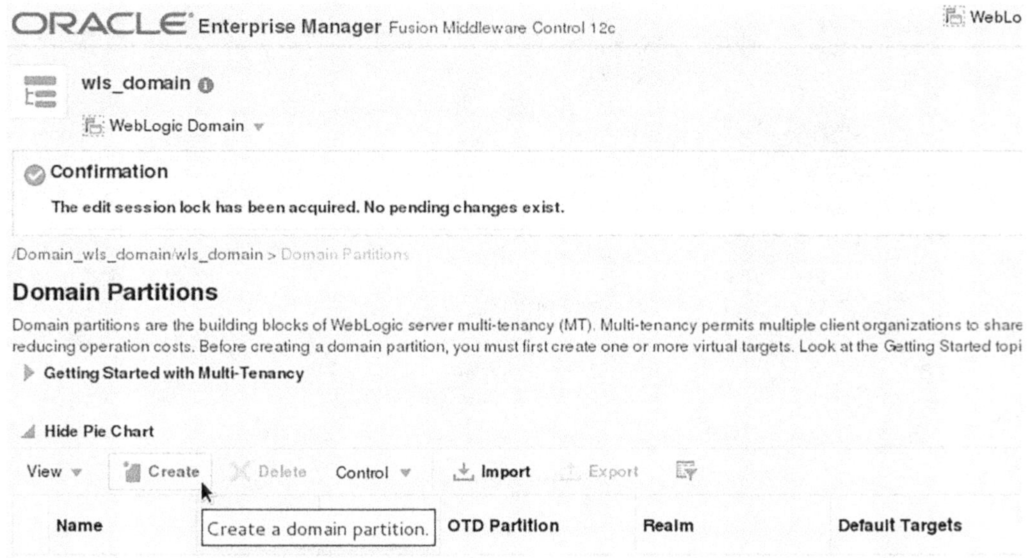

Figure 36-20; Create a new partition using the EM console

It is also possible to use an automated WLST script to create the partition. The first step offers a possibility to enable OTD load-balancing and to select the OTD runtime link which should be used to update the remote OTD (figure 36-21).

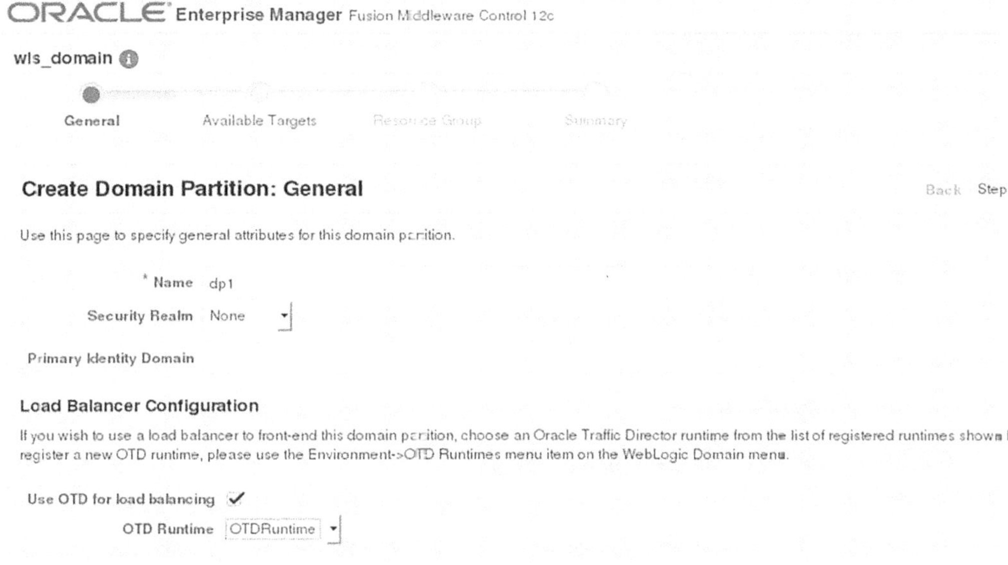
ORACLE Enterprise Manager Fusion Middleware Control 12c
wls_domain
General
Available Targets
Create Domain Partition: General
Back
Step
Use this page to specify general attributes for this domain partition.
* Name dp1
Security Realm None
Primary Identity Domain
Load Balancer Configuration
If you wish to use a load balancer to front-end this domain partition, choose an Oracle Traffic Director runtime from the list of registered runtimes shown
register a new OTD runtime, please use the Environment->OTD Runtimes menu item on the WebLogic Domain menu.
Use OTD for load balancing
OTD Runtime OTDRuntime

Figure 36-21: Configure the remote OTD runtime link

With this setup on partition level, the OTD load-balancing setup has been completed. The multitenancy domain will automatically update the OTD domain whenever partition instances are started or stopped.

Automatic OTD update from the multitenancy domain

After the setup of both domains has been completed and the link between both domains has been established, the administrator can start the partition clusters. After the partitions have been started, you can see the automatic update in the OTD domain (figure 36-22).

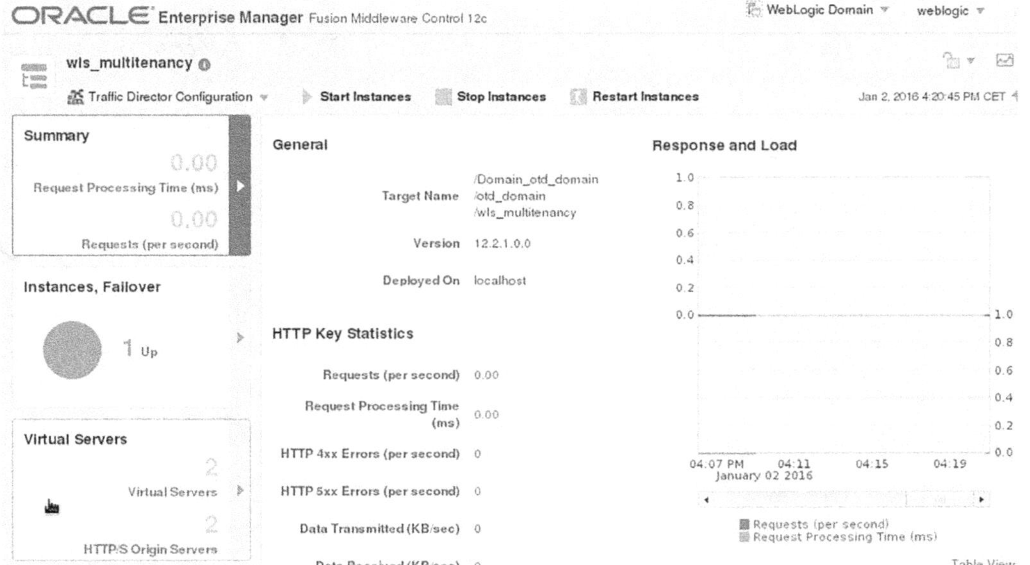

Figure 36-22: OTD domain was updated

As you can see in the screenshot above, the OTD runtime now shows two virtual servers.

The tab called "Origin Servers" provides a list of destination servers. In our case these are the virtual targets for our two partitions in the multitenancy domain. If the administrator would shutdown a partition or start additional partitions, this list will be updated (figure 36-23).

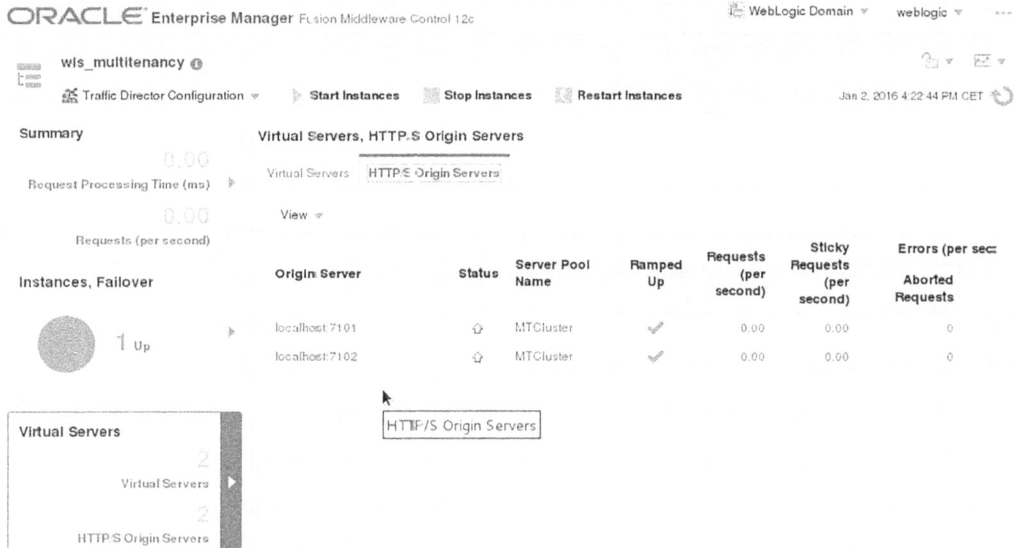

Figure 36-23: List of original servers

The above information, including the cluster name, is provided by the multitenancy domain. The configured link is used in order to contact the OTD domain and to update the information in the OTD runtime associated with this link.

The OTD portal also provides information about the setup of the routing. Select the "virtual server" link to see these details (figure 36-24).

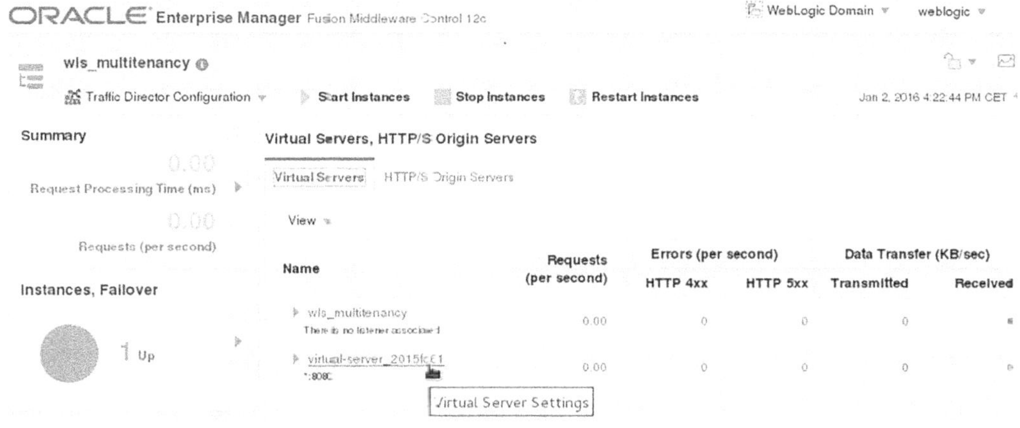

Figure 36-24: Select the virtual server link

The routing information displays the routing rule and the destination cluster, including all the destination servers (figure 36-25).

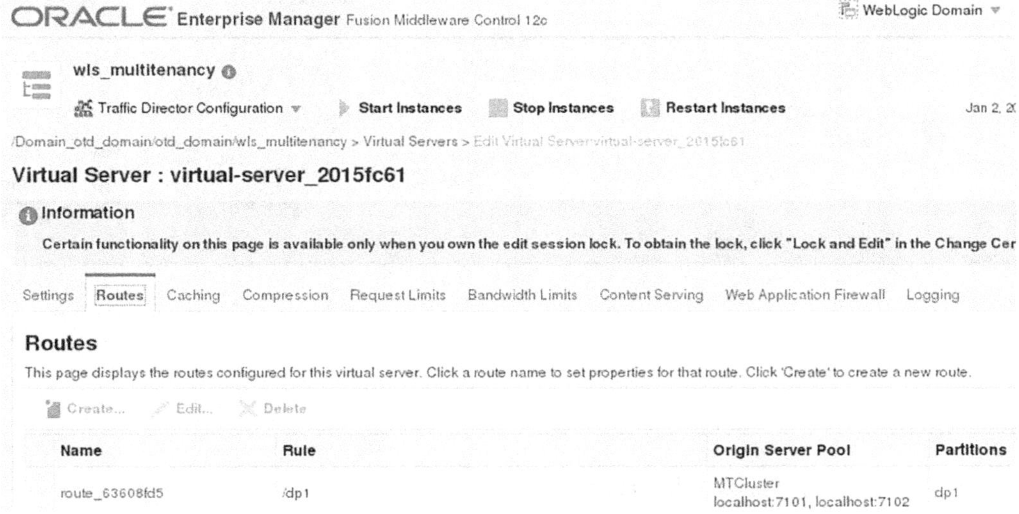

Figure 36-25: Routing information

Shortcuts of the OTD

Oracle has implemented a nice integration between OTD and partition based multitenancy domains.

For many real-world infrastructure setup the OTD provides a very valuable setup. But the OTD integration also has a number of potential disadvantages.

One of the first disadvantage is the dependency on Oracle Linux, because the OTD is only certified for this operation system.

A second disadvantage is the way Oracle has implemented this integration. The multitenancy domain establishes a remote connection to the OTD domain. Usually the OTD domain would reside in the DMZ network and the multitenancy domain in the core network. Any link from the core network to the DMZ is suspicious and not wanted for any company.

If the OTD is running in the DMZ, this also means that the administrators need to install, patch and maintain a full WebLogic and OTD installation. Usually companies try to avoid application server installations in the DMZ and tend to use reverse proxies to tunnel incoming communication to core network.

Summary

The Oracle Traffic Director fills an important gab in the Oracle multitenancy strategy. There are other http load-balancer which could forward traffic to WebLogic instances, like Apache with the WebLogic proxy or the Oracle http server which is based on Apache.

The Oracle Traffic Directors provides a number of business advantages for customers. The most important one is the link between the multitenancy domain and the OTD domain. The OTD setup can be automatically updated as soon as the partition cluster changes. Another unique advantage is that OTD domains can be managed by the familiar WebLogic administration server and the corresponding administrative consoles.

The multitenancy integration of Oracle Traffic Director also has a number of disadvantages with regards to firewall setup and installation.

Especially in combination with dynamic clusters, the use of the multitenancy integration simplifies the administration of the load-balancing setup for partition clusters.

Extending Multitenancy into Coherence Caches

CHAPTER

Introduction

After looking at the multitenancy integration into the load-balancing frontend provided with the Oracle Traffic Director, this chapter discusses the Oracle multitenancy support of the attached backend systems. In order to offer a complete multitenancy story, Oracle also offers multitenancy support for Coherence caches and also for Oracle databases. This chapter discusses the multitenancy support of Coherence caches (figure 37-1).

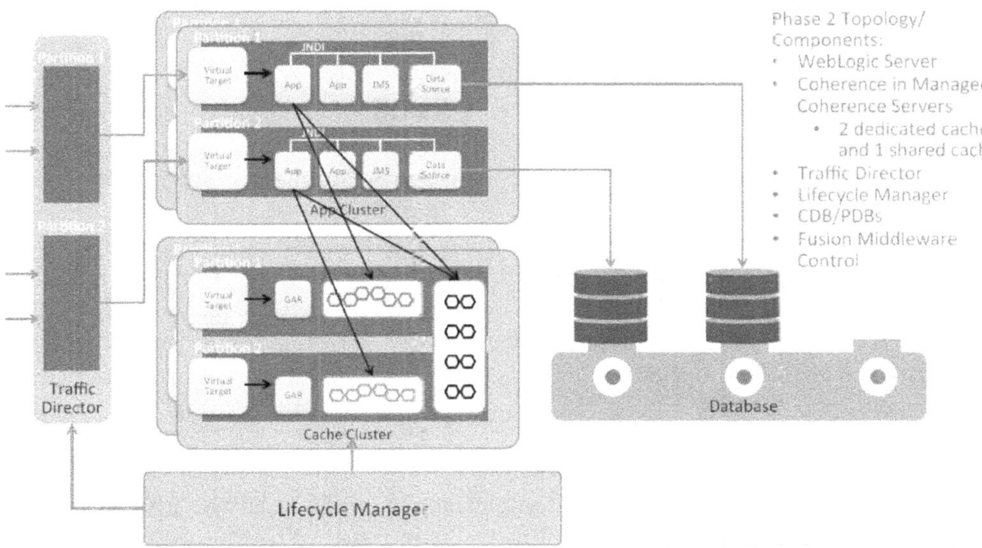

Figure 37-1: Key concepts © Oracle

Oracle Coherence

With Coherence, Oracle provides an in-memory data grid and a distributed caching solution. Many applications require frequent and/or fast access to data. Distributed caches are especially useful for data which does not need to be persisted, or for data which is (mostly) read-only. Coherence implements an abstraction layer with a large number of different cache configuration options. Coherence also provides a database integration which allows external database changes to be fed back into the cache. Coherence is composed of many individual nodes or JVMs which together implement a distributed caching environment.

Coherence can be used as standalone application from a number of different clients. It is also possible to use manage Coherence with the WebLogic administration environment. WebLogic also supports a special way to deploy a Coherence client using a deployment unit called "GAR". GAR stands for "**G**rid **Ar**chive" and conserves the appropriate directory structure.

Please refer to the detailed Coherence documentation available from Oracle for more details. The rest of this chapter concentrates on the multitenancy support and the integration into WebLogic partitions.

Coherence and WebLogic Partitions

Coherence Multitenancy allows WebLogic Server Multitenant applications to share a cluster across a set of tenants and applications, consolidating infrastructure requirements. Multitenancy provides tenant-specific caches as well as shared caches for hosting reference data. Oracle provides a full integration with Oracle Traffic Director and WebLogic Server in order to allow customers to implement an end-to-end multitenant solution. WebLogic partitions can be extended in order to work with distributed caches. Coherence Caches used within a partition can be either private or shared.

J2EE applications which uses Coherence caches can take full advantages of all the benefits added by the WebLogic multitenancy layer. This includes for example density, isolation, migration and others. Please refer to part five of the book that explained a number of common use-cases. Adding support and access to a Coherence cache for a "WebLogic application" which is deployed to a partition does not require any change to the application implementation. Partition clusters can be configured to use a common (usually shared) Coherence cluster (figure 37-2).

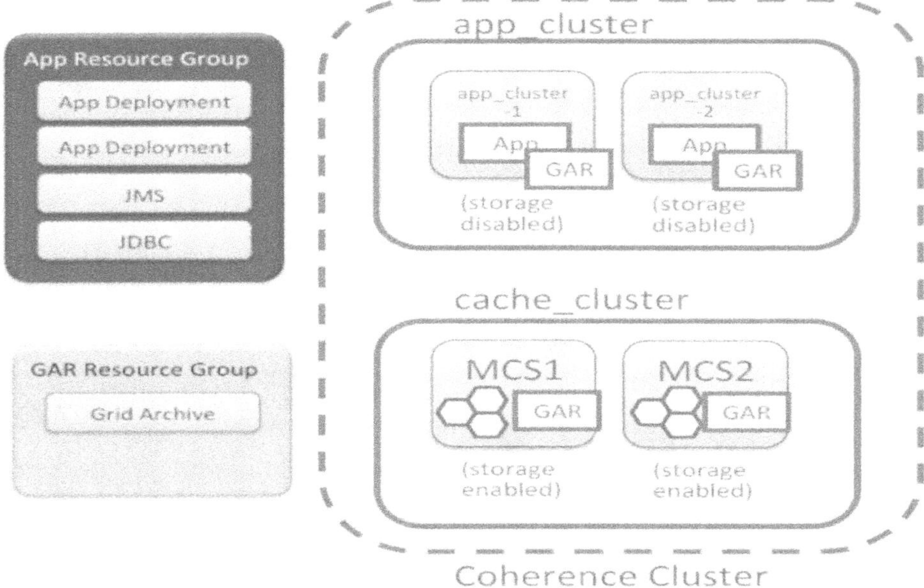

Figure 37-2: Common setup with distinct partition and cache clusters

Multitenancy environments require administrators to setup own clusters of managed Coherence servers. The coherence application itself needs to be provided as Coherence specific grid archive (GAR) deployment module.

Typically caches used in different partition clusters are isolated against each other. Note that this also means that all partition instances get their own cache instance, even if the same GAR is deployed to all partitions. Isolation is provided at the domain partition level and is transparent to the application.

For each GAR that is deployed to a partition, the partition will create a new instance of the cache. This is achieved by creating a partition specific tenant-id. Very similar to the partition resource overrides discussed earlier in the book, it is also possible to override cache configuration properties (figure 37-3).

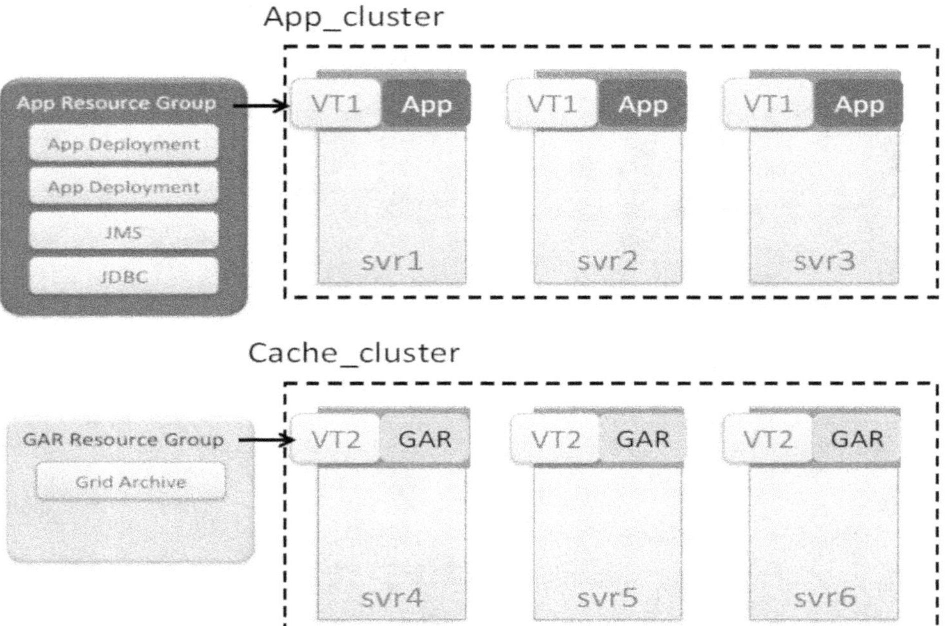

Figure 37-3: Deploying Coherence applications as part of resource groups

The following WLST script can be used to define partition specific cache overrides. A method called "createCoherencePartitionCacheProperty" is available on partition level in order to define override properties.

```
Connect("weblogic","xxxxx","t3://localhost:12001")

# start an edit session
edit()
startEdit()

# change to the partition
cd('/')
cd('/Partitions/MartinTestPartition')

# create a new cache configuration
cmo.createCoherencePartitionCacheConfig('SessionConfig')
cd('CoherencePartitionCacheConfigs/SessionConfig')

# within the new configuration, you can create your properties and set the override values
cmo.createCoherencePartitionCacheProperty('<my-property>')
cd('CoherencePartitionCacheProperties/<my-property>')
cmo.setValue('<my-value>')

# save and active your changes
save()
```

In many cases it is required that multiple partitions share the same cache instance. Typical examples include access to the same sessions from different instances. Partitions can be configured to allow the sharing of the caches. Cache sharing is of course transparent to the application. Whenever caches do not contain data which is specific to one partition instance, it is advisable to share the caches in order to maximize the efficient usage of resources.

Summary

With multitenancy support built into Oracle Coherence, Oracle extends its multitenancy strategy into attached backend applications. Depending on the isolation requirements of the application, partition can be configured to use instance specific caches or shared caches.

Elastic Services combine WLDF and elastic clusters

CHAPTER

Introduction

The first 5 parts of the book were dedicated to multitenancy topics and the new partition technology. In the current advanced section, we are looking beyond the core WebLogic at the extension of the multitenancy approach into the load balancing frontend (OTD) and into the caching backend (Coherence). Both are part of the Oracle middleware stack and are integrated together nicely.

Cloud services and similar setups are also based on the capability to scale out or shrink based on load. WebLogic has started with version 12.1.2 to offer a new concept called dynamic clusters where cluster members are created from a single template definition. This feature alone does not fulfill the need of modern scaling. Based on WLDF and new actions WebLogic has extended this concept to allow automated cluster scaling. WLDF has also be extended to be embedded into a partition. This allows automated scaling for clusters based on the need (policy rules) of special partitions. This combined with infrastructure interceptors form the new "Elastic Framework" that extend dynamic clusters into so-called elastic clusters.

WLDF Overview

WLDF (WebLogic Diagnostic Framework) is an integrated framework in WebLogic in order to collect, save and analyze runtime data for monitoring or troubleshooting. It provides a number of services which will be executed within the WebLogic server virtual machine. Using these services, you will be able to gather information which will help you to get a detailed view into the runtime performance of our server instances and also inside the deployed applications.

It is a very valuable tool for error location and diagnostic operations. Note that it does not provide access to the ConfigurationMBeans, only to the runtime MBeans. WLDF is not meant to be a tool for creating reports about the configuration. WLDF is targeted to work with runtime information. WLDF can be used to collect data from different

MBeans or create state snapshots. Other WLDF components can perform certain analysis or actions based on the collected data. The data can be access via external tools or displayed using the integrated dashboard. Main goal of WLDF is it to provide access to insight information into the runtime state of servers and applications in order to monitor health or detect and analyze problem situations and finally to react if necessary with specified actions. Starting with WebLogic 12.2.x Oracle has added new features to WLDF which enable dynamic cluster scaling.

WLDF Components

Logger, Harvester (and also the image capture feature) collect and consume runtime information which is created by the different data creators. Normally data creators are the different runtime MBeans inside the runtime MBeanServer of the WebLogic instances. Its collected data is used by the "*Archive*" component for persistence and by the "*Watch*" (now called "*Policy*") and "*Notification*" (now called "*Action*") components for monitoring and analysis. The data access subsystem communicates with the harvester and the logger for getting real time information and with the archive for historical data (figure 38-1).

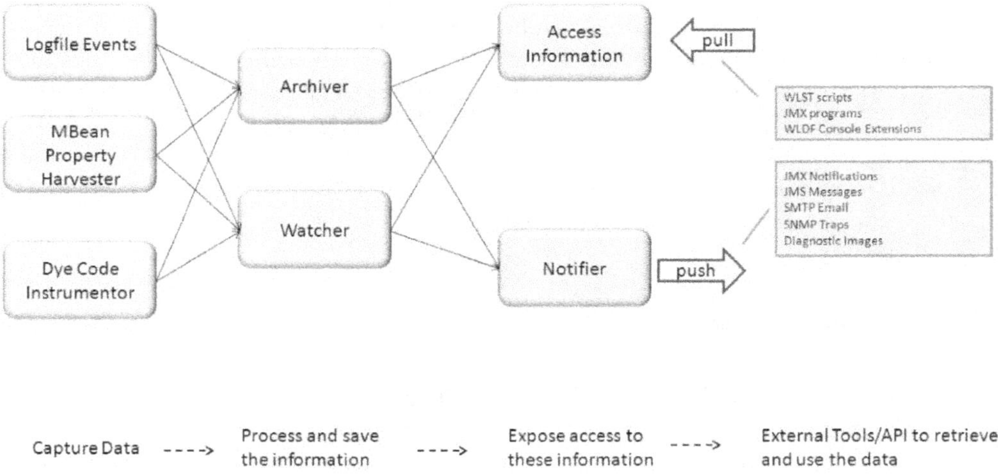

Figure 38-1: Simplified view on WLDF

For an in-depth explanation of WLDF, please refer to my book about WLDF. This chapter focus on the integration of WLDF into a partition and the new features added to WLDF to even better support multitenancy.

WLDF Extensions to better support Multitenancy

The WLDF book is based on WebLogic 12.1.x. Oracle has implemented a number of changes in WLDF for its latest version of WebLogic. These changes were mainly done in order to support partitions and to honor the fact that the former notifications can now also be real activities. The components watch and notification have been renamed to policy and action. The names of the WLDF components have be adapted to reflect the extended usages.

WLDF already did support JMX notifications, SMTP traps, JMS notifications and diagnostic image actions. With 12.2.1 Oracle has added a number of new types, which extend the power of WLDF even further.

The following actions have been added in WebLogic 12.2.1:

- Scaling up and scaling down dynamic clusters when a certain policy evaluates to true. These are called "*Elastic actions*" and provide a powerful way to interact directly with the domain structure.
- As Oracle has added REST management to WebLogic, a new action is now available that can send a REST notification. This can be used for management activities using the WebLogic REST interface or for custom REST messages
- A generic script based on WLST can be executed.
- A custom log message can be created

Another new and very powerful addition to WLDF are the new smart rules that have been added to WebLogic 12.2.1. Smart rules are prepackaged policy expressions with a set of configurable parameters that allow the end user to create a complex policy expression just by specifying the values for these configurable parameters.

WLDF Embedded into Partitions

Up to WebLogic 12.1.x WLDF could only scoped to WebLogic servers (or clusters). In order to support application scoped diagnostics and to honor the new concept of "WebLogic Applications", it is now possible to embed WLDF components into partitions and therefore scope them to partition level.

Monitoring, logging, debugging, diagnostic data access, image capturing and application instrumentation is now supported at partition level.

Diagnostic modules can now be embedded into partitions. WebLogic follows the new model that was discussed throughout the book and provides the capability to add harvester, policies and actions components to a resource group or a resource group template.

Differently to the previous watches, policies are rules that are defined in Java Expression Language for conditions that need to be monitored.

Elastic Services for Elastic Clusters

Clusters have ever been a central configuration and runtime feature of WebLogic. Version 12.1.2 added a completely new way of creating cluster member. The features was called dynamic cluster because their size could be changed and their members were created based on a managed-server template. Dynamic clusters offered a way to dynamically assign servers to machines and therefore provide a better usage of resources. WebLogic 12.2.1 extend this concept and adds elastic scaling to dynamic clusters, allowing them to be scaled up or down based on conditions identified by the user. Scaling a cluster can be done interactively on demand, or based on rules/policies and corresponding actions. It is even possible to create calendar based rules - e.g. for scaling up during Monday to Friday during business hours and scaling down during night hours. At the weekends the system can be scaled down even further to save power and costs.

Oracle defines these two ways of elastic scaling in the following way:

- Manually adding or removing a running dynamic server instance from an active dynamic cluster. This is called **on-demand scaling**. You can perform on-demand scaling using the Fusion Middleware component of Enterprise Manager, the WebLogic Server Administration Console, or the WebLogic Scripting Tool (WLST).
- Establishing policies that set the conditions under which a dynamic cluster should be scaled up or down and actions that define the scaling operations themselves. When the conditions defined in the scaling policy occur, the corresponding scaling action is triggered automatically. This is called automatic (rule-based) scaling.

(© Oracle documentation)

The elasticity framework which was added to WebLogic 12.2.1 implements a very flexible way to optimize the capacity used by your dynamic clusters. Oracle added even another feature called script interceptors. These interceptors allow you to provide custom code which could for example communicate with your hosting provider or own internal virtual hosting framework to even add a new virtual machine (or Docker container) before doing the scale-up of your cluster. In combination with the new WLDF actions and policies this can be used as a foundation for a completely automated and resource optimized cluster and capacity management.

Elasticity enables the automatic scaling of dynamic clusters and re-provisioning of associated resources (figure 38-2):

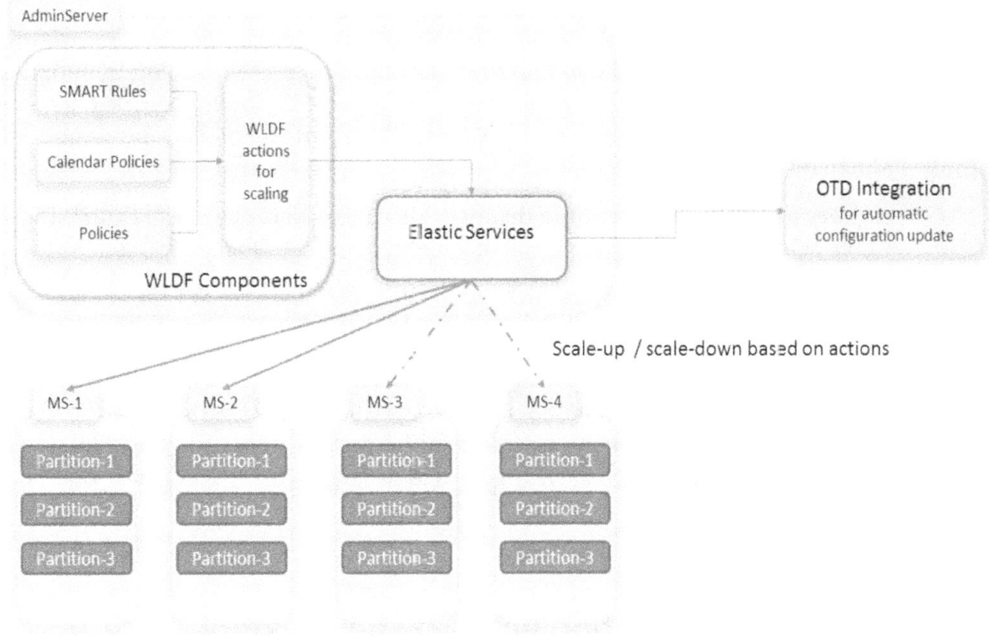

Figure 38-2: Automatic scaling using the elastic framework

WebLogic supports three different ways to scale dynamic clusters.

1) The manual scaling option, which involves human intervention by using the WebLogic console or one of the new WLST commands like scaleUp(…) or scaleDown(…). This also includes external triggering which then uses e.g. the WLST commands
2) Time boxed scaling options which will be applied to certain times. Based on calendar entries scaling up/down can happen to well defined times (like weekend / workdays)

3) Fully automated scaling based on policy rules and corresponding WLDF actions. This is the most advanced and most automated way of scaling

As the diagram above depicts, the elastic framework consists of a number of different components. It is also important to understand that the elastic framework only runs within the admin server so that the scaling features are not available while the admin server is down.

The following components together represent the elastic framework:

- The already mentioned new actions provided by the WLDF framework for automated scaling
- A number of additional configuration items in order to set scaling boundaries and defines advanced configuration like cooling times. Cooling times here mean a minimum time between scaling events. Most of them can be found in the DynamicServerMBean.
- A very new interceptor feature that provides hooks in order to call external systems. This can be used to create virtual machines, bring up Docker container or more.
- WebLogic internal services that will be called by the WLDF actions which ultimately implement the scaling activities
- As discussed in a previous chapter the integration into Oracle Traffic Director (OTD). This allows the admin server to update the OTD configuration about the additional servers (or remove servers in the case of a scale-down). Please refer to the OTD chapter (chapter 36) for more details about the OTD and what needs to be done to activate it.

Infrastructure Integration with Elastic Clusters

Two potential issues are commonly asked for when discussion the elastic features. Both have been addressed by WebLogic in the 12.2.1 release.

Infrastructure availability and readiness:

Scaling up a cluster means extending the cluster to additional machines. Are these machines ready for that? Is WebLogic installed? Is the machines – in case of a virtual machine or Docker container available and running at all? WebLogic itself cannot provide answers to these questions. Nevertheless a scale-out can only be successful if these questions gets addressed before the scale-out happens. WebLogic introduces an interceptor approach with a number of callbacks. Administrators can provide custom implementations which can hook into the scaling process and do the needful to make sure that scaling up will be successful or to do cleanups after a shrink activity.

Avoid overloading resources:

Another example from real life. Every cluster member hosts a datasource. The maximum number of concurrent connections per datasource is configured to be 20. The database itself does not support more than 100 concurrent connections. This means that more than 5 managed-servers in this cluster will overload the database and result in JDBC errors and issues. Scaling up clusters – even if automated policies indicate that it is needed – should fail if a scale-up will result into new issues with the database backend. In order to support that WebLogic has added the concept of a database interceptor. This can be configured to check if the planned scale out will violate resource limits. In case of a violation, this interceptor will stop the scale-up and reject it.

WLST Support

WebLogic has added two new commands to the WLST scripting environment which support the scale-up and scale-down activities. The following provides the online help coming with WebLogic WLST:

Output of help('scaleUp')

```
number of specified servers. The non-running server number with the lowest server id starts first,
followed by the next highest non-running server id. The user can optionally specify that the dynamic
cluster configuration should also be increased if there are not enough non-running servers in the
cluster to start. If so, then the maximum size of the cluster is increased by the additional number
of servers needed and the specified number of servers is started.

Syntax:

scaleUp (clusterName, numServers, [updateConfiguration], [block], [timeoutSeconds], [type])
- clusterName = Name of the dynamic cluster.

- numServers = Number of servers to start.

- updateConfiguration = Optional. Boolean value specifying whether WLST should increase the maximum
size of the cluster if there are not enough non-running servers. If not specified, this argument
defaults to false.

- block = Optional. Boolean value specifying whether WLST should block user interaction until the
system component is restarted. This argument defaults to true, indicating that user interaction is
blocked until the operation completes. If set to false, WLST returns control to the user after
issuing the command and assigns the task MBean associate with the current task to a variable that you
can use to check its status. If you are importing WLST as a Jython module, block is always set to
true.

- timeoutSeconds = Optional. Time (in seconds) that WLST waits for the server(s) to start before
canceling the operation. The default value is 600 seconds.

- type = Optional. If specified, the argument value must be DynamicCluster.

Example:

wls:/mydomain/serverConfig> scaleUp ("myCluster", 3, true, true)
          Starting server(s) in cluster 'myCluster' ...
```

```
The server(s) started successfully.
```

Output of help('scaleDown')

```
cluster by the specified number of servers. The server with the highest server id will be shutdown
first, then the next highest, etc. until the specified number of servers is shutdown. The user can
optionally specify that the dynamic cluster configuration should also be decreased. If so, then the
maximum size of the cluster will be decreased.

Syntax:

scaleDown (clusterName, numServers, [updateConfiguration], [block], [timeoutSeconds], [type])
- clusterName = Name of the dynamic cluster.

- numServers = Number of servers to shutdown.

- updateConfiguration = Optional. Boolean value specifying whether WLST should decrease the maximum
size of the cluster. If not specified, this argument defaults to false.

- block = Optional. Boolean value specifying whether WLST should block user interaction until the
system component is restarted. This argument defaults to true, indicating that user interaction is
blocked until the operation completes. If set to false, WLST returns control to the user after
issuing the command and assigns the task MBean associate with the current task to a variable that you
can use to check its status. If you are importing WLST as a Jython module, block is always set to
true.

- timeoutSeconds = Optional. Time (in seconds) that WLST waits for the server(s) to start before
canceling the operation. The default value is 300 seconds.

- type = Optional. If specified, the argument value must be DynamicCluster.

Example:

wls:/mydomain/serverConfig> scaleDown ("myCluster", 3, true, true)
          Shutting down servers from 'myCluster' ...
          Server(s) stopped successfully.
```

Summary

The elastic services in WebLogic implement a feature that is highly needed in modern cloud based services or hosted services. Automatic scaling based on policies and rules are a vital for dynamic and cost driven infrastructures. WebLogic cannot provide answers to all challenges but provides interceptor approaches in order to hook in custom code.

In combination with the new and extended WLDF implementation, the scaling can be executed automatically based on policies, smart rules and actions. It is also possible to provide calendar based scaling – e.g. weekend / weekday load adoptions.

Multitenancy and Docker – Complementary but also competitive Technologies

CHAPTER

Introduction

The entire book up to now focused on the new partition technology, which offers a new isolation layer to WebLogic. This isolation layer adds a number of advantages to the WebLogic administration.

Isolation technologies are not new (see section three of the book that talks about the different layers of isolation). The partition technology is the new answer from Oracle that acts as the foundation for multitenant systems, cloud and cloud based architectures and in general adds a bunch of new administration features to WebLogic.

But Multitenancy is not the only technology on the market offering these kind of features, albeit the only one integrated into WebLogic. Another new technology is getting more and more popular, which is called "Docker". The focus of Docker is similar but different. It is also possible to combine both technologies. As many companies are either already using Docker or looking at Docker, it is worthwhile to compare these two technologies.

Docker overview

Docker is an open-source project that automates the deployment of applications inside software containers, by providing an additional layer of abstraction and automation of operating-system-level virtualization on Linux. Docker uses the resource isolation features of the Linux kernel such as "cgroups" and kernel namespaces, and a union-capable file system such as "aufs" and others to allow independent "containers" to run within a single Linux instance, avoiding the overhead of starting and maintaining virtual machines. The Linux kernel's support for namespaces mostly isolates an application's view of the operating environment, including process trees, network, user IDs and mounted file systems, while the kernel's cgroups provide resource limiting, including the CPU, memory, block I/O and network. (© Wikipedia) See figure 39-1:

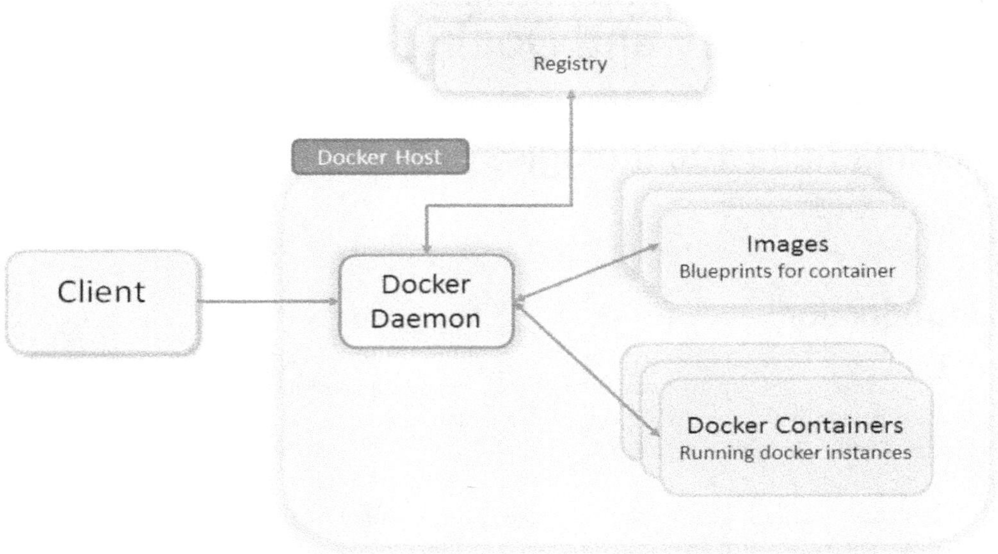

Figure 39-1: Main Docker components

Docker is designed as a client-server architecture. The client provides an administrative interface with operations like "build", "pull", "run" and more. This client communicates with the daemon, which needs to run on the machine where you want to run the containers. The daemon is the central component that works with the containers (like build, run, distribute). It is possible albeit not required that the client runs on the same machine than the daemon as the communicate using a REST based API.

Docker components:

Daemon	Central component that runs on the host where you want to operate the containers. Communication is done via the client.
Client	Primary user interface to communicate with the daemon
Image	Is a template or blueprint. It can contain a pure OS but also software like a WebLogic instance or Tomcat. Every Docker container is created based on an image.
Registry	Repository for images. They can be made available for the public or can be private (e.g. company internal). The public Docker registry is provided with the Docker Hub.
Container	A container is a running instance created based on an image. Containers can be run, started, stopped, moved, and deleted. Each container is an isolated and secure application platform.

Docker containers are processes of the operating system. One part of the isolation is done by the so called "*cgroups*". Cgroups have been invented by Google and it is an abbreviation of "control groups". But the isolation of a Docker container would be not be complete without "*namespaces*", which wrap global system resources in an abstraction. To the processes within a particular namespace, all global resources appear to them as their own resources.

All Docker containers have to share the same physical resources like network, disk I/O, CPU, etc., but any change of a resource of the same namespace is only visible to the processes of the very same namespace. For all other processes outside this namespace, the changes are invisible!

With Docker we can define a so called "*overlay network*" and with this feature, it is possible to have these containers running on different hosts, different datacenters or even in different countries; if you like . It is also possible to simulate a whole datacenter on a single host, by defining different overlay networks, e.g. "dev-network", "UAT-network" or "production".

Docker Swarms

Docker containers can be clustered together. This clustering is done by a Docker tool called "*Docker swarm*". The Docker swarm technology enables administrators to treat a cluster of Docker nodes as a single virtual system. The Docker nodes may run on the same or different machines. Clustering is important as it is the foundation for load-balancing and failover. It is also the foundation for system scaling.

Swarm uses different technologies for pre-checks and testing in order to make sure that the Docker hosts always have enough resources for all the distributed containers. Swarm assigns containers to underlying nodes. It also contains algorithms to choose the best (most likely, the host with the lowest load) host for the new workload. The administrator may pre-define which policy to choose for the automatically distribution of the containers across the cluster.

Comparison of Docker and virtual machines

A Docker container is an instance/process of a Docker image. A Docker image contains all information and files to start a Docker container. It contains literally everything from the OS up to the application that will be used by the users. Albeit similar Docker is not a virtual machine (figure 39-2).

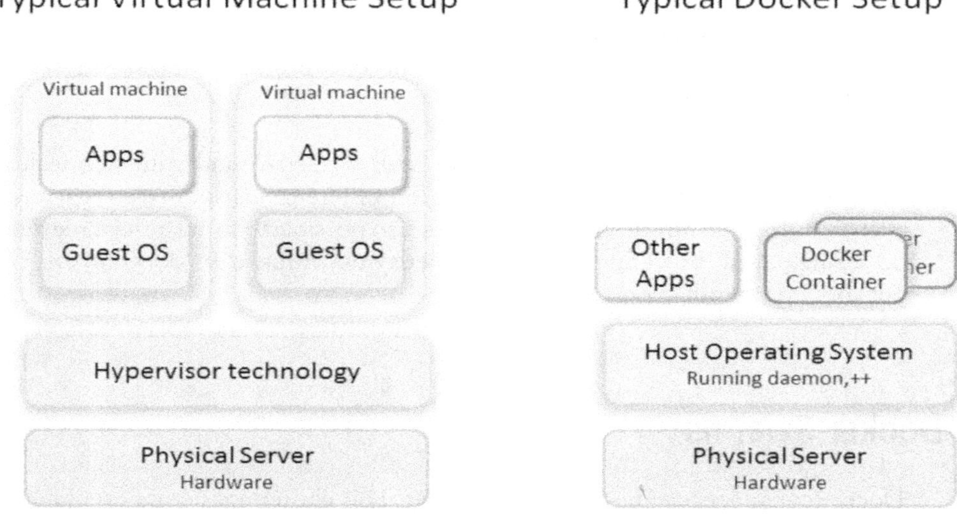

Figure 39-2: Docker vs. VMs

Typical virtual machines are complete operating systems with all applications. Each virtual machine comes with its own full operating system. Containers on the other hand are very small (depending on the application). They focus on applications and contain mainly all application dependencies.

Docker images are built up in layers in a union file-system. The first layer of an image usually is the OS layer. Then there are the server and/or application layers. If one adds some features to an existing image, a new layer will be added.

Docker compared to Partitions

As we already know, partitions live inside a managed WebLogic server, which itself lives in a JVM. This JVM runs on an operating system and this runs on a chosen hardware platform. This applies, more or less for Docker containers too. They are processes, actually special processes, which run on an operating system on a chosen hardware. There is a daemon, which is controlling these special processes, aka Docker containers. WebLogic's partitions and Docker container have some isolation features in common. They live on the same ground, share some resources and they do not know about the other units. (Unless you make them aware of each other.)

One can move or clone a partition to another managed server; the same applies to Docker containers. They can be "moved" (fired up on the new box and killed on the former one) or cloned as well. There also is a tool to migrate running Docker containers from one to another host.

The following list provides a technology comparison. Please take it as high-level comparison and not a detailed technical one:

Component	WebLogic + Partitions	Docker
Core component and administration	Admin Server	Daemon
Access to technology and infrastructure	WLST, JMX, WLS Console, REST API	Docker client, REST API
Central repository feature	---	Docker repository
Blueprints for runtime instances	Exported partitions, Resource group templates, resource deployment plans, partition overrides	Docker image
Runtime instance	WebLogic Partition or in general a WebLogic managed server	Docker container
Getting runtimes	Import partitions	Client pull / run
Load-balancing	OTD integration	--
Dynamic clustering	Elastic framework, elastic clusters, infrastructure and database interceptors	Swarm technology
Isolation	Resource manager, service isolation on partition level, security isolation	Cgroups, namespaces

WebLogic in a Docker container

It is possible to run a WebLogic Server inside a Docker container and this is certified by Oracle. This means, you will get support, depending on your contract and can benefit from all the advantages. Oracle has also published the corresponding Docker files in order to create WebLogic install images and WebLogic domain images. These images are built as an extension of existing Oracle Linux images (figure 39-3).

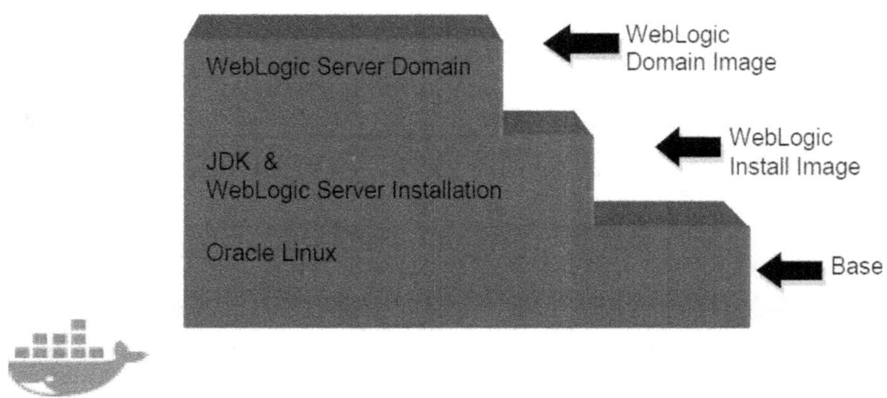

Figure 39-3: WebLogic Docker Images (© Oracle)

Based on these images two different types of containers can be created. Either a container that contains a WebLogic admin server or a container that acts as a managed-node and contains a NodeManager and managed server.

However, why should you run a WebLogic server inside a Docker container? One of the big advantages of Docker containers is their isolation. It is not strict as a common virtual machine, but most of the time the offered features are sufficient.

This does not mean that the WebLogic instances in a Docker container should not host partitions. Docker really adds additional isolation features on a lower level that WebLogic does not offer. See chapter 8 – Operating System Isolation. Docker can fill a gap especially on this layer (figure 39-4).

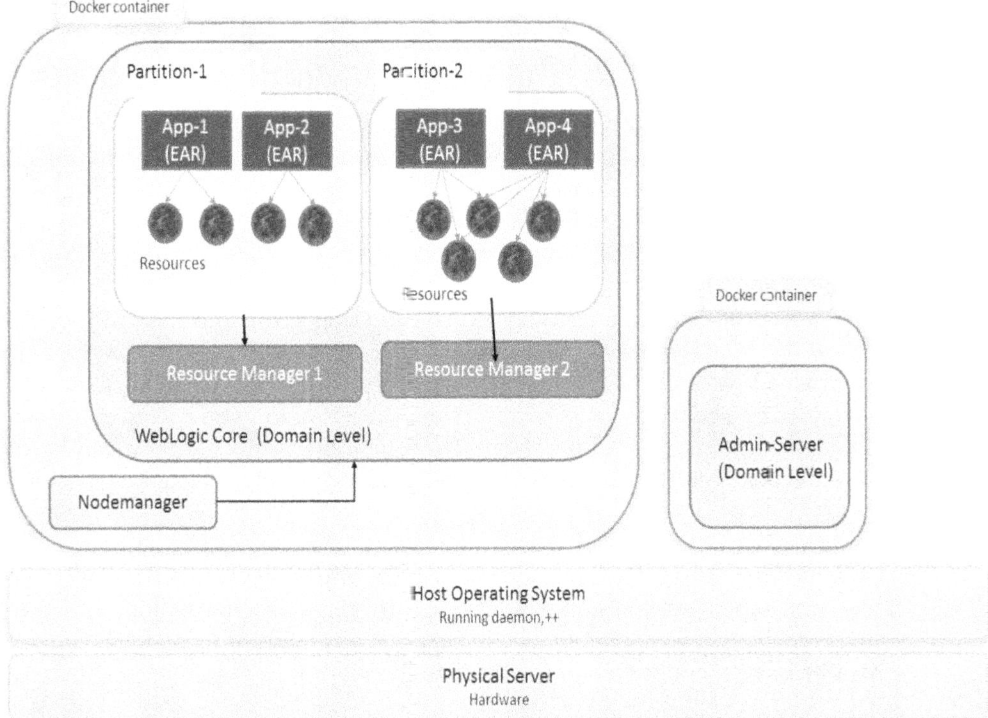

Figure 39-4: WebLogic in a Docker container

The above picture – also see chapter 8 – depicts that Docker offers another layer of isolation between the operating system and the java virtual machine.

Docker containers as WebLogic machines

One of the basic administration concepts in WebLogic is the "machine" arrangement. Every managed-server can be assigned to a machine. A WebLogic machine is represented by a node manager. Therefore a WebLogic machine is very often referred to as a "Node".

Using a combination of Docker and WebLogic dynamic clusters, a number of different operation models are possible (depending on your needs).

Traditional domain model:

Whenever needed the administrator brings up an additional Docker container (WebLogic node) and then adds the new node to the domain and extends the existing cluster if needed.

Standard Dynamic cluster:

The WebLogic domain is setup to use dynamic clusters. Whenever needed, the administrator can bring up a new Docker container. Then the dynamic cluster can be extended into the new Docker container.

Elastic clusters:

The new elastic features of WLS 12.2.x can bring automation to a different level. Triggered by calendar or smart rules, scale-up or scale-down activities can be performed. WLDF policies can be even embedded into a partition so that scaling activities can be triggered based on managed server or even partition. If scaling is triggered by a partition, only the cluster which hosts this partition can be scaled-up or down. Many other options and setups are possible.

Combine elastic clusters and Docker swarm:

The ultimate automation and scaling combination is achieved if the elastic services get combined with Docker swarm clustering. Infrastructure and database interceptors prevent uncontrolled scaling. Communication with Docker swarm can be implemented as an infrastructure interceptor.

WebLogic support for Docker

Oracle has published Dockerfiles and supporting scripts to the GitHub repository that can be used to build WebLogic Docker images. In addition scripts have been published to extend these images to create WebLogic domain images.

The following scripts are provided together with the Docker files. Both together are needed to build WebLogic domain images.

buildDockerImage.sh:

builds the WLS image using the WLS installation Dockerfile instructions.

createMachine.sh

starts a Node Manager in the container and calls addMachine.sh to start Node Manager and add the Node Manager machine.

createServer.sh

starts a Node Manager in the container and calls add-server.py to configure a Managed Server in the machine create by add-machine.py.

create-wls-domain.py

WLST script configures a base domain with one Admin server, JMS server, JSP, Data Source.

add-machine.py
: WLST scripts to create a machine using the Managed Server container name.

add-server.py
: WLST scripts to create a Managed Server.

rm_containers.sh
: removes all running containers

clean-up-docker.sh
: removes all ghost containers and all ghost images

commEnv.sh
: enable JPA 2.1 support

jaxrs2-template.jar
: template to configure JAX-RS

(List © by Oracle)

Summary

As we discussed above, the WebLogic partitions are offering a way to easily provide multitenancy and much better utilization of the WebLogic servers. There is no need to change the processes about how to build and deploy software. The upgrade can be done quite easy and the advantages pay off very fast.

With Docker containers, which are similar in some ways, there is the chance to extend the flexibility and the utilization of the given (hardware-) environment even more. It is now possible to deploy not only an application, but a whole sets of servers, databases, small tools and anything else, that is needed. It can be prepared, tested and deployed without any changes in the setup, unless you want to change something by intention.

As more and more well-known software becomes available and certified for Docker containers, there will be more scenarios, where one can benefit from the advantages of the combination of the provided features.

Partitions and Docker – albeit in some degree similar – can work together. Docker offers a better isolation for the Java JVM instance (called WebLogic server) which cannot be provide by WebLogic itself. Elastic services together with the Docker swarm technology and the WebLogic interceptors enable administrators to create a very powerful and dynamic infrastructure.

Part VII

Putting it all together

WebLogic as a Platform and Foundation for Cloud Services

CHAPTER

Bringing it all together

Well, you nearly finished reading this book. As a last step let us put all the topics and technologies discussed in this book in a common and broader context (figure 40-1).

Figure 40-1: Technologies discussed throughout the book

The book focuses on the new partition technology and surrounding components. The partition technology has by nature nothing to with cloud computing but it provides a very interesting platform for cloud services. Oracle has added the multitenancy technology in the context of a far bigger offering – the Oracle java Cloud services (JCS).

WebLogic Server Multitenant and its partition technology

As discussed in detailed in section 3, 4 and 5 of this book, Oracle has added the new partition technology to WebLogic. This technology adds a number of isolation features on different levels to WebLogic. Applications together with their resources can be bundled as "WebLogic application" and can be deployed to microcontainers which are implemented as partitions. Tools like the Domain to Partition Conversion Tool (DPCT) have been implemented to help with the migration (figure 40-2).

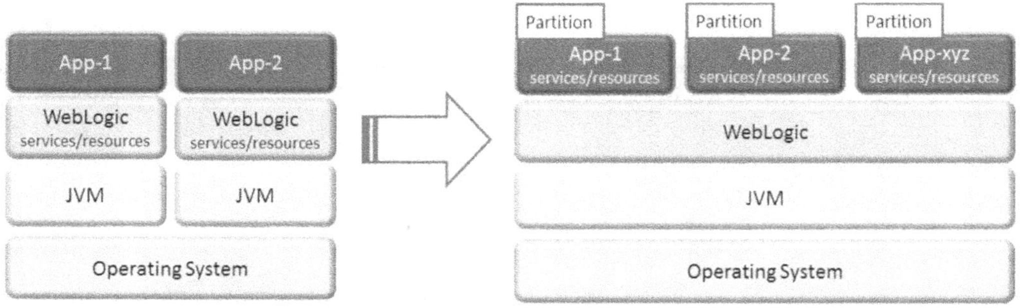

Figure 40-2: Microcontainer technology (partitions)

WebLogic has also been extended to support elastic services which can scale-up or scale down dynamic clusters based on resource events captured by the diagnostic framework (WLDF). Actions (formally known as notifications) are provided for elastic services.

In addition to WLST and the different consoles a new management API based on REST has been added.

Integration into other Technologies

WebLogic applications always need frontend (e.g. load-balancer) or backend (database, caching or other) services.

Especially the integration between WebLogic partitions and the OTD has been extended by a new service running in WebLogic called Lifecycle manager. This service can inform and update the OTD configuration about changes in the cluster of a certain partition (scale up/down). Also live migration events that changes the hosting details of a partition can be published to the OTD in order to update the OTD configuration (figure 40-3).

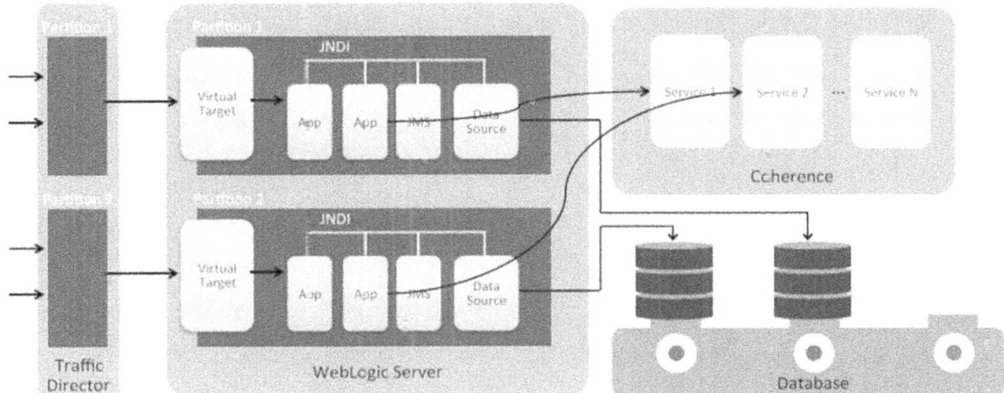

Figure 40-3: Extending Mult tenancy into the OTD load balancer © Oracle

Also backends like caches (Coherence) or Oracle database (pluggable database) have been extended to support multitenancy.

Java Cloud Service (JCS)

Oracle offers cloud services for different cloud levels (IaaS, PaaS, SaaS and special combinations). It goes far beyond the scope of this chapter to describe the complete offering which contains (among others) a java cloud (JCS), database cloud, container cloud, mobile cloud, management cloud and many others. All based on Docker with Docker images getting generated during deployment to the cloud.

The basic idea behind all cloud service is that the deployment process will merge the deployment artifacts handed over by the user together with a selected Docker base images and create a new Docker image. This new image will then we run in the cloud. Base images include for example the JDK versions or in case of a higher stack the WebLogic, Tomcat or JBoss version.

As soon as new technology stacks (e.g. patches) are available the user can upgrade to that patch. During upgrade the original deployments will be merged with the new base images and the cloud deployment process will create a new deployment Docker image.

The complete administration of all cloud services can be done using a web portal or using the REST API. REST is the technology of choice for all cloud automations. As

WebLogic also supports administration using REST, the same technology used to automate the cloud activities can be used to configure and operate your WebLogic instances in the cloud (figure 40-4).

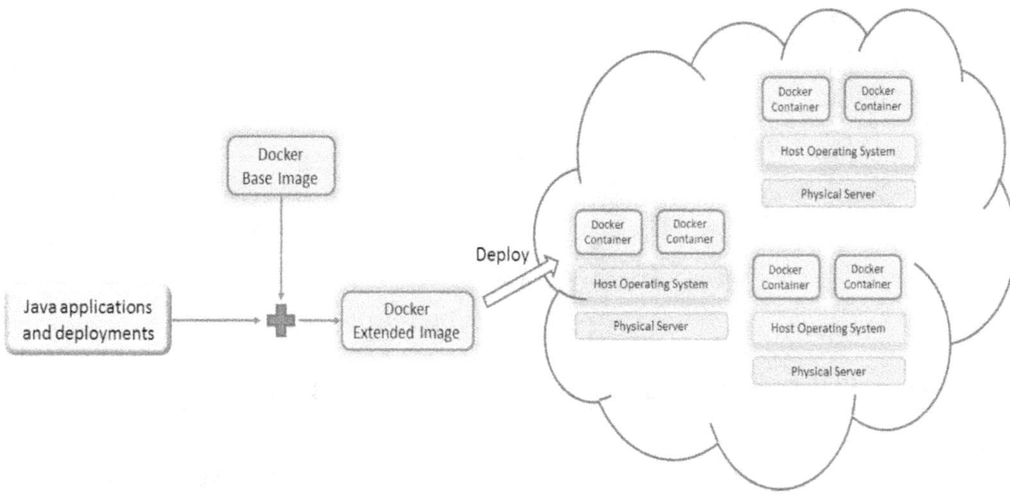

Figure 40-4: Java Cloud Services (JCS)

Instead of application deployments a JCS instance can also be for example a WebLogic domain with one or more partitions. Deployments can be done to a partition as Oracle has already added WebLogic 12.2.x and the partition technology to its cloud service.

CloudMachine

Many companies – especially in the financial industries – cannot move to a public cloud due to security and legal constraints or concerns. With a new CloudMachine offering Oracle has created an integrated offering including hardware and cloud software which can be hosted on premise in your own datacenter. The very interesting fact is that this CloudMachine is running the identical software as being used in the public cloud.

All technologies, processes and automations are identical for the private (on premise) and the public cloud.

Interchangeable Environments

The technology stack is designed to support applications being moved back and forward between traditional setup, public and local cloud environments. Due to its new abstraction layer, the new partition microcontainers are providing an especially seamless migration technology.

Even though development could also be done in a development cloud service, consider a local development environment based on a standalone WebLogic domain. For simplicity the following example focus on WebLogic only (figure 40-5):

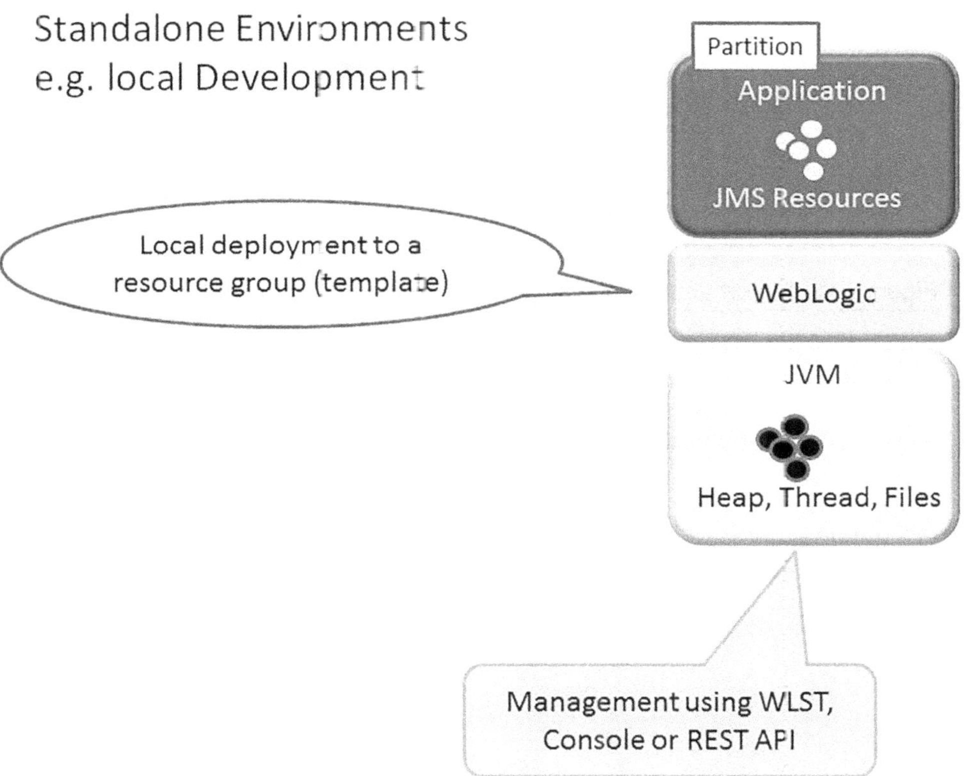

Figure 40-5: Local standard development environment

In order to move your application to other environments like tests, integration, non-functional-test or others, the partition will be exported (WLST, REST or Console). Resource deployment plans can be now created based on infrastructure differences in the other environments (like datasource URLs or credentials), see figure 40-6.

Export partitions from local domains and add resource deployment plans

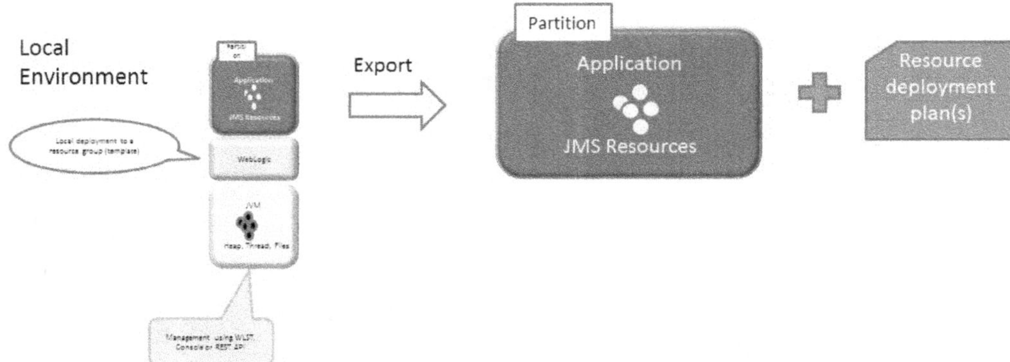

Figure 40-6: Export your local partition and prepare the migration

Now the exported partition can be migrated either to other standard WebLogic domains. It is also possible to migrate this partition – note without any change in the partition or the application itself – to a cloud environment.

For this example let us assume that your test and integration environments are located in a public cloud. Using the cloud portal or REST the partition can now be imported into a cloud instance based on WebLogic 12.2.x (figure 40-7).

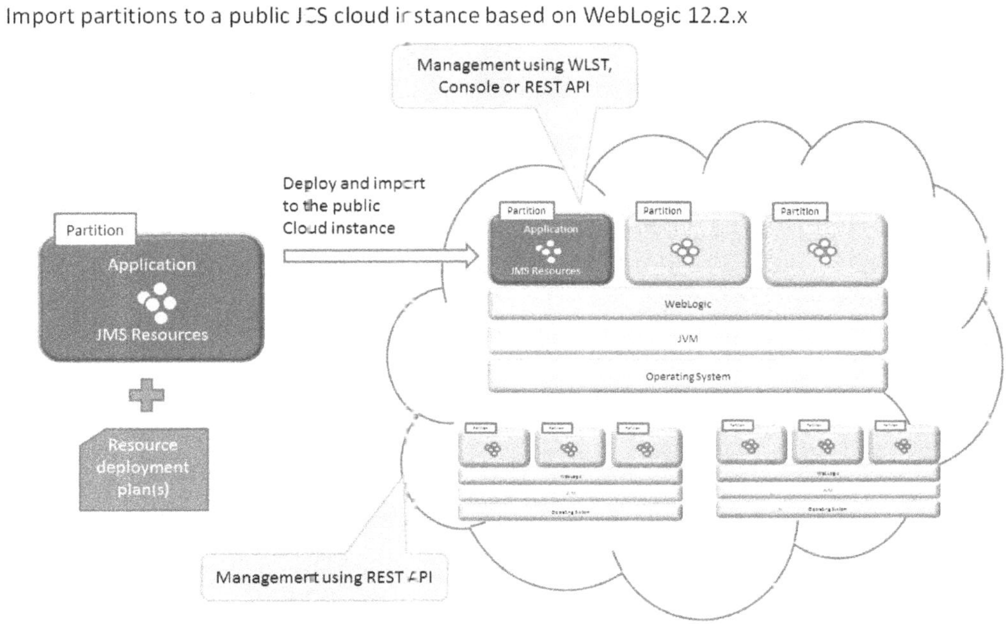

Import partitions to a public JCS cloud instance based on WebLogic 12.2.x

Management using WLST, Console or REST API

Deploy and import to the public Cloud instance

Partition

Application

JMS Resources

Resource deployment plan(s)

WebLogic

JVM

Operating System

Management using REST API

Figure 40-7: Import the partition into a public cloud instance

Remember that this is a simplified picture. Cloud instances are usually multi-node instances. For multi-node instances load-balancer technologies are needed. The cloud has automatically added a configuration to the OTD using the WebLogic lifecycle manager so that the OTD can balance the load to the new partition cluster.

Also scaling up/down actions are provided and could be also triggered by REST calls.

For legal reasons let us assume that your production environment must be located within your own datacenter. In this case it is no problem to export the partition from the public cloud, create an appropriate resource deployment plan and import the partition to your private cloud in your datacenter (e.g. on a CloudMachine).

It would of course also be possible to import this partition you have exported from the public cloud to a standalone (non-cloud) WebLogic production cluster. The steps are surprisingly similar in both cases.

In case a private cloud is used, the same technologies, the same web portals and the same process can be used to deploy the partition to the private cloud as you did previously to import it to the public cloud (figure 40-8).

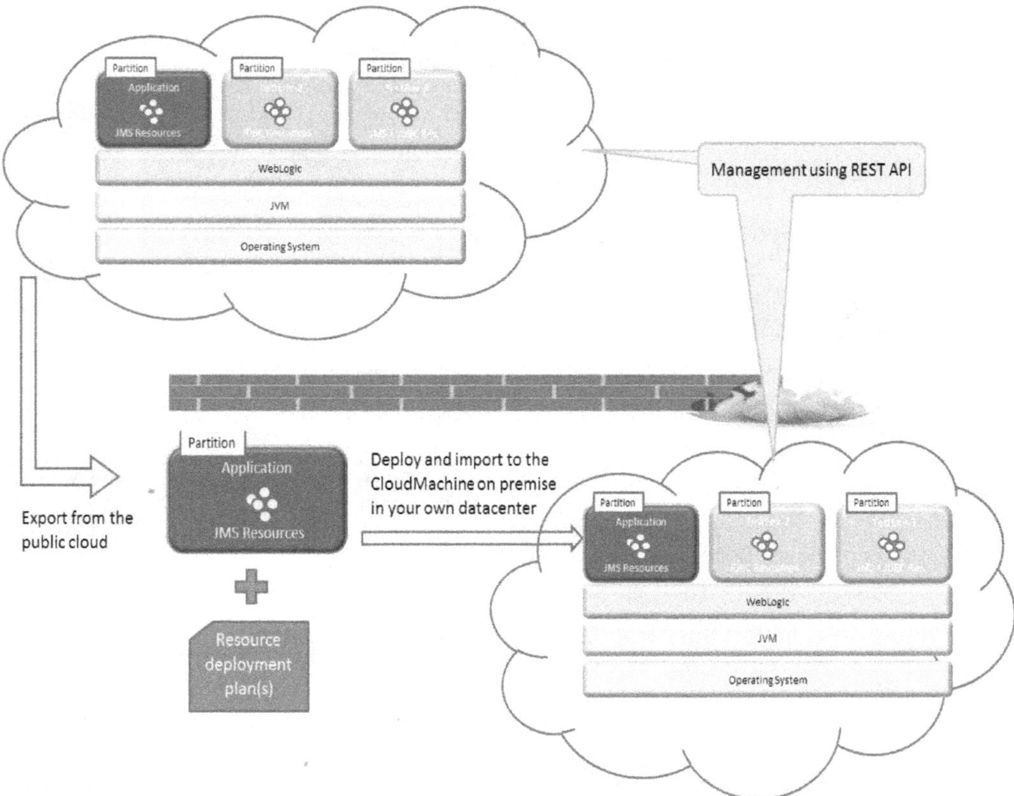

Figure 40-8: Migrating a partition from the public to a private cloud

Summary

WebLogic Server Multitenant and its partition technology is a big new milestone in the history of WebLogic and has started a completely new way of deploying, bundling and isolating applications. This technology – even if used with only a single partition per domain – has a number a new benefits. The new technology offers new architectures for a number of use-cases (see section 5) which could have been solved in the same way before.

As said in the foreword, the partition technology has by nature nothing to with cloud computing but it provides a very interesting platform for cloud services. Oracle has added the multitenancy technology (as well as the REST API, elastic services, OTD integration, Docker certification and more) also in the context of a far bigger offering – the Oracle java Cloud services (JCS).

Applications bundled as partitions together with resource deployment plans can be very easily moved to the Oracle public cloud Java services or to an Oracle Cloud machine which offers a private cloud on premise. A flexible management, upgrading and patching is provided as all cloud applications are running on Docker images.

Part VIII

Appendix

Resources and Links

CHAPTER

Books

Advanced WebLogic Server Automation

Administration and Monitoring with WLST and JMX

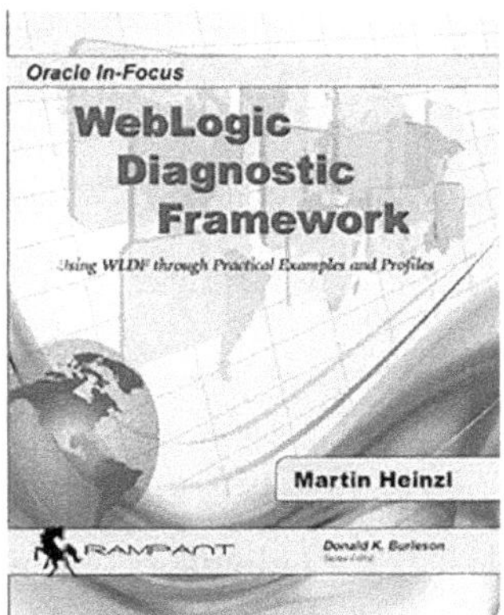

WebLogic Diagnostic Framework

Using WLDF through Practical Examples and Profiles

Links

Oracle Product documentation

- http://www.oracle.com/us/products/middleware/cloud-app-foundation/weblogic/weblogic-server-multitenant-ds-2742664.pdf
- https://docs.oracle.com/middleware/1221/wls/wls-multitenancy.htm
- https://docs.oracle.com/middleware/1221/wls/WLSMT/toc.htm
- https://blogs.oracle.com/WebLogicServer/entry/domain_partitions_for_multi_tenancy

Youtube

- https://www.youtube.com/watch?v=C5GP_JB88VY
- https://www.youtube.com/watch?v=6b7dySBC-mk
- https://www.youtube.com/watch?v=1sTA1VdLkow
- https://www.youtube.com/watch?v=D1vQJrFfz9Q

Multitenancy

- http://www.gartner.com/it-glossary/multitenancy
- http://en.wikipedia.org/wiki/Multitenancy
- https://vikashazrati.wordpress.com/2008/06/23/multi-tenancy-explained/
- https://developer.salesforce.com/page/Multi_Tenant_Architecture
- http://www.computerworld.com/article/2517005/data-center/multi-tenancy-in-the-cloud--why-it-matters.html
- http://whatis.techtarget.com/definition/multi-tenancy
- http://www.oraworld.co.uk/oracle-weblogic-12cr2-12-2-1-what-is-multitenancy/
- http://www.fabriziomarini.com/2015/12/weblogic-1221-multitenancy-example-of.html

XaaS:

- http://de.wikipedia.org/wiki/Everything_as_a_Service
- http://apprenda.com/library/paas/iaas-paas-saas-explained-compared/

- http://www.rackspace.com/knowledge_center/whitepaper/understanding-the-cloud-computing-stack-saas-paas-iaas
- https://www.linkedin.com/pulse/20140730172610-9679881-pizza-as-a-service (Albert Barron)
- https://www.computenext.com/blog/when-to-use-saas-paas-and-iaas/
- http://ad-hoc.net/blogs/2010/12/la-nube-iaas-paas-saas-itaa-un-breve-repaso-de-conceptos/
- http://www.ijarcsse.com/docs/papers/Volume_4/6_June2014/V4I6-0158.pdf

Coherence

- http://docs.oracle.com/middleware/1221/coherence/index.html
- http://docs.oracle.com/middleware/1221/coherence/release-notes/technotes.htm#COHRY173

Oracle Traffic Director

- http://docs.oracle.com/middleware/1221/otd/index.html
- http://docs.oracle.com/middleware/1221/otd/admin/get_started.htm#OTAD G24030

Oracle HTTP Server

- http://docs.oracle.com/middleware/1221/webtier/index.html
- http://docs.oracle.com/middleware/1221/webtier/administer-ohs/whats_new.htm#HSADM1172

Elastic Framework and elastic Clusters

- https://docs.oracle.com/middleware/1221/wls/ELAST.pdf
- https://blogs.oracle.com/WebLogicServer/entry/elasticity_for_dynamic_clusters
- http://docs.oracle.com/middleware/1221/wls/ELAST/overview.htm#ELAST5 29
-

- WebLogic Server 12.2.1 Elastic Cluster Scaling with WLST
    - https://www.youtube.com/watch?v=6PHYfVd9Oh4
- WebLogic Server 12.2.1 Elastic Cluster Scaling with WebLogic Console
    - https://www.youtube.com/watch?v=HkG0Uw14Dak
- WebLogic Server 12.2.1 Automated Elastic Cluster Scaling
    - https://www.youtube.com/watch?v=6b7dySBC-mk

Docker

- http://www.oracle.com/us/products/middleware/cloud-app-foundation/weblogic/weblogic-server-on-docker-wp-2742665.pdf

About the Author

Martin Heinzl is a principal consultant and middleware expert, working in the areas of architecture, middleware and enterprise landscapes and systems. Over the last 16 years he has built up extensive experience in enterprise middleware technologies and distributed systems. His main areas of focus include architecture, integration, application server and middleware technologies, J2EE, CORBA, distributed systems and security. His project involvement has included architecture, design, analysis, SOA (like) systems, configuration, security, deployment, automation, management and monitoring. This experience has given him a thorough knowledge of all parts of the application lifecycle.

In the past Martin was responsible for a complete, huge application server infrastructure and for the automation of a complex web service security layer including single-sign-on, SAML, OWSM, Oracle Service Bus and other technologies. With a few thousand WLS server instances. He was also responsible for the WebLogic architecture and infrastructure (including monitoring and security) of different high risk / high volume financial systems. He is working in an expert team of a world-wide company internal hosting platform with different technology stacks deployed on a large number of servers with several thousand application (server) instances.

In 2013, Martin joined the Oracle Customer Advisory Board for WebLogic and he always tries to be up to date on middleware technologies by attending conferences and taking part in beta programs. Martin is located in the Frankfurt/Main are in Germany and you can reach him at multitenancy@mh-enterpriseconsulting.de

He is also the author of the books "Advanced WebLogic Server Automation" and "WebLogic Diagnostic Framework" by Rampant TechPress.

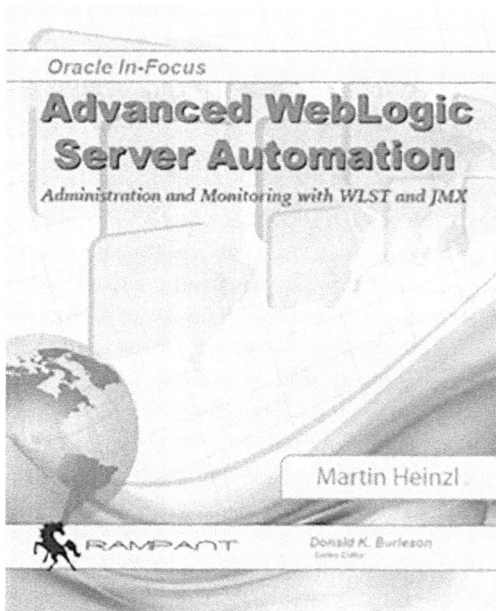

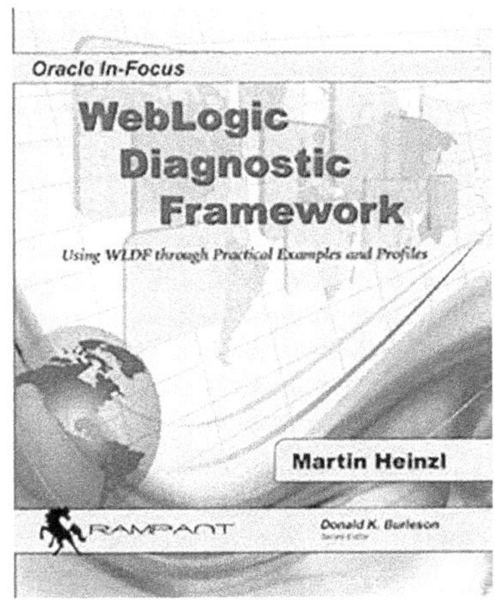

WebLogic Diagnostic Framework

Using WLDF through Practical Examples and Profiles

Martin Heinzl

ISBN: 978-0-9861194-0-8

Publisher: Rampant TechPress

WebLogic is a complex, professional application server environment with a complex and powerful security environment. WebLogic server at its core implements the J2EE specification stack and its main purpose is to offer a hosting environment for J2EE applications.

But WebLogic is much more than that. Like most professional J2EE server WebLogic also offers a large number of extended features like comprehensive management, clustering and failover functionality on different levels, plus a number of extended enterprise features not required by J2EE but very useful in the enterprise world, enterprise features that are required by many companies.

Index

A

B

C

D

E

F

G

H

I

J

K

L

M

N

O

P

Need more
horsepower?
Call the Oracle Experts.
Expert Oracle Support
• Remote DBA Services
• Remote Oracle Health Checks
• Oracle Tuning
• RAC & Grid Support
On-Site Oracle Training
• Oracle RAC and Grid Training
• Oracle Tuning Expert Secrets
• Customized Oracle Training
• Follow-up Mentoring
Slow Oracle
Performance?
BC is a leading provider of Remote
Oracle Database Healthchecks
Help!
BURLESON
Consulting
BC
BURLESON
CONSULTING
800.766.1884
www.dba-oracle.com

www.ingramcontent.com/pod-product-compliance
Lightning Source LLC
Chambersburg PA
CBHW080126220326
41598CB00032B/4965

* 9 7 8 0 9 8 6 1 1 9 4 2 2 *